Light!

Light!

The Industrial Age 1750–1900
Art & Science, Technology & Society

Andreas Blühm Louise Lippincott

With 304 illustrations, 195 in colour

Thames & Hudson

Note to the reader

The entries further explore the issues raised in the introductory essay. They roughly follow the chronology of events and inventions, and the dating of the works of art. Cross references are only made where specific works are concerned. Please make use of the index of proper names at the end of the book for more information.

Works listed in the bibliography are abbreviated in the footnotes. However, since the extensive bibliography is divided into sections, readers may have some difficulty locating a specific reference. We apologize for the inconvenience.

Foreign quotations are given in the authors' translation unless otherwise indicated.

A few footnotes refer to websites. Further links are available on the Light! website. You are welcome to bookmark <www.vangoghmuseum.nl/light> and join the forum.

Frontispiece
Giovanni Segantini, *My Models*, 1888, Kunsthaus Zurich (detail)

First published in the United Kingdom in 2000 by Thames & Hudson Ltd, 181A High Holborn, London WC1V 7QX, on the occasion of the exhibition *Light! The Industrial Age 1750-1900, Art & Science, Technology & Society* (Van Gogh Museum, Amsterdam, October 2000-February 2001, and Carnegie Museum of Art, Pittsburgh, April 2001-July 2001)

Designed by Pieter Roozen

British Library Cataloguing-in-Publication Data
A catalogue record for this book is available from the British Library

ISBN 0-500-51029-6

Printed and bound in Italy by Artegrafica

Contents

Foreword

Light is integral to the making and enjoyment of any work of art, yet it rarely has been the subject of art historical scholarship or museum exhibitions. This project examines 150 years of scientific, technological, and artistic innovation in the field of light. Scientists from Newton to Einstein; inventors from Argand to Edison; artists from Chardin to Van Gogh – the story is complex, fascinating, and still evolving. The exhibition demonstrates that although light is a constant presence in our lives, the understanding and interpretation of it has changed significantly over time, with consequences for every field of human endeavor. We hope that *Light!* will stimulate further thought and research on the subject in many fields and disciplines.

Light! originated as separate projects in our respective museums. We combined forces in 1997, merging the Van Gogh Museum's project on light, art, and science with the Carnegie Museum's interest in light, art and technology. The result is a more comprehensive and challenging exhibition than either museum would have accomplished alone.

Andreas Blühm, Head of Exhibitions & Display at the Van Gogh Museum, and Louise Lippincott, Curator of Fine Arts at the Carnegie Museum of Art, have served as exhibition curators and catalogue authors. They have benefited from the museological insights of James Bradburne, Director of the Museum für Angewandte Kunst in Frankfurt am Main, as they ventured into multi-disciplinary territory. Throughout, they have relied on the expertise and assistance of the staffs of both museums, especially as international co-workers are now only an e-mail message away. In the end, such ambitious and unusual projects depend heavily on the willingness and imagination of all involved, and we recognize with respect the contribution of so many staff members to the exhibition's success.

Equally crucial is the generosity of lenders, for without their help, our story would have been a thin one indeed. We trust that the presentation of their objects in interesting and provocative new contexts will in some measure mitigate the pain of their absence.

In Pittsburgh, the Carnegie Museum of Art salutes the Women's Committee for its early and generous support of this project. Bayer Foundation responded to our request for support, as did PNC Financial Services Inc. and an anonymous local foundation. To these principal donors, we owe much.

Richard Armstrong
Henry J. Heinz II Director
Carnegie Museum of Art

John Leighton
Director
Van Gogh Museum

Acknowledgments

The roots of this project in Amsterdam can be traced back to Caryl Marsh. Her combined interest in science, art history and museology first provided us with an idea for the exhibition. James Bradburne, at the time Head of Design at the newMetropolis Science and Technology Center in Amsterdam, worked with us on the concept, and was always ready to provide both advice and encouragement. Without his enthusiasm and inspiration neither the exhibition nor the book would have become what they are today. And, finally, it was Joseph Rishel who brought Amsterdam and Pittsburgh together, setting the stage for our cooperative enterprise.

In Pittsburgh, *Light!* originated as a more limited inquiry into the impact of artificial lighting on nineteenth-century painting. The early enthusiasm of Phillip Johnston made it possible to later embrace the partnership with the Van Gogh Museum. Richard Armstrong's energy and support has ensured its successful implementation in the United States.

Without the knowledge of a variety of "light experts," their written works as well as their personal interest and involvement, we would still be entirely in the dark. Johan Jansen, who has been concerned with light and illumination for many decades, is a pioneer in his field and gave us invaluable suggestions. He is also the founder of the Artificial Light in Art Foundation in Eindhoven. His successor, Bernadette Reijs-Nieuwenhuis, allowed us access to its rich archives.

Wolfgang Schivelbusch, the doyen of light history, lent us a patient ear. He has published more or less everything one needs to know on the subject, and our recognition and respect are demonstrated by the fact that we have been able to add little to his contributions.

Ara Kebapcioglu unites an immense knowledge of the subject with a fantastic network. His tiny shop in the rue Flatters in Paris provided more information than many a museum. He brought petroleum and gas to life for us.

Dan Mattausch, president of the Rushlight Club in the United States, was a constant source of expert information and advice on historical lighting. We are also grateful for his help with identifying a variety of lamps for the first time.

Nico Brederoo and Henk Boelmans Kranenburg led us to the magic lantern and awakened our enthusiasm for this old, but thoroughly entertaining technique. From him we learned that it is not the medium that is the message, but what one makes of it.

Among the preservers of ancient lighting we cannot fail to mention EnergeticA, Museum voor Energietechniek, in Amsterdam, where a group of volunteers continues to work tirelessly to save an almost unknown treasure-trove of light history. Cor Wagemakers, Sjaak Linsen, Bart Mackor and Klaas Zaal helped us to discover it. It was here that we first encountered functioning gas and arc lights. At the National Museum of American History, Smithsonian Institution, Bernard Finn and Steven Turner shared their unparalleled collections of lighting technology and science, as well as their work in progress. William Andrewes of the Collection of Historical Scientific Instruments, Harvard University, demonstrated the workings of the orrery, camera obscura, and other eighteenth-century instruments related to light, vastly increasing our understanding of these complex devices.

Kevin McGuire, on the other hand, showed us light's future. At Tailored Lighting, Inc. in Rochester, New York, we felt something of the spirit that must have pervaded Edison's laboratory at the beginning of the last century. During a visit to Museum EnergeticA he measured the spectrum of both gas and arc lights, which he then recreated electrically to illuminate a work by Van Gogh in the exhibition. Light sources based on his patents have been successfully installed in a number of museums, and will – we hope – make complaints about museum lighting a thing of the past. It was Gordon Anson of the National Gallery of Art in Washington who brought him to our attention.

The future also belongs to Jelle Post Koen Vroejenstijn and Eric Hiensch of VLM Computer Graphics in Amsterdam. We have them to thank for the street animations and the computerized lighting experiments based on works in the exhibition.

Computers are as much a part of public life today as gas lamps were in 1850. We would like to express our gratitude to the e-company, Amsterdam, for the conception and realization of our Internet site (www.vangoghmuseum.nl/light) which we hope will continue to flourish even after the exhibition is over, independent of space and time: Jurriënne Ossewold, Dick van Dijk, Hank van Dijk, Valerie Kranenburg, Harriet Onderstal, Marc Rouffaer, and Margo Rouwhorst. Andrea Bandelli provided additional advice.

We are grateful to Leesa Rittelman, research assistant for the exhibition, for much of the original source material presented in this book, as well as for her valuable advice and assistance in the selection of photographs, cameras, and films for the Pittsburgh venue. Without her encouragement and persistence, this aspect of our project would be less rich.

For further suggestions and information we would like to thank: Carrie Asman, Georges Berne, Harm Beukers, Elger Blühm, Reimund Blühm, Holger Böhning, Stephen Cannon-Brookes, Elizabeth Clegg, Peter de Clercq, Vittoria Crespi, Iris M. van Daalen, Andreas Daum, Luca Delfini, Marina Ducrey, Sally Duensing, Thomas Elsaesser, Betty Binns Esner, David Esner, Isabelle Farçat, David Fraser, Thomas W. Gaehtgens, John Gage, Beatrice B. Garvan, Nancy Harrison, Patrick Heurley, Annemieke Hogervorst, Annemieke Hoogenboom, Dick van der Horst, Annemarie Hürlimann, Thomas Humphrey, Mieke Ijzermans, Bruno Jacomy, Gerlof Janzen, Astrid Kwakernaak, Alastair Laing, Fred Leeman, Ingeborg Leijerzapf, Katherine Liapi, Theresa Levitt, Laurent Mannoni, Volker Manuth, Laure de Margerie, Chris Miele, Alexandra R. Murphy, Cornelia Peres, Joachim Pissarro, Jan Theun van Rees, Paul Ries, Falk Riess, Joseph Rishel, Christopher Riopelle, Alexander Robertson, Joseph Ruzicka, Niek Scheeres, William Sharpe, Wim van Sinderen, H. J. Smit, John P. Smith, Beate Söntgen, Abigail Solomon-Godeau, Ingrid Stilijanov-Nedo, Margret Stuffmann, Joel Tarr, Richard Thomson, Susan Vogel, Martha Ward, Johannes Weber, Wolfgang Westphal, Stephen White, Hans Wolff, Christopher Wray, Hans Ph. Ypma, Hendrik Ziegler, and Harro Zimmermann.

Every exhibition depends on loans and thus on the generosity of both private collectors and public institutions. The reactions to our – frequently slightly unorthodox – requests were always extremely friendly, even when they could not be fulfilled. We would like to extend our thanks to: Henry Adams, Fabienne Aellen, Graham Allen, Cathleen Anderson, William Andrewes, Jean-Pierre Angremy, Charles Anston, Robert Arpots, Luisa Arrigoni, Anthony Bannon, Anne Barz, Margrit Bauer, William E. Baxter, Laure Beaumont-Maillet, René van Beek, Stephanie Belt, Ernst Beyeler, Helen Bieri Thomson, Willem Bijleveld, H. F. Bill, Jim Bobick, J. E. A. Boogaard, Mattie Boom, R. Bosveld, James Bradburne, Christopher Brown, Neil Brown, Rainer Budde, Tim Burgard, Uwe Busch, Virginia Button, Françoise Cachin, Sarah Cash, Anne-Laure Carré, Edward Carter, Phillip Dennis Cate, Antonia Charlton, François Cheval, Catherine Clément, Peter de Clercq, Bruno Contardi, Sir Neil Cossons O.B.E., Elisabeth Cumbler, Jean-Pierre Cuzin, Götz Czymmek, Diane DeGrazia, Jan Deiman, Christiane Delpy, John De Santis, Alain Di Stefano, Gerdine van den Dool, Amy P. Dowe, Judith Durrer, E. Ebbinge, Tara Emsley, Anne Fahy, Hélène Fauré, Marc Fehlmann, Larry J. Feinberg, Joanne Fenn, Dominique Ferriot, Jan Piet Filedt Kok, Maria Teresa Fiorio, Catherine Fournier, David Fraser, Flemming Friborg, Rob van Gaal, Thomas W. Gaehtgens, Amber Woods Germano, Burkhardt Göres, Catherine Goeres, Vincent Willem van Gogh, Ray Goodman, Heide Grape-Albers, Richard Green, Marcia Grodsky, Janine Grünfeld, Tod Gustafson, Peter de Haan, Deborah Harding, Anne d'Harnoncourt, Anne van Helden, Allis Helleland, Christoph Heilmann, Freek Heijbroek, Wim Hoeben, Hanna Hohl, Marijn van Hoorn, Annie Jacques, Gerda Jansen, Phillip Johnston, Annemiek de Jong, Samuel Josefowitz, Ara Kebapcioglu, Claude Keisch, Dorothy Kellett, Margaret Kelly, Peter M. Kenny, Hans van Keulen, Dragan Klaic, Christian Klemm, Femke Koens, Pauline Krusemann, Evert Kwaadgras, Madame Le Couteur, Ronald de Leeuw, Frans Leidelmeijer, Serge Lemoine, Ray Anne Lockhard, Stephen Lockwood, Henri Loyrette, Ger Luijten, Julia W. Marlow, Danila Marsure Rosso, Olivier Meslay, Emmanuel Moatti, Bart Molenaar, Hanne Møller, Philippe de Montebello, W. F. J. Mörzer Bruyns, Christa Moorkamp, Therese Mulligan, Martin Myrone, Sandy Nairne, Stephen Nash, Nathalie Naudi, Susanne Netzer, Ann Newmark, Isabella Nitze,

Barbara O'Connor, Claire I. R. O'Mahony, Pieter van Oordt, Y. W. Ordelman, Harry S. Parker, Christian Passeri, Joke van Pelt, Ian F. Pollard, Earl A. Powell III, Miriam Pragt, Maxime Préaud, Mary Sue Sweeney Price, Greg Priori, Bernadette Reijs-Nieuwenhuis, Martha Richardson, Joseph Rishel, Pam Roberts, Malcolm Rogers, Duncan Robinson, Anne Röver-Kann, Pierre Rosenberg, Anton van Run, David Saker, Bernd Schälicke, Peter Schatborn, Margarete Schauß, Uwe M. Schneede, J. Schrofer, Daniel Schulman, Emmanuel Schwartz, David Scrase, Sir Nicholas Serota, George Shackelford, Wendy Sheridan, Peter Sigmond, Elizabeth Smallwood, Mary Solt, The Rt Hon Lord Somerleyton GCVO, Bonny Sousa, MaryAnne Stevens, Susan A. Stein, Roger Stoddard, Toni Stooss, Hannie Straver, Doron Swade, Robert Jan te Rijdt, Gary Tinterow, Barbara Trelstad, Julian Treuherz, Helen Valentine, Rafael Valls, Stephen Van Dyk, Isabelle Varloteaux, G. A. C. Veeneman, Nol Verhagen, Birgit Verwiebe, Rik Vos, Cor Wagemakers, Jane Wallis, Malcolm Warner, Cindy van Weele, Ute-G. Weickardt, Catherine Whistler, Stephen White, Oliver Wick, James N. Wood, Liz Woods, Nancy Wulbrecht, Lisa Yeung, and Tamra Yost.

Almost all our colleagues at our respective museums were involved in the project in one way or another. In Amsterdam we would like to thank Aly Noordermeer and Sara Verboven in particular, who were responsible for the safe transport of a huge variety of often unusual objects. The following also provided further suggestions, advice, and support: Edwin Becker, Hans Beets, Saskia Beukers, Ton Boxma, Caroline Breunesse, Rene Caïro, Monique Hageman, Ella Hendriks, Sjraar van Heugten, Ton Hoofwijk, Leo Jansen, Cor Krelekamp, John Leighton, Hans Luijten, Mireille Melchers, Rianne Norbart, Fieke Pabst, Kees Posthuma, Sjoukje Posthuma, Jan Samuelsz, Frans Stive, Chris Stolwijk, Benno Tempel, Louis van Tilborgh, Cees Tournier, Heidi Vandamme, Marije Vellekoop, Melanie Verhoeven, Anita Vriend, and Roelie Zwikker. The installation of the show in the Van Gogh Museum in Amsterdam lay in the capable hands of Henk van der Geest and Peter de Kimpe, assisted by Bart van der Linden, Wim Plas and Pieter Roozen.

In Pittsburgh we are grateful to staff members of the Museum of Art and its sister institutions, Carnegie Science Center, Carnegie Museum of Natural History, and Carnegie Library: Elisabeth Agro, Linda Batis, Ellen Baxter, Seddon Bennington, Meg Bernard, Elissa Curcio, Bill Devlin, Heidi Domine, Ruth Edelstein, Michael Fahlund, Lauren Friedman, Bob Gangewere, Rhonda Goldblatt, Patty Jaconetta, Bill Judson, Jennifer Kersting, Champ Knecht, Beth Levanti, Cathy Logan, Dennis McFadden, Charlene Shang Miller, Barbara Merrin, Tracy Myers, Sarah Nicolls, Wendy Osher, Susan Palamara, Chris Rauhoff, Will Real, Allison Revello, Janice Reyes, Maureen Rolla, Marilyn Russell, Lucy Stewart, Tey Stiteler, Monika Tomko, Heather Wahl, and Rhonda Wozniak. Leonard Tena and Roger Wei have assisted us with physics and optics in the installation, which has been designed by Paul Rosenblatt of Damianos + Anthony with Maguire Hilbisch Associates. Gaea Leinhardt of the University of Pittsburgh has worked with Museum of Art staff on interpretation and presentation.

This book was made possible in large part by Rachel Esner, Jacob Groot, Peter Harholdt, Erik and Petra Hesmerg, Sjaak de Jong, Laura Munster, Jan Robert, Julie van Roden, Pieter Roozen, Monique Smulders, Walter van der Star, and Richard Stoner. Thomas Neurath and Simon Mason of Thames & Hudson supervised the production with enthusiasm and professionalism.

Andreas Blühm
Louise Lippincott

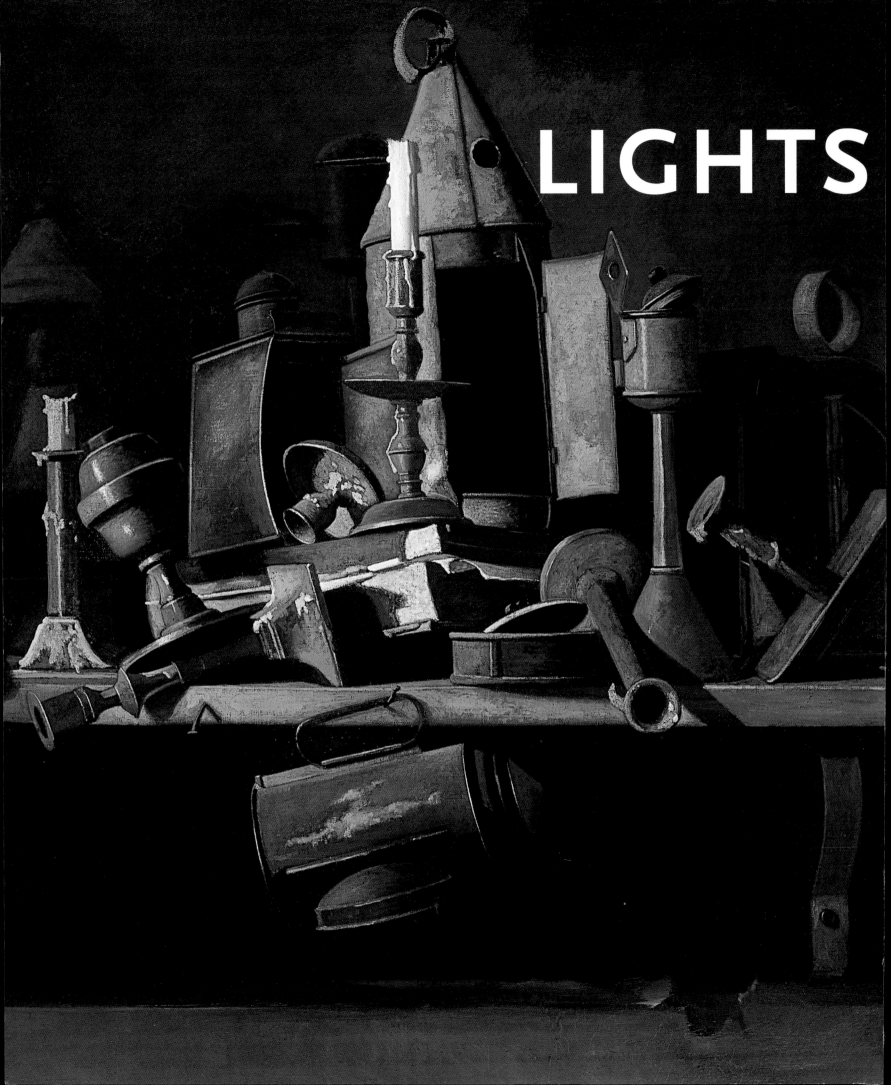

LIGHTS

# of Other Days

Light is the measure of all things. Immaterial as it appears to the human eye, light makes our world visible. In our era, when the question of light's materiality is more confusing than ever – not just particles, not just waves, but both according to how you look at it – it is time to consider its equally varied history. But what is a history of light? Light itself has not changed physically. Therefore, a history of light is really a history of the human perception, understanding, and manipulation of light.

This book and exhibition came into being because we wished to point out that the light we see and live by today is not what others saw and lived by one hundred years ago, nor what might be lighting peoples' lives fifty years into the future. Our great-grandparents lit their houses with flaming gas jets. Our children seem to be lighting their rooms with cathode ray tubes, fiber optics, and liquid crystal display screens. The days of the familiar incandescent light bulb might be numbered! Light today, especially artificial light, is so taken for granted that we barely notice it. Is natural light necessary anymore? Some people seem to use it as an optional health benefit, like regular exercise.

Why should all of this be of concern to art museums? As holders and interpreters of great works of art, we have always known that light plays an integral role in art's making, meaning, and display. We also know, from cleaning skylights or changing the light track in our galleries, that each time the light changes, so does our experience of art and its environment. And with such loss and change, come losses and changes in our ability to comprehend the visual effect, meaning, and accomplishment of great paintings. As we surveyed the eighteenth- and nine-teenth-century paintings in our collections, we realized that their painters' light was not the same as ours. The artists who created them knew, believed, and saw different aspects of light than we do today. As a result, we cannot understand their work without exploring topics that the artists themselves took for granted. This book presents the results of our research; an attempt to recre-ate, for today's audiences, lights of an earlier time that illuminate masterpieces of the past.

Kerosene table lamp, Austrian, ca. 1875–1900, Lumière de l'oeil, Paris

"I am much in the *Dark* about *Light*."

– *Benjamin Franklin*[1]

"People speak about Enlightenment and wish for more light.
My God, of what use is light if people have no eyes or if those who have, keep them deliberately closed?"

– *Georg Christoph Lichtenberg*[2]

"It is true that the sun illuminates the painter's canvas, but it is the painter who illuminates his painting."

– *Charles Blanc*[3]

John Frederick Peto, *Lights of Other Days*, 1906, The Art Institute of Chicago, Goodman Fund (detail)

Searching for light

Researching the history of light turned out to be a more challenging project than we anticipated. How does one show today's viewers light from long ago? How do we describe it? How do we immerse people in old-fashioned light environments, and how do we recover the lost meanings and values these lights held? Finding answers to these questions became our goal as we realized just how much of light's history is disappearing in our modern time. Firsthand experience of old light is hard to obtain in the twenty-first century. How can one enjoy starlight when our skies are so light-polluted? How many of us now see the sun without an obscuring industrial haze? Who still rises with the sun instead of the alarm clock? If we do experience natural light in old-fashioned ways, it is almost always due to a disaster: a power failure, or losing one's matches in the wilderness, or forgetting the sunscreen. The old artificial lights are even more remote from our daily lives. When attempting to switch on an antique lamp, could you find the switch? What would you do when you realize it never had one? Would you value light more if it was harder to make?

Joshua Reynolds, *Self-portrait*, ca. 1747, National Portrait Gallery, London

When we turned to the libraries for precedents, we discovered there are no all-embracing histories of light available, although numerous specialist studies have been written. Since antiquity, light has been a topic not only for philosophers, but also artists, doctors, psychologists, poets, chemists, religious visionaries, physicists, nudists, astronomers, and socialists. While we have enjoyed our forays into the literature of these exotic fields, our objective could never be encyclopedic. Overwhelmed by the material and myriad points of view, we decided to concentrate on a limited period, the era of industrialization. We believe no other era saw such thoroughgoing revolutions in light and lighting than the years between 1750 and 1900.

Although the story traditionally begins in the second half of the seventeenth century with the legendary discoveries of Antoni van Leeuwenhoek, René Descartes, Isaac Newton, and Christiaan Huygens, we have begun our account of the revolution in light in the middle of the eighteenth century. By that date, the scientific revolution had penetrated the public sphere and was changing the lives, work and thoughts of many in Europe and the future United States. The literate public could read about the new science in dictionaries and encyclopedias, especially the great French *Encyclopédie*, published from 1752–65. Artists, still shedding the stigmas of trade and craft, were taking a new interest in what was then "high tech" as a source of subject matter, practical ideas, and prestige. Scientists, anxious to establish their intellectual and professional credentials, and manufacturers seeking markets, publicized their inventions for an increasingly literate and wealthy populace. For the next 150 years, light science and technology (along with science and technology in general) enjoyed a golden age of general enthusiasm and interest and many artists joined in this public fascination. Most of the concepts and technology developed during this time could be communicated in basic language, with relatively simple mathematics and easily discerned diagrams. Natural phenomena could still be created, measured, and displayed in the home, laboratory and lecture hall, and be seen by the naked eye. The public, at the height of the positivist era, believed that science and industry would improve the lot of humanity everywhere. However, that story begins to dissipate with the development of relativity theory at the turn of the nineteenth century. Einstein's ideas suddenly removed science and light from the realm of the mundane and placed them in the strange and exotic universe that we struggle to imagine today.

Villeneuve ?, *Diogenes Guides Marat towards Daylight*, 1793, etching, Bibliothèque Nationale de France, Cabinet des Estampes, Paris

The ancient philosopher Diogenes, who went about in the daytime with a lit lantern searching for reasonable men, was one of the idols of the French Revolution.

Edgar Degas, *Interior*, 1868–69, Philadelphia Museum of Art, The Henry P. McIlhenny Collection in memory of Frances P. McIlhenny (detail)

Vincent van Gogh, *The Potato Eaters*, 1885, Amsterdam, Van Gogh Museum (Vincent van Gogh Foundation) (detail)

Even when restricted to the time frame of roughly 1750–1900, however, the relevant bibliography turned out to be immense, but often peripheral to our main subject. Instead of covering every detail of this profuse history of illumination, we aim to highlight significant inventions and tensions and to raise readers' awareness of light's pervasive, changing role in our lives and thoughts. Even so, certain aspects of light are *not* addressed in this project, although they are also extremely important. The first is the study of color, a phenomenon so closely tied to light that the two cannot be separated easily. However, art historian John Gage has written two excellent books on the history of color, so the subject is not suffering from the neglect that hampers our knowledge of light.[4]

Throughout, we have concentrated on those aspects of science, technology, and art that were understood by eighteenth- and nineteenth-century publics. Consequently, twentieth-century light science with its arcane mathematics receives little attention here. In the end, the dependable discipline of art history, seemed most appropriate to the subject and seriously underrepresented in the existing literature.

Light history and art history

One of the oldest and simplest methods of art history is the comparison. Art historians are trained to compare picture with picture, detail with detail, technique with technique, in order to answer basic connoisseurship questions: Is this work authentic? Is it by this or that artist? Is it early or late in date? Is it more successful than other works; is it better than a rival's? We carried out these exercises with light in art but met with unilluminating results. In fact, we discovered that we could not even honestly answer such simple questions, such as whether Degas painted lamplight better than Van Gogh. Never having seen nineteenth-century oil lamps in use, how could we judge? Despite professional sensitivity to light in art and the environment, we had no clue about the appearance of lights of the past. Our questions became: what did old forms of light look like? Why did artists depict some kinds of light effects, but not others? How well does their art represent light as it was observed or experienced in the past? How do these lights of the past compare with the way people use or experience light today? Eventually, we realized that the important comparisons for this project were not between works of art at all. What we wanted to compare was art with experience: the experience of light – how we see it, how they saw it, and how they portrayed it.

This book and the exhibition it accompanies make these comparisons within the limits imposed by ink on paper and museum-standard environmental controls. Our method may be conservative, but our comparisons are somewhat mad. We compare a painting of a stuffed bat and Gallé lamps, *Gauguin's Chair* by Van Gogh seen in four different lights, telescopes and textbooks, a camera and a camera obscura. These juxtapositions consistently present older experiences of light that we cannot now understand by other means. For a concrete example, let us return to the question of the nineteenth-century oil lamp. Can the experience of its light be visualized best through the emotionally-charged scene in Degas's *Interior*, or Charles Dickens's description of a cozy evening gathering, or a household manual with instructions for cleaning and filling oil lamps, or by lighting a real antique lamp in a museum laboratory? Our response is an emphatic "all of the above."

By comparing these different representations of the past's experience of light, we learned a great deal about oil lamps. We also found out much about traditional family life, the reasons householders turned thankfully to gaslight, and what is so troubling about Degas's most famous genre scene. We found ourselves wondering if the television set and computer were the twentieth-century equivalent of the oil lamp and fireplace – the glowing light at the center of every family evening at home. Such comparisons and juxtapositions open our eyes to lights from other times and from our own. Our multifaceted approach, with its emphasis on personal experience, is actually older than art history. In the eighteenth and nineteenth centuries, lectures, demonstrations, and exhibitions jumbled together the new science, the new technologies, and sometimes – often unwittingly – new art, for the enlightenment and entertainment of the general public. We are attempting to do the same.

Light sources

The earliest studies of artificial lighting concentrated on antiquarian preservation and theatrical simulations as electricity replaced older technologies. Most old lights – kerosene lamps, gaslights, arc lamps – fell out of use because they are difficult and dangerous to operate. In fact, they are so dangerous that even the most accurate period rooms in museums must use simulations of doubtful authenticity. But understanding the old lights is not simply a matter of finding and igniting the original devices and fuels. One also needs great patience and skill to keep the old lights going. We no longer have social customs or manual skills dedicated to maintaining burning lights. And, after all that work, the paltry amounts of illumination actually produced hardly seem worth the effort. Even the early incandescent lamps seem hopelessly dim when compared to their contemporary successors. Thus, in our attempts to experience the old light directly, we faced a challenge: even if reconstructions were perfect, our eyes are so accustomed to bright, modern, ambient light, we can scarcely recognize the differences between the candlelight and gaslight that stunned and dazzled our ancestors.

Our next step in exploring the experience of light took us on a search for firsthand written descriptions. But we were surprised to discover a limited number of such accounts in the thousands of pages turned. As long as individuals are ignorant of future possibilities, they cannot predict what experience to record for posterity. Who wrote about sitting in a carriage before it was possible to take the train? Who wrote about retyping a manuscript before backspacing on a word-processing computer became possible? The silence of the written sources has already been noted by the historian William O'Dea, whose groundbreaking book on the social history of light drew the right conclusion: "It is obvious, therefore, that light – or the absence of it after dark – was a most important factor in social history. It is, however, one that has been almost completely ignored. This is no doubt due to the scarcity of references to lighting in both literature and art, and the fact that most of the references that do exist are to the unusual rather than the ordinary."[5] As O'Dea recognized, flicking the light switch is another daily activity too banal to mention unless it is accompanied by a flash fire in the wiring.

Artificial light is a central literary theme only in the genres of horror and science fiction, where once again we face the problem of writers who describe or invent the exception, not the norm. An example is the cinematic thriller, *Wait Until Dark*, featuring drug dealer Alan Arkin and blind woman Audrey Hepburn battling for hours over a light switch. Our horror grows until the drug dealer suffers the final consequence of his unthinking dependence on light – he dies, unable to defend himself in the dark. As this example suggests, light can and does become more visible in imaginative works and writings: fiction, drama, and poetry. Yet, we had to train ourselves to find it in scenic descriptions, symbolic passages, and obscure allusions.

Next to the written documents, there are the paintings, drawings, prints, and photographs that are prime material for research on the light of the past. Looking back to O'Dea's comment above, we believe that art historians' sensitivities have been dulled, too. Once the authors, both art historians, started to look for light in the visual arts, we found it everywhere. But, as we became aware of selected art's value for our topic, we came to realize that we could not necessarily depend on what we observed in objects and images as historically reliable. Both making and observing art are acts of interpretation. When artists – and we believe they are more sensitive to light than most of us – treated light as their subject, their work interested us greatly. But at the same time, the reliability of their images as sources of information about old

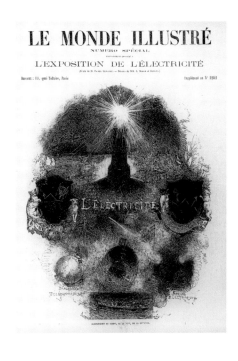

C. H. Koning, *Electrical discharge*, engraving from Martinus van Marum, *Description d'une très grande machine électrique [...]*, Haarlem 1785, Teylers Museum, Haarlem

lighting sometimes actually decreased. We learned that artists' materials and techniques lacked the intensity or subtlety to match natural effects, that an artist would alter a light effect to enhance a dramatic moment, or a pigment had faded to a ghost of its former self. Artists rarely left records of their intentions or working process, nor of the political or religious views that influenced their light symbolism. Thus, we could not be sure if the location of a light source in an interior scene or landscape represented what the artist saw, or followed a stylistic rule about the distribution of "lights" upon the picture plane. We could not be sure where art began and history ended in the images we found.

The field of art history has been surprisingly silent on the topic of light. This is especially puzzling if one thinks about the crucial role of light in the production and display of art. Although there are hundreds of art book titles containing the word "light" – *Masters of ...*, *Northern...*, *Drawn into...*, *American...* – the subject of light itself, whether artificial, natural or scientific, is rarely discussed in any of these volumes. This has been noted by Wolfgang Schöne, the author of the only comprehensive study of light in art, but he, in turn, does not reflect upon the development of artificial lighting, partly due to his concentration on art before 1800.[6] Many art historians have described painterly light effects that characterize particular historical styles or techniques; for example, the theatrical light effects typical of baroque painting. However, very few have written in depth about the light in which art was produced and

Auguste Lepère after Edmond Morin, *Electricity*, title page of *Le Monde Illustré, Numéro spécial exclusivement consacré à l'Exposition de l'Electricité*, 1881, Van Gogh Museum, Amsterdam

displayed. The truism still holds that daylight is accepted as the best, if not only, suitable illumination. With that in mind, art historians have not dedicated their time to comparing the differences between typical studio lighting (cool, even light from the north) and display lighting, which was often quite different, whether in homes, palaces, churches, galleries, or museums. Even art museums, obsessed with issues of preservation and fiscal economy, place low priority on displaying works of art in historically appropriate, sympathetic lights.

When we focus more specifically on art historians' recent discussions of light during the period 1750–1900, we encounter several trends in the field that both stimulate and complicate our work. The first is the burgeoning popularity of impressionist and post-impressionist art, which has cemented in the popular mind the notion of nineteenth-century French landscape painters as discoverers of "light" at its sunniest. The conventional history of French impressionism, beginning with the rustic iconoclast Corot, the outdoorsy Barbizon School, and moving on to the incipient modernism of the impressionists and Cézanne, is now coming under revision. For example, recently, art historian Peter Galassi has traced the origins of nineteenth-century outdoor painting to eighteenth-century Rome. Even so, landscape painters' depictions of light are still discussed in isolation from broader cultural contexts.[7]

A. Müller, *Die Gasbeleuchtung im Haus*, Vienna, Pest & Leipzig 1881, Carnegie Library, Pittsburgh

Secondly, a misconception develops from stereotypes of Paris as the capital of the nineteenth century, the birthplace of modernism, and the city of light. These celebrated epithets for this great city are certainly appropriate for the last thirty years of the nineteenth century, but they are wide of the mark for the rest of our period, 1750–1870. This is especially true of Paris's reputation for light. In fact, most of the innovative technology related to light was developed outside of France; Paris was actually backward in adopting modern lighting compared to other capitals; and some science and most technologies were not "popularized" in French as rapidly as in English or German. We began to wonder whether artists in other countries, exposed to modern ideas about light decades before their French colleagues, might have discovered "modern light" on their own and then brought it to Paris.

Thirdly, intertwining art and science has become trendy among art historians, notorious for their antipathy to higher mathematics and the hard sciences. While many useful studies seem to come into print almost daily, most betray a certain timidity (which we share) with scientific sources. The tendency to rely on the familiar material in artists' treatises and published criticism ignores the obvious and important fact that artists had access to knowledge from many other sources, including ephemeral publications, popular literature, public lectures, and general conversation. We have turned to these sources as much as possible and found them to be extremely relevant.

Art, science, technology

The historiography of science and technology actually parallels that of art. An early emphasis on great men, a concentration on stories of progress and success within limited fields of endeavor, and attempts at broader perspectives that place the subject in cultural contexts; this progression could describe both art history and the history of science over the last seventy-five years. Historians of science and technology have surpassed art historians in addressing reception issues, however. As a result of modern attempts to industrialize the world, the problem of how different cultures, publics or populaces respond to scientific and technological change has stimulated extensive and sophisticated research. Now, historians, such as Wolfgang

Julia Margaret Cameron, *Sir John Frederick William Herschel*, 1867, albumen print, Carnegie Museum of Art, Pittsburgh, Director's Discretionary Fund

While artists and scientists regarded each others' work with respect, there was no longer a sense that one person could master the complexities of both disciplines. Thus, Julia Margaret Cameron's fine photographic portrait of the astronomer John Herschel concentrates on the intangible connections between their respective disciplines: the responsibilities of genius, the inner life of the imagination, and visionary creativity. Significantly, she drapes him in velvet like a Renaissance sage.

Schivelbusch, also recognize that curious and unpredictable interactions between people and new technology characterized the Industrial Era in Europe and the United States. Unfortunately, *Disenchanted Night*, Schivelbusch's eye-opening study of the effect of artificial lighting on many aspects of nineteenth-century life, including theater, neglected the visual arts.[8]

At the beginning of the twenty-first century, it appears that art and science were becoming reacquainted again, at least in popular perception. To some, contemporary art and physics seem equally remote from routine reality. Others point out that digital technology has created new connections between the public and everything from rocket science to video art to home

Thomas A. Edison's office in West Orange, with Aurelio Bordiga's marble sculpture *The Genius of Electricity* of 1888 in the background, West Orange, New Jersey, Edison National Historic Site.

Edison bought this sculpture after seeing it on display at the Universal Exposition in Paris in 1889. Edison added the lightbulb himself after the sculpture arrived in New Jersey.

shopping. Such interconnections between art and science were common in the history of light before 1900, which is full of people whose specialty was not to specialize. The archetypal renaissance man, Leonardo da Vinci, painted timeless pictures, excelled in chiaroscuro (i.e., the relation between light and shadow), and invented an oil lamp with a projecting lens. His amazing combination of intellectual genius, manual skill, and mechanical inventiveness were equally admired in his time and now.

Following in Leonardo's footsteps and partly hidden by his shadow, were Jan van der Heyden, the Dutch seventeenth-century cityscape painter, inventor of the fire hose and street lights; later Philippe Jacques de Loutherbourg, painter of sublime landscapes and inventor of the moving image; Louis-Jacques-Mandé Daguerre, Romantic painter, stage designer and pioneer of photography; Samuel Morse, painter and inventor of telegraphy; as well as Alvan Clark, a telescope maker and portraitist. Unlike Leonardo, these men have never been considered artistic geniuses. Most were thought of as failures at different stages in their careers, and today are esteemed as second rank painters whose efforts to make a living induced them to experiment and innovate with whatever came to hand. Despite their flawed reputations, these artist/inventors are critical for this project because they exemplify the many connections that existed between the sciences and the arts in previous centuries.

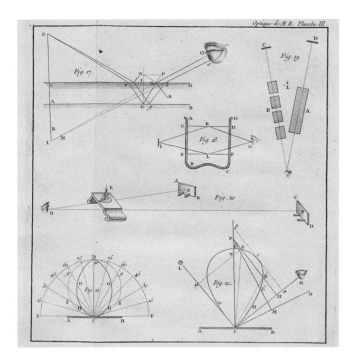

Diagram explaining refraction, engraving from Pierre Bouguer, *Traité d'optique sur la gradation de la lumière,* Paris 1760, Carnegie Library, Pittsburgh

Eugène Cicéri after Karl Girardet, *Sunrise from the Right,* chromolithograph from Camille Flammarion, *The Atmosphere,* New York 1874, Carnegie Library, Pittsburgh

How did the scientists and artists see their relationship? In 1799, more than one hundred years after Newton published his *Opticks,* the author John Wood still felt that he had to explain the basic Newtonian postulates about light to the artist/readers of his treatise on perspective.[9] The landscape painter Pierre-Henri de Valenciennes reassured his colleagues and readers of his 1800 treatise: "We will not attempt to discuss whether light emanates from the sun, or if it is material. Our aim is not a treatise on physics; we limit ourselves to a discussion of painting."[10] When Jacques Nicolas Paillot de Montabert, a painter and author of a multi-volume treatise on painting (1829–51), writes about light he eagerly points out that it is not his or his readers' job to really understand the physics: "It is not a matter of instructing painters in the conjectures of physicists regarding certain peculiar characteristics of light, [...]."[11]

The painters, trained at their academies according to methods of the seventeenth century, had learned little if any mathematics or science beyond the geometry of space and shadow. The memoirs and letters by the artists themselves – or rather the lack thereof – reflect their ignorance and confusion about the importance of light. A wonderfully preposterous example of such ignorance is the poet Coleridge's confession: "To me, I confess, Newton's positions, first, of a Ray of Light, as a physical synodical Individuum, secondly, that 7 specific individua are co-existent (by what copula?) In the complex yet divisible Ray; thirdly that the Prism is a mere mechanic Dissector of the Ray; and lastly, that Light, as the common result, is = confusion."[12] No wonder a famous artistic dinner in London in 1817 ended up with a toast to "the confusion of Newton!" Some saw light in color, others saw color in light, some saw only light, others saw only color. Cézanne, in a letter to Emile Bernard, even went so far as to state: "Light does not exist for the painter."[13] Ruskin, at last, proclaimed that the artists' isolation from scientific development was advantageous. In his essay, *The Artist and the Man of Science,* he wrote that the artist "should be illiterate, but well read in the best books, and thoroughly high bred, both in heart and in bearing. In a word, he should be fit for the best society, *and should keep out of it.*"[14] One thing was sure, the Renaissance ideal of the artist-scientist was over.

Most scientists ignored the fine arts altogether. There were, however, exceptions to the rule: An example was the French physicist François Arago when he praised the invention of photography in 1839. Others boasted proudly when their discipline surpassed art as a means of recording or interpreting nature, or they expressed frustration when artists ignored new scientific discoveries (e.g., lightning bolts did not conform to the traditional zigzag). Eventually, there was no avoiding science. In 1873, Gaston Tissandier stated in the first edition of his popular magazine *La Nature* of 1873: "Science is everywhere; it is evident in every moment, it has become so widespread it even appears in novels."[15] Hermann von Helmholtz addressed the growing gap between the arts and sciences in his seminal essays, *On the Physiological Causes of Harmony in Music* (1857) and *On the Relation of Optics to Painting* (1871), and certainly exercised influence on painters, such as Whistler and Seurat. In spite of these signs of mutual interest, science (physics in particular) had become increasingly mathematical just as art was becoming less so, with the abandonment of geometrical perspective. Even artists who boasted of the relationship between science and their art – Seurat and Signac come to mind – got much of their scientific knowledge second or third hand and at a very basic level of understanding.

Natural light

In the eighteenth and nineteenth centuries, artists and scientists invented natural light. They began to distinguish the light of nature – produced in some unknown fashion by sun, moon, and stars – from divine light, artificial light, studio light, and the lights that artists distributed across canvas according to abstract aesthetic principles. Whatever it was shining down upon earth, it had a character of its own worthy of observation and analysis. It was something that had physical presence and physical effects, and could be measured or painted like any other substance. When artificial lighting became widespread in European and American cities in the early 1800s, natural light could be contrasted with the unnatural light generated by Argand burners and gas jets. At that point, natural light acquired a moral identity – pure, healthy, truthful – as well as a physical one.

Throughout the nineteenth century, artificial light continued to encroach on the environment, and artistic conceptions of natural light changed as a consequence. By the 1870s, what some considered to be the "natural" light for select environments and populations was actually artificial. Prostitutes in 1870s Paris, for example, were allowed out on the streets only after the gaslights came on (a perverse sort of sunrise). The poet Stephane Mallarmé considered gaslight to be the natural ambiance for city women, and he praised the impressionists for making special efforts to paint their female subjects in rural daylight, where their complexions looked better.[16] By the 1880s, natural light had become just one of many distinctive types of light available for daily life (just as it is today), and in the urban environment it was becoming increasingly rare. The decadents of the 1890s, typified by the recluse des Esseintes in Huysmans's novel *Against the Grain* (*A rebours*) tried to avoid the glare of daylight at all costs.

The scrupulous, detached observation of natural phenomena, especially natural light, is one of the hallmarks of the age of enlightenment. At first, scientists and amateurs far outnumbered artists as light observers. The names of the great eighteenth-century painters of natural light can almost be counted on the fingers of one hand: Chardin, Liotard, Valenciennes, Loutherbourg, Vernet, Canaletto. They were brilliant painters, *now* considered to be original naturalists. Chardin and Liotard restricted their light studies to the domestic laboratory of the kitchen still life, but Valenciennes left the studio to paint oil sketches of landscapes. Valenciennes subjected his observations to careful geometric analysis, like any enlightened student of optics. However, the purpose of these small images as records of transient light effects is documented by frequent inscriptions of the date, the time of day and the weather conditions. These studies served as a database for elements of finished compositions. Artists exchanged these little studies with each other and eventually they were actively collected, as connoisseurs came to appreciate the art of observation as highly as the art of invention. Real outdoor painting – the execution of the painting entirely on the spot – was the next logical step. The art historian and critic Richard Muther explained this move into nature as a reaction against urbanization. As cities became larger, denser, and increasingly urban in character, the more artists and their patrons yearned nostalgically for the countryside. This is why, according to Muther, the 1800s became the century for painting light, meaning natural light.[17]

Daylight

This move to the outdoors coincided with growing public interest in the scientific investigations and controversies surrounding natural light. J. M. W. Turner, in England, and Caspar David Friedrich, in Germany, rendered the movement of the sun and its striking coloristic effects with unprecedented precision. Turner's annotations to Joseph Priestley's *History and Present State of Discoveries Relating to Vision, Light, and Colours* (1767) testify to the genuine scientific interest that accompanies his artistic production, while his attempts to observe the sun directly nearly led to blindness. In the 1850s and 1860s, the next generation of English painters, the Pre-Raphaelites, pioneered genuine plein-air painting. If one compares the meticulous description of every detail of the grass or the wool of a sheep – as in Ford Madox Brown's *Pretty Baa-Lambs* of 1851-59 – with the impressionists' attempt in the early 1870s to depict the brightness of daylight with loose brush strokes, two things become evident. First, natural light, as such, has become a subject of advanced painting. Second, artists claiming to paint natural light with scientific objectivity nevertheless produced extremely diverse results.

Both the impressionists and Pre-Raphaelites claimed to be "objective" observers of nature, only interested in the true rendering of what their eyes saw. William Holman Hunt summarized their position: "When we Pre-Raphaelites were charged with exaggeration in our key of colour, and were told that our pictures had all the hues of the rainbow, we replied that the brown shadows of old professors did not give the impression of open-air effect which we had been surprised to discover while searching for the truth before Nature herself. We registered prismatic hues because we found that each terrestrial feature mirrored the blue sky and the tints of its neighbouring creations; and we maintained that while a part of our picture by itself might appear over-coloured, it was consistent in the impression it gave of truth."[18] He then continues to bash the impressionists whose method, he believed, simply disguised technical inability.

The impressionists in turn, represented here by their most eloquent spokesperson, Edmond Duranty, were also too happy to use or accept the jargon of modern science when their art was discussed: "Proceeding by intuition, they little by little succeeded in splitting sunlight into its rays, and then reestablishing its unity in the general harmony of the iridescent color that they scatter over their canvases. With regard to visual subtleties and delicate blending of colors, the result is utterly extraordinary. Even the most learned physicists could find nothing to criticize in these painters' analysis of light."[19] Both Hunt and Duranty talk about prisms and splitting sunlight in order to explain their respective artistic positions toward natural light. Georges Clemenceau stated in his 1928 monograph *Claude Monet: Les Nymphéas*, that impressionism was depending upon electromagnetic theory. However, since it is impossible now to determine the depth of the impressionists' knowledge of science, we cannot tell if the statements above are true.

Did artists feel so left behind by the public debate, that they needed to incorporate such references to science in their work? John Adkins Richardson, whose *Modern Art and Scientific Thought* of 1971 is still an extremely valid study, pointed out that the impressionists may actually have known the latest theories of light and used them to their own artistic goals: "The contemporary physiologist Hermann von Helmholtz noted that 'not every illumination is suitable for representing a landscape.' His studies imply that painters should not light objects from behind since that would cause the thing to appear flat, surrounded by a nimbus of light, and continuous with its own shade. Moreover, the artist's vision would be impaired by *mouches volantes* and fugitive sensations dancing within the silhouette of the form. In his haystack pictures, Monet did exactly what he was supposed not to, and with precisely the results Helmholtz predicted. That was what he *wanted* to have happen. Monet did not discover such phenomena; they were well known. Impressionism simply made them part of an aesthetic currency."[20]

These paradoxes may be explained by the fact that the early, radical plein-air painters in England and France believed that scientific ideas and objective observations of nature offered powerful modern alternatives to traditional academic painting formulas. In England, the

Jean Siméon Chardin, *Glass of Water and Coffee Pot*, ca. 1761, Carnegie Museum of Art, Pittsburgh, Howard A. Noble Collection (detail)

Pre-Raphaelites turned to the outdoors in order to escape from the "brown soup," or "sauce," style of painting typical of the painterly, monochromatic modes of Joshua Reynolds and Thomas Lawrence. Not surprisingly, when the British rebels exchanged studio north light for unmodulated sunshine, they saw brilliant color, blue shadow, and extraordinary detail. The impressionists, too, claimed that the objectivity of sunlight enabled them to see and paint nature in a new, anti-academic way. However, the academic style they were rejecting was the colorful, highly finished and detailed manner of Jacques-Louis David and Jean Auguste Dominique Ingres. Consequently, impressionist daylight scenes go in the opposite direction from both Ingres and the Pre-Raphaelites with bold brushwork, patches of raw color, and absence of detail.

Like the Pre-Raphaelites the impressionists also painted their shadows with tones of blue for two possible reasons. French academic painters had painted their shadows with shades of black, and scientists had established the blueness of shadow on firm optical principles. The impressionist's practice of giving such titles as "effet de soleil" etc. to their paintings was meant to point out the modern scientific treatment of the subject to audiences who were already sensitized by science to light's varying effects on climate, environment, perception, and psychology.

In viewing science – in this case light science – as the essence of the modern and the opposite of the traditional, these avant-garde painters differed very little from the rest of positivist nineteenth-century society. Painters found modernity in the same places everyone else did – the innovations and discoveries of science and technology that promised to liberate humanity from the ignorance, conflict, and miseries of the past. Common sense (not high end physics) and public optimism about all things scientific and technological; these were the roots of "scientific" painting, just as they were the roots of scientific housekeeping (read on). One should not be surprised to find the impressionist's science also described (and described better) in housekeeping manuals. A case in point is *The Handbook of Household Science: A Popular Account of Heat, Light, Air, Aliment, and Cleansing*, published in London and New York in 1860. The author Edward L. Youmans, a popularizer of science, was to be instrumental in inviting Nicholas Tyndall to give his epoch-making lectures on energy and light in the United States in 1872. In his *Handbook*, Youmans painstakingly described Newtonian optics and color theory, and their application to everything from the arrangement of lighting fixtures to the selection of complementary and contrasting hues for flower arrangements and bonnet trim. This way, housewives and artists learned basic optics in order to apply their individual crafts (housework or painting) in modern, scientific ways.

There also seems little doubt that the nineteenth-century landscape painters' obsession with brightness is related to increasingly accurate scientific measurements of the brightness of sunlight, starlight, artificial lights, and artistic effects. Development of the photometer (light meter) began in the early eighteenth century with simple systems for comparing different light sources with a common uniform standard, such as the light generated by a wax candle set at a fixed distance from the observer. By the middle of the nineteenth century, far more sophisticated photometers gauged the relative brightness of stars or the illuminating power of lighting fuels, such as gas. It is yet another paradox of painters' struggles with natural light that, just as they were attempting to depict its visual effects, scientists were proving that some of these effects were impossible to capture. When in 1857, physics teacher Jules Jamin turned his photometer toward the paintings of Granet, Barbizon landscapes, and works of the French realists, he proved that no artist's pigment could match the intensity of sunlight.[21] Duranty, in his advocacy of the impressionists, also brought up the issue of brightness as measured by scientists, as opposed to brightness as perceived by the human eye.[22] One can argue that the history of landscape painting in the second half of the nineteenth century is the story of artists' attempts to trick the eye and brain into perceiving brightness that could not truly be matched with pigment alone.

There were interesting shifts in preferences of the sort of natural light painters preferred over the years: bright daylight (Turner, impressionists), cloudy to overcast skies (realists from Constable to Courbet), sunrises and sunsets (Romantics, symbolists, sometimes even impressionists, Van Gogh) or night (Romantics, symbolists again). The possible connections between artists' choices and developments in contemporary light science have not been fully explored. Twilight alone, physically and artistically, deserves a thorough study. During the period under consideration here, the scientific explanation of twilight's effects depended on both sophisticated understanding of the wave theory of light and research into the makeup and depth of the earth's atmosphere. The astronomer and popular science writer Camille Flammarion published the first account of the atmosphere for general readers in 1872. He proposed that on worlds with no atmospheres, such as the moon, visual details would be seen clearly from great distances, and the sky would have no color whatsoever. Earth's atmosphere, on the other hand, lent itself to a number of astonishing and beautiful light effects as a result of its unique atmosphere, the subject of an entire chapter on "Light and Optical Phenomena of the Air."

Observers were also gradually realizing that atmospheric light effects differed from place to place as well as from time to time during the day. In his epochal description of the known universe, *Cosmos*, the explorer and naturalist Alexander von Humboldt wrote, "The idea which the artist wishes to indicate by the expressions 'Swiss nature' or 'Italian skies,' is based on a vague sense of some local characteristic. The azure of the sky, the form of the clouds, the vapory mist resting in the distance, the luxurious development of plants, the beauty of the foliage, and the outline of the mountains, are the elements which determine the total impression produced by any particular region."[23] These regional atmospheric effects were most powerfully expressed during the twilight hours. Artists traveled long distances to capture exotic lights: Van Gogh to Provence, Monet to Holland, and Delacroix and Renoir to Algeria.

Twilight

Northern Romantic painters such as Friedrich and Church observed twilight with the intensity of positivist scientists, but the purpose of their poetic masterpieces was to cause awe in the mind of the beholder. Their art is more about reflecting the divinity of creation than about skillfully rendering realistic descriptions of nature. In this sense, they reflect their generation's philosophical debate

over the connections between scientific discovery and religious belief. Did the study of nature heighten one's appreciation of God's creation, or destroy belief in it altogether? The impressionists ridiculed the Romantics' attempts at portraying the subtleties of twilight. According to Duranty, the Romantic painter depicted artificial conventions rather than real light; he "knew nothing but the orange-tinted band of the setting sun over somber hills, or the white impasto tinged with chrome yellow or rose lake, which he threw across the opaque bitumen of his woods."[24]

Sunrises and sunsets, with their striking and short-lived color ranges, were loved by late nineteenth-century dreamers and visionaries, the symbolists. The melancholy of evening was a theme not only in painting, but also in poetry and music. In this kind of work, the twilight often expresses a subjective mood that appears antithetical to scientific treatment. The dreamer who stares into the setting sun will not consider or produce an explanation of the physical phenomena causing the sky to turn red; in fact, he or she would rather not even hear about it. The neo-Romantic symbolists, who delighted in ambiguity, viewed the physics of light as just another banality that stood in the way of the creative imagination. Even so, some of the better symbolist images of evening and twilight reveal a striking control, not only of the painterly techniques, but also of naturalistic light and atmospheric effects. As with the earlier generation of Romantics, the symbolists used scientific naturalism as the means to a more spiritual end, i.e., the evocation of subjective, almost mystical moods.[25]

Like many scientists of the time, Helmholtz drew close comparisons between the different waves of light that constituted colors, and the waves of sound that produced musical tones. Helmholtz showed how the shapes of sound waves explained musical harmony; did Whistler think about the shapes of light waves that might produce color harmony? It would be interesting to investigate whether the fin de siècle concept of synesthesia, the creation of a secondary sensation in one sense by a stimulus to another, also depended upon the wave theories of nineteenth-century physics. Not until the end of the nineteenth century would Lord Rayleigh be able to unite atmospheric studies with the wave theory to explain why the sky is blue, and why sunsets vary in color and intensity from place to place and time to time. Rayleigh observed that as the sun descended toward the horizon, its light had to penetrate a steadily thickening atmosphere. As light scattered off air molecules and particles of dust, quantities of the shorter wavelengths (blue, indigo, violet) scatter and are lost in the upper atmosphere, while the longer, reddish wavelengths break through, imparting the distinctive coloration of sunset.

Darkness

Before the advent of modern outdoor lighting, night was a time of real or imagined danger, rest, and intimate social gatherings. Yet, despite the often negative connotations of nocturnal darkness, night scenes were popular in painting during the sixteenth and seventeenth centuries, with some Dutch masters even specialized in the somber theme. Therefore, we must ask what the difference is between a nocturne by an old master and a modern one. Before we look at the visual evidence note the numbers: between 1820 and 1850 there were more autonomous night scenes painted than in any other given period. By autonomous we mean a night scene not connected to a dramatic nocturnal event, such as the captivity of Christ. Rather, the painter's true subject is night itself. And when compared, the Romantic nights are often darker than those of their predecessors. Whereas the old masters illuminated their landscapes with a full moon or a blazing fire, Friedrich, Church and later even Millet sometimes restricted themselves to the sickle moon only. In other words, they were painting darkness itself, unlike their seventeenth- and eighteenth-century predecessors, showing warm firelight and cool moonlight contrasted against a dark background. Did nineteenth-century painters feel a greater sensibility for nuances of light or could they simply be more subtle because of better light in the studio or in the gallery where the work was destined to hang?

Nobody would assume that nineteenth-century painters were actually more physiologically sensitive than their colleagues in previous centuries. In fact, many of them may have become less so as they lived increasingly in well-lit urban environments. Thus, in 1849, the Paris-based artist Gustave Courbet describes finding his way home during a visit to the provincial town of Ornans: "[...] I heard the clock strike eleven. I was taking my leave of them and thanking them when, stepping outside, we found ourselves in such complete darkness that all three of them insisted that I should spend the night there. However, I prevailed by pointing out to them that they might perhaps be depriving me of some fine emotions (as I love the night so much). M. Ordinaire walked a few steps with me, then we tried to find each other in the dark to shake hands, God, what a dark night it was!"[26]

Painting darker thus requires perceiving darkness differently. Darkness had become a distinctive and conscious experience when it ceased to be the only option at night. In order to appreciate the darkness one has to first appreciate brightness, whether of daylight or artificial light. For Courbet, for example, getting lost in Ornans was an unusual comic experience that he enjoyed recounting to a friend, whereas his evening companions simply avoided it by staying home. Like the nineteenth-century pastoral, the nocturne expresses the modern urbanized observer's nostalgic sense of a lost past. And even if we think that an Argand lamp or the flickering gas flame are dim, to the eye of the nineteenth-century beholder the contrast with total darkness was obvious. Thrusting all subtle differentiations aside, we propose that the Argand lamp, the photometer, and the introduction of gaslight in some measure inspired Byron's poem *Darkness* (1816), Caspar David Friedrich's painted nights and Chopin's *Nocturnes* (1829 and later). If the light consumers were blinded by the new light, as innumerable sources reveal, just imagine the effect on sensitive painters. With light becoming a commonplace commodity, the darkness of night offered respite.

Later in the nineteenth century, the symbolists reacted directly against the banal glare of modern light, or as Richard Muther described it in retrospect: "Finally, after looking into the light for so long, the moment arrived when the eye started hurting. From the brightness of sunlight and the electrically lit Salons one fled into the shadow of the evening and felt most comfortable at the hour of dawn, when grey-black veils covered all things."[27]

Lights of other worlds

The growing interest in night and darkness in the eighteenth and nineteenth centuries is also connected with advances in physics and astronomy. Beginning with Newton's formulation of the concept of gravity to explain the motions of the solar system, as well as improvements in telescope design, thanks to his work in optics, astronomy transformed people's understanding of the universe and their place within it. The light of the night sky became the primary source of information about the cosmos at this time, and a source of endless fascination and controversy for all.

Between 1750–1900, astronomers entered a new realm of thought and discovery. They speculated on the presence of atmosphere and life on the stars and planets; they discovered that the Milky Way was actually composed of millions of stars, not luminous vapor; they measured the age of the cosmos in thousands and millions of years instead of centuries; they, for the first time, estimated the distance between the earth and several nearby stars; and they ascertained that stars not only moved away from the earth, but also experienced a cycle of birth and death. The excitement generated by these ideas supported a new breed of science popularizers, notably Ralph Proctor in England and Camille Flammarion in France. In the arts, it stimulated the invention of a new genre, science fiction, in both literature and cinema. It was a difficult time for those who believed in the biblical account of creation that begins with God's first command, "Let there be light."

The staggering impact of these ideas is still felt today, and remains controversial. Without doubt, it changed the night sky from "heaven" into a battleground for scientists, religious leaders, spiritualists, and atheists. It is difficult now to assess how well-versed artists were in astronomical science, although given the high level of public interest in the topic, it would have been nearly impossible to ignore the subject. Throughout the nineteenth century, as they had done for centuries, artists continued to draw heavily upon the Bible for subject matter, including such light-related subjects as the creation, the crucifixion, and the appearance of heaven. Astronomical controversies may in fact have given these ancient themes a new life as artists, such as William Blake, Gustave Doré, and Jean-Léon Gérôme, struggled to visualize or reconcile these conflicting descriptions of the universe.

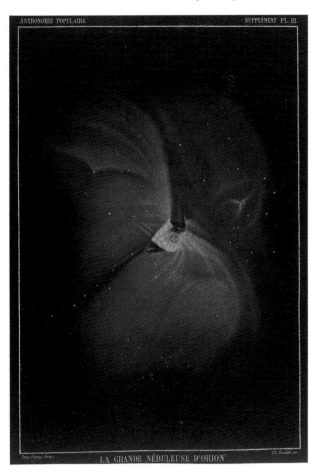

Th. Toulet, *The Orion Nebula*, chromolithograph from Camille Flammarion, *Les Etoiles et les curiosités du ciel*, Paris 1882, Van Gogh Museum, Amsterdam

Lunar Day, wood engraving from Camille Flammarion, *The Atmosphere*, New York 1874, Carnegie Library, Pittsburgh

Turning night into day

There is an age-old question whose answer appears to shift according to the latest fashion or ideology. What came first: the invention that caused a demand, or the demand that caused an invention? The history of public lighting is an example of the dialectical relationship between possible needs and possible solutions. If enlightenment and positivist science were transforming people's understanding of natural light, technology and capitalism were doing the same for artificial light. Between 1750 and 1900, Europeans and Americans discovered how to turn night into day. New methods of making light and distributing fuel and power forever shifted the concept of night from its traditional associations with seclusion, rest, and fear. From the invention of the Argand lamp (1783) through the introductions of gas (ca. 1800) and electricity (ca. 1880), night gradually acquired its modern identity as a time of additional work, public entertainment, and education.

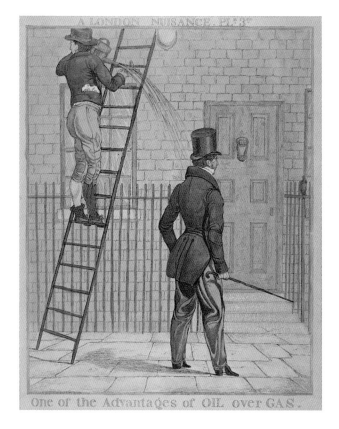 

Richard Dighton, *One of the Advantages of Oil over Gas*, 1826, etching, Guildhall Collection, London

Richard Dighton, *One of the Advantages of Oil over Gas*, 1826, etching, Guildhall Collection, London

If Argand's innovation was a response to a clearly articulated public demand, the next public lighting innovation, gaslight, was actually discovered almost two hundred years before people figured out how to use it. Jean Tardin had noticed the illuminating power of gas in 1618.[28] But gas was neither reliable nor efficient until engineers, utilizing their experience of harnessing and distributing steam and water power, began piping gas from a central supply to numerous burners. The shift from the freestanding oil lamp, with its own fuel supply, to gaslighting, with its city-wide infrastructure, revolutionized the concepts of production, energy supply and consumption even before the networks of railroads or electric power lines. In the eighteenth century, in laboratories all over Europe, independent researchers experimented with lighting fuels and techniques. It may be curious, but not astonishing, that several countries honor their own inventors of gaslight: James Clayton and William Murdoch in England, Johann Peter Minckelers in the Netherlands, Johann Georg Pickel and Wilhelm August Lampadius in Germany, and Philippe Lebon in France.

The confusion about the origin of gaslight does not relate to the presumed origin of the word "gas" from the Greek "chaos," although this association is tempting.[29] Rather, we blame the competitive nationalism of the early writers of industrial history. Friedrich Ludwig Knapp, in one of the first historiographies of the element, written in 1860, attempts to date the introduction of gaslight into daily life for the year 1803.[30] British industrial historians, however, tend to date the event in 1792, when William Murdoch built a small coal gas plant to illuminate his house. The important point for us is that, once the basic chemistry of gas production was known, many engineers developed methods to produce it.

Although engineers solved the problems of gas production and distribution, it took capitalists, politicians, and artists to introduce the technology to the public. Artist-entrepreneurs Rudolph Ackermann in London and Rembrandt Peale in Baltimore were among the first to install gaslighting in their workshops and galleries, and they publicized the new technology in advertisements and publications. It was up to the capitalists to organize investors into private gaslighting companies, and the politicians had to find the public moneys for urban improvement. All those who were employed in the traditional oil lighting trade opposed the new technology, dealers in whale oil and lamplighters alike. Public enthusiasm for the new technology proved stronger.

Between 1812 and about 1880, gas engineers and entrepreneurs had to solve numerous problems associated with the development of the world's first centralized public lighting method. These included establishing uniform standards of purity and brightness for their light, inventing a fair means to measure consumption, allaying public panics over gas leaks and explosions, moralizing over private profit-making from public amenities, and teaching consumers how to use this new fuel safely. (In the beginning, many gas users believed that flames shot through the gaspipes and emerged at the jet. Some extinguished their gaslights by blowing out the flame as if it were a candle, with catastrophic results.) Great Britain, leading in industrialization due to its natural resources, scientific and mechanical acumen, and entrepreneurial spirit, became the pioneer in gas technology and urban streetlighting, with other countries only catching up in the 1840s or 1850s.[31]

The huge successes enjoyed by the early gaslighting companies, railroads, and other industrial enterprises created a positive environment for further experimentation and innovation for its own sake. As the German architect Gottfried Semper stated while under the impression of the first Universal Exposition in London of 1851, the paradigms had shifted: "It appears already that inventions are not anymore means to satisfy an existing necessity or means for enjoyment; now inventions rather create the need and enjoyment. The order of things is reversed."[32] Gaslighting resembled the other great networked systems constructed in the early Industrial Revolution, including municipal water systems, railroads, and telegraph lines. Rather like waterworks, gas pipes connected households and businesses to a central reservoir that was constantly renewed. Consumers of water and gas could obtain these essential commodities without awareness of the complex industrial, chemical, and engineering processes that went into their production.

Compared to the enormous cultural changes wrought during the shift from candlelight and lamplight to gaslighting systems, the introduction of electric lighting in the 1870s and 1880s was far less traumatic. Thomas Edison and his competitors did not have to educate their public on a whole new concept of urban planning and life, they just had to prove that electric light was cheaper and better than gaslight. Their battle was more technical and commercial than cultural. At first, electric arc lighting was too powerful for widespread use. Consequently, the writer of an article in *La Nature* of 1873 did not foresee success: "The interest of these experiments is incontestable from the scientific point of view, but we strongly doubt that the arc light will penetrate the practical realm, for its brilliance is too striking."[33] Only when Edison, Swann, and other innovators found ways to distribute electrical power to separate fixtures and reduce its brightness to familiar levels in the late 1870s, did electric lighting become natural and more common at home. It had become more like gaslight.

Electricity versus Art

The early electricians, as they were called, enjoyed a second advantage over the pioneers of gas. Beginning with the 1851 Crystal Palace exhibition where Gottfried Semper pondered the novelties of gas jets, Universal Expositions, staged throughout the remainder of the century, offered inventors and entrepreneurs the ideal showcases for new products and technologies, especially lighting.[35] Beams, palaces and fountains of lights were major attractions for crowds, and no costs were spared to surpass the most extravagant features of the preceding fair. The visitors to the Universal Expositions – millions of people of all classes – were shown an array of modern light sources displayed in the most luxurious fashion. Other exhibitions, which are much less known today, were dedicated to electricity alone, perhaps the most influential of which was the 1881 fair in Paris. As many as 758,214 visitors (8,382 visitors per day, according to the official report) saw 164 exhibitors from 19 firms showing 159 different lamps. Approaching the exhibition at night must have been quite exciting, only to be surpassed by the experience inside the Palais des Champs-Elysées: "Once one has penetrated the grand entrance, the spectacle becomes magical. It is best to ascend immediately to the second floor; the view embraces the grand hall and its countless lights; the splendor of the illumination is incomparable.[...] the building's cupola resembles an immense vault of fire. The Champs-Elysées palace has become a veritable palace of Light."[36]

It may be worthwhile wondering at this stage what such an experience could have meant for artists. In the early nineteenth century, they had been among the earliest developers and popularizers of artificial lighting systems, and like the general public, some were overwhelmed by the glory of the big exposition displays.[37] However, the explosion of industrialization and technological innovation rapidly diminished opportunities for non-specialists as the century progressed. In fact, we would propose that the institution of electric power and electric lighting gradually undermined and replaced some of art's traditional public roles in advertising and production of public

spectacles. In 1893, excited by the latest developments, Arthur Wilke wrote a voluminous book on electricity and its applications. He claimed that the "artist may think that he is independent, but the progress of technology does nonetheless have an influence on the development of art."[38]

In the 1880s, electricity left the artists in total confusion. Electric light even threatened to replace painting and sculpture as the main instrument for public propaganda. As Marshall McLuhan has pointed out in his classic treatise on communications, electric light was the new information medium.[39] With enormous spectacles, illuminated advertisements, Morse code flashing to the sky, and signal beams in bright colors, the Universal Expositions displayed the publicity value of electricity. The 1893 World's Columbian Exposition in Chicago illuminated 90,000 arc and incandescent lights every night, with Edison's brilliant Tower of Light in its center. And Carolyn Marvin reminds us of the most grandiose project of all: Camille Flammarion's proposal "to group immensely powerful lights in the pattern of a familiar constellation like the Big Dipper for extraterrestrial observers. Its dimensions would require lights at Bordeaux, Marseille, Strasbourg, Paris, Amsterdam, Copenhagen, and Stockholm."[40] At that time, globalization was not an issue, it was already a fact. But back to the question of how painters, once privileged in the visual sphere, could match the impact of all this. The answer is simple: they could not. With gaslights, arc lamps and light bulbs, all competing with each other at the Paris Fair of 1889, the public was exposed to a sensory overload unparalleled even in our time. A hundred years after Ami Argand's oil lamp with the hollow wick had revolutionized the artificial light for the first time, all limits were broken. In the second half of the nineteenth century, light seemed to be everywhere and in immeasurable quantities.

The new electrical systems marginalized art in yet another, more subtle and disturbing sense. As Arthur Wilke observed, "Nowadays electricity arrives in neighborhoods where it would not be allowed to enter in plain work clothes. [...] The Germans especially require that electricity appear only if perfectly dressed for the occasion. Electricity has a much easier life in America. There it is liked, even if the wire is bare and the light shines from a primitive wooden post [...]. Electricity may not do that in Germany; here it must show itself to the public only in its Sunday dress, otherwise the political and the aesthetic police will appear immediately."[41] Wilke's concerns were two-fold. He not only recognized the subordination of artists to technology, evidenced by their

The Electrical Exhibition Paris 1881,
wood engraving from *Le Monde
Illustré, Numéro spécial exclusivement consacré à l'Exposition de
l'Électricité, 1881,* Van Gogh
Museum, Amsterdam

diminished role as decorators of light fixtures, but also the beginnings of the aesthetic of early
twentieth-century modernism, stripped-down, industrial, unadorned, and seemingly without art.

The historical importance of the 1881 exhibition was underlined by a display of electric
engines of the past. The Dutch member of the Awards Jury, Elisa van der Ven, marked the occasion by taking a number of the new light bulbs back home for the collection of Teylers Museum
in Haarlem. Despite his enthusiasm, Henri de Parville, who wrote a detailed account of this
groundbreaking exhibition, noted a curious and disturbing side effect. For the first time, the public was confronted with many machines whose appearance did not express their function: "We
are not yet in the habit of observing machines that function without any apparent cause. Their
occult workings baffle us. The secret of their existence escapes us."[42] The mechanism of a steam
engine had been obvious from the movement of its parts. An electrical generator, however, hid
the sources, causes, and actions of its seemingly magical power. And it appeared that light bulbs
glowed independent of any power source. Thus, after natural philosophers had stolen the secrets
of the Gods, engineers became magicians again, at least in the eyes of the amazed public. While
Wilke's concern was design, Parville's observations went further, to the new and disturbing
abstraction of modern life. Although by 1900 artificial light was more available than ever, it was
also harder than ever to see how it was made or where it came from. Some artists gave expression
to the alienation felt by the common man on the one hand, and technology and science on the
other. It is here where one may find the roots of the abstractions of a Picasso or a Kandinsky.

Work at night in the fields, wood engraving from Em. Alglave and J. Boulard, *La Lumière électrique*, Paris 1882, Universiteits-bibliotheek van Amsterdam

The exploitation of light

Who utilized new and brighter light? The earliest and biggest investors in artificial lighting systems were factory owners. By the early 1780s, Richard Arkwright was operating his cotton mills by candlelight or lamplight. The luminous buildings were beautiful enough to inspire a painting by Joseph Wright of Derby in 1782 (private collection) and an admiring comment from a visitor to the mill at Cromford in 1790. "These cotton mills, seven stories high, and fill'd with inhabitants, remind me of a first rate man of war; and when they are lighted up, on a dark night, look most luminously beautiful."[43] In 1805, William Murdoch installed gaslighting in a cotton mill near Halifax, and other large textile makers followed suit soon thereafter. Although gaslighting seems incredibly dangerous to us today, it was preferred then because it actually reduced the danger of fire as compared to candles or oil lamps.

Beginning in 1810, large factory owners in Manchester and Birmingham started installing gaslighting in their buildings. Investing in better light greatly improved productivity and efficiency. And, as a significant natural consequence, the night shift became economically feasible; the high cost of candles, fuel oil, and insurance before the gaslight era had made operating at night prohibitively expensive. Another economic consequence of gas-lit factories was that the high cost of installing gas plants limited their use and benefits to only big capitalist operations, giving these larger companies yet another advantage over the small, individual manufacturers. Sweatshops were gas-lit, and while workers benefitted from the increased light and some improvement in safety, they also suffered ever-longer working hours in poisonous, overheated conditions. Too much light was also thought to be unhealthy, as Forbes Winslow stated in 1867: "Persons exposed for an undue length of time to the glare of brilliantly-lighted rooms often suffer from chronic ophthalmia and other affections of the organ of vision. [...] Tailors, seamstresses, shoemakers, jewellers, watchmakers, and, in fact, all who work by artificial light, are subject to serious disorders of the eye."[44]

Most painters had to wait for the creation of municipal gas companies in order to install their own lighting systems. Although he was not the first artist to do so, Vincent van Gogh exploited the possibilities of extended working hours under strong artificial light. As a young man in The

Hague, he dreamt of becoming an illustrator for *The Graphic*. In the 1882 Christmas supplement of that magazine, he noted a double page devoted to the publication's print shop, showing work in the evening under artificial light.[45] Later, he had a gas pipeline installed at the Yellow House in Arles in order to work at night with Gauguin. He was convinced that this investment in greater efficiency would pay off.

With the success of gaslight, businessmen continued to experiment with new lighting technologies, especially for work in large open spaces. Sometimes, lighting for efficiency could even turn into a spectacle: When a Bremen brewery installed electric floodlights at the construction site of its new facilities, this spectacle attracted lots of curious onlookers.[46]

Selling (by) light

Following close on the heels of the factory owners in the use of commercial light were the urban merchants, who rapidly discovered that brilliantly lit goods, displayed in big shop windows, sold far better than items stocked in a dim interior. One of the first entrepreneurs to build his own gas plant and publicize it was London printseller Rudolph Ackermann. Ackermann had published an article on the benefits of gaslighting as early as 1809, had put a gas plant in his home-workshop-printshop-library complex by 1811, and published the first treatise on gaslight in 1815. As municipal gas plants made the new lights more accessible to shop owners, glowing windows became increasingly common in urban areas, brightening up the streets and encouraging increased pedestrian traffic at night. In 1848, author Elizabeth Gaskell described the gaslight effects in Manchester in *Mary Barton*: "It is a pretty sight to walk through a street with lighted shops; the gas is so brilliant, the display of goods so much more vividly shown than by day, and of all shops a druggist's looks the most like the tales of our childhood, from Aladdin's garden of enchanted fruits to the charming Rosamund with her purple jar."[47]

Emile Zola made the connection between lighting and commerce a major theme in his novel about the rise of the department store *Au Bonheur des dames*. When the owner of the new store adopts gaslighting in his windows, he forces the surrounding shopowners to do the same or face ruin. The novel culminates when the department store closes for renovations and reopens in blazing glory with new electric lights. Window-shopping at night even became a major tourist attraction.[48]

Light entertainment

In the Enlightenment and industrial eras, art, science and technology collaborated most fruitfully in the fields of popular education and entertainment. Once it could be controlled with lenses and created at will, illumination became an essential element of showmanship in all its forms. Then as now, dramatic lighting technologies attracted mass audiences and stunned them with spectacular visual effects. The magic lantern, forerunner of the modern slide projector, facilitated demonstrations of the miracles of knowledge by using visual and playful examples that instructed and entertained at the same time. Surviving lantern slides from the eighteenth and nineteenth centuries include images of specters and demons to frighten the superstitious, mechanical slides that demonstrated the relative motions of the planets to teach the young, and scenic views for the armchair tourist. The theater

Hippolyte Camille Delpy, *The Boulevard Barbès Rochechouart in Winter*, 1879, Elisabeth Cumbler (detail)

Hippolyte Michaud, *Spectators at the Theater*, ca. 1840–60, Rijksmuseum, Amsterdam

Footlights illuminated the actors and, as we see here, the audience as well. The shadows thus created from below had always been considered particularly unflattering. In numerous treatises, painters were warned against the effect. Michaud's aim was apparently to caricature the audience.

became a center for innovative combinations of art and technology, as stage designers and lighting engineers competed to create ever more spectacular effects with the new gaslights, limelights, and arcs. Light effects became so important, that audiences were plunged into darkness for the first time, so the stage would appear even more brilliant. The new possibilities for visual spectacles, such as sunsets, moonrises, and rainbows, at times overwhelmed other theatrical considerations, such as plot.

Artists were among the most enthusiastic collaborators and innovators in the use of light for the creation of entertaining spectacles. Charles Willson Peale, for example, created the huge candle- and lamp-lit transparencies that celebrated heroes and victories in eighteenth-century Philadelphia. He was one of many to promote the panorama, a huge circular or semicircular scenic painting of deceptive realism. Exotic locales and historic battles were favored subjects. Executed with the help of optical devices, such as the camera obscura, the panorama could be transformed from a day to a night scene, or from calm to storm, by lighting, at first with Argand lamps, then gas and limelight. When these technologically advanced spectacles were combined with the new art of photography (invented by panorama showman Daguerre), the result would be the greatest form of public entertainment invented in the nineteenth century – the moving picture.

Some artists tried to distance themselves from mass entertainment and its vulgar light, but like everyone else they were soon seduced. A wonderful case in point was the first use of electric lighting in the galleries of the Paris Salon of 1878. That year, the Avenue de l'Opéra and the Folies-Bergère had been lit with electric Jablochkoff candles, and so were some Parisian department stores. Academic painters were appalled that the exhibition organizers, Republican government officials, illuminated their precious works of art with arc lamps hitherto confined to the shop and the popular theatre. Likewise, Monsieur Walter, the nouveau riche newspaper magnate in Maupassant's novel *Bel-Ami* (1884), betrayed his vulgar origins by proudly displaying his newest painting in glaring electric light.[49] However, in 1879, only one year after the electric light outraged Salon artists, Edgar Degas was inquiring about its availability for the fourth impressionist exhibition. By 1880, early Edison light bulbs could be seen in a New York art gallery, and in 1890, electric light was established in Theo van Gogh's gallery on the Boulevard Montmartre for an exhibition of works by Jean-François Raffaëlli.[50]

Modern artists attempted to render the new lights, attracted by both the night life and the visual effects they engendered. Manet, Degas, and Toulouse-Lautrec painted the eerily-lit bars and brothels, often exaggerating the odd color spectra of gas or electricity. They also loved to paint the new life on the streets at night – people working, playing, or just lounging about in pools of light that became larger and brighter over the course of the century. Realist painters revelled in the commercialized vulgarity of it all. Today their images of working class night life spark feelings of romantic nostalgia, raffish glamour, and sexual adventure.

Light and learning

Projecting an image, wood engraving from François-Napoléon-Marie Moigno, *L'Art des projections*, Paris 1872

Working, shopping, playing, and learning – all sectors of life were affected by the new light. Learning and lighting were even associated in a metaphorical sense when Sherlock Holmes called the new board schools in England the "Lighthouses of the future."[51] The educational ideals of the French Revolution could be realized after new technologies extended the day, not only for work or entertainment, but for learning too. Obviously, gaslighting installed in schools and working men's coffee houses and clubs allowed workers to read or study at night. However, on a more sophisticated level, new light technologies transformed teaching itself. The effect of this change has been continuous from the early eighteenth century to the present.[52] At first, the magic lantern, introduced by 's Gravesande in the 1720s for demonstrations of natural philosophy (or natural science), was favored after more powerful light sources enabled its use in large spaces. What had been a privilege for few became a means of mass instruction and entertainment. Public magic lantern lectures were followed in the nineteenth century by the use of increasingly sophisticated projectors for what were more than simple slide shows. Great nineteenth-century lectures were "illustrated" by actual demonstrations of important experiments. Manuals for teachers and lecturers emphasized the importance of experiments to prove points; projected light was essential for presentations of physics, astronomy, biology, art, and geography. Today, these demonstrations are available on film in movies, video, and television.

Magic Lantern, ca. 1875– 1900, Haags Documentatie Centrum Nieuwe Media, The Hague

When a handle at the side of the slide's frame is turned, the stars rotate and the sun rays start to flicker.

At home

Before the industrial era, most artificial lighting was employed in the home. Ever since humanity learned to use fire, the domestic hearth has been the center, both physically and symbolically, of family life for a number of reasons. For many, up to and including the twentieth century, a fire was the primary source of heat and light after dark. Unlit streets and countryside were considered extremely dangerous, and so togetherness was usually an unavoidable necessity. Candles, wood and coal were expensive, and therefore, most families shared a single light or fire in the evenings.

The old lights were dim, flickering, and high maintenance, but they sufficed for storytelling, conversation, reading, sewing, mending, and card games. As much as they allowed for evening activities, they were the bane of every housewife's existence, as their delicate materials (glass chimneys), volatile fuels, and perpetual dirtiness (dripping tallow, greasy smoke) made their cleaning dangerous, dirty, labor intensive and absolutely necessary on a frequent basis. Consequently, householders switched to new fuels, such as whale oil, kerosene, and gas, which provided steadier, cleaner, slightly brighter flames. Despite their many advantages, the new lights had some drawbacks. Some feared that the brightness of the lights could damage the eyes, and others feared explosions. Over time, even as the purity, piping, and regulation of gas improved, other concerns discouraged general domestic use: excessive heat, the pollutants and

poisonous byproducts of combustion that created health problems and tarnished silver, and, cosmetically speaking, the eerie color of the flames were thought to be unflattering to women's complexions and the colors of jewels. But most significantly, as gaslight proliferated in the commercial and public spheres, many found it too vulgar to use in the home. Edgar Allan Poe railed against its "false principles" in his *Philosophy of Furniture* as early as 1840.[53] By the end of the nineteenth century, the wealthy restricted gaslighting to hallways, the servants' quarters and workspaces, while lighting their own rooms with outmoded, labor intensive, but high-status candles and oil lamps. What is most remarkable is that over the course of the Industrial Revolution, with gas and electricity transforming public and economic life, light levels in the average household changed relatively little.

It seems bizarre today to think that people once considered relatively dim lights (equivalent to twenty watts or less) to be dangerously bright. It is another paradox of modern lighting that every time inventors found a way to make a brighter light, householders reciprocated with denser lampshades. Thus, the invention of the Argand lamp stimulated Count Rumford to invent the lampshade and publicize it in a pamphlet of 1811.[54] Count Rumford made his shades of translucent silk, but with subsequent improvements in oil and gas lights, shades were made of porcelain, metal, and colored glass. The electric light bulb called for extreme measures, such as the gorgeous, but semi-opaque stained glass masterpieces of Louis Comfort Tiffany. Householders' worries about damaging their eyes with light also led them to cover windows with layers of blinds, curtains, and potted plants (the green leaves imparted a soothing atmosphere). Light absorbing colors and fabrics were intended to create restful environments that contrasted with the glare of the world outside. As a contemporary observer stated: "With horror many have realized the effect of the electrically lit streets with the difference in color between the blue electrical and the yellow gas and lamplight. [...] Yes, the bright light of the street shines even into the apartments and forces us to use thick curtains."[55] In contrast, eighteenth-century householders expended much of their decorating energy on amplifying the available light by filling their interiors with mirrors, crystal chandeliers, and gilded lighting fixtures, carved and gilded picture frames, and gilt bronze ornamented furniture.

The meaning of light

From ancient sunworship to modern nudism, light has symbolized goodness in all its perfection. In almost every era and culture, it has represented inspiration, power, truth, and beauty. The ancient Greeks used the same word for light and truth.[56] Between 1750 and 1900, light also came to represent the most cherished values of western civilization: democratic forms of government, enlightenment for the masses, and industrial progress. The Victorian philosopher and poet Matthew Arnold coined the famous phrase "sweetness and light" to describe the ideals of modern civilization; and the image of the lightbearer – some ideal being carrying a torch, a sun, or a lightbulb – became a hallmark of the era.

Light symbols have been heavily contested in modern ideological and political struggles. Most famously, in France, the Sun King Louis XIV was supplanted by the *lumières* of the enlightenment and the dazzling brilliance of the revolutionary god of Reason. Religious leaders, especially those of the Catholic and Protestant revival movements, claimed that divine light was the only true light in the nineteenth century. For them, daylight was now the slave of materialistic scientists, and artificial light was commercial and corrupting. In the United States and Britain, politicians and capitalists claimed light for their own by incorporating light symbols on coins, bills, and stock certificates. British prime minister William Gladstone declaimed in the House of Commons in 1858, "Decision by majorities is as much expedient as lighting by gas."[57] Alglave and Boulard, two French witnesses of the 1881 Electrical Exposition in Paris expressed their hope

Hugo Höppener, called Fidus, *Prayer to Light*, 1894, Deutsches Historisches Museum, Berlin

that their government would establish a general distribution of electric light so the spirits of democracy and science would unite: "It is essential that we retain from the 1881 Exposition a widespread distribution of the power and light from electricity. One must hope that the municipal council of Paris will not hesitate where the democratic and scientific spirits are so happily allied."[58]

The socialists, who fought for more natural light in the life of the working classes, through modern housing and more free time, frequently used the sun as a sign of hope and a better future. As early as 1867, a thorough study had linked lighting conditions at home and work with public health. The author, Forbes Winslow, complained that 30,000 to 40,000 people lived in lightless cellars in Liverpool alone. The lack of light in their housing was considered a major threat to their well-being. In fact, many nineteenth-century deformed bone samples in current medical collections testifiy today to the most unpleasant consequences of vitamin D deficiency.[59] Early public health initiatives also recognized that daylight contributed to cleanliness, and higher living standards; capitalists then invented brand names such as "Sunlight," "Sun," "Lux" and, later, "Electrolux," to sell their household products.

The nineteenth century saw a proliferation of monumental, symbolic lightbearers in public art. It is astonishing to see how the most advanced technologies were given a sculptural or painterly expression that appear comical, or just plain bizarre, to modern eyes. Yet, their very awkwardness testifies to the odd, new, and not always successful mixtures of old conventions and modern innovations that typify the period. Edison himself admired Aurelio Bordiga's statue *The Genius of Electricity* at the 1889 World's Fair in Paris, bought it and put it in his office in West Orange, New Jersey. Other examples are Antonio Rossetti's sculpture with the same title, shown at the Philadelphia Centennial (1876), and Reinhold Begas's group *The Electric Spark*, showing a couple energized by high voltage in marble (present location unknown). Pierre Puvis de Chavannes painted the stairway walls of Boston's Public Library in 1895 with a large fresco called *The Inspirational Muses Acclaiming Genius, Messenger of Light*, and Jean-Baptiste Carpeaux's group *Imperial France Enlightening the World and Protecting Agriculture and Science* of 1866 still adorns the Louvre. And the biggest lightbearer of all, the *Statue of Liberty*, installed in New York harbor in 1886, is yet another member of this artistic family.[60]

Invisible lights

Perhaps the most strange and telling example of the confusions of old and new ideas about light was the problem of invisible light. When William Herschel discovered infrared light (the invisible rays that we sense as heat) in 1800, Pandora's box was opened. Discoveries of other invisible lightwaves, such as ultraviolet and x-rays, and James Clerk Maxwell's ether theory, suggested to many that invisible worlds existed parallel with ours, but literally "on a different wavelength." As scientists proved there was light beyond visible light, they created scientific justifications for any sort of mysticism. In fact, many of the era's leading scientists dabbled in, or seriously explored, spiritualism as a professional concern.

Photography, the objective art, seemed to provide physical evidence of the invisible. If one could photograph the bones beneath the flesh, or glimpse the invisible with infrared or ultraviolet illumination, could not other intangibles (thoughts, spirits, ghosts) also exist in the ethereal world? In 1898, the Shroud of Turin, photographed, revealed a negative image that could be read as a face. Was there still more light out there that did not meet the eye? Even Sir Oliver Lodge, the physicist, and Camille Flammarion, the astronomer, took part in the occult rage at the end of the nineteenth century and witnessed pictures being taken of auras. Andreas Fischer, who researched extensively on the photography of the invisible, informs us of about two million followers of this movement in North America alone.[61] None of the cases withstood scientific tests, but that did not seem to deter many, among them avant-garde artists such as Kandinsky and Munch, who in one way or another joined the search for the invisible.

X-ray photograph of a hand of a lady with a bunch of flowers, photogravure print, from Walter König, 14 Photographien mit Röntgen-Strahlen aufgenommen im Physikalischen Verein zu Frankfurt a. M., Leipzig 1896, Deutsches Röntgen-Museum, Remscheid

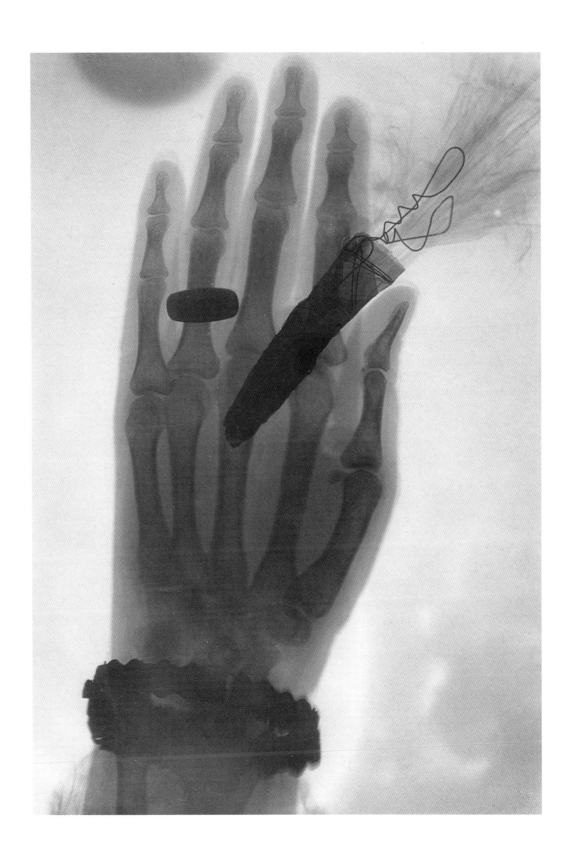

The future of light

We still do not know what light is. Modern physicists, astronomers and cosmologists, building on the achievements of Newton, Herschel, Helmholtz, and Maxwell, among others, have measured its speed (it seems to be constant), named its basic component (the ambiguous, changeable photon), tied it to matter ($e = mc^2$), and thrown up their hands in despair. They have resolved the debate over its particle or wave nature by admitting that it can be both or either, depending on how one looks at it. The latest research adds even more complexity. Scientists have invented the single atom laser, discovered that neutrons and photons actually have mass, slowed light down and claim that a single photon of light can exist in two places at the same time. They would agree that as their knowledge progresses, light's mysteries become deeper. Several recent authors have pointed out that today's public thinks contemporary art and contemporary physics have much in common: they are esoteric, full of strange people, and completely detached from everyone else's real world.

In the mundane world, light is now so easy to obtain that we hardly notice it at all. In this respect, the situation is the opposite of the common experience of all previous eras. We have tried to chronicle the curious transitions and transformations that artificial light wrought on art, culture and society in the eighteenth and nineteenth centuries, when such light was introduced. The process has been recorded in the images, books, and objects that have been assembled and reunited for our project. Through them, one can see the beginnings of modern life as we know it today – night life, movies, the second and third work shifts, and spotlights, both real and metaphorical. Yet, in order to really understand what light meant and did to people's lives in the eighteenth and nineteenth centuries, it may be more instructive to compare it with the technology that is transforming every aspect of life today, the suddenly ubiquitous computer. Like the streetlight, computers are creating new forms and concepts of night life and sociability. Like the humble oil lamp, they are becoming the glowing centers of family life. Like the telescope and the spectroscope, they are producing scientific descriptions of a universe, or universes, of unimaginable size. They are acquiring new symbolic power, too, becoming (as light once did) symbols of democracy, intellectual power, and connectedness. Like gaslight in factories, they are changing work places and work habits. They are transforming the worlds of art, entertainment, and communication – as did limelight, neon, and the cinema over one hundred years ago. And, to take the analysis one step further, the computer is also a source of light, serving as both the tool and its illumination.

This book and the exhibition it accompanies, were created first on computers. Our software incompatibilities, e-mail viruses, and hardware upgrades hampered the planning and production process every step of the way. As a result, we sympathize with the housewives who had to retrain themselves when gas pipes replaced oil lamps at home in the 1850s. We recognize the confusion of the exposition visitors who could not understand how a motionless lump of metal generated power and light. We share the metaphysical bewilderment of observers of a universe moving at unheard of speeds, generating measurements unimaginably large and small. We envy the capitalists who bet on the new technologies before their potential was obvious to all. We cheer for the artists who invented new painting techniques that would succeed whatever the technology that lit them, and that would show the world in its constantly changing lights.

The history of light continues into the twenty-first century with new discoveries, new technologies, and new uses that we cannot yet imagine. At the same time, light links us with the traditions of the past. We think it is significant that New Years Eve 1999–2000 was celebrated, from New Zealand to Hawaii, with a worldwide competition of light spectacles. Despite the many recent breakthroughs in lighting technology, tried and true fireworks prove to be the most awe inspiring of all. We will end with one safe prediction: In all its manifestations, light remains a source of wonder.

Jan Caspar Philips, *Fireworks on the Vijver, The Hague, 13 June 1749, in Celebration of the Peace of Aix-la-Chapelle*, 1749, engraving, Rijksmuseum, Rijksprentenkabinet, Amsterdam (detail)

Notes

1 Letter to Cadwallader Colden, 23 April 1752, *The Papers of Benjamin Franklin*, vol. 4, New Haven 1961, p. 299.

2 *Aphorismen* 1796/99.

3 Blanc 1867, p. 581.

4 Gage 1993; Gage 1999.

5 O'Dea 1958, p. 2.

6 Schöne 1954, p. 19; compare Sedlmayr 1960, p. 312.

7 Peter Galassi, *Corot in Italy: Open-Air Painting and the Classical Landscape Tradition*, New Haven & London 1991, passim.

8 Schivelbusch 1986/1988.

9 Wood 1799, pp. 1-2.

10 Valenciennes 1800, p. 250.

11 Paillot de Montabert 1829-51, vol. 7, chap. 336 "De la lumière et de ses principaux caractères optiques," p. 17.

12 Quoted after Dawkins 1998, p. 40.

13 Letter to Emile Bernard, 23 December 1904, quoted in P. M. Doran (ed.), *Conversations avec Cézanne*, Paris 1978, pp. 44-45.

14 John Ruskin, "The Artist and the Man of Science," *Selections of the Writings of John Ruskin*, First series 1843-1860, 7th ed., London 1904, no. 79, p. 207.

15 p. V.

16 "The complexion, the special beauty which springs from the very source of life, changes with artificial lights, and it is probably from the desire to preserve this grace in all its integrity, that painting – which concerns itself more about this flesh-pollen than any other human attraction – insists on the mental operation to which I have lately alluded, and demands daylight – that is space with the transparence of air alone." Quoted in Moffett 1986, p. 30.

17 Muther 1925, p. 381.

18 Hunt 1905, vol. 2, pp. 470-71.

19 Quoted after Moffett 1986, pp. 42-43.

20 Richardson 1971, pp. 12-13; compare Asendorf 1989, a brilliant analysis of the tendencies towards fragmentation in art and technology after 1880, represented by among other things, the photographs of Muybridge, the painting of impressionism, autotype, the division of sound waves into electrical impulses that enables telephony and image transfer.

21 Jamin 1857; compare Sheon 1971.

22 Quoted after Moffett 1986, p. 30.

23 Alexander von Humboldt, *Cosmos: A Sketch of a Physical Description of the Universe* (1847), Baltimore & London 1997, p. 97.

24 Quoted after Moffett 1986, p. 43.

25 The love-hate relationship between realism and positivism on one side and romanticism and subjectivity on the other, had its parallels in literature and on stage, where the lighting became either clear and sharp or diffuse, according to the stylistic preference of the author or director, cf. Bergman 1977, p. 315. Even photography, this seemingly objective technique, was influenced in the direction of Romantic twilight. With the pictorialists of the late nineteenth century soft focus became an artistic and expressive choice.

26 Gustave Courbet, *Letters of Gustave Courbet*, trans. and ed. Petra ten-Doesschate Chu, Chicago & London 1992, p. 90.

27 Richard Muther, *Geschichte der Malerei*, Berlin 1922, pp. 242-43.

28 Mackenzie 1947.

29 Compare Griffith 1992, p. 238. We leave aside here that natural gas was a source of light in China 3,000 years earlier.

30 Knapp 1879, p. 6.

31 Interestingly enough, it was not always the center that starts and the provinces that follow, almost the opposite: In the case of electric lighting the French countryside was more advanced than Paris thanks to watermills driving the turbines, and in England it all started with Joseph Swan's first light bulb in 1861 in Newcastle-on-Tyne, rather than in London. Compare Harrison 1963, p. 2.

32 Semper 1851, p. 9.

33 *La Nature* 1 (1873), p. 158.

34 Alglave and Boulard 1882, p. 424.

35 The first Universal Exposition of 1851 was, by the way, a triumph of natural light. Paxton's Crystal Palace allowed for "shadowless brightness" while the glass was prepared to diffuse the light in order to avoid glare. Compare Eugene S. Ferguson, "Expositions of Technology, 1851-1900," Kranzberg 1967, p. 714, and Maag 1986, pp. 100-01.

36 Parville 1882, p. 5; compare also Alglave and Boulard 1882.

37 At the 1900 Paris Fair, the Palais d'Electricité "thrilled everyone, not least the future Futurist Giacomo Balla, who included the Palace, lit up like Harrod's, in the centre of one of his paintings, and later gave two of his unfortunate daughters names that remined him of the experience: Luce (light) and Elettricità (electricity)." Frank Whitford, "The best was yet to come," *Times Literary Supplement*, 4 February 2000, p. 18.

38 Wilke 1893, p. 594.

39 Marshall McLuhan, *Understanding Media: The Extensions of Man*, New York 1965; compare Marvin 1988.

40 Marvin 1998, p. 188.

41 Wilke 1893, p. 595.

42 Parville 1882, p. 14.

43 Egerton 1990, no. 127, quotation ibid., p. 200.

44 Winslow 1867, pp. 273-74.

45 Letter to his brother Theo, ca. 11 December 1882 (294/252). Thanks to Hans Luijten.

46 Achim Saur, "Eine 'Elektrische Centralanlage' für Bremen: Die Anfänge der Elektrizität in der Hansestadt," *Bremen wird hell* 1993, p. 19.

47 Elizabeth Gaskell, *Mary Barton: A Tale of Manchester Life* (1848), London 1970, p. 101.

48 K. Baedeker, *Paris: ses environs et les principaux itinéraires des pays limitrophes à Paris*, 3rd ed., Paris 1874, p. 69, compare Clayson 1991, p. 95. When Pittsburgher Mary Roswell Scaife visited Paris in 1878 she noted that some shops already had electric lighting (probably with the Jablachkoff candle, a form of arc light), which she preferred to yellow gaslight. The stores themselves stayed open until midnight. Mary Roswell Scaife, "A Pittsburgh Lady on the Grand Tour (1878)," *Carnegie Magazine* 28 (October 1954), pp. 265-72, 275, here p. 265.

49 Chap. II, 7.

50 Letter from Theo van Gogh to his sister Willemien of 2 June 1890 (Amsterdam, Van Gogh Museum, Vincent van Gogh Foundation, inv. b931V/1962). Thanks to Chris Stolwijk.

51 Harrison 1963, p. 74.

52 In this respect we disagree with observers like Barbara Stafford, who considers today's digital world to be a revival of eighteenth-century oral visual culture, see Stafford 1994, p. XXV.

53 Poe 1840.

54 Schivelbusch 1988, p. 167.

55 Cornelius Gurlitt, *Im Bürgerhause: Plaudereien über Kunst, Kunstgewerbe und Wohnungs-Ausstattung*, Dresden 1888, p. 188.

56 Thanks to Michael Nedo.

57 O'Dea 1958, p. 230

58 Alglave and Boulard 1882, p. X.

59 Winslow 1867, pp. 240-41.

60 This kind of symbolism was not confined to the artistic and industrial elites. We only need to recall the numerous *tableaux vivants* of the Statue of Liberty performed by patriotic Americans all over the country. In 1884 250 Edison workers marched through New York City with each a light bulb attached to their helmets, demonstrating for Grover Cleveland's election as President. The power supply was carried by horses. Cf. Rebske 1962, p. 146.

61 Andreas Fischer, "Ein Nachtgebiet der Fotografie," *Okkultismus und Avantgarde* 1995, pp. 503-21.

Entries

Discovering light

Joseph Priestley's *Biographical Chart* vividly illustrates the explosion of scientific interest in light during the seventeenth and eighteenth centuries in Europe. It gives the names of more than forty researchers, as compared to less than ten for the preceding six centuries. Among the forty are the most distinguished intellects of their era: Galileo, Kepler, Descartes, Boyle, Leeuwenhoek, Roemer, Huygens, and Newton. These men are famous today not only for their discoveries about light, but also for their contributions to mathematics, astronomy, microscopy, chemistry, physics, and philosophy. For some, the astronomers and microscopists, light served as a tool for observing and analyzing nature. But for others, notably Isaac Newton and Christiaan Huygens, light was a subject worthy of study in its own right. Their books on light, published in 1690 and 1704, defined the subject for the next two centuries.

The *Opticks* and the *Traité de la lumière* broke new scientific ground in several ways. For one thing, they were written in the vernacular, not Latin, the traditional language for scientific discourse since the middle ages. Clearly both authors wished their discoveries to reach beyond the universities and learned societies. Both rely heavily on mathematics, including geometry and the new calculus, to explain observations or support hypotheses. And, both emphasize the importance of experiments as the basis for observations, reasoning, and the formation of new theories. Consequently, these books are among the founding works of modern science.

Newton and Huygens disagreed fundamentally about the nature of light. Newton argued that light consisted of particles like other forms of matter, that moved in straight lines and bounced at mathematically predictable angles. Huygens believed that light was a wave-like disturbance in an air-like medium, the ether. According to Huygens, it radiated outwards from its source like ripples after a stone drops into a pond, or like the sound vibrations produced by a musical instrument. Each scientist based his theories on careful experiments backed up by mathematical analysis, and each is correct. Modern physics combines their basic ideas in a new theory of light's dual nature as wave and particle. However, during the 150-year period covered here, Newton's particle concept dominated until the early nineteenth century, at which point several key experiments suddenly provided support for Huygens. As we shall see in the following pages, their different theories of light influenced many aspects of life and art in the eighteenth and nineteenth centuries.

Title page of Christiaan Huygens, *Traité de la lumière*, Leiden 1690, Universiteitsbibliotheek Amsterdam

A Biographical Chart of Those Who Have Most Distinguished Themselves by their Discoveries Relating to Vision, Light, and Colours, frontispiece to Joseph Priestley, *The History and Present State of Discoveries Relating to Vision, Light, and Colours*, London 1772, Carnegie Library, Pittsburgh

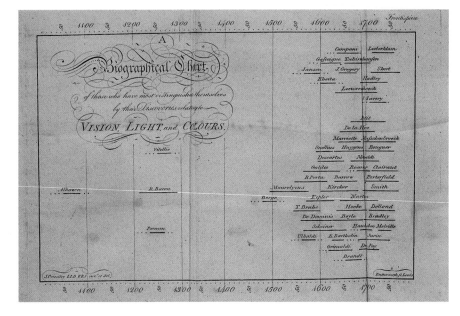

Title page of Isaac Newton, *Opticks*, London 1704, Universiteitsbibliotheek Amsterdam

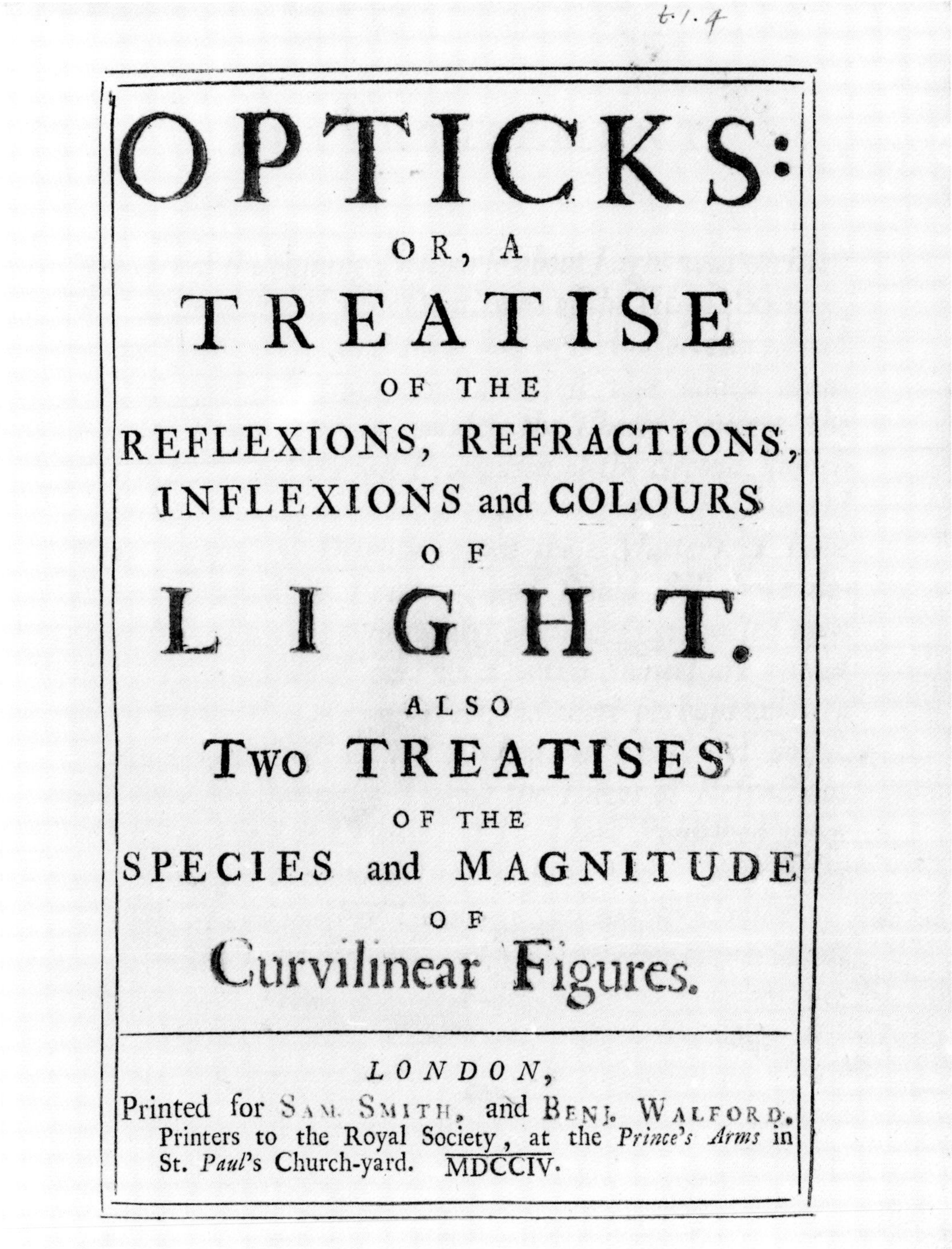

OPTICKS:
OR, A
TREATISE
OF THE
REFLEXIONS, REFRACTIONS,
INFLEXIONS and COLOURS
OF
LIGHT.
ALSO
Two TREATISES
OF THE
SPECIES and MAGNITUDE
OF
Curvilinear Figures.

LONDON,
Printed for SAM. SMITH, and BENJ. WALFORD,
Printers to the Royal Society, at the *Prince's Arms* in
St. *Paul's* Church-yard. MDCCIV.

The prism experiment

Of Newton's many discoveries, the prism experiment proved the most important to artists. In this famous demonstration, still an essential element of secondary school physics courses, a beam of sunlight is directed through a prism. The light refracts, with different colored rays refracting at different angles, creating a spectrum. This demonstration conclusively proved that white light is composed of different colored lights arranged in a fixed sequence, conventionally described as progressing from red to orange, yellow, green, blue, indigo and violet. Newton's analysis and explanation of the spectrum eventually became the basis of every important theory of color in nature and art up to 1900, although it took decades for his ideas to reach artists and the general public.

In the early eighteenth century, many artists had not yet grasped the full implications of the science they celebrated in paintings and prints. Giovanni Battista Pittoni's famous *Allegorical Monument to Sir Isaac Newton* is a strange blend of old religion and new science. Pittoni painted a series of these allegorical tombs or monuments dedicated to the great men of Britain, including the exceptional natural philosopher. It represents a quasi-religious ceremony: an annual gathering of symbolic divinities, antique philosophers and learned men around the tomb of Newton to celebrate his great achievements. Pittoni's principal model for this idea seems to have been a Renaissance glorification of learning and philosophy, Raphael's fresco of the *School of Athens* in the Vatican. However, Pittoni centers his composition on a scientific demonstration rather than the learned conversation featured in the fresco. This demonstration is Newton's famous prism experiment on a grand scale. However, Pittoni's version is physically impossible to achieve, especially with eighteenth-century equipment. For one thing, no ray of sunlight can traverse the distance between the oculus above the tomb and the first focusing lens without spreading. For another, the light is deflected at an angle that defies the laws of optics. Finally, as it passes through the prism, it once again bends at an angle unknown in nature. It is ironic that a painter glorifying Newton misunderstood his fundamental ideas about light. Pittoni's mistake is even more surprising, given that Newton's nephew had sent him detailed and explicit instructions about the content of the scene. The artist might also have consulted the famous library of Consul John Smith, his patron, for an accurate illustration of the experiment.

Lens, Dutch, ca. 1750–75, Teylers Museum, Haarlem

Prism in holder, Dutch ca. 1750–75, and *Prism with decorative shape*, Dutch, ca. 1775–1800, Universiteits-museum Utrecht

Giovanni Battista Pittoni,
*An Allegorical Monument to Sir
Isaac Newton*, 1727–30,
Fitzwilliam Museum, Cambridge

47 **The prism experiment**

Newton for the public

The influence of Newton's writings and the almost religious admiration he experienced during his lifetime did, in fact, continue for decades after his death.[1] Newton's *Opticks*, the fruit of years of research, was first published in 1704 and quickly went through a number of editions. Despite this, the work remained inaccessible to the larger public, as it required knowledge of mathematics that few at the time possessed. Voltaire, who was present at the Englishman's extravagant funeral, took his writings and "translated" them for the educated layman. In the introduction, the philosopher proclaimed – not without some satisfaction – that his work would finally disprove the ridiculous theories of the ancients. Their time was past, and Voltaire was proud of the part he himself had played in the emergence of a new era: "Thus, we cannot congratulate ourselves enough for being born at a time and in a nation where people are beginning to open their eyes, and to have made such a contribution to humanity and the use of reason."[2]

Still more popular than Voltaire's *Elémens de la philosophie de Neuton* was Francesco Algarotti's *Newtonianism for Women*, first published in Italian in 1737. It appeared in a number of languages over several decades, and was widely disseminated and read. Knowledge of Newton's theories was *bon ton* among the social elite, as demonstrated by the introduction to a later Dutch edition, which states that some basic understanding of natural science was a requirement for anyone wishing to be a worthy member of society. Voltaire's aims seem to have been fulfilled.

The triumph of truth over ignorance and the dawn of a new age are also the subjects of the strange painting by Januarius Zick, *Newton's Contribution to Optics*. Its theme matches its title, while a pendant picture (also in Hanover) treats the scientist's role in the development of the theory of gravity. Zick certainly had a special interest in such topics, as did his father, Johann Zick, who was not only a painter and his first teacher, but also an astronomer and mathematician. Here, the young, idealistic Newton is shown tearing away the mask of false belief, revealing the distorted face of ignorance. To the right, we see Euclid and Diogenes leaving the stage, making way for their venerable follower in the disciplines of mathematics and philosophy. Newton's science itself, which Giovanni Battista Pittoni had attempted to capture in paint a few decades earlier, retreats here in favor of a mixture of classical apotheosis and Enlightenment propaganda, similar to that found in the pamphlets of the French Revolution.

Frontispiece to Voltaire, *Elémens de la philosophie de Neuton, mis à la portée de tout le monde*, Amsterdam 1738, Universiteitsbibliotheek Amsterdam

1 Haskell 1970; Wagner 1974.
2 Voltaire 1738, p. 15.

Januarius Zick, *Newton's Contribution to Optics*, ca. 1790, Niedersächsisches Landesmuseum, Hanover

Projections I

No other instrument united serious science and popular entertainment as perfectly as the magic lantern. It was invented in the seventeenth century, but the oldest surviving example is the one shown here, probably built by the instrument maker Jan van Musschenbroek for Willem Jacob 's Gravesande. 's Gravesande was a famous physicist and perhaps the most important propagator of Newton's teachings – Voltaire even came to him for advice while translating the Englishman's writings. As director of the Leiden Physics Theater in 1724, he purchased the latest instruments for his demonstration lectures. When 's Gravesande died in 1742, the university acquired his entire collection, an act of great foresight and inestimable value: "With this formidable acquisition, the Leiden Cabinet of Physics became the finest and most comprehensive collection of philosophical instruments in the world."[1]

Jean Ouvrier after Johann Eleazar Schenau, *The Magic Lantern*, before 1784, engraving, Rijksmuseum, Rijksprentenkabinet, Amsterdam

In the eighteenth century, oil lamps were used to create the projections, while a concave mirror helped to strengthen the beam. Thanks to an ingenious system of lenses, it was possible to project the pictures at a distance of up to 30 feet. These images had little artistic pretension, and often showed nothing more than monstrous figures – perhaps to help assure the public's attention. Thomas L. Hankins and Robert J. Silverman have noted that by the eighteenth century such demonstrations, which had simply been part of the proof of an experiment a hundred years earlier, were now used primarily for pedagogical purposes.[2]

It was 's Gravesande himself who first introduced projectors into his scientific lectures: "'s Gravesande continued Newton's mathematical emphasis, but with experiments that were meant to illustrate and confirm rather than to initiate inquiry. It was with 's Gravesande that the 'demonstration' lecture using instruments became a standard method

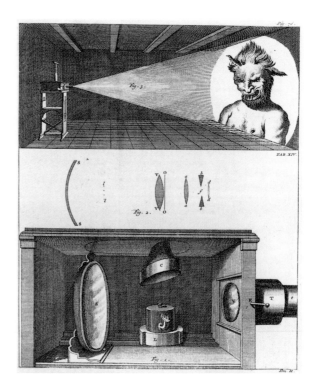

The mechanism of Jan van Musschenbroek's projection lantern, engraving from Willem Jacob 's Gravesande, *Physices elementa mathematica, experimentis confirmata*, Leiden 1721, Universiteitsbibliotheek Amsterdam

of instruction in natural philosophy." As the authors further indicate, 's Gravesande's method had an effect on how things were actually taught: "As the 'demonstration' part of the physics lecture passed from geometrical proof to the exhibition of phenomena, the rhetorical geometrical form also disappeared from the textbooks."[3] With demonstration as a new form of teaching, one is tempted to make a comparison with the advent of educational television and the Internet. Learning by reading and calculating was expanded to include learning by doing and seeing. However, one can also look at this advancement, from another angle: 's Gravesande's popularization grew from the gap between progressive scientific knowledge and the non-specialists' ability to absorb the new information. The general public now had the opportunity to take an interest in these revolutionary discoveries and demanded that they be easy to understand.

Jan van Musschenbroek, *Projection lantern*, ca. 1720, Museum Boerhaave, Leiden

1 De Clercq 1997, p. 11.
2 Hankins and Silverman 1995, pp. 42-43.
3 Ibid., p. 53.

Enlightened painting

'LIGHT, (*Painting*) This term in PAINTING signifies not light in itself, but the imitation of its effects represented in a composition...'[1] Thus the great French *Encyclopédie* of 1751–56 draws the essential distinction between the light of nature as studied by natural philosophers, and the light of art as manipulated by painters, a distinction rarely questioned during the following century. There is little doubt about which light the Encyclopedists found more interesting: LIGHT (*Painting*) rates two perfunctory paragraphs and one cross-reference to reflection, whereas LIGHT (*Optic.*) occupies eight full pages of text and numerous cross-references to scientific and philosophical subjects.[2] Encyclopedists described the latter as "the sensation that the sight of luminous bodies conveys to the soul, or equally, the properties of these bodies that enable them to excite this sensation in us."[3] The *Encyclopédie* discussion of light in painting is dominated by the shadow and the different colors of natural and artificial light, elaborated in artists' texts and training since the Renaissance. In contrast, shadow is of little significance in the pages on optical light, the basic problems having been considered solved. Of far more importance throughout the text are the ongoing debates over theories of light as ray or particle, and the phenomena of the spectrum, refraction, diffraction, and polarization. Here, Newton's revolutionary theories of optics dominate.

Given the *Encyclopédie*'s priorities, it is obvious why Chardin's paintings appealed so highly to enlightenment critics despite their humble subject matter. *Glass of Water and Coffeepot*, like so many late Chardin still lifes, offers a beautifully realized examination of the behavior of "light in itself," that owes little to the artificial distribution of lights and darks characteristic of "LIGHT (*Painting*)." The diffused overall light, falling from upper left and largely absorbed by the opaque stone ledge and backdrop, minimizes shadow. The water glass is a brilliant case study of the central optical problem of the eighteenth century: refraction, the bending of light as it passes through transparent materials of differing densities. On the most practical level, refraction was an essential study of lensmakers, makers of telescopes and microscopes, including the great Huygens and Newton, but its mathematical analysis was also yielding crucial information about light's fundamental nature and speed. The materials of Chardin's composition – air, glass, and water – are identical to those employed in the eighteenth century's most advanced experimental equipment, such as the optical boxes and troughs and prismatic glass cells preserved in the Boerhaave Museum, Leiden. Judging from critical praise of a water glass in a different Chardin still life (*Glass of Water and Bucket of Plums*, Musée des Beaux-Arts, Rennes, Salon of 1759), his scientific acumen was easily recognized by contemporaries ("half filled with water which creates two kinds of transparencies perfectly rendered")[4]. The remaining elements of Chardin's composition, the glazed earthenware coffeepot, papery bulbs of garlic, and smooth leaves from the same plant, deal with the more difficult problem of diffraction, the behavior of light as it bounces and scatters off uneven surfaces of differing opacities and textures.

This is not to suggest that Chardin was himself an optical scientist. Much of eighteenth-century science, including the study of light, was based primarily on keen observation, description and measurement of easily visible phenomena – practices not far removed from those of art. The description of Chardin as an observational painter is extremely just, with the added proviso that Chardin seems to have observed most carefully the cutting-edge topic of enlightened natural philosophy.

Large prismatic cell and *Optical trough*, ca. 1720–40, Museum Boerhaave, Leiden

When the trough was filled with water, the circular watch glasses functioned like lenses. Placed in relationship to a half-filled trough, it demonstrated the different refractions of light through air and water.

Benjamin Martin, attributed, *Apparatus for measuring the angle of incidence*, ca. 1765, Harvard University Collection of Historical Scientific Instruments, Cambridge, Massachusetts

A mirror, container of liquid, or prism could be placed in the center of this instrument. The sliding metal arms recorded the angle of light approaching and leaving the central device.

1 Diderot and d'Alembert 1751-80, vol. 2, t. VII-XII, p. 724.
2 Ibid., pp. 717-24.
3 Ibid., p. 717.
4 Pierre Rosenberg, *Chardin 1669-1769*, exh. cat. Paris (Galeries nationales du Grand Palais) 1979, p. 314.

Jean Siméon Chardin, *Glass of Water and Coffeepot*, ca. 1760, Carnegie Museum of Art, Pittsburgh, Howard A. Noble Collection

Glitter

Candelabrum, British, ca. 1725,
Carnegie Museum of Art,
Pittsburgh, Gift of Ailsa Mellon
Bruce

One candle makes very little light. Its flickering impedes focused vision. With one candle, it is possible to grope one's way through the house, or read a book, one line at a time. It is not possible to see one's spouse at the other end of the dinner table, nor will one candle illuminate even a very small room. For a long time, the only way to achieve more light was to light more candles. However, candles were formidably expensive. Although they came in many sizes and qualities, no one, not even kings, could afford to light up entire buildings, or even rooms, except on the grandest occasions. As a result, great effort, expense, and ingenuity went into the development of devices that amplified candlelight.

These devices worked by reflecting, refracting or diffusing light – optical principles better understood following the work of Newton and Huygens at the end of the seventeenth century. Polished metal, glass, and reflective textiles, such as silk or metallic threads, all perform these optical functions, and were used extensively in the interior decoration of great houses during the seventeenth and eighteenth centuries. These materials epitomized luxury – not only were mirrors, plate glass, gilt bronze, and silk damask expensive in themselves – they also symbolized the even greater extravagance of lighting up the house after dark.

These devices reached their most elegant and effective form in the eighteenth century, following major improvements in mirror and glass making, and before Argand lamps superceded the candle. Chandeliers amplified light from candles by refracting it from hundreds of prismatically cut drops of glass. The development of lead glass in the mid-eighteenth century increased their propensity to sparkle, because the new glass was relatively white in color, more transparent, and free of flaws. (It had been invented to improve the quality of lenses in telescopes.) Mirrors became larger after French and English mirror makers developed new techniques for making glass in huge, smooth sheets suitable for architecturally-scaled pier glasses and larger windows with fewer mullions. Gilding on architectural ornament, picture frames, candlesticks, and wall lights brought sparkle to ceilings, walls, and furniture. The magical effect of light glittering off rich and costly materials was the eighteenth century's ultimate expression of power and wealth.

Thomas Hope (designer) and Alexis Decaix (maker), attributed, *Pair of candlesticks*, ca. 1807, Carnegie Museum of Art, Pittsburgh, Museum purchase, Gift of Ailsa Mellon Bruce, by exchange, and Ailsa Mellon Bruce Fund

Microscopes

Beginning in the seventeenth century, scientific research depended increasingly on experiments, and the instruments with which they were conducted, and the results, measured and recorded. It was not enough for the natural philosopher to think and write; it was also necessary to test ideas in the real world of nature. The first scientists adopting the new method had to design their own instruments. Just as Newton and Huygens ground lenses and built telescopes for their work in optics and astronomy, natural philosophers, investigating the microcosm (Antoni van Leeuwenhoek, Robert Hooke) made the first microscopes.

At first, the poor quality of the glass and mirrors in microscopes (and telescopes) limited their effectiveness. To the modern observer, the view through the bubbly, clouded glass lenses is extemely foggy and not much enlarged. The great improvements in eighteenth-century instruments resulted from new glass- and mirror-making processes that enhanced transmission and reflection of light, and from the adoption of the technical precision of clock making. The heliostat, a complicated clockwork mechanism made – in this example – by a clockmaker, allowed a small, light-focusing mirror to follow the sun across the sky. As a result, the mirror could project a steady beam of light useful for a time-consuming experiment, such as the microscopic examination of the circulation of the blood through the translucent tail fin of a fish. As a result, eighteenth-century scientific instruments are works of art that actually worked. Expensive, delicate, and precious, they became prized possessions of the elite.

The new experimental approach turned science into a group activity. Previously isolated researchers now worked with sophisticated craftsmen; university professors taught students in lectures and public demonstrations; amateurs uncapped their microscopes and telescopes to instruct and entertain family and friends. Some of the most curious and bizarre instruments of the later eighteenth century were designed to project on a public scale the tiny images captured in microscope and telescope lenses. The solar microscope projected sunlight to display an image. Set into a window shutter, it captured sunlight on the exterior mirror, focused it through lenses in its barrel, and projected it through a glass slide, creating on the opposite wall, seven-foot-wide images of algae, fleas, and dust, just to name a few. Until the invention of the Argand lamp at the end of eighteenth century, only sunlight was strong enough to project an image with enough scale and clarity for even a small audience to see.

Microscope, Dutch, ca. 1750–75, Museum Boerhaave, Leiden

Jacob van der Cloesen, *Heliostat*, ca. 1720–40, Museum Boerhaave, Leiden

Projecting an image with the solar microscope and *Microscopic image*, colored engravings from Martin Frobenius Ledermüller and Adam Wolfang Winterschmidt, *Mikroskoopische vermaaklykheden*, [...], Amsterdam 1776, Universiteitsbibliotheek Amsterdam

Solar microscope, Dutch, ca. 1750–1800, Museum Boerhaave, Leiden

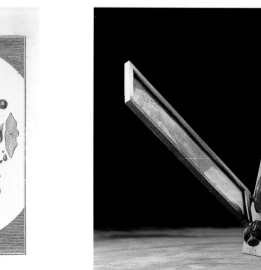

Seeing stars

Nathaniel Hill and George
Adams, Sr., *Orrery*, 1754,
Nederlands Scheepvaartmuseum,
Amsterdam

This orrery was constructed by
the firm of George Adams,
one of the leading and most
productive instrument makers
in England at the time. He
continually revised his planetary model according to the
latest discoveries.

William Pether after Joseph
Wright of Derby, *The Orrery*, 1768,
mezzotint, Carnegie Museum of
Art, Pittsburgh

As patron of the invention, the
Earl of Orrery gave his name
to all similar planetary models. This mezzotint (after a
painting in Derby) illustrates a
demonstration of the instrument, emphasizing the
absorption of the participants
as they are experiencing an
entirely new vision of the
universe.

It is futile to debate which is more
fascinating: to view the world from close-up
through a microscope, or to discover the
enormous distances of space with the help of a
telescope. Both instruments can trace their
origins back to the seventeenth century, and
their flourishing success throughout the
eighteenth. The improvement in lens-making
technology naturally played an important role.
Telescopes could now scan the remote regions
of the solar system and explore depths of space
that were frightening to contemporaries. The
new instrument gave its user the feeling of
coming into contact with the Creator himself.
Despite all the exact scientific knowledge on
which his instruments were based, George
Adams regarded them above all as proof of the
existence of God: "[...] natural philosophy
affords no support to the wretched system of
materialism, but concours with religion in
endeavouring to enlighten the mind, to comfort the heart, to establish the welfare of society, and promote the love of order."[1] The telescope thus became an attribute of wisdom,
and kings and princes felt it was their duty to
know something about astronomy.[2] In addition to its scientific purpose, and thus its function as a status symbol, the telescope also had
an economic value – namely in navigation.

Exact knowledge of the stars and planets
made it possible for instrument makers to
build extraordinarily accurate planetariums,
operated with the aid of cranks, clockwork
mechanisms and cogs. These – often highly
elaborate – objects were used for popular
scientific demonstrations, where, once again,
it was sometimes difficult to distinguish
between pedagogy and entertainment. Joseph
Wright of Derby twice depicted such demonstrations, reproducing the images in mezzotint for wider dissemination. Wright was
a member of the Lunar Society, a group of
gentry who, on each Monday nearest the full
moon, would meet to carry out various experiments. The painter's interests indicate clearly
that he believed in the unity of science and art.

Jan van Deijl, *Achromatic
telescope*, 1781, Teylers Museum,
Haarlem

In 1758, the English instrument maker John Dollond
discovered the solution to a
problem that hitherto prevented the full development
of the telescope, namely, the
chromatic aberration of the
objective lens. Combining two
lenses, each with a different
refractive index, provided the
answer. Here, his Dutch colleagues Jan van Deijl and his
son, Harmanus, took up the
idea, equipping their telescope with both double-
convex and concavo-convex
lenses. They proudly signed
their masterpiece *Jan van Deijl
& Zoon Fecit Amsterdam Ao
1781*, much as an artist would
a painting.

1 *Lectures on Natural and
   Experimental Philosophy* (1794),
   quoted after Turner and Levere
   1973, p. 6.
2 Klamt 1979; Klamt 1999.

Allegories of light

These two allegories of light were painted at more or less the same time and yet could not be more different. Maulbertsch is considered one of the most important representatives of the late Baroque in Austria. His work is apparently an oil sketch for a ceiling painting. The viewer looks into the sky, where Phoebus Apollo – the sun god – is shown storming in on his golden chariot, expelling darkness with the help of his divine comrades. Between Apollo and Mercury we see Aurora, placing the morning star in the heavens. In the foreground, a figure of Truth drives the forces of evil into a chasm. Maulbertsch freely mixed the iconographical traditions of Christianity and the antique: he would have used the same visual elements in a composition depicting the Archangel Michael battling the dragon, or an apotheosis of a saint.

While Maulbertsch remained faithful to traditional forms of allegory, Lantara abandoned the figural altogether. This Frenchman specialized in landscapes with striking light effects. In contrast to others of his generation, Lantara's fame was short-lived. In the nineteenth century, he was rediscovered as a kind of bohemian *avant la lettre*, but to this day there have been no serious examinations of his work.[1] This is unfortunate, as he was an extraordinary and original artist. His work not only presages the abstract iconography, but even the style of the Romantics, whose endless horizons symbolize the grandeur of creation. The triangle inscribed with the Hebrew letters JAHWE is a sign of the Holy Trinity, introduced by the Renaissance mystic Jakob Böhme. The painting here illustrates Genesis 1:2: "And the earth was without form, and void; and darkness was upon the face of the

deep. And the spirit of God moved upon the face of the waters." The next line, Genesis 1:3, reads: "And God said, Let there be light: and there was light." In his bold painting, Lantara shows us the breaking of the first dawn, thus inventing an allegory of the origins of the world. This ambitious attempt to make the invisible visible is also a statement about the role and position of the artist, who alone was capable of imitating creation.

Franz Anton Maulbertsch, *Allegory of Light and Truth*, ca. 1750, Wallraf-Richartz-Museum, Cologne

1 George Levitine, 'Les Origines du mythe de l'artiste bohème en France: Lantara,' *Gazette des Beaux-Arts* 86 (1975), pp. 49-60.

Simon-Mathurin Lantara, *The Spirit of
God Moved Upon the Face of the
Waters*, 1751, Musée de Grenoble

Work lights

For many centuries, bizarre-looking devices such as these lit the majority of households that had any lighting at all. The basic oil lamp, a shallow bowl with a spout or support for a wick, plus a handle, dates back to antiquity. Candlesticks are also many hundreds of years old, while the origin of the splint holder is unknown. Their forms and functions changed little before the advent of new fuels and lighting technologies in the middle of the nineteenth century which rapidly rendered them obsolete. Today, it takes an expert to make them work again, or even to recognize some of them as lights.

Despite their form, they were very efficiently adapted for their functions. They were work lights for poor, middle class, and rural homes, and for the kitchens and servants' quarters of wealthy households, in the epoch preceding gas and electric lighting. Their common features tell much about their everyday uses. Their crude and simple forms reflect the skills of the local blacksmiths who made them. Each is made of iron, a relatively inexpensive, unbreakable, and nonflammable material. Fire resistance was important because open flames generated the light. The material had to be unbreakable as each device was portable and bound to be dropped now and then. The double crusie lamp and the splint holder have handles, while the flat tray under the candlestick made it easy to lift. Broad bases or spreading legs guaranteed stability. However, hooks on the candleholder and double crusie lamp allowed them to be hung on walls or furniture such as chairs. Finally, the candleholder and the crusie lamp were adjustable so the light source could be raised or lowered as needed. In their portability, durability, and flexibility, these lights can be compared to modern task lights or flashlights.

These lights are also similar in their dependence on finite amounts of fuel: batteries today, candles, wood splints, or pools of grease or lard, then. Unlike batteries, the fuels for these primitive lamps could be made in the home. Splints were chips or slivers of wood that burned relatively cleanly. Rushlights were single reeds saturated with animal fat to render them more flammable. Rushlight and splint holders supported their fuels in narrow slits or pincers, exposing the entire piece to the air, enabling it to burn completely. Candles and oil (or grease or lard) lamps relied on animal fat that burned off a wick made of cloth or vegetable fibers. The simple and inexpensive candles used in the iron candleholder were made most probably from tallow, a hard form of animal fat, instead of the cleaner, better burning, and far more costly beeswax. The double crusie lamp burned grease.

The fuels indicate how tightly these designs were tied to pre-industrial, rural economies. They relied on the gathering of fuel from the surrounding countryside, and the slaughter of animals for their meat, fat, and hide. The rendering of fat to make tallow was a smelly, messy process best accomplished outdoors; and the end product smelled and smoked when burned. Grease, tallow and lard were abandoned as soon as more economical alternatives were discovered, such as whale oil, kerosene and other petroleum byproducts. These volatile fuels would change lamp design completely. And by the end of the nineteenth century, as industrialization both radically changed city life and prompted nostalgia for traditional rural existence, the primitive iron lamps acquired unexpected significance. In 1889, Van Gogh painted such a lamp hanging from a bedpost in a peasant cottage, illuminating the evening's work. Its radiant light, far surpassing the dim and flickering historical reality, symbolizes the spiritual value of a disappearing way of life.

Vincent van Gogh, *The Wake (after Millet)*, 1889, Van Gogh Museum, Amsterdam (Vincent van Gogh Foundation)

Double crusie grease lamp, American, ca. 1750, *Splint holder* and *Candleholder*, both American, ca. 1800–50, Carnegie Museum of Natural History, Pittsburgh, Gifts of Arthur B. Van Buskirk and George and Lilian Ball

The camera obscura

Artists have always been reluctant to admit their use of technical aids. As individualism and the cult of genius grew in the eighteenth century, it became increasingly important to hide the fact that the inspired hand occasionally needed a little assistance. Many painters despised photography because it robbed them of their exclusive claim to the imitation of reality. In the case of landscape painting, however, this prerogative had been under threat for centuries. The camera obscura, known in principle since antiquity and as an actual optical instrument since at least the sixteenth century, seemed to make an exact reproduction of the external world possible: "the prettiest landskip I ever saw was drawn on the walls of a dark room," an eyewitness reported in 1712.[1] The technique is as primitive as it is astonishing: light enters a darkened box or room through an opening so small that it prevents the rays from scattering. These rays then travel in a straight line, projecting what is outside onto the opposite wall – although turned upside down and reversed.

Enough camera obscuras and similar perspective devices have come down to us from artists' studios to indicate that they were an essential tool for the landscape painter, stressing the scientific nature of art. There is no way of knowing, however, how regularly they were used. Only in the cases of Vermeer and Canaletto, one is relatively certain of the device's application. While the camera obscura could help painters recreate a topographical situation, the light was too weak for anything more. Many treatises, for example those by the pioneer of plein-air painting Pierre-Henri de Valenciennes, advised against its use because of its tendency to distort.[2] Even Sir Joshua Reynolds, who once owned the example we see here, probably employed it less in his art (after all, he was not a landscape painter) than in technical experiments. The founding director of the Royal Academy discussed light regularly in his discourses, if only in rather vague

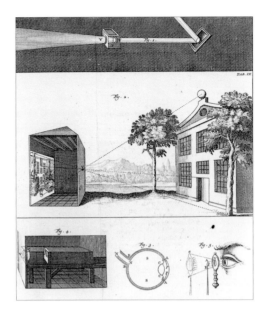

A *camera obscura*, engraving from Willem Jacob 's Gravesande, *Physices elementa mathematica, experimentis confirmata*, Leiden 1721, Universiteitsbibliotheek Amsterdam

terms. For example, he spent much time calculating the relationship between dark and light areas in paintings by the Old Masters. His wonderfully crafted camera obscura, with its mirrors, lenses and elaborate folding mechanism, was probably designed to impress rather than to be used. When folded, it appears to be a book, turning the instrument itself into as much of an illusion as the pictures it produced.

The camera obscura earned its place as the mother of photography. However, as soon as it was possible to fix the images produced in the little black box, the device grew to be superfluous as a painter's tool. On the other hand, as a form of entertainment, it has lost nothing of its fascination. Thanks to better lenses, the projections could be enlarged and camera obscuras were built that could actually be entered. Illusionists made regular use of the camera obscura throughout the nineteenth century, and even the prehistory of the fax machine can be traced back to it: in a treatise of 1880, entitled *La Télescopie électrique*, the Portuguese professor Adriano de Paiva suggested coating the projection surface with selenium; the images, he believed, could then be transmitted using telegraph lines.

1 Brennan n.d., p. 14.
2 Valenciennes (1800), p. 208.

Camera obscura, British, ca. 1760–80,
Science Museum, London

Early street lights

William Hogarth, *Cruelty in Perfection*, 1785, etching and engraving, Rijksmuseum, Rijksprentenkabinet, Amsterdam

Jan ter Gouw, *City Lighting: Candle 1550, [oil] Lamp 1750, Gas 1850*, 1851, pen and ink, Gemeentearchief Amsterdam

Beginning in the seventeenth century, some of Europe's most progressive cities, such as Amsterdam, began systematically lighting their major streets, usually with strategically located candle-lit lamps, which acted as beacons to guide the traveler from place to place. Before this, people had been dependent either on their own lanterns or hired lantern carriers, and the light moved along with them. In Paris, Louis XIV set his mark by providing permanent illumination on the Place des Victoires. It was some time, however, before it became obvious that more, and less expensive, lighting could also produce enormous *public* benefits, notably in the reduction of crime and popular unrest. Even in the eighteenth century, the London street-

lights were already in the hands of private companies, which competed with one another.[1] In 1765, the city of Paris announced a competition for the development of more efficient street lamps. The famous French chemist Antoine Laurent Lavoisier took part. He had recently employed Pierre Bouguer's "lucimètre" in order to measure the lanterns' luminosity. Improved street lighting had clearly become a great necessity, one that Paris shared with all the other great cities of Europe. A few years later, Ami Argand's hollow wick oil lamp would help fill this huge gap in the market.

The light of these oil lamps, which today would hardly be considered serviceable, made a great impression on contemporaries. Already in 1746, Valois d'Orville honored the inventors of Paris's new lanterns, Preigney and Bourgeois, with a poem celebrating their triumph over the powers of darkness. In it, Jupiter seeks to calm the Sun, exhausted by her struggle with the Night, by announcing that mortals had finally put an end to her enemy's empire.[2] There are, however, few eyewitness accounts of the period's lighting. The new technology was barely in widespread use before its charms had faded; progress had become a matter of course, and lamps and lighting were only noticed when they failed to work. When Simon Morley, the hero of Jack Finney's *Time and Again* (1970), returns from his time travel to the New York of the 1880s, one of his supervisors asks him: "'Well, what about streetlamps? [...] Were they gas or electric? That's not hard to tell.'" And Morley replies: "'Oscar, I no more paid any attention to streetlights than *you* do when you go out at night.'"

Petrus van Schendel, *Night Market in Antwerp*, 1861, The Richard Green Gallery, London

Depictions of the nighttime streets were rare in the eighteenth century. And indeed, why would an artist have been interested in painting them? They were entirely dark and there was nothing to see. In the nineteenth century, however, there developed a kind of yearning for the sleepy half-light of days gone by. The Dutch artist Petrus van Schendel specialized in evening market scenes. His views are imbued with this nostalgia and had little to do with contemporary reality.

1 Falkus 1976.
2 Drien-Joseph le Valois d'Orville, *Les nouvelles lanternes*, Paris 1746.

By the light of a candle

"Morceau de réception" was the term used to describe a painting or sculpture submitted to the French Academy in order to achieve full membership. In general, painters and sculptors put a great deal of effort into these works, placing particular emphasis on the demonstration of technical skill in their chosen medium. Complex subjects or compositions were also popular as a way of convincing the jury that the artist took his métier seriously.

A female artist – particularly one who was a foreigner – must have had an especially difficult time in the Paris of 1767. Anna Therbusch, born Lisiewska, received her early training in Berlin, under the auspices of her Polish father. She became court painter to both the king of Prussia and the Elector Palatine before moving to France in 1766. This painting was to gain her entry into the leading art academy in Europe. Given that she was already a mature painter, there was no need to employ all the various tricks of the trade in order to astound the jury. Instead, she concentrated on a variety of lighting effects in an intimate interior setting, giving the work

Georges de La Tour,
Christ in the Carpenter's Shop,
1645, Musée du Louvre,
Département des Peintures, Paris

the purely descriptive title "A man with a glass in his hand, lit by a candle". The candle itself is invisible to the viewer, hidden behind a shade – creating an atmosphere similar to that found in paintings by Caravaggio and his followers, particularly the French painter Georges de La Tour. The candlelight illuminates the young man, who regards the viewer through somewhat glazed eyes, holding his wine glass casually, even carelessly, in his left hand. The candle is the only source of light, effectively emphasizing the shadows and throwing the man's face and clothes into relief. The shadows cast by the other objects in the picture are also reproduced realistically.

The picture achieved its aim, and Therbusch was admitted to the Academy. This does not mean, however, that everybody was equally pleased with the painting and its execution. None other than the Enlightenment philosopher Denis Diderot subjected the work to a detailed examination, in which he concentrated primarily on the lighting. He quickly came to what he perceived as the painting's greatest problem: "The light is not that of a candle. It is the blazing light of an inferno. There is none of that velvety blackness, that softness, that delicate harmony characteristic of artificial light. None of that haziness which surrounds the light source and the objects it illuminates. None of those passages or insubstantial half-tones that multiply to infinity in nocturnes, and whose imperceptible and varying shades are so difficult to render. They should be there and they are not. The skin, the fabrics have retained nothing of their natural color. [...] I do not sense anything of that invisible darkness which mixes with light and makes it almost luminous."[1] It is hardly important whether anti-Prussian sentiments or a distaste for women painters played a role in this harsh judgment. What the critic sought to show was that the artist had failed in her central ambition, namely in the rendition of the lighting. More could have been accomplished in this area, so he seems to believe, than the painter was capable of.

1 Quoted after *Diderot et l'art de Boucher à David, Les Salons: 1759-1781*, exh. cat. Paris (Hôtel de la Monnaie) 1984-85, p. 360.

Anna Dorothea Therbusch, *A Drinker – Light Effect*, 1767, Ecole nationale supérieure des beaux-arts, Paris

Night effects

Until the middle of the nineteenth century, the workday was divided between the daylight hours and the hours of darkness. The culture was still pre-industrial – few clocks, no night shifts, no closing hours, and almost nothing in the way of night life. Artists worked at night, like shopkeepers, weavers, farmers, and everyone else, by the light of fires, candles, oil lamps, or the moon. The warm, dim, flickering lights severely limited the type of work that artists might do, for details lose themselves in shadows, colors are muted and warmed, architectural space vanishes into vast reaches of darkness. Wright of Derby exploited these effects brilliantly in *An Academy by Lamplight*. The warm light seems to animate the monochromatic statue, as it reduces the richly garbed students to sculpture.

Artists working by lamplight usually made drawings rather than paintings, and they concentrated on single figures, often monochromatic sculptures and casts. Night was the time to study chiaroscuro, the use of light and shade to model form. This is the occupation of some of the young gentlemen clustered around the graceful *Nymph with Seashell*. The student in the foreground draws the dramatically-lit figure with black and white chalk on blue paper, materials that lend themselves to describing form with highlights and shadows. Wright's own drawings from the 1760s and 1770s are often in this medium. From the painting's title, we know that the students belong to an academy, which in the eighteenth century could be anything from an aristocratic social club to a professional association of working artists perfecting their manual skills. Although the youthful countenances of the students suggest they might be apprentices in training, their elaborate costumes, with frilled collars and cuffs, belong to the English tradition of the "fancy picture" based on imagination, not real life.

There is still controversy over the realism of Wright's forge paintings, of which *The Blacksmith Shop* in Derby is the second of four. In terms of artificial lighting effects, they may be Wright's boldest, for he placed the glowing

ingot in full view instead of shielding its brilliance, as occurs with the ceiling lamp hidden behind a swag of drapery in the *Academy*. As a result, the forge pictures contain the extremes of light and darkness achievable in the eighteenth century, both in real life and in art. But, did blacksmiths in Derbyshire really set up shop in Renaissance ruins? Would the smith's family and friends normally be in attendance in the workshop? Wright made some effort to explain why blacksmiths would work after dark by including a waiting traveller whose horse presumably lost a shoe. The moonlight not only gave Wright a chance to show his skill with cool and warm lights, but also supports his story – nocturnal travel was limited to nights when the moon was full.

Joseph Wright of Derby, *An Academy by Lamplight*, ca. 1769, Lord Somerleyton, Somerleyton Hall, Lowestoft, Suffolk

Joseph Wright of Derby, *The Blacksmith Shop*, 1771. Derby Museum and Art Gallery

Enlightenment

Anonymous, French, *Liberty, Equality, Reason*, 1794, lead

"It seems to be the fate of humankind that those things furthest from our understanding are those which our sensual faculties encounter most often," wrote the mathematician, physicist, and astronomer Johann Heinrich Lambert in the introduction to his treatise on "photometrics" of 1760. In what follows, he goes on to complain of the lack of a physical theory of light.[1] Lambert himself did much to overcome this problem. His words are, however, somewhat astounding, considering that they were preceded by a century in which more had been done to solve the mystery of light than ever before. This was the period of the Enlightenment, the only historical epoch to include the word "light" in its name.

The roots of the Enlightenment lay in the seventeenth century. René Descartes was the first to not only define the properties of light, but also to regard it as a manageable material.[2] This prepared the way for the actual measurement of fire and light, and novel optical instruments were constructed. In the symbolic language of the period, light and reason were inseparable. Voltaire, who helped popularize Newton's theories, Burke and Schiller, all used metaphors of light to describe and praise the new "Age of Reason." Werner Hofmann has noted how the demystification of light produced new gods – men such as Benjamin Franklin who, as the conqueror of lightning, was as venerated as Isaac Newton himself.[3]

The "Enlightenment" was not only a philosophical concept, but a political one as well. In

the eighteenth century, even kings and popes wanted to be regarded as "enlightened." They encouraged the sciences out of genuine interest, and they occasionally enacted reforms designed to help the general populace participate more easily in society and the political process. Thus, the "Enlightenment" was always more than a historical period. It was and still is an intellectual force that seeks to promote education and science and combat prejudice and religious fanaticism.

B.L. Prevost after C.N. Cochin fils, frontispiece to the *Encyclopédie ou Dictionnaire raisonné des sciences, des arts et des métiers*, 1772, Private collection

Diderot's *Encyclopédie*, one of the first efforts to codify the knowledge of the period, was introduced by a motto taken from Lucretius's *De rerum natura*: "O you who first amid so great a darkness were able to raise aloft a light so clear, illumining the blessings of life, you I follow [...]."[4] Even the frontispiece relates to light and was expounded in detail: "In an Ionic temple, sanctuary of Truth, we see Truth herself wrapped in a veil and bathed in a light that parts the clouds and disperses them. To her right, Reason and Philosophy seek to lift and remove her veil. [...]"

1 Lambert 1892, pp. 3-4.
2 Cf. Blumenberg 1957.
3 Hofmann 1989, pp. 24-25.
4 Lucretius, *De rerum natura*, with an English translation by W. H. D. Rouse, ed. Martin Ferguson Smith, Cambridge & London 1975, Book 3, 1, pp. 188-89.

Declaration of the Rights of Man, French, 1793, engraving, Bibliothèque Nationale de France, Cabinet des Estampes, Paris

Rays of light are included in all the early paintings and prints of the *Declaration of the Rights of Man*. Here, the symbolism of the Enlightenment is combined with a concrete program: reason and human rights were considered one.

Freemasonry

Freemasonry flowered during the eighteenth century. After it emerged in London, 1717, it took some ten years to develop a tri-gradual system of Entered Apprentice, Fellow Craft and Master Mason, after the example of the old craft, or guild corporations, which it emulated.[1] These caught on, and after 1760, especially in France, there was a veritable proliferation of degrees, many of them exalting their candidates to ranks with resounding titles and qualities, all of them purely imaginative and fictitious. In fact, some of these degrees were set up by people whose object was little more than taking advantage of human vanity and making money out of selling impressive charters and diplomas. Recurrent themes in the symbolic language of Freemasonry include the building or rebuilding of King Solomon's Temple in Jerusalem, and all kinds of legends and traditions forming the lore of this temple. Equally important is "Light" as a source of illu-mination: it can be explained piously as salvation, mystically as the *unio mystica* with the Deity or Supreme Being, or rationally as "insight, knowledge, understanding, enlightenment." Most of these degrees are now merely a matter of Masonic history, but some of those considered more serious have proved fit enough to survive and are still practiced today.

Freemasonry's light symbolism is drawn from a number of sources, makes extensive use of relevant quotations from the Bible, and is closely related to the symbolic language of the French Revolution. Many Enlightenment philosophers and scientists – even Isaac Newton himself – were members of the order. The 1770s saw the foundation of so-called *Illuminatenbünde* in Germany, secret societies that fought for freedom and equality based on morality and ethics. The initiates' knowledge, that is, their "enlightenment," gave them the power to achieve their goals.

The Initiated, French, ca. 1785, pen and ink, watercolor, Verzameling van de Orde van Vrijmetselaren (CMC), The Hague

The caption reads "post tenebras lux," light after darkness, which is indeed a universal conception of any kind of initiation. It might even be applied to the very first Masonic degree, that of the Entered Apprentice, who enters the lodge blindfolded and undergoes a ritual which culminates in "giving back" light to him.

Decoration for a Master of the Masonic Lodge "L'Union Frédéric" in The Hague, ca. 1816, silver, Verzameling van de Orde van Vrijmetselaren (CMC), The Hague

1 The authors are grateful to Evert Kwaadgras for his comments and contributions.

The Degree of the Royal Arches, French, ca. 1785, pen and ink, watercolor, Verzameling van de Orde van Vrijmetselaren (CMC), The Hague

The Grand Lodge of The Netherlands possesses a manuscript in five volumes known as the *Maçonnerie des Hommes*, datable to ca. 1785, originating from France. The manuscript contains many illustrations to support the descriptions. Here, the rays of the sun shine into the "seventh arch" underneath the temple of Jerusalem. They light up a golden plate in the form of a triangle, which bears the Tetragrammaton, the holy and ineffable Hebrew name of God.

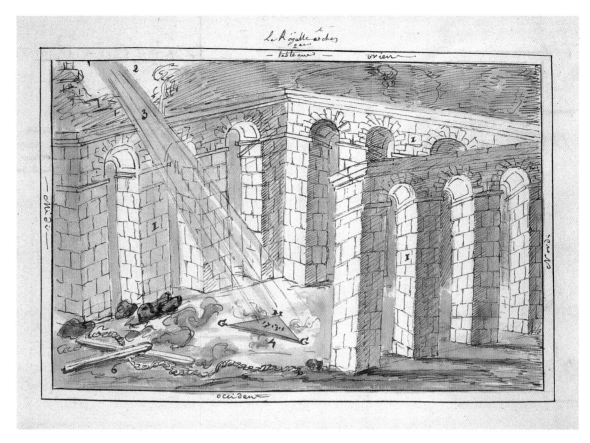

Chamber of Preparation for the Knight of Phoenix, French, ca. 1785, watercolor, Verzameling van de Orde van Vrijmetselaren (CMC), The Hague

Many Masonic initiations start with a preparatory stay in a "cabinet of reflection," or "chamber of preparation." To earn this degree, the candidate was invited to ponder on the unity of arts and sciences with nature. Clearly, illumination in this degree was equated with culture, learning and knowledge of nature. Nature, with its cycles of life, presents a scientific image of the possibility of deathlessness and resurrection, of which the phoenix, an emblem of Christ, is the symbol.

Fireworks

Fireworks are practically the only light spectacles that, through the centuries, have neither lost any of their original fascination nor been transformed beyond recognition by modern technology. Joseph Wright of Derby was responsible for what is probably the most convincing representation of a fireworks display in the history of art. The painter, a genius in many genres, captured the annual *girandola* above the Castel Sant'Angelo in Rome in what we must assume were its proper colors. On 30 June 1787, Goethe described the event in the dairy of his Italian journey: "Yesterday we saw the illuminated dome and the fireworks of Castel Sant'Angelo. The illuminations are spectacular, like a scene from fairyland; one can hardly believe one's eyes."[1] What even the great poet seems unable to describe in words – the splendor of the display, its ephemerality and plasticity, and the incredible noise – is almost impossible to capture in a picture, even one that moves. However, Wright succeeded in making the motion of the flying sparks appear convincing. The painting is an unequalled and brilliant coup, fitting seamlessly into the artist's long line of works depicting forges, scientific experiments, erupting volcanoes and other phenomena that fascinated the gentlemen and women of the Enlightenment.

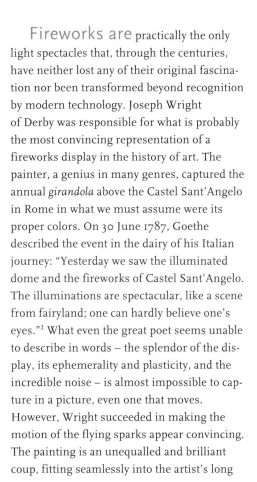

Anonymous, *Fireworks*, ca. 1780–90, colored engraving, Theater Instituut Nederland, Amsterdam

The use of the transparency technique for this sheet strengthens its evocative power; it was designed to be used in a viewer of optical prints.

Portable theater, ca. 1750–75, oil on glass, Theater Instituut Nederland, Amsterdam

The transparency of this extraordinary glass model, depicting a fireworks scene on stage, makes the light effect truly palpable. A sense of movement would have been achieved by a flickering candle or oil lamp.

Jan Caspar Philips, *Fireworks Theater on the Vyver, The Hague, 13 June 1749, in Celebration of the Peace of Aix-la-Chapelle*, engraving, Rijksmuseum, Rijksprentenkabinet, Amsterdam

What was already a difficult task for the painter, was almost impossible for the graphic artist, restricted only to black and white.[2] Nonetheless, the eighteenth century produced a large number of excellent prints illustrating fireworks. Here, the engraver's skill was challenged to the maximum. For those who witnessed the display, the sheet was a perfect souvenir, while for others it gave an impression of the event they had missed.

1   Johann Wolfgang von Goethe, *Italian Journey, 1768-1788*, trans. W. H. Auden and Elizabeth Mayer, San Francisco 1962, p. 344.
2   Salatino 1997-98; Kohler 1988.

Joseph Wright of Derby, *The
Annual Girandola at the Castel
Sant'Angelo, Rome*, 1775–76,
Walker Art Gallery, Liverpool

Vesuvius

Witnessing the eruption of Mount Vesuvius was one of the high points of the eighteenth-century Grand Tour, a young Englishman's introductory visit to the principal sights and attractions of the continent.[1] Although it was impossible to predict, the chances of actually seeing an eruption were actually quite good, as the volcano apparently erupted regularly every few years.[2] The Bay of Naples was all the more ravishing when seen by the light of a fire-spewing mountain and the glow of lava. The sense of frisson was heightened by the knowledge that this natural event was not only spectacular but also potentially deadly. For the observers, this made the eruption all the more sublime, which in the eighteenth century was understood as the union of the beautiful and the terrifying.

Countless painters tried their hand at the subject, and some were even specialists in the genre. Many were contented simply to make souvenirs. These ranged from naïve, mass-produced watercolors on the one hand, to large canvases depicting not only the eruption but also a variety of other phenomena as well. Volaire was among those who produced the latter type. In his repetitions and variations on the Vesuvius theme, he was rarely satisfied with simply illustrating the event itself. An ambitious artist, he sought to demonstrate his skill, and to this end often combined diverse sources of light in a single composition. Incorporating moonlight, campfires and reflections in water, his canvases are sometimes almost too elaborate. Diderot complained of this trend among contemporary painters, whom he felt misused their talents and sacrificed "truth of effect."[3] Volaire, however, was simply following the precepts of his teachers and the authors of contemporary treatises, who all recommended that night scenes include various types of lighting.

1 Beat Wyss, "Der Vesuv von Wörlitz: Illuminierte Aufklärung im kleinstaatlichen Deutschland," in Kohler 1988, pp. 135-42, here p. 140.
2 A detailed statistical analysis of Vesuvius's eruptions can be found at www.geo.mtu.edu/~boris/VESUVIO_1631-1944.html.
3 Denis Diderot, *Essai sur la peinture* (1765), chap. III.

Pierre-Jacques Volaire, *Eruption of Vesuvius*, 1771, Private collection, courtesy Rafael Valls Limited, London

Fire and air

This modest little lamp represents nothing less than the birth of modern artificial lighting.[1] Its simple, but revolutionary, principle is based on the discovery of the great French chemist, Antoine Laurent Lavoisier, that flames are fed by oxygen. He disproved the so-called phlogiston theory, according to which fire was an element in itself. In true Enlightenment spirit, Lavoisier could be said to have stolen fire from the gods, making it controllable and measurable, much as Newton had done for light. The chemist was particularly interested in practical matters, such as improving the lighting of streets and the stage. The Swiss inventor Ami Argand worked in his immediate circle. He put the new theory of combustion to use in 1780, surrounding the wick of an oil lamp with air by placing it in a cylindrical glass tube, itself positioned in a perforated holder to allow for even more air circulation. The oil could thus burn both brightly and economically, and produced no smoke. By the end of the eighteenth century, the widespread interest in the physical properties and appearance of light, that had dominated science since Newton, had found a technical expression.

It is impossible to overexaggerate the importance of the Argand principle. It led to enormous progress in all areas of lighting. Argand lamps were employed whereever bright and stable light was required. From street to stage, the hollow wick provided a solution to the problem of flickering and weak light. Microscopes no longer needed mirrors to capture sunlight; magic lantern performances experienced a surge in popularity; and, thanks to the Argand lamp, which Benjamin Franklin brought to America, the country's first museum – Peale's museum in Philadelphia – was able to stay open into the evening beginning in 1797.

However, the new technology brought its inventors little luck, both economically and otherwise. On several occasions, doubts were cast on their authorship. Argand was forced to defend his invention against the plagiarism of his competitors, who produced and marketed almost identical models. Legal proceedings were held in England and France and lasted many years. It is, therefore, not surprising that this lamp, from the Teylers Museum in Haarlem, is clearly inscribed with the words "Argand's Patent." The French Revolution, finally, led to Argand's complete ruin. In contrast to his patron, however, he did manage to survive it. Lavoisier, who had done so much for his country, was sentenced to death and executed in 1794.

Argand lamp, British, 1784-89, Teylers Museum, Haarlem

Georg Friedrich Kersting, *Man Reading by Lamplight*, 1812, Kunstsammlungen Weimar, Schlossmuseum

In domestic settings, too, the Argand lamp provided better light for reading and working.

1 Schrøder 1968; Wolfe 1999.

From a Newtonian perspective

Pierre-Henri de Valenciennes
was the leading neoclassical landscape painter
in France from 1787 until his death in 1819.
His large idealized landscape compositions
were greatly admired in his lifetime. His
importance now rests on his plein-air sketches
and his treatise on perspective, the first comprehensive manual for landscape painters. In
his sketches and writings, Valenciennes developed a new vision of landscape that is based
on Newtonian physics and the direct observation of nature. It is summed up in one sen-
tence: "[...] the least falsehood is not permitted
in Painting, and even less in Perspective; that
science has its basis in the truth and exactitude of Geometry, which could only be established in its principles by the profoundest
study of Nature." This conception of Nature,
organized according to known mathematical
laws, served as a foundation of Enlightenment
science and philosophy from the early eighteenth century. With the publication of the
first edition of Valenciennes's treatise in 1800,
it formally entered the world of art.

In the treatise, Valenciennes disclaims any
interest in teaching actual physics. Valenciennes concentrates on how perspective and modern scientific ideas about light and color affect
landscape painting. He frequently backs up
his assertions – especially in regard to light
and color – by referring his readers to Newton:
"[In his works, readers] will see with what wisdom and exactitude the English philosopher
has developed the causes and its different
effects."[1] His discussion of geometrical perspective is based on the concept of visual rays:
beams of light that transmit an image to the
eye. These beams are straight, reflect and
refract in mathematically consistent ways, and
form the structure of the perspective system
advocated in the treatise.

Valenciennes's ideas about aerial perspective are the most original and influential
aspect of his work. Aerial perspective is based
on the perception that distant objects appear
paler in color than foreground objects; this difference is caused by the intervening air, which
(according to Valenciennes) blocked more colored visual rays coming from distant objects.
Although he learned aerial perspective from
other painters, notably Joseph Vernet,
Valenciennes explained it with Newtonian science. Newton's discovery of how light decom-
poses into a spectrum of colors that reflect and
refract differently, causes, according to
Valenciennes in his writings, the effects of
aerial perspective, as well as the blueness of
the sky, sunsets, reflections and refractions
from pools or drops of water, rainbows, and
the effects of fog and mist.

Like any good Newtonian, Valenciennes
developed and tested his ideas with experiments, the numerous oil sketches he made on
the spot. These were private studies, never
exhibited in his lifetime. The two selected here
demonstrate several of his basic principles.
They show the same scene at different times of
day – an idea recommended in the treatise that
anticipates the cathedrals and haystacks of
Monet in the 1890s. They show different kinds
of light (cool morning and warm evening)
falling on different types of objects (a geometrical building and an irregular tree). The light
moves in relation to the viewer, too. In the
morning scene, we can tell by the shadows that
the sun is located behind, above, and to the left
of the viewer. In the evening scene, the sun has
moved to the right (west) and is before the
viewer, low on the horizon. The size, shapes,
and colors of the shadows in each have been
worked out with mathematical precision.
Valenciennes diagrammed this progression in
plate XXXI of the treatise, but he brought it to
life in the sketches. Although he considered his
study of light in nature as private preparation
for the real work of composing ideal landscapes, his ideas and methods transformed
landscape painting in the nineteenth century.

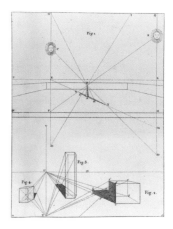

*Diagrams of Shadows Projected
Toward the Horizon, the Sun
behind the Spectator*, engraving
from Pierre-Henri de
Valenciennes, *Elémens de perspec-
tive pratique, à l'usage des artistes*,
Paris 1820 (first edition 1800),
University of Pittsburgh, Frick
Fine Arts Library

1 Valenciennes 1820, p. 177.

Pierre-Henri de Valenciennes,
View of Ara Coeli, ca. 1785, Musée
du Louvre, Département des
Peintures, Paris

Pierre-Henri de Valenciennes,
View of Ara Coeli, ca. 1785, Musée
du Louvre, Département des
Peintures, Paris

Enlightenment and revolution

Despite its Enlightenment roots, the French Revolution's relationship to light and light sources was anything but straightforward. Street lamps, introduced by the king and monitored by the police in the seventeenth century, were viewed by many as instruments of repression, and destroyed by the mob in the first phase of the Revolution. A popular song demanded the aristocrats be hung from them, and broadsheets often caricatured the nobility as winged lanterns. This trend, however, was soon reversed. The humble Greek philosopher Diogenes, who walked through Athens in bright daylight equipped with a lantern, searching for human beings, became a hero of the Revolution. Camille Desmoulins, who had led the storming of the Bastille, liked to compare himself to Diogenes; in his *Discours de la Lanterne aux Parisiens*, published in Year I of the Revolution (1790), he wrote: "He looked for one man, and found two-hundred thousand. [...] Yes, I am the queen of the lanterns."[1]

The revolutionaries referred to light in countless propaganda paintings, often transforming Christian allegories into personifications of virtue or worldly figures. The highpoint of this obsession with light came in 1790 when, on 18 July (a little more than a year after the fall of the Bastille), a great celebration was held on the Champs-Elysées. These grand illuminations were a reflection of those commissioned by Louis XIV who, as the Sun King, often had himself portrayed as a bearer of light.

Jean-Baptiste Chapuy after Louis Simon Boizot, *Liberty Armed with the Scepter of Reason Suppresses Ignorance and Fanaticism*, 1793–95, etching

In the course of the revolution, morals became stricter and pictures more austere. The all-seeing eye surrounded by rays of light was a motif employed ad nauseam. Here, bolts of lightning put the enemies of reason to flight. The print is apparently a reproduction of a relief; Boizot was a sculptor who lived on church commissions before the Revolution, but had an official position after 1791.

Anonymous, *In the Midst of the Purest Light, You, Obstinate Clergy, Remain in Darkness*, ca. 1790, etching

The Return of the Aristocrats from the London Racetrack, French, ca. 1790, colored etching

This is an early print depicting aristocrats as winged lanterns – an obvious association at the time. A standard-bearer with a fool's flag and a torch leads them forward. However, lamps and torches were soon to be reinterpreted as symbols of reason and reform.

Pierre Gabriel Berthault after Jean Louis Prieur, *Celebrations and Illuminations on the Champs-Elysées on 18 July 1790*, 1790–91, etching

The French revolutionaries made light their most important symbol with the illumination of the Champs-Elysées a year after the storming of the Bastille. Garlands and obelisks of light illuminated the huge square, which was filled with countless Parisians. Prieur sought to give an impression of the brilliance of hundreds, if not thousands, of oil lamps by emphasizing the shadows. The artist was to pay for his revolutionary élan with his life during the Reign of Terror.

1 Camille Desmoulins, "Discours de la Lanterne aux Parisiens (An I)," *Oeuvres*, ed. Jules Claretie, Paris 1874, pp. 133-95, here pp. 141-42.

Michel Honoré Bounieu, *France Sacrificing to Reason*, 1791–92, mezzotint

In this print, which Bounieu made after a now-lost painting, the artist depicts France in a manner usually reserved for the Virgin in an Annunciation scene. Her attributes have merely been changed to conform to the new ideology. Bounieu himself managed to survive the confusions of the period, keeping his post as a drawing teacher at the Ecole royale des ponts-et-chaussées, which he had obtained in 1772, until his death in 1814.

Le Général d'Alton poursuivi par les Reverberes Patriotiques.

James Gillray, *The Zenith of French Glory – The Pinnacle of Liberty*, 1793, colored etching

This is a famous English caricature criticizing the French Revolution and the Terror; once again, street lamps play a central role.

Anonymous, *General d'Alton Pursued by Patriotic Street Lamps*, 1790, etching

Street lamps, destroyed during the early Revolution as signs of authority, soon came to have more positive associations. Here, they pursue the infamous General d'Alton, responsible for the bloody suppression of rebellious uprisings in the Hapsburg-controlled Netherlands.

Silhouettes

Title page of Johann Caspar Lavater, *Over de physiognomie*, Amsterdam 1784, vol. 1, Rijksmuseum, Amsterdam

Joseph Adolf Schmetterling, *Couple Sitting at a Tea Table*, ca. 1790, pen and ink, Rijksmuseum, Rijksprentenkabinet, Amsterdam

When the Swiss writer and theologian Johann Caspar Lavater published his study of human physiognomy, he could not have imagined the furor the book would create. This multi-volume, richly illustrated work was translated into many languages, and appeared in numerous editions. His lectures were attended with an almost religious fervor. Lavater's theory of physiognomy was based on the assumption that it was possible to "read" a person's soul, or rather character, through certain details of his or her physical appearance. In order to support this hypothesis and to give it a scientific foundation, Lavater availed himself of contour drawings of the human profile, still known today as "silhouettes." The name originated with Etienne de Silhouette, Louis XV's finance minister, whose tax regime forced the buyers of miniatures to switch to the cheaper medium.

Lavater made use of this new fashion, introduced in the 1760s, and with his theories, even gave it a certain cachet. He was determined to deliver physiognomy from the charge of pseudo-science. Goethe supported him in his efforts. The silhouette was a particularly useful medium in this respect, as the reduction of the head to a simple contour meant that one would not be distracted by unimportant details: "There is no better, more irrefutable proof of physiognomy's objective truth than the silhouette," he wrote. For Lavater, shadows were a reflection of divine light: "[...] if a shadow is the voice of truth, the word of God, then that which has a soul and is filled with God's light is its living model."[1]

Looking back, the gravity with which the Enlightenment treated physiognomy – today no longer considered a science at all – is certainly astonishing. What now seems irrational was determined by a will to categorize, to make the human measurable and thus to discover the secret of creation. Silhouettes, however, were not always created for such serious philosophical purposes. They were often simply a means of passing the time in making something decorative. Silhouettes could be painted, and were most usually made of paper. Goethe himself cut an extraordinary number of silhouettes, and the painter Philipp Otto Runge was particularly skilled in the art. Unusual examples, such as those shown here enhanced the technique.

Samuel Mohn, *Covered cup with silhouettes*, 1807, Museum für Angewandte Kunst, Frankfurt am Main

Silhouettes faciles, ombres amusantes produites par l'arrangement des mains et les doigts placés entre une lumière et la murailles dessinés par Darjou, Paris ca. 1840, Cooper-Hewitt, National Design Museum Branch, Smithsonian Institution Libraries, New York

1 Quoted after Ilsebill Berta Fliedl, "Goethe und Lavater," in Sabine Schulze (ed.), *Goethe und die Kunst*, exh. cat. Frankfurt am Main (Schirn Kunsthalle) 1994, pp. 192-203, here p. 194.

Lighting for the enlightened

In the eighteenth century, Amsterdam set about enjoying the wealth it had amassed during the recent Golden Age. The spirit of enterprise appears to have been more or less stifled by luxury. Travelers commented on the complacency of the country's inhabitants, and would have had little fresh to report had it not been for a palatial new building on the Keizersgracht. In her travel diary of 1791, Princess Louise of Mecklenburg-Strelitz, who was later to become queen of Prussia, referred to it as the largest and most beautiful structure in the entire city – an opinion shared by many. The name of the building was written in gold letters above the entrance: FELIX MERITIS (Happiness Through Merit). It was built in 1787 by the architect Jacob Otten to house the society of the same name, founded "to provide wealthy citizens with a venue in which they could avail themselves of the civilized pleasures of artistic and scientific pursuit."[1]

Felix Meritis was a kind of club for like-minded representatives of the various branches of the arts and sciences. In the members' opinion, it was not religion, but knowledge, that would lead to improvement in the human condition. The society's manifold activities took place in four large halls, and combined education, experiment and entertainment – a typical Enlightenment phenomenon, as we have had occasion to note elsewhere. Their belief in progress was also expressed in the lighting, which made use of the most modern technology available at the time. A series of four etchings captures the association's pride in both their building and their ideals. Each of the rooms is differently lit. The Music Room was illuminated by light from thirteen windows during the day and by three large chandeliers equipped with twenty-eight Argand lamps at night. In the center of the foreground a visitor points to the new lighting system. The Auditorium is lit from windows facing the canal to the East. More Argand lamps are installed for artificial lighting. The Natural Science Reading Room contained a chandelier made of Argand lamps, with a large reflector used to direct the light downwards; one sector of the reflector is opened and allows to look at the lamps. This opening may have served to illuminate a board on an easel where notes and formulas would have been written. The windows could be closed with shutters. The Drawing Salon was lit from above and provided with a long rod on which curtains and various lamps could be hung in order to control and direct the light.

Noach van der Meer the Younger and Reinier Vinkeles after Jacques Kuijper and Pieter Barbiers, *Felix Meritis*, 1791/1801, four etchings and engravings, Rijksmuseum, Rijksprentenkabinet, Amsterdam

1 *Gedenkstuk der feestviering van het vijftig-jarig bestaan der Maatschappij Felix Meritis*, Amsterdam 1827; Max Bruinsma (ed.), *Felix Meritis 1787-1987*, Amsterdam 1987. With thanks to Roelie Zwikker.

MUZYK ZAAL
IN HET GEBOUW der MAATSCHAPPYE FELIX MERITIS
BINNEN AMSTERDAM.

SALLE de CONCERT
DANS L'EDIFICE de la SOCIÉTÉ FELIX MERITIS
A AMSTERDAM.

GEHOOR ZAAL
IN HET GEBOUW der MAATSCHAPPYE FELIX MERITIS
BINNEN AMSTERDAM.

AUDITOIRE
DANS L'EDIFICE de la SOCIÉTÉ FELIX MERITIS
A AMSTERDAM.

ZAAL DER NATUURKUNDE
IN HET GEBOUW der MAATSCHAPPYE FELIX MERITIS
BINNEN AMSTERDAM.

SALLE DE PHYSIQUE
DANS L'EDIFICE de la SOCIÉTÉ FELIX MERITIS
A AMSTERDAM.

TEKEN ZAAL
IN HET GEBOUW der MAATSCHAPPYE FELIX MERITIS
BINNEN AMSTERDAM.

SALLE de DESSIN
DANS L'EDIFICE de la SOCIÉTÉ FELIX MERITIS
A AMSTERDAM.

The forges of Vulcan

At the end of the eighteenth century, Coalbrookdale's coke and iron works were renowned for their great size, complexity, and large scale production; the British navy's cannons, the great boilers of steam engines, and the struts of the early iron bridges were all made in Coalbrookdale. The place was featured in picturesque tours and landscape painting because its nightmarish topography, disfigured by decades of industrial pollution, exemplified the poetic concept of the terrible and the sublime. The novel immensity, horror, and frightening power of the furnaces and mills thrilled and challenged Loutherbourg's generation of artists, writers, and visitors. Loutherbourg's lurid evocation of the coke hearths at Bedlam Furnaces, spewing flames and sulphurous smoke, has since come to represent the region as a whole, and early industrial England in general.

Comparisons of *Coalbrookdale by Night* with eighteenth-century paintings, such as Wright of Derby's *Girandola* or Volaire's *Eruption of Vesuvius* (pp. 77 and 79), place it within a genre of nocturnal spectacle painting. The paintings exhibit similar devices – buildings silhouetted against glowing clouds of smoke, tiny figures dwarfed by violent forces, and convincing detail – to capture the experience of "being there" for the imaginative viewer. At the heart of each picture is a hidden explosion.

Explosions, annihilating bursts of heat and light, have symbolized superhuman destructive powers ever since Zeus, king of the gods, threw his first thunderbolt. At first, such power was restricted to natural catastrophes, such as storms, volcanoes, and raging fires. According to Greek myth, humans acquired the divine power to blow things up when the Titan Prometheus stole fire from the heavens. In early modern Europe, cannons and fireworks expressed princely power in both real and symbolic terms – if one believes the painters, the pope's fireworks could explode as impressively as Mount Vesuvius. *Coalbrookdale by Night* shows another step in the transformation of mind-shattering explosions, from unpredictable natural catastrophe to a controlled routine. Loutherbourg's painting marks the passage of power from gods, to kings, to the middle-class industrialists who would dominate the nineteenth century.

But Loutherbourg's explosion comes from a forge, the province of another classical god, Hephaistos. His Roman name of Vulcan was given to the volcano spouting smoke, flames and sparks said to come from his subterranean manufactory. Hephaistos was above all a great artificer and a master of fire and metal. He forged arms and weapons – the equipment of the hero Achilles, for example – like a mythical precursor of the Coalbrookdale industrialists, whose cannons gave the British fleet its power. Eighteenth- and early nineteenth-century images of explosive power and light, Loutherbourg's above all, seem to represent humankind's efforts to come to terms with its new understanding and increasing mastery of natural forces. The ability to make light, not yet challenging the power of the sun but approaching the force of lightning and volcanic action, seemed to promise new benefts and new terrors simultaneously.

Philippe Jacques de
Loutherbourg, *Coalbrookdale by
Night*, 1801, Science Museum,
London

Seeing the light

William Blake and Francisco Goya were the greatest visionary artists of their generation. Neither portrayed the light of nature according to the geometrical precepts of eighteenth-century science or art theory. The lights in prints by Blake and Goya symbolize intellect, imagination, and spiritual truth. *Sleep Delivers Them* and *When the Morning Stars Sang Together* belong to sets of prints in which the artists expressed their most personal beliefs about humanity's ability to perceive and live by these enduring truths. The theme of both is "seeing the light."

In *Sleep Delivers Them*, all are immersed in darkness and sleep. The hooded figures in the foreground, probably Capuchin nuns, turn their backs to the brilliant light flooding the cave-like prison. A conventionally dressed woman in half shadow is also oblivious. As the title implies, sleep delivers them from the dreary, dark prison but also prevents them seeing the light. Further interpretation depends on the possible meanings of darkness and light. Goya provides some clues in *The Sleep of Reason Begets Monsters*, probably the most famous image of this series, the *Caprichos*. If darkness and sleep are here associated with irrational horror, then their opposites, light and wakefulness, must represent reason, enlightenment, and truth. It is also probable that Goya was commenting upon specific historical circumstances. The sleeping nuns may represent Spanish Catholicism and the Inquisition. If so, this image alludes to Catholic Spain's willful denial of the glories of the European Enlightenment.

Blake's print employs some of the same motifs and ideas of *Sleep Delivers Them*, but conveys the opposite message about religion and the Enlightenment. In this scene from the Old Testament Book of Job, Job and his family inhabit another dark, cave-like space. But unlike Goya's nuns, they are enthralled by the divine light emanating from God the Father in the space above them. God appears in the act of creating the sun and moon, while above him four androgynous winged figures, emblematic of the stars, rejoice at the miracle of creation. Light is a product of divine power and religious revelation, not disciplined and rational human inquiry. As we know from Blake's voluminous writings, the darkened cave probably represents earthly materialism, the world of science and rationalism of the Enlightenment (created, according to Blake, by Newton). Job and his family can glimpse the spiritual light beyond its cloudy edges as a result of the many physical and spiritual trials that they have suffered.

"Seeing the light" is a metaphor for discovering truth or obtaining enlightenment, seeing beyond the mundane facts of daily life. Both of these images transcend the mundane to present us with the ultimate joys and horrors confronting the human spirit. Light and darkness, brilliantly manipulated by these master printmakers, communicate their meanings directly to us.

Francisco Goya, *The Sleep of Reason Begets Monsters*, 1799, etching and aquatint, Carnegie Museum of Art, Pittsburgh, Gift of Mr. and Mrs. Charles J. Rosenbloom

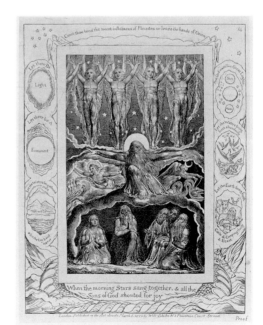

William Blake, *When the Morning Stars Sang Together, & All the Sons of God Shouted for Joy*, 1825, engraving, plate 14 of *Illustrations for the Book of Job*, Carnegie Museum of Art, Pittsburgh, Purchase

Francisco Goya, *Sleep Delivers Them*, 1799, etching and aquatint, plate 34 of the *Caprichos*, Carnegie Museum of Art, Pittsburgh, Gift of Mr. and Mrs. Charles J. Rosenbloom

Goya's use of aquatint to create deep, rich shadows in this etching contributes to its visionary effect.

Daylight in the studio

Bright daylight enters through a window into the painter's studio. The easel is turned slightly to catch the light without casting shadows from the painter's right hand. A screen covers the lower part of the window to let the light come mainly from above. We may assume that the window faces north.

For all artists, whether of the past or present, good lighting is an essential ingredient in the creative process. Throughout the centuries, daylight's brightness and stability have been particularly important. Initially, painters and sculptors concentrated their efforts on manipulating the influx of natural light; later, they made use of artificial illumination. The most constant daylight comes from the north, where the movements of the sun have the least disturbing consequences. For this reason, studio windows tend to face in this direction and, at least in the case of right-handed painters, are to the left of the easel. Opaque curtains or oiled paper helped soften direct sunlight and maintain stability even in changing weather. On the other hand, by opening or closing the shutters, special lighting situations and effects could be produced that were not possible with daylight alone.

Professional opinions about studio lighting were varied. In 1829, Jacques Nicolas Paillot de Montabert, for example, suggested – in contrast to most of his colleagues – that artists install shutters, which would allow the influx of light from more than one direction. The aim was to produce a more natural effect, particularly in landscape painting. For history painting, however, which set great store by an easily readable message, unidirectional lighting remained the most desirable.[1] It was also recommended that light enter the studio from above, preferably at a 45° angle. The influential critic Charles Blanc believed it should come from even higher, to give man's upright posture its full due.[2]

The German Romantic Georg Friedrich Kersting executed a number of works depicting an artist's studio. Contemporary descriptions by eyewitnesses confirm that these provide a realistic glimpse of the painter at work. They are, however, also cleverly thought-out compositions, which transform seemingly simple scenes into complex treatises on the origins of art and artistic creativity. The painter is shown as an isolated figure – a lonely genius. He is Friedrich Matthäi, a Dresden neoclassicist, at work.[3] The tiny room is filled with props and painter's tools. In the background stands a sculptor's bench and on it is a set of model figures arranged around a table. These figures were used for studying perspective and for preparing compositions, in this case a Last Supper. A huge canvas, rolled up at the top and bottom and almost too big to have entered the studio at all, stands behind. Its enormous emptiness has something almost threatening about it, demanding to be filled. The picture on which Matthäi is working is turned towards the window. Judging by his utensils, he is in the process of executing the underdrawing. The lower quarter of the window is adjusted so that more light can enter from above, and so that the artist's hand casts no irritating shadows.

1 Paillot 1829-51, vol. 9, pp. 603-07; Couture 1867, pp. 285-87; Callen 1995, pp. 117-18.
2 Callen 1995, p. 117.
3 Werner Schnell, *Georg Friedrich Kersting (1785-1847): Das zeichnerische und malerische Werk mit Oeuvrekatalog*, Munich 1994, no. A 49, pp. 31-35.

Georg Friedrich Kersting, *Friedrich Matthäi in the Studio*, 1812, Städtische Kunstsammlungen Chemnitz

Romantic transparencies

The transparency is a medium particularly well suited to reproducing effects of light. Light, shining from a candle or an oil lamp through the glass or translucent paper, illuminates the landscape drawn or painted on the surface. The images depict various times of day or the moon shining, and create a mysterious and sublime atmosphere. Masters, such as Gainsborough, Turner and Friedrich, all created these extremely fragile works of art. The Romantics and their light-obsessed predecessors in the eighteenth century, elevated the transparency to new artistic heights. The sublimity of nature, so often conjured up in literature and art, could be both demonstrated and intensified using transparencies. In 1767, the president of the Royal Society ardently thanked the archaeologist and antiquarian William Hamilton for the gift of a transparency depicting an eruption at Vesuvius: "The representation of that grand and terrible scene, by means of transparent colours, was so lively and so striking, that there seemed to be nothing wanting in us distant spectators but the fright that everybody must have been fired with who was so near."[1]

Transparencies were so popular that the technique began to be used not only by artists. As prints, produced in large series, they became available to a wider audience. In the introduction to his *Instructions for Painting Transparencies*, which first appeared in 1799, the London bookseller and publisher Rudolph Ackermann wrote: "The effect produced by Transparencies, if managed with judgment, is wonderful, particularly in fire and moon lights, where brilliancy of light and strength of shade are so easily attainable, and ever must be superior to that of painting with opake colours. The very great expence attending the purchase of stained glass, and the risk of keeping it secure from accident, often precludes almost the possibility of ornamenting rooms, grottos, cottages, &c. with it; but now by the introduction of this beautiful style of painting, so deservedly admired by the fashionable world, we may obtain a substitute nearly equal, and can appropriate it to different uses, as well ornamental as useful, at a comparatively small expence."[2] The book was clearly designed to promote transparent painting as a hobby. For those who did not wish to take the trouble of making transparencies themselves, a large selection was readily available from Ackermann or one of his competitors. In addition to Romantic landscapes, depictions of historical events were among the most fashionable motifs. Ackermann did not limit himself to small formats either: in 1802, he commissioned a thirty-foot high transparency, which he had placed in front of his bookshop on the Strand and illuminated with gaslight.[3]

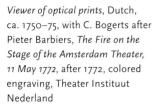

Viewer of optical prints, Dutch, ca. 1750–75, with C. Bogerts after Pieter Barbiers, *The Fire on the Stage of the Amsterdam Theater, 11 May 1772*, after 1772, colored engraving, Theater Instituut Nederland

Franz Niklaus König, *The St. James Fires at Lake Brienz*, ca. 1815, watercolor, Kunstmuseum Bern

Franz Niklaus König's display case for diaphanoramas, ca. 1815, Kunstmuseum Bern

The Swiss artist Franz Niklaus König was a typical minor painter and stage designer forced to follow the fashions of the period. König is assumed to have produced around one hundred transparencies, among them landscape motifs, but also a series depicting folk costumes. In 1815 he began to exhibit these works in his apartment in Berne with great success; in 1820 he even took them on tour in Germany and France. Here the transparency is shown in Königs display case, which is kept in the Kunstmuseum Bern as well.[4]

1 Salatino 1997-98, p. 96.
2 Ackermann 1800, pp. 3-4.
3 Ford 1983, p. 49.
4 Marcus Bourquin, *Franz Niklaus König: Leben und Werk*, Bern 1963, pp. 52-54; Verwiebe 1997, pp. 70-76.

Artists' little helpers

For centuries, artists have used various visual aids to both learn and improve their technical skills. Before students at an academy were allowed to copy plaster casts – let alone living models – they had to master basic geometric forms and the details of anatomy. The study of light and shadow was the main focus of these often rather dull exercises.

Lay figures, plaster models and three-dimensional wooden volumes had been used for this purpose since the Renaissance. They were designed to help the artist recreate the idealized anatomy of classical statuary in perspective. As long as the works of antiquity continued to determine the canon of beauty, the pupils' assignments changed little. Art students only occasionally rebelled against the constant and benumbing reproduction of these lifeless objects. Until the end of the nineteenth century, however, only a small minority dared cast doubt on this particular practice. Even Van Gogh felt it was necessary to submit himself – alone or under supervision – to these academic rigors, considered essential before embarking on an artistic career.

The Institute of Art History at the University of Utrecht owns an exemplary collection of nineteenth-century devices of this sort. The wooden egg, which can be arranged in a variety of positions on its stand, was especially useful for studying the effects of light and shade. It was no easy task to reproduce its elliptical form. Using a directional light source, numerous variations in chiaroscuro could be created. The cast of a foot served as a model in more advanced exercises, while the lay figure and so-called *écorché* united the study of anatomy and light. The *écorché* was used to learn about musculature and its workings. Only with knowledge of what went on below the skin, it was thought, could an artist properly model the human figure, i.e., reproduce the play of light and shadow. New sources of light helped increase the contrast between the two.

Cast of a foot, lay figure, écorché with measuring device, and wooden egg on a stand, eighteenth and nineteenth centuries, Rijksuniversiteit Utrecht, Kunsthistorisch Instituut

Perspective model, ca. 1860, plaster, Musée des arts et métiers du CNAM, Paris

This model is not so much a tool for artists as for mathematicians; it does, however, remind us that the study of perspective had helped raise painting from a craft to a science.

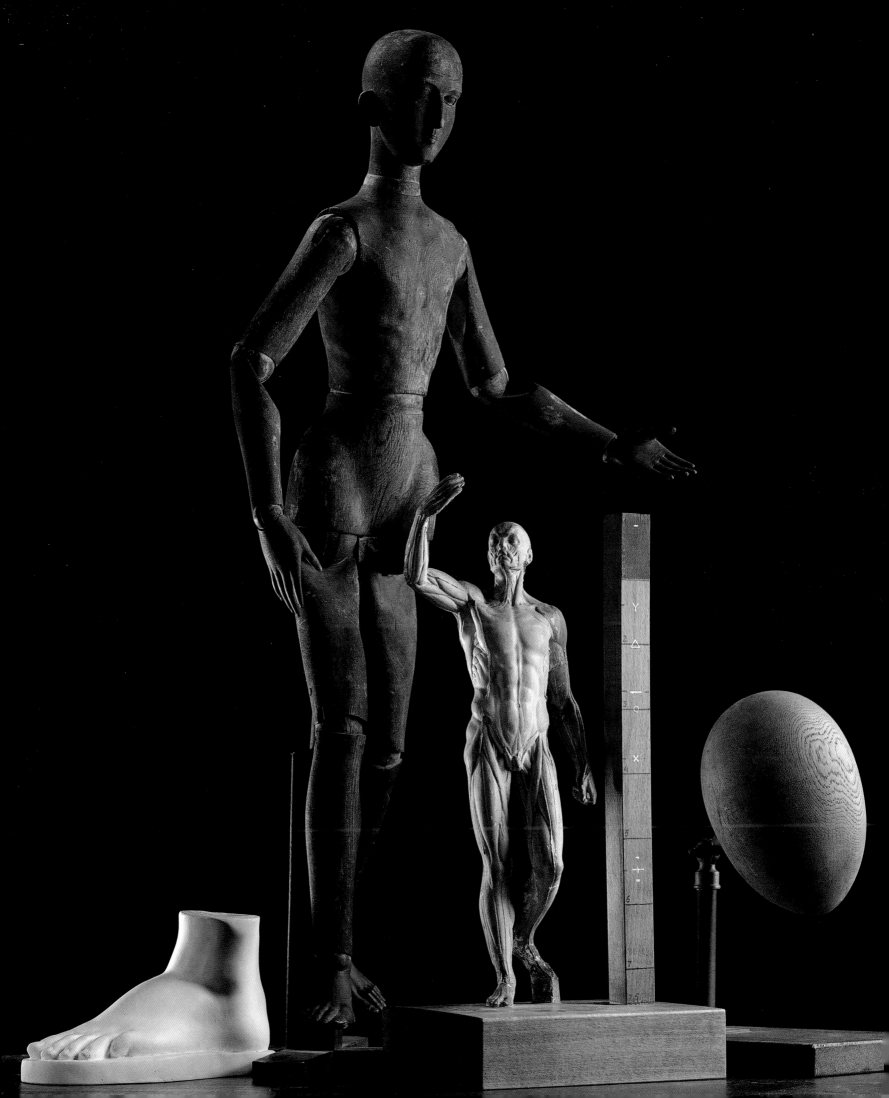

Perspective at night

European painters first depicted interiors lit by candles in the seventeenth century. Caravaggio, Georges de La Tour and Gerard van Honthorst were among the most famous specialists in the genre. Their work defined the theme for succeeding generations: dim, shadowy spaces with a single brilliant candle or lamp illuminating one or more figures, often saints (such as Mary Magdalen in meditation) or biblical characters. Musicians, card players, and carousers also appear, sometimes with symbolic allusions to the five senses or moralizing proverbs. The artists manipulated their lighting effects to suggest tranquility and spirituality, intimate sociability, or violence and confusion, depending on their subject.

Nineteenth-century artists, such as the Danish genre painter Wilhelm Bendz, brought the tradition into the modern era. His group of young men enjoying tobacco, music, cards and conversation seems to bear no religious or moral message as seventeenth-century scenes often did. The only action depicted here is two musicians' efforts to hush the card players by raising their hands. In fact, Bendz reversed the seventeenth-century device of using light effects to enhance the religious or moral message. In the *Tobacco Party*, as in most of Bendz's works, the characters' activities justify the lighting effects, the real subject of most of his painting, and certainly of this one.[1]

Analysis demonstrates how this unpretentious scene is a tour-de-force of lighting and perspective. Begin with the lights themselves, and move outward. Two candle flames light the narrow, crowded, high-ceilinged room. One of the flames, that on the right, is visible, while the second is blocked by the tablet held by the young man in glasses. Note that the light from the second candle appears more intense as a result of being reflected off the tablet. Furthermore, the smoke of the pipes also affects the light, damping and diffusing it in the murky space between the smoker on the

left and the mirror on the wall above and beyond him. Bendz sensitively depicted the way the light bounces off more solid materials, also: the porcelain coffee cup near the left-hand candle glows; pages of sheet music at far left catch the light evenly; but on larger surfaces such as the walls, light fades gradually into shadow. In the mirror to the left of the window, the three panes of glass reflect light at slightly different angles, creating a disjointed reflection.

The shadows themselves are fascinating. By working with two light sources, Bendz caused himself a complex problem in perspective. The light of the right-hand candle is reflected upwards and toward the back wall. The two men standing in front of the window cast shadows on the back and side walls of the room. As a result of the rules of perspective, the shadow of the standing smoker is darker but shorter than that of his leaning companion, whose huge shadow falls on the wall farther from the candle flame. The candle on the left is closer to the viewer, and because of the screening effect of the seated smoker's raised hand, its light falls mostly downward. The shadows on the floor of the room are cast from this light source alone. These shadows radiate out and away from the light source. Thus, the shadowy hand at the center of the painting's lower edge is projected from the proper right hand (grasping the pipe) of the seated smoker.

Whether working by daylight or candlelight, Bendz revelled in complex light effects. This painting appears to be an indoor equivalent of Pierre-Henri de Valenciennes's landscapes in Newtonian perspective (p. 83). It self-consciously updates the seventeenth-century tradition according to modern aesthetic and scientific principles. Bendz's interest in light and perspective was characteristic of the pupils of Danish landscapist C. W. Eckersberg, an early advocate of plein-air painting and perspective theory who had worked in Italy.

Wilhelm Bendz, *A Tobacco Party: Justitsråd Jürgensen's Sunday Gathering*, 1827–28, Ny Carlsberg Glyptotek, Copenhagen

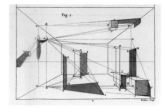

Perspective drawing of a room lit by lamplight, from Pierre-Henri de Valenciennes, *Elémens de perspective pratique, à l'usage des artistes*, [...], 2nd ed., Paris 1820

1 *Bendz* 1996, no. 34.

101 Perspective at night

New light in Britain

Rudolph Ackermann was one of the first print and booksellers in nineteenth-century London to address the new market of affluent consumers created by the early Industrial Revolution. His *Microcosm of London*, London 1808-11, is still a primary source of information and images of the principal buildings and sights of Regency London. The text frequently and proudly enumerates lighting devices and the activities they facilitated: huge glass skylights at the exhibition rooms of the Royal Watercolour Society; 37,000 colored lamps for the nocturnal festivities at Vauxhall Gardens; a magnificent chandelier with fifty patent lamps at Astley's Amphitheatre; single Argand lamps to brighten the surfaces of the gaming tables at Brooks' club. The book's attention to these details reminds us how differently light was used and experienced before the advent of twenty-four-hour-a-day ambient lighting. The quality and quantity of available light measured the modernity, wealth, and taste of a city.

Frederick Accum's *Practical Treatise on Gas-Light* was the first book published on the new lighting technology developed in England in 1797 and in France in 1802. By 1815 it was clear that gas-lighting would supplant many of the artificial lighting devices illustrated in Ackermann's *Microcosm*. Ackermann himself had installed a gas-lighting system in his workshop, print gallery, and home by 1811, and testified in this publication that the new lights were cleaner, brighter, cheaper, and more efficient than candles or lamps. His gas-lighting apparatus, built by England's first real gas engineer Samuel Clegg, served as the model for the illustrations to the treatise. The first edition sold out within four months, and a second was hastily prepared. Why such popularity? The accurate illustrations and technical descriptions assisted those building their own gas plants, as did the analyses of economic costs and benefits. The book was also essential for investors in the newly formed Gas-Lighting Company in London, whose claims had been tested (on behalf of Parliament) by the author, chemist Frederick Accum, and whose systems had been designed by none other than Samuel Clegg. The speculative excitement generated by the Gas-Lighting Company's activities in 1815 compares with that surrounding internet companies today; investors saw a technology that not only would change the way people lived and worked, but might also make them a fortune.

Augustus Welby Pugin and Thomas Rowlandson, *Gaming House: Great Subscription Room at Brooks's, St. James Street*, colored aquatint from Rudolph Ackermann, *The Microcosm of London*, 3 vols., London [1808-11], University of Pittsburgh, Darlington Memorial Library

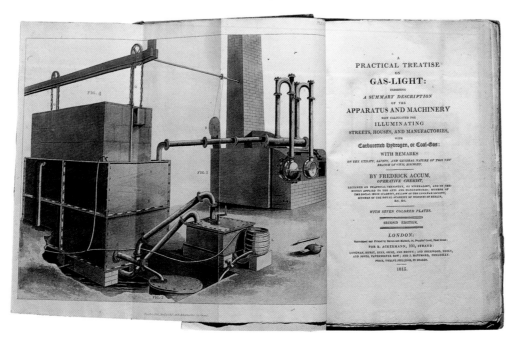

Neo-gothic gas lamp designs (detail on the right page) and *A perspective view of a gaslight apparatus*, 1815, engravings, from Frederick Accum, *A Practical Treatise on Gas-Light*, London 1815, Carnegie Museum of Art, Pittsburgh, Heinz Architectural Center

The illustration on the left represents the actual gas manufacturing plant installed in art publisher Rudolph Ackermann's premises.

Pl. V. faci

4

a

c

b

b   b

a

a

7

8

The discovery of skylight

At the beginning of the nineteenth century, observers began to distinguish between daylight and sunlight. Sunlight is the warm yellow light shining directly down from the sun. Daylight is the overall, bluish light of the earth's atmosphere – the light that we see by when the sun is overcast by clouds, for example.[1] In 1817, the artist Henry James Richter wrote a remarkable treatise on the subject: *Day-Light; a recent discovery in the art of painting: with hints on the philosophy of The Fine Arts, and on that of the human mind, as first dissected by Emanuel Kant.*[2] Richter carefully described the ways in which daylight and sunlight define and limit an observer's knowledge of the physical world: "If the Sun's rays strike the *surface* of a body, we know that there is a surface that reflects it to our sight; if the *dark side* of this body receive some light from a neighbouring object on which the Sun also shines, we immediately perceive the surface on that side; and if the light of the SKY shine down upon all bodies it will distinguish to us their upper surfaces, though not illumined by the Sun, and thus determine their solidity in that direction."[3] In other words, according to Richter, we do not see the object itself; we see only different kinds of light reflecting off some of its surfaces – and our knowledge of the visual world is based entirely on these partial and transient observations. Thus the visual knowledge involved in making or looking at art is based on fleeting perceptions specific to precise moments in time and space. These fleeting perceptions, Richter argued, should be the basis for a new form of modern art, true to nature and human perception and free from the academic generalities and time-hardened traditions that resulted in artificial, unnatural paintings.

Although we do not know whether Constable read Richter's book, or knew him professionally, certainly he agreed with Richter's argument about daylight when he wrote, "The sky is the source of light in nature – and governs everything."[4] His cloud studies – over 200 oil sketches made between 1820 and 1822 – demonstrate Richter's notion of how light creates our knowledge of the physical world. What are clouds but impalpable, ephemeral masses of vapor, knowable to earthbound human senses only when daylight and skylight strike or shadow their changing forms? They defy the systematic laws of geometry, perspective, and classical landscape, as exemplified in the work of French landscape painter and theorist Pierre-Henri de Valenciennes (p. 83). Changing perceptions of space, through light, over time, are the true subject of the Constable cloud studies. Constable's precise notations of time, light, and weather conditions on his sketches – this example is inscribed *Noon 27 Sept very bright after rain wind West* – also indicate a Richter-like view that these perceptions were valid only for specific times and places. In fact, using his own observations, Constable occasionally disputed the generalized descriptions of clouds invented by Luke Howard and Thomas Forster, pioneer meteorologists.

Constable's philosophy of art coincided with Richter's on one final point – the importance of direct observation and representation of light in nature as the key to modernity. In much of his work he aimed to invent a "natural painture" that accurately depicted the world as he saw it, nothing more and nothing less.

John Constable, *The Laundry Line*, ca. 1821, Carnegie Museum of Art, Pittsburgh, Heinz Family Acquisition Fund

Constable is believed to have painted this sky study while looking out the window of his house in Hampstead.

1 The blue light of the sky is caused by light waves scattering off air molecules. The shorter the wavelength (or bluer the light), the more likely it is to scatter, thus in any part of the sky except toward the sun, we are more likely to see blue light than any other color. Cf. Lynch and Livingston 1995, pp. 22-23.
2 Richter 1817.
3 Ibid., p. 8.
4 Quoted after Kristen Lippincott, et al., *The Story of Time*, exh. cat. London (National Maritime Museum) 1999, p. 209.

John Constable, *Cloud Study with Horizon of Trees*, 1821, Royal Academy of Arts, London

The kaleidoscope

Today, the kaleidoscope is seen as a toy, and its serious scientific origins have long been forgotten. Its inventor, the Scottish physicist David Brewster, had carried out a number of experiments on polarization of light, using a variety of glass fragments. In his *Treatise on the Kaleidoscope* of 1819, he presented various mathematical calculations to demonstrate the underlying principles of the multifaceted reflections. In his opinion, the instrument would be useful to artists, architects and textile designers, who would be drawn to the symmetrical and abstract patterns. The name is derived from the Greek, and combines the words "beautiful," "shape," and "to see." The kaleidoscope is tangible proof that the belief in the unity of art and science, and education and entertainment, lived on into the nineteenth century. Barbara Stafford wrote: "Kaleidoscopic visions were the romantic culmination of a hermetic and ingenious *ars combinatoria*. [...] Rational recreations succeeded in turning visual pleasures into moral philosophy and optical games into meditative icons."[1] They were apparently a great success – if it is true that in the first month alone after its introduction into the market in 1819 200,000 were sold in Paris and London.[2] However, Brewster gained little from this invention – the patent was incomplete and the instrument soon found numerous imitators.

Brewster's interest in optics was indeed multifaceted. In addition to his research into polarization, with the resulting entertaining side effect of the kaleidoscope, he was also interested in stereoscopy and the theory of primary colors. He promoted William Henry Fox Talbot's photographic calotype process, and was responsible for the introduction of the Fresnel lens in British lighthouses. His research into the phenomenon of afterimages, however, led to permanent damage to his eyesight.

Robert Bate, *Polyangular kaleidoscope with stand*, ca. 1820, brass and glass, Science Museum, London

Spherical mirror reflecting a statuette of the Venus de Milo, wood engraving from Amedée Guillemin, *La Lumière*, Paris 1886, Private collection

Much like kaleidoscopes, concave and convex mirrors were used for both scientific and entertaining purposes.

Mirror, French, ca. 1750–1800, Musée des arts et métiers du CNAM, Paris

1 Stafford, *Artful Science*, 1994, p. 67.
2 Weiss 1996, p. 40.

Painting at night

As night fell, the painter's work came to an end. Candles and oil lamps provided only enough light to draw by. This was often recommended as a kind of exercise, as these sources of illumination were excellent for studying the effects of light and shadow. Already in the seventeenth century, Willem Goeree had demonstrated how oiled paper shades reduced the flickering of lamplight.[1] Working in color, however, would have been unthinkable.

The first documented painting to have been executed under artificial light is Anne-Louis Girodet's *Pygmalion*, which after six years of work was finally presented to the public at the Salon of 1819. It had been commissioned by Count Sommariva, and he was so proud of his new acquisition that he had himself painted as if on a visit to Girodet's studio. The picture clearly illustrates the particular circumstances of the artist's working environment. A sharply defined beam of light shines on the canvas. The painter is shown on a ladder in front of it, holding his palette and brush. In order not to leave any doubt as to the work's true subject, moonlight shines through the skylight. Further, a small version of Girodet's *Endymion* hangs in the background to the right; painted in 1792, its most fascinating feature is the effect of wan moonlight. The light source employed was very likely an Argand oil lamp, whose beam was so strong that it could easily be directed with the help of reflectors. In the years that Girodet was at work on his picture, there was a general feeling that French art was in crisis. Perhaps the painter hoped that by employing this new technology he could provide an impulse to creativity, and thus help improve the general artistic situation.[2]

The critics, however, were unconvinced, and Girodet's experiment remained an exception. Artificial light and daylight could, after all, also complement one another in the studio. The most important thing was that painters now had a choice. Thomas Couture, a colleague of the next generation, found daylight alone boring, and set out in search of a light source "that would give strong definition to forms."[3] In general, though, artists took few risks in their choice of illumination. Gaslight, for example, found its way into the studio rather slowly. In use in English and American studios by the 1840s, it was hesitantly accepted in France. As late as 1867, Jean-Louis Gérôme was still discussing the advantages of painting by gas, almost forty years after it had been introduced into museums.[4]

Adèle Chavassieu d'Audebert after François-Louis Dejuinne, *Girodet Painting "Pygmalion and his Statue"*, 1822, Milan, Pinacoteca di Brera, on loan to the Galleria d'Arte Moderna

Anne-Louis Girodet, *Endymion*, 1785, Musée du Louvre, Département des Peintures, Paris

1 Willem Goeree, *Inleydinge tot de algemene teyken-konst* (1668), 3rd ed., Amsterdam 1697. Thanks to Volker Manuth.
2 Cf. Andreas Blühm, *Pygmalion: Die Ikonographie eines Künstlermythos zwischen 1500 und 1900*, Frankfurt am Main 1988, pp. 128-36, 246-51.
3 Couture 1867, pp. 286-87.
4 Fanny Field Hering, *The Life and Works of Jean-Léon Gérôme*, New York 1892, pp. 166-67.

109 Painting at night

Johann Friedrich Jügel after Karl
Friedrich Schinkel, *Stage design for
Friedrich Schiller's "Don Carlos,"*
1822, aquatint, Theater Instituut
Nederland, Amsterdam

Lighting the stage I

The Berlin architect Karl
Friedrich Schinkel was a master of histori-
cism in all the arts he practiced, including
theatrical design. Here, the empty set is
reproduced in Gothic style. The light comes
in from the left, that is, from the direction
the actors would normally enter the stage.
Schinkel's design could be built today,
although this type of scenery is no longer in
fashion. On the other hand, the rather conventional design disguises what amounted to
a revolution in stage lighting.

Around the middle of the eighteenth century, stage designers began to differentiate
between the illumination of the stage and the
auditorium. "The illuminations, the luminous
transparencies, the glittering effects, the
bejewelled ornamentation of sparkling precious stones were gradually to be replaced by
the picturesque and pictorial world of the historical and exotic milieus in *atmospherical*
light," wrote the theater historian Gösta
Bergman.[1] Directors drew inspiration from
painting. One of the pioneers of this new
approach was the same Francesco Algarotti
whose best-seller *Il Newtonianismo per le dame*
helped disseminate the latest theories of light
like no other book of the period.

However, it was only with the introduction
of the Argand lamp that it became possible to
truly use and direct light to dramatic effect. For
the first time, the depths of the stage could be
illuminated. This had an enormous impact on
acting style: actors were no longer forced to
stand at the edge of the stage in order to
declaim their text in the unflattering glare of the
footlights, but could move about and speak
more naturally. In Schinkel's time, stage lighting experienced yet another technical transformation: the introduction of gaslight, first in the
United States – in 1816 at the Chestnut Street
Theater in Philadelphia – and then in England
in 1817. Its effect was described as being as mild
as it is splendid-white, regular, and pervading.
Gaslight had its Paris premiere at the Odéon in
1821. Nowadays it is difficult to judge the precise difference between gas and oil lamps; creative designers, however, were quick to make
use of the new technology. In February 1822,
for example, the Paris opera opened – most
appropriately – with a production of Niccolo
Isouard's *Aladdin's Magic Lamp.*[2] The press was
enthusiastic about the lighting. One of the two
designers was none other than Louis-Jacques-
Mandé Daguerre, the diorama painter who later
became the co-inventor of photography.[3]

1 Bergman 1977, p. 177.
2 Ibid., pp. 256-59.
3 Gernsheim 1968, pp. 11-12.

Flickering images

In the early nineteenth century, even painters such as Gainsborough, Turner and Friedrich did not hesitate to turn their hand to transparent painting, a technique that also had a long tradition in the decorative arts.[1] A wide variety of techniques were used in entire branches of the craft industry to make light shine through transparent or translucent materials. Lithophanes were probably the most popular form, particularly among the middle classes. The procedure, in which figural reliefs are pressed into porcelain, was invented in 1827 by the Frenchman Paul de Bourgoing, and soon became fashionable throughout Europe and America. Moralizing scenes and reproductions after both the old masters and modern artists were reproduced to great effect. The flickering candle gave an impression of movement – much as torchlight did in sculpture galleries – making the figures seem almost lifelike. The flame, which is both free and controlled, and the sense of motion in light – these were, and are, endlessly fascinating.

Franz Anton Siebel, *David and Samson*, 1825, enamel painting on glass, wood, Rijksmuseum, Amsterdam

This colorful little screen with its monumental subject is a typical example of the way the middle classes sought to bring the pathos of high art into the domestic sphere in the early nineteenth century. The craftsmanship is of high quality, and the object was clearly meant to astound the visitor – and indeed it would have made quite an impression in the sober interiors of the Biedermeier period.

Anton Kothgasser, *Night cup*, ca. 1820, enamel painting on glass, Staatliche Museen zu Berlin, Preussischer Kulturbesitz, Kunstgewerbemuseum

This original cup with a nocturnal motif may have had its place on a nightstand. A last drink before snuffing out the candle would have reminded the tired owner of the late hour, and perhaps helped him to get to sleep. The decorative technique – in which the glass was first painted and then etched – is an elaborate one, and made the cup a luxury item. Kothgasser was a leading craftsman in this genre.

Candleholder with lithophane shade, German, ca. 1835-44, iron and biscuit porcelain, Carnegie Museum of Natural History, Pittsburgh, George and Lilian Ball Memorial Fund

1 Verwiebe 1997, pp. 93-95.

Turning on the light

As these group portraits clearly show, turning on the lights was a tedious process before the introduction of gas and electricity. In Wilhelm Bendz's painting of the life class at the Charlottenborg art academy, students practice or fidget or doggedly begin work as a man on a ladder makes final adjustments to the lights directed at the model. Almost simultaneously, American painter Samuel Morse used the same theme in his monumental portrait of members of the United States Congress. The symbolism of both paintings is the same: the idea that good work, be it artistic production or national legislation, could only be done in proper light. Thus the focus in each composition on the lamplighters, and the enlightening effects of lighting technology, the Argand-type lamp in particular.

Artists' night classes orginated for practical reasons. They extended the available working hours beyond sunset and they distributed the heavy costs of models and fuel among the participants. The complex system of lamps, reflectors, and shutters installed in the academy permitted specific, controlled lighting on the subject. (Who selected the pose and light-ing was often a subject of intense negotiation.) By eliminating the transient effects of daylight and reducing the distraction of color, artists concentrated attention on the pure effects of light and shade essential to drawing, the foundation of academic practice. Under stable lighting conditions, they could draw complex studies of incredible refinement and realism. Students and mature artists participated in the evening classes, perfecting their skills or accumulating a vocabulary of poses for use in larger compositions.

Their choice of subjects was limited, however, to one or two monochromatic figures, either living models or casts of antique sculpture. For many artists, the difficulties of organizing compositions from many separate and differently lit figure studies proved insurmountable. Merciless critics enjoyed pointing out when the direction of light in a landscape or interior failed to match that on a figure, or when a figure in sharp chiaroscuro seemed to float before a flatly lit background. Neither Morse nor Bendz made such mistakes, being masters of perspective systems that unified light, space, and action within carefully worked out geometric structures. The coherence of their scenes gives them their realism.

As artificial lighting technologies improved steadily over the course of the nineteenth century, artists worked more and more at night, both in academies and in their homes. They bought the expensive Argand lamps, and they installed gas lights. What began as private study and preparation, however, gradually developed into the execution of independent works of art, sometimes radically realistic in their subject matter. Bendz and his contemporaries anticipated the later nineteenth-century naturalists in this respect, by showing their subjects casually awaiting the start of their professional activities, rather than in formally posed arrangements.

Samuel Morse, *The House of Representatives*, 1822–23, The Corcoran Gallery of Art

The start of an unusual evening session is delayed as the janitor painstakingly prepares the chandelier composed of dozens of Argand lamps, each needing to be filled with oil, trimmed, and lit before being hauled back up to its place under the ceiling.

Wilhelm Bendz, *The Life Class in
the Academy of Fine Arts*, 1826,
Statens Museum for Kunst,
Copenhagen

Lighthouses

The beneficial effects of new lighting technologies are nowhere more obvious than in the case of lighthouses. New reflectors and lenses were directly translated into greater scope and thus improved safety. No invention was more important in this regard than that of the French physicist Augustin-Jean Fresnel in 1821. His compound lens has remained the standard to this day. The lens is made up of concentric circles calibrated to capture and direct the spread of light. Prisms line the exterior edges, which point the light horizontally. The beam is not concentrated into a small area – as with a burning glass – but rather forms a ray of any length or breadth desired. Not only lighthouses, but also other kinds of light projection instruments and floodlights profited from Fresnel's invention. Its roots, however, went back to an earlier discovery by Georges-Louis Leclerc de Buffon (1748). As so often, the Industrial Age adopted a "pure" invention of the Enlightenment and transformed it into a commodity, which in turn helped further stimulate the development of transport and the growth of the economy. The importance of Fresnel's lens for both shipping in general and for the lives of the sailors and their families cannot be overestimated.

This example, from the Musée des arts et métiers in Paris, was probably made for the purposes of exhibition and demonstration. The word on the practicality of the new invention had not yet gotten out, and some form of advertising was deemed necessary. By the middle of the century, however, lighthouses equipped with the Fresnel lens were springing up all over the world. Factories devoted their entire production to making the new lens. A single specimen could cost as much as $12,000, but with a range of up to eighteen miles, it was apparently well worth the investment.[1] Once the introduction of electricity further improved the overall luminosity, practically the only limitation was the curve of the earth itself: In 1893, the city of Chicago constructed a searchlight whose beam could be seen in Milwaukee, 84 miles away; at ten miles it was possible to read a newspaper by it.[2]

In the course of the nineteenth century, lighthouses came to have a certain mystical aura, particularly in seafaring regions with rocky coasts, such as Scotland. From Turner to Seurat, we find the lighthouse as a symbol of calm and security. The notion of the lighthouse as a "bringer of light" finds perhaps its best expression in the Statue of Liberty in New York. The association between freedom, light and guidance goes back to the Enlightenment, and even today can still give rise to feelings of nostalgia.

François jeune, Fresnel lens, 1835, glass, wood, brass, Musée des arts et métiers du CNAM, Paris

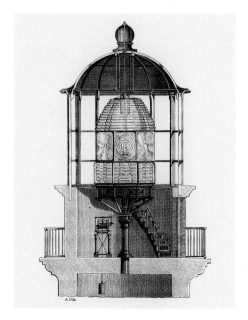

Lighthouse lantern, wood engraving from Amedée Guillemin, *La Lumière*, Paris 1882, Private collection

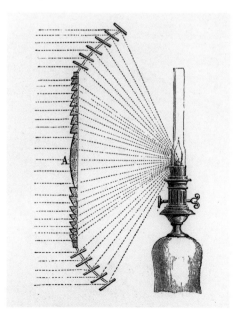

Light beams emanating from a Fresnel lens, wood engraving from Amedée Guillemin, *La Lumière*, Paris 1882, Private collection

1 http://www.west.net/~pamass
   /htmfiles/freslens.htm.
2 Rebske 1962, p. 173.

The pencil of Nature

A camera lucida attached to a working table, engraving from Ernest Hareux, *L'Outillage et le matériel nécessaires à l'atelier ou en plein-air*, Paris ca. 1870–90, Van Gogh Museum, Amsterdam

Camera lucida, ca. 1825–75, Musée Nicéphore Niépce, Ville de Chalons-sur-Saône, France

Photography was not invented out of the blue in the 1820s and 1830s. Already a century earlier, in 1725, Johann Heinrich Schulze demonstrated that certain chemicals were sensitive to light. William Lewis repeated his experiments in 1763, and passed his notes on to the famous ceramicist Josaiah Wedgwood. In 1802, the latter's son Thomas, a chemist, published a method for reproducing silhouettes on paper coated with silver salts – a kind of photography without a camera. One great disadvantage, however, was that these images could not be permanently fixed, so they faded on exposure to light. The information pertaining to the various chemicals was already available, but no one was then able make a connection between them.[1]

The breakthrough came in the following generation. The most important figures were John Herschel, the physicist and astronomer, and the university professor and polymath William Henry Fox Talbot. One of Herschel's typical diary entries, dated 3 January 1826, reads: "Talbot called ... stayed from 2 till 5, much talk about Light."[2] David Brewster and William Hyde Wollaston also belonged to their circle. These "light scientists," from a variety of disciplines, prepared the way for a revolution. Herschel had discovered the correct fixing chemicals in 1819, but even twenty years later no one felt photography was yet ready to make its stage debut. Then, news arrived from Paris: the French Academy had recognized and published Daguerre's invention, the daguerreotype. Suddenly, the era of gentlemanly scholarly reflection was over. Talbot found himself forced to speed up his research. He was ahead of Daguerre in one respect, however, as he was looking for a method that would allow images to be printed over and over again. Talbot invented the reproducible negative, which was to remain the standard until the introduction of digital imaging.

The new medium was quickly improved. The chemical components of the photographic plates and papers became both more sensitive and stable. One of the major goals was to shorten the exposure time in order to achieve

more flexibility and efficiency. A decisive step was taken in 1851, when it became possible to fix photographic images on paper.

Photographs could now be endlessly reproduced. Improvements in artificial lighting were naturally of decisive importance, and it is therefore surprising that no one has yet examined exactly how these two areas interacted. For several decades, however, artificial light sources were not strong enough to be any use to photography. Photographers were thus among those who sought to exploit even the most minor developments to the fullest. In 1877, a dynamo by the German firm Siemens was installed by the photographer Henry van der Weyde in his studio in London's Regent Street, and, with the help of an electric arc light, was able to reduce the exposure time from half a minute or more to between two and ten seconds. Swindlers, unable to afford such expensive investments, used gun powder to imitate the effect, something serious photographers found unacceptable.[3]

It was not until the end of the century, with the introduction of better lenses, that photographers were able to take pictures at twilight, at night or in artificially lit interiors. Fred Holland Day and Alfred Stieglitz experimented with gaslighting in their work, for the first time achieving truly aesthetically pleasing results. Before this, photography had merely been an aid to artists – and one they were even ashamed of. By 1890, however, photography had found its own artistic voice. It no longer simply recorded light; it interpreted it.

William Henry Fox Talbot, *View towards Lecco*, ca. 1833, camera lucida drawing, The Royal Photographic Society, Bath

Talbot's fascination with all aspects of light is demonstrated by his adoption of Wollaston's camera lucida, patented in 1806. It was designed to enable the artist or amateur to create landscape views in almost perfect perspective. Talbot's disappointment with the results led him to think of alternatives.

1 Koschatzky 1987, pp. 43-47; Batchen 1997.
2 Quoted after Schaaf 1992, p. 1.
3 Rebske 1962, pp. 83-84.

Bust of Patroclus, calotype from William Henry Fox Talbot, *The Pencil of Nature*, London 1844, The Royal Photographic Society, Bath

In the early days, statues were a favorite motif among photographers because, unlike living creatures, they stood still. As Talbot noted: "Statues, busts, and other specimens of sculpture, are generally well represented by the Photographic Art; and also very rapidly, in consequence of their whiteness. These delineations are susceptible of an almost unlimited variety: since in the first place, a statue may be placed in any position with regard to the sun, either directly opposite to it, or at any angle: the directness or obliquity of the illumination causing of course an immense difference in the effect. [...] With regard to many statues, however, a better effect is obtained by delineating them in cloudy weather than in sunshine. For, the sunshine causes such strong shadows as sometimes to confuse the subject."

Sun worship

"The sun is god," are said to have been Turner's last words.[1] No painter before or after has painted the sun with such brilliance, daring, and profound emotional power. Observers recorded how he did it, finishing a painting for exhibition in 1837. "He was absorbed in his work, did not look about him, but kept on scumbling a lot of white into his picture – nearly all over it [...]. The picture was a mass of red and yellow of all varieties. Every object was in this fiery state. He had a large palette, nothing on it but a huge lump of flake-white; he had two or three hog tools to work with, and with these he was driving the white into all the hollows, and every part of the surface. This was the only work he did, and it was the finishing stroke. The sun, as I have said, was in the centre; from it were drawn – ruled – lines to mark the rays; these lines were rather strongly marked, I suppose to guide his eye. The picture gradually became wonderfully effective, just the effect of brilliant sunlight absorbing everything and throwing a misty haze over every object. Standing sideways of the canvas, I saw that the sun was a lump of white standing out like a boss on a shield."[2]

Turner knew light science and color theory. He read and annotated Joseph Priestley's *History and Present State of Knowledge Relating to Vision, Light, and Colours* (1772) and Goethe's *Theory of Color* (translated 1840), and he owned a copy of astronomer Mary Somerville's *Mechanism of the Heavens* (1830). With his friends, scientists Humphry Davy and David Brewster, he debated the properties and action of light, color, and the spectrum. One of Turner's acquaintances, the Reverend James Skene, believed that, "aided by the dis-coveries daily making in the mysteries of light, [Turner's] scrutinising genius seems to tremble on the verge of some new discovery in colour, which may prove of the first importance in art."[3]

The artist's "scrutinising genius" led him to spend hours flat on his back on Hampstead Heath observing the sky. He drew sunrises and sunsets, studied the solar eclipse of 1804, and endured appalling weather to experience light in every atmospheric condition. Even nearly abstract compositions, such as *Sun Setting Over a Lake,* are true to nature. The arcs of red and yellow light above the horizon are well known twilight effects, as are the crepuscular rays emanating from the blob of yellow paint that is the sun. The painting is also "true" to human perception, in the way that the light's glare and intensity seem to blot out all recognizable detail in the landscape (an observation that the French impressionists adopted after seeing Turner's work).

Yet, Turner's paintings, for all their naturalistic and optical effects, act primarily on the emotions. The viewer reacts viscerally to overwhelming color – brilliant chrome yellows and reds, blinding whites – that, according to Goethe's theory, symbolized and evoked positive emotions, such as gaiety, warmth, and happiness. Throughout Romantic poetry, including that written by Turner himself, the sun's passage across the sky symbolized time and mortality. Its setting represented the waning of earthly glory, the ending of life, and the coming of night. Like so many of Turner's sublime late landscapes, *Sun Setting Over a Lake* inspires awe at the power and beauty of light – connecting art and nature with humanity's deepest religious feelings.

James Mallord William Turner, *Sun Setting Over a Lake*, ca. 1840, Tate Gallery, London, Turner Bequest

Sunset at Sea, color lithograph from Camille Flammarion, *The Atmosphere*, New York 1874, Carnegie Library, Pittsburgh

1 Andrew Wilton, *Turner and the Sublime*, Chicago 1980, p. 102.
2 Bailey 1997, pp. 301-02.
3 Hamilton 1998, p. 65.

Torchlight effects

While for everyday situations and domestic use, bright and constant light was preferred, when it came to spectacles, moving lights were extremely popular. The use of flickering torchlight in sculpture galleries was considered particularly effective, as its motion and warm color made the marble or plaster statues appear to be alive. During the eighteenth century, it was fashionable among the educated elite to tour museums in the dead of night: the sublimity of the artworks illuminated by torches and the eerie atmosphere combined to create an unforgettable experience. Royal nocturnal visits had a kind of tradition in France, originating with Napoleon's nighttime viewing of the Laocoön group, recently arrived from Italy in 1810. In 1837, Louis-Philippe paid a visit to the Louvre at night, and in 1839 to the sculpture gallery at Versailles. As eyewitnesses report, twenty lantern-bearers, armed with concave reflectors, transformed the darkness into light.[1] Vinchon's

painting shows the royal family admiring a statue of Joan of Arc, created by the king's youngest daughter. The visit appears to have an almost ritual nature, and the overall mood is solemn, even sacred.

This nocturnal practice continued even during the Third Republic. As late as 1873, we find a wood engraving of the liberal and westernized shah of Persia, Naser od-Din, visiting the Louvre. The print, published in *Le Monde Illustré*, shows the official guest admiring the most famous sculpture of antiquity, the *Venus de Milo*, a work that had belonged to the museum since 1821. The sculpture, which is in two parts, had recently been restored to what is now thought to be its original appearance except, of course, for the missing arms. The flickering light playing over the compact form shows the figure to its best advantage: the fine modeling of the body and drapery are emphasized, and her walking motion seems prolonged.

Louis-Joseph-Amédée Daudenarde after Frédéric Lix, *Visit of H. M. Naser od-Din Shah to the Louvre*, wood engraving from *Le Monde Illustré* (26 July 1873), Foundation Artificial Light in Art, Eindhoven

Auguste Vinchon, *Louis-Philippe and the Royal Family Viewing Marie d'Orléans's Statue of Joan of Arc in the Galerie de Pierre (1839)*, 1848, Musée National des Châteaux de Versailles et de Trianon

Two views of a cast of the *Venus de Milo*, ca. 1850–1900, plaster, Collectie Rijksakademie, on loan to the Allard Pierson Museum, Amsterdam

1 "Article de 1837, republiée dans La Sarthe, 10 février 1938," quoted after Jean Galard (ed.), *Visiteurs du Louvre: un florilège*, Paris 1993, pp. 107-08.

123 **Torchlight effects**

The invention of painting

According to an antique myth, the origin of painting can be traced back to the play of darkness and light. Pliny recorded the legend in his *Natural History* (XXXV, 12). Debutades' lover was forced to take leave of her, and in order to preserve his presence she traced his shadow on a wall. The history of the transmission of the story is complex, but since the Renaissance it has never again been forgotten. Paintings illustrating the tale were produced in great quantity during the second half of the eighteenth century; this is no surprise, of course, as the neoclassical artists were especially fond of ancient stories relating to their métier. The art historian Hans Wille has shown that in the years before 1800 the shadow itself was generally depicted with great precision.[1] This was probably the result of the improvements in light projection made possible by the development of the Argand lamp.

Daege's painting is an excellent example of the genre, ambitious in both size and execution. The painter, a young man at the time, apparently hoped to prove himself with this work. In terms of style, the picture is rather conservative, a piece in the academic tradition with no trace of Romantic influence – except perhaps that the scene is set outdoors. The composition is well balanced, and the poses are somewhat too obviously derived from Antique statuary. The fashion for silhouettes – which is clearly related to both the subject in general and this painting in particular – was far from over at this time. The popularity in this period of both the story of the invention of painting and the silhouette grew out of the Enlightenment's obsession with light. In the minds of contemporaries, light had become completely controllable; it had been robbed of its last shreds of mystery. Only one thing had still not been achieved: the mechanical fixing of a shadow. But many were hard at work on this task, and only a few years after Daege painted his picture, the first breakthrough had already been made. The inventions of Daguerre, his comrades-in-arms and competitors, standing at the origins of photography, ended the silhouette era. After 1840, artists lost interest in the story of Debutades and her lover.

Eduard Daege, *The Invention of Painting*, 1832, Staatliche Museen zu Berlin, Preussischer Kulturbesitz, Nationalgalerie

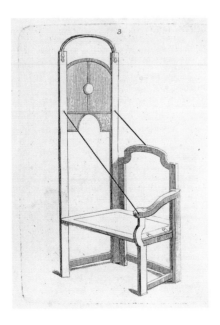 

Silhouette machine, engravings from Johann Caspar Lavater, *Over de physiognomie*, Amsterdam 1784, vol. 2, Rijksmuseum, Amsterdam

1 Wille 1960; compare Rosenblum 1957.

Daguerre

Louis-Jacques-Mandé Daguerre, *Portrait of an Artist*, 1843, daguerreotype, George Eastman House, Rochester, New York, gift of Eastman Kodak Company

Eduard Isaac Asser, *Daguerreotype*, ca. 1840–50, Rijksmuseum, Rijksprentenkabinet, Amsterdam

The daguerreotype process was complicated and did not always work. Here the plate has failed to reproduce the intended image, which was captured by the camera under special lighting conditions.

Photography's pioneers combined theories of light with the discoveries of chemists, astronomers, painters and stage designers. Centuries before, the camera obscura had made it possible for light to travel through a small opening and thus produce reversed projections of images. Only in the 1830s, however, was a way found to fix these images on sensitized metal plates. The process entailed placing a polished silvered copperplate in a box filled with the fumes of iodine, thus creating a tarnish that was actually light-sensitive silver iodide. This plate was then placed in a camera and exposed to light for about a quarter of an hour. The exposed plate was then subjected to mercury fumes, whereby a discernible image was formed in the areas struck by light. This was then fixed in a bath of common salt. The picture produced was a unique image that only appeared when the plate was held at a certain angle.[1]

Like the railroad, steam ships and the telegraph, photography was hailed as a sign of progress; its uses were immediately recognized and contemporaries greeted it with great enthusiasm. The inventors, William Henry Fox Talbot, Nicéphore Niépce and Louis-Jacques-Mandé Daguerre, all came to prominence in the 1830s. Their biographies bear witness to enormous curiosity and perseverance. Another contributor was the physicist and astronomer François Arago. In 1811, he found proof of Thomas Young's wave theory of light, thus ending the dominance of the Newtonian concept of light as consisting of particles. Arago's research led to the development of polarizing filters, which enabled scientists to measure the intensity of light. It is therefore not surprising that he immediately understood the significance of the discoveries made by Niépce and Daguerre. Thanks to his

excellent argumentation, the French parliament awarded Daguerre a stipend, enabling him to continue his activities without financial worries. Arago persuaded the members by suggesting they consider four issues when judging the invention, in the following order: Was it original? Would it serve the needs of archaeology and the fine arts? Did it have practical applications? And, finally, would it help advance science?[2]

These questions arose not only from Arago's own system of thought, but also from the origins of photography itself, in which art and science were intimately connected. His protégé Daguerre was a man of the theater. As a stage designer, he had created spectacular decors depicting all kinds of atmospheric light effects: "In this field Daguerre's ability proved incomparable, for he understood better than anyone else how to vary the play of light and shade on the *décor* in order to animate the scene – effects, it must not be forgotten, that had to be achieved with oil lamps. If the painter P. H. Valenciennes had cause to complain some years previously that when an actor says 'Night is coming on' the stagehands invariably turns out all the lights at once, Daguerre taught them the art of producing subtle and gradually changing light effects."[3] In the 1820s, Daguerre had turned to painting dioramas, which transformed these theatrical effects into an independent and popular genre. While painting them, the artist probably relied heavily on a camera obscura.

In the beginning, the weakness of artificial light sources hampered photography's full development. However, an alliance between chemists and physicists soon helped still the public's new-found hunger for images. The era of the daguerreotype was brief; it ended when photographs could finally be reproduced.

Soleil Opticien, Paris, *Daguerreotype set*, ca. 1840, Universiteitsmuseum Utrecht

Louis-Auguste Bisson, *Portrait of a Man*, ca. 1843, daguerreotype, Rijksmuseum, Rijksprentenkabinet, Amsterdam

1 Schaaf 1992, p. 45; for a detailed description see George M. Hopkins, "Reminiscences of Daguerreotypy," *Scientific American* 56 (22 January 1887), pp. 47, 52; the text can be found at www.daguerre.org/resource/process/remin.html.
2 Cf. Sheon 1971, pp. 435-50.
3 Gernsheim 1968, p. 10.

127 **Daguerre**

Modern hell

In this spectacular vision of the palace of Satan, John Martin depicts the flaming torches of Hell in the guise of London gaslights, the very opposite of pure divine light. Thus, light symbolism and lighting technology are key to an understanding of this work as an allegory of vice and corruption in the modern city in general, and London's Pall Mall in particular.

Pandemonium is Satan's palace and gathering point for the legions of Hell preparing their assault on humankind. John Milton's epic poem *Paradise Lost* (first published 1670) described the satanic palace with its Doric columns, echoes of pagan Babylon, Cairo, and Assyria, and flaring torches fueled by "Naptha and asphaltus," volatile and dangerous petroleum derivatives still in use in nineteenth-century lamps. In Martin's interpretation of the subject in this 1841 Royal Academy exhibition painting, Pandemonium itself resembles a neoclassical arcade and its antique torches seem to have been replaced by gas street lamps. The art historian Christopher Newall has plausibly suggested that the new buildings of Carlton House Terrace, recently constructed on Pall Mall, provided the architectural prototype for this version of Satan's palace.[1] The fact that Pall Mall was notorious as the first gaslit London street (in 1808), and also became a favorite playground of the libertine Prince Regent, enhances the likeliness of Newall's identification. By 1841, portraying a gaslit hell was not an original idea. As every regency satirist from Thomas Rowlandson on down had noted, Pall Mall's gaslights proved irresistible to nocturnal thrill-seekers.[2]

Installed in centers of commerce, entertainment, and crime, the new lights drew fascinated innocents into the urban underworld as surely as satanic fires trapped lost souls in the poetic hells of Dante and Milton. Lord Byron, regency London's premier hell-raiser, seems to have been the first to explicitly describe Pall Mall as a modern Pandemonium, as we read in Canto XXVI of his poem "Don Juan," published in 1818: "And smooth'd the brimstone of that street / of hell / Which bears the greatest likeness to Pall / Mall."[3] Byron's damned hero spends his nights rattling up and down the brilliantly illuminated street populated by expensive prostitutes and lined with high-stakes gambling clubs, known to the initiated as "hells." Subsequently, in art and literature, flaring gas jets inevitably accompany scenes of vice, crime, and sedition. Some of the more lurid urban guidebooks, *New York by Gas-Light* and its imitators, *London by Gas-Light* and *Paris par le gaz*, warned their readers that they would in fact, be touring the modern hell.

John Martin was himself an urban engineer of sorts who devoted a significant portion of his life to the design of a water supply system for the city of London. Like few artists of his generation, he was aware of the physical implications of the city's extraordinary growth, and he must have understood the costs and benefits of a public lighting system based on underground pipes connected to a central production plant. But, it is equally tempting to read his image of Pandemonium, erupting volcanically from the ground, as a comment on the explosive development of the West End. Certainly, by pairing this artificially illuminated hell with the sweet daylight of *The Celestial City* in the 1841 Royal Academy exhibition, Martin suggests that one of the attractions of gaslight is its exciting potential for moral and physical destruction.

1 Newall 1998, p. 167.
2 Stella Margetson, *Regency London*, New York 1971, pp. 125-27; see, for example, the anonymous *An Heroic Epistle to Mr. Winsor [...]*, London 1808, p. 7: "They walk, Pall-Mall! Might every evening boast / A head illumin'd for each illumin'd post, / Might count a scavant tenant to each house, / and London rival Laputa in NOUS."
3 George, Lord Byron, "Don Juan," in *The Poetical Works of Lord Byron*, London 1966.

John Martin, *Pandemonium*, 1841,
The FORBES Magazine
Collection, New York

Liquid gold

Oil is probably the oldest source of artificial light, and the oil lamp is the most common object that has come down to us from antiquity. Its design hardly changed at all until Ami Argand's invention of the hollow wick. Following this development, however, there were a number of enhancements: wicks were improved, and the fuel supply was mechanized using clockwork and pumps, making it possible to deliver the oil from below. The tank could thus be incorporated into the foot of the lamp, and no longer cast annoying shadows.

Although oil soon faced competition from gas, it remained the most widespread source of domestic lighting during the entire nineteenth century. Naturally, this was a question of economics. In the beginning, whales were the major source of lamp oil, but the animals were on the brink of extinction. Fossil oil was discovered in the 1820s in Ohio but it took until 1859 when the first oil was drilled from underground, this time in Pennsylvania. From now on, fossil oil was available in sheer abundance and soon the sea mammals were relieved of some of their worst enemies. Consequently, once the refined fossil oil had become available for mass consumption, the kerosene lamp triumphed over its more expensive rivals. Wolfgang Schivelbusch has claimed its entry into the bourgeois salon a perfect indicator of the lighting psychology of the nineteenth century. For him, it was precisely the archaic – anti-modern – nature of the technique that gave the kerosene lamp its deeper meaning for the consumer: it was independent of any network and its light was warm and comforting.[1] Other advantages – which should not be underestimated – were the fact that it was much less dangerous than gas, and that one could move the lamps around, placing them where they were most needed. It is also important to remember that gaslighting was not available to everyone everywhere.

Kerosene, which was lightweight and relatively inexpensive, brought real advances in lighting to a large segment of the population. In this context, the ageing German painter Wilhelm Kügelgen wrote in a letter of 1864: "Now I, too, have a kerosene lamp, bought yesterday in Quedlinburg, and today I have a terrible headache because the light is so strong. I'm going to replace the porcelain shade with one made of thick paper."[2] Clearly, many advances in technology also had a negative side. It was only towards the end of the century that the oil lamp began to be pushed slowly from the market, this time by completely safe electric light – the first light source without an open flame. It finally put an end to the soot, smoke and lampblack commonly associated with candles, oil lamps and gas.

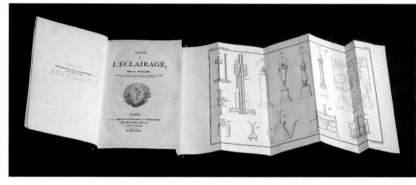

1 Schivelbusch 1986, p. 155.
2 Quoted in Rebske 1962, p. 68.

Menzel, Monet and modern light

In the 1840s, the German artist Adolph Menzel painted intimate, spontaneous oil sketches that represented natural and artificial light in new and vastly significant ways. His work differs crucially from that of Bendz, Hummel, and other Biedermeier painters – his predecessors and contemporaries – because it directly records his observation of light phenomena, and is not constructed according to the geometrical principles of Newtonian physics or traditional perspective. In fact, critics have pointed out that Menzel's construction of space in *Living Room with the Sister of the Artist* is awkward, if not faulty. At the same time, they recognize that his brilliant depiction of light and atmosphere in these small rooms is totally convincing and astoundingly modern. Because Menzel's view of reality was based on his perceptions rather than on any scientific system, his work introduces subjectivity, the artist's personal vision, into nineteenth-century painting. He underscores the immediacy of this vision by painting with free, loose brushstrokes, at odds with the prevailing European taste for highly colored and finished compositions.

Living Room with the Sister of the Artist is lit by four lights, two of which we cannot see. In the foreground, the candle in the sister's hand casts a gleaming light on the door frame. The second light source visible on the table in the background is probably an oil lamp, whose even glow was ideal for sewing and other "close work" at night. As for the invisible lights, one would seem to be a chandelier or hanging lamp concealed by the wall and doorway on the left. It lights up the ceiling and creates the overall brightness in the space. The presence of a fourth light source is suggested by the dark shadow that falls on the lower right hand corner. This would have been cast by the artist himself, working by lamplight in the hallway. The muted color scheme of browns, dull reds, and greens, is consistent with the effect of the warm light generated by candle and lamp flames.

Menzel's sketches from the 1840s are admired today, somewhat nervously, as precursors of the freely worked light studies of the French impressionists. It is unclear whether Menzel introduced these motifs and techniques to French painters during visits to Paris in 1855 and 1867, when he stayed for several months. By then, French painters had also seen paintings by Turner, Constable, and the Pre-Raphaelites, with the their equally original approaches to light, color, and brushwork. Claude Monet's *Interior after Dinner* was painted more than twenty years after Menzel's *Living Room*. Monet has drastically simplified his composition by depicting only one light source and casting much of the room into opaque shadow. The lamplight is more brilliant and cooler in hue than Menzel's, and it outshines the orange-red light from the fire. Although still some years from adopting the characteristic impressionist brushstroke, Monet's thick application of paint and minimal detail differ from Menzel's, as does his detached, indeed impersonal, portrayal of his preoccupied friends, the painter Alfred Sisley and his family.

Claude Monet, *An Interior after Dinner*, 1868–69, National Gallery of Art, Washington, D.C., Mr. and Mrs. P. Mellon 1983

Adolph Menzel, *Living Room with the Sister of the Artist*, 1847, Bayerische Staatsgemälde-sammlungen, Neue Pinakothek, Munich

How bright is bright?

In 1855, a teacher from the Ecole poly-technique in Paris wondered how a realist painter would react to this hypothetical offer from a physicist: "You observe the play of light, and I study it like you; you do it with your eyes, whose witness sometimes leads you astray; me, I employ precise instruments that do not lie; these instruments might be useful to you, I will lend them to you; I will share with you the knowledge acquired by science, and I am confident that the practice of your art will benefit somehow, and you may better approach that perfection which you pursue."[1] One of the instruments this teacher, Jules Jamin, had in mind was the photometer, a simple device for measuring relative brightness that had been invented in the early eighteenth century. During the first half of the nineteenth century, photometers had greatly improved in accuracy and refinement, thanks to astronomers attempting to measure stellar distances, and gas engineers testing the quality and strength of the new gaslights. Forerunner of today's photographic light meter, the photometer permitted an observer to compare one source of light with another. By adjusting the instrument, the observer could measure the difference in brightness between the two lights. If the second light were of known or fixed brightness, such as a candle, different light sources could be compared to the uniform standard and then to each other.

Jamin, armed with his photometer, then posed another question, or perhaps we should say, challenge: "Now let us see if, truly, paintings do represent natural scenes faithfully, or can they only aspire to the verities of convention."[2] Selecting artists known for realistic lighting, he conclusively proved that their work could not approach the effects found in nature. After numerous measurements, he found that in landscape paintings, the brightest sunlight appeared to be, on average, only two to four times brighter than its surroundings, whereas in nature the actual difference was roughly eighty percent greater. When he measured the effect of lamplight in a painted night scene, he found it generally appeared twenty to thirty times brighter than surrounding bright areas; in real life, however, a candle proved 1,500 times brighter than a nearby sheet of paper.[3] Such contrasts could not be achieved in art, so the vaunted realism of many such paintings is an illusion created by artistic convention.

Yet, if painters would recognize that the scale of light and dark possible in painting was strictly limited, some realism could be achieved: "[...] artists of the modern school have made enormous progress in the direction of accuracy; everyone has noticed that their paintings contain shadows that are dark and blue and more vivid lights, and there are some paintings by Decamps, for example, where the effect of the sun measured by a photometer falls within the limits of nature."[4] Alexandre-Gabriel Decamps is usually described as a respectable mid-nineteenth century painter of oriental scenery and genre subjects. Although his interest in light has been noticed, no one has considered that to be a central subject of his, or considered him to be – even unwittingly – a scientific artist. His accuracy of observation and representation has been overshadowed by the spectacular (and thanks to Jamin, demonstrably artificial) effects of the British landscapists Constable and Turner, and the later generation of French impressionists.

A Turkish School, painted in 1846 as Decamps's interest shifted from color to light effects, allows us to appreciate both his modesty and his subtlety. Modesty, in that he does not seek to represent extremes of light and dark, sensibly limiting himself to a shadowy room brightened by a few strips of direct sunlight. Subtlety, in the extremely refined nuances of shadow in the foreground and the beautiful variations of light reflecting off the corner in the background. Decamps's painstaking gradation of values (dark and light) simulates the much larger range of values found in nature or, even, a humble Turkish school. In the past, it has been easy to dismiss his coloring as dull, or be distracted by his exotic subjects. Perhaps he is a painter only a physicist could love.

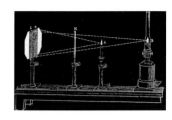

Rumford type photometer, wood engraving from Jules Jamin, *Cours de physique de l'Ecole polytechnique*, Paris 1869, Carnegie Library, Pittsburgh

1 Jamin 1855, p. 627. Cf. Sheon 1971.
2 Jamin 1855, p. 636.
3 Ibid., pp. 636-37.
4 Ibid., p. 637.

Alexandre-Gabriel Decamps, *A Turkish School*, 1846, Amsterdams Historisch Museum (Fodor Collection), on loan to the Van Gogh Museum, Amsterdam

Light engineering
in the home

Nineteenth-century housekeeping manuals devoted lengthy chapters to the subject of lighting. There were several reasons for this profusion. First of all, in the age of positivism, some writers felt compelled to provide histories and scientific theories of light, giving far more complete descriptions of the wave theory or photometry, for example, than are to be found in many art treatises. Secondly, nineteenth-century lighting technologies were incredibly varied and complex. In one household, candles, oil lamps, and gaslighting might have been found in different spaces destined for different purposes; after 1880, electric lighting may have been added to the mix. It was necessary, according to domestic theory and practice of the time, to explain how each lamp was constructed and operated, what illuminating properties, safety hazards, and economic costs and benefits were associated with each fuel, and the social conventions determining location and use of different lights. Any housekeeper conversant with one of these manuals became, of necessity, an expert chemist, engineer, and economist – a domestic scientist.

The introduction of gaslighting into dwellings in Europe and America can be dated from the 1820s, when the construction of municipal gas plants and piping systems provided a central supply available in urban areas. Gaslighting functioned on completely different principles than all previous forms of lighting, and required careful explanation for consumers. First and strangest of all, gas lamps did not contain their fuel, but drew it from pipes within the walls. This caused great difficulties for those accustomed to carrying their lights about with them, although eventually a limited amount of flexibility was achieved by connecting gas lamps to outlets by rubber tubes. People had to be reminded to turn their lights off by disconnecting the gas rather than blowing out the flame. However, a benefit of the new system was the obsolescence of ungainly fuel reservoirs, so it was possible to design lamps of elegant slenderness or ornamental complexity. The Renaissance revival style of the wall bracket was especially appropriate for the torch-like flame from the gas-jet.

Like more traditional lamps, gas lamps produced light from flames, although no wicks were involved. This was a major benefit to housekeepers, who were spared the labor of trimming and adjusting wicks, and replacing them when used up. However, the flames generated by gas were far brighter than most domestic consumers were accustomed to; therefore, expensive and elaborate shades were needed. The heat generated by combustion called for durable and nonflammable glass shades – the homemade paper and silk used with Argand lamps became fire hazards with gas. Moreover, the chemistry of gas combustion produced water and smelly, sometimes poisonous fumes. Small gaslit rooms became unhealthy very rapidly. The fumes frequently damaged fabric, metal, and oil paintings, and left unsightly stains and deposits on walls and ceilings. The manuals recommended that gaslighting be restricted to large spaces, such as halls, where more heat and smoke could escape upward or be ventilated outward. The late nineteenth-century mania for ventilation and fresh air was closely connected with the polluting effects of gas.

Allegorical gas bracket, British, 1880–1900, Lumière de l'oeil, Paris

The coming of night

Twilight is the transition from day to night, and light to dark. As such, it is a potent symbol that can endow a landscape painting with the intellectual depth and emotional charge that are traditionally the province of historical subjects. In the first half of the nineteenth century, wracked by revolution and war in Europe, and increasingly troubled by contentious issues of slavery in the United States, paintings of twilight evoked associations with the failure of the Enlightenment, the threat of barbarism, and preoccupation with death.

For Caspar David Friedrich, Germany's greatest Romantic artist, twilight marked the ending of life's voyage, symbolized by the small sailing ship heading for land in *Cross on the Baltic Sea*. The cross is both a marker for the harbor and a consoling reminder of Christ's sacrifice; the anchor represents the promise of redemption. The full moon is a symbol of Christ himself, lighting the traveler's way to final peace and safety. Friedrich repeated this composition with variations several times, using one version to memorialize the death of a friend. The symbols appear frequently in different combinations and arrangements in many other Friedrich landscapes. The starkness of this scene, with "no church, no tree, no plants, no blade of grass," means that much of its emotional impact derives from the delicately lit sky, whose fading, greying colors suggest the fading of life.[1]

Friedrich's work is often compared to that of Frederic Edwin Church, the American master of symbolic landscape. A generation younger than Friedrich, Church united a grand vision of the vast American wilderness with grandiloquent light symbolism. However, the elements of his landscapes are not linked to specific Christian concepts, thus opening them up to any kind of religious, moral, political or personal interpretations. In *Twilight*, the Vermont countryside and its tiny cottage are overwhelmed by a sunset of intense drama. The contrast between flaming sunset and the tiny cottage lights stimulate meditations upon human insignificance in the face of nature, and the feebleness of human efforts to emulate the works of God. In 1850, Church titled this work *Twilight, "Short arbiter 'twixt day and night."* The quotation comes from Milton's *Paradise Lost* describing Satan's return to the Garden of Eden and suggests that this is, above all, a moral landscape.[2] In the light of the Miltonic reference, we may interpret the illuminated cottage as a symbol of humanity's effort to keep a light burning even as clouds of darkness blot out the sun.

Caspar David Friedrich, *The Cross on the Baltic Sea*, 1815, Stiftung Preussische Schlösser und Gärten Berlin-Brandenburg, Potsdam (Schloss Charlottenburg, Berlin)

1 Caspar David Friedrich, quoted in Werner Hofmann (ed.), *Caspar David Friedrich 1774-1840*, exh. cat., Hamburg (Hamburger Kunsthalle) 1974, p. 200.
2 Franklin Kelly, *Frederic Edwin Church*, exh. cat. Washington, D.C. (National Gallery of Art) 1989, p. 43.

Frederic Edwin Church, *Twilight,*
"Short arbiter 'twixt day and night,"
1850, The Newark Museum,
Wallace M. Scudder Bequest Fund

Drawing in the dark

As gas street lamps were installed in cities throughout Europe and the United States, artists could, for the first time, work *en plein air* – outdoors – at night. And, for the first time, they had interesting things to draw, as increasing numbers of people took to streets that were becoming safer and easier to navigate. Adolph Menzel's continuous interest in contemporary night life and artificial light supports his reputation as a modernist painter in spite of the traditionalism of his methods.

Departure after the Party describes the new visual effects and night life engendered by gaslighting. The final moments of an evening party at Menzel's house spill out onto the pavement. The artist Paul Meyerheim was there and later described Menzel ordering the departing guests to stand still while he sketched frantically under a lamppost. The cab-driver charged extra for his wait. Menzel drew him twice, catching his bent stance, strong profile and rumpled blanket. Significantly, the drawing of the cabdriver differs in finish and emphasis from a study of the cloaked woman on the right that was probably executed in the studio in daylight. The brighter, more even natural light created rich, subtle patterns of shadow in the cloak, and Menzel had the time to capture their complexity.

When it came to composing the finished painting, Menzel had to combine these and other studies made under different lighting conditions into a unified and believable whole. He achieves coherence with a frieze-like arrangement of figures illuminated from above by a single powerful source. Light and dark divide the compositon into two parts. Menzel enhanced the distinction between lit and shadowed areas by working in gouache, a luminous medium, in the bright spaces. Gum arabic adds depth and translucency to the shadows. On the left, gaslight falls directly on the embracing women, the sleeping child, and dignified matron – who provide anecdotal information about the nature of the party. On the right, dappled shadows conceal the cab driver and some departing guests. They also mask the differences between figures that are so obvious in the preliminary drawings.

Adolph Menzel, *Departure after the Party*, 1860, Carnegie Museum of Art, Pittsburgh, Heinz Family Acquisition Fund

Adolph Menzel, *Two studies, man with a plaid blanket*, 1860, pencil on paper, Staatliche Museen zu Berlin, Preussischer Kulturbesitz, Kupferstichkabinett

This is a preliminary study, sketched on the street, for the figure of the cab driver in the shadows slightly to the right of center in *Departure after the Party*. The *x* in the left margin indicates the pose chosen for the final work.

Adolph Menzel, *Woman in a Cloak and Headshawl*, ca. 1860, pencil on paper, Staatliche Museen zu Berlin, Preussischer Kulturbesitz, Kupferstichkabinett

This carefully finished, detailed drawing is brightly lit and was probably executed in the studio. Menzel used it for the figure of the female pedestrian on the far right of *Departure after the Party*.

141 **Drawing in the dark**

Deceptive daylight

Ford Madox Brown, *The Pretty Baa Lambs*, 1851-59, Birmingham City Museums and Art Gallery

Plein-air painting could be hazardous. While working on *The Pretty Baa-Lambs* in the hot sun, Ford Madox Brown twice came down with fevers, then the sheep ate the flowers in his garden. Moreover, his lay-figure in its elaborate costume had to be hauled in and out every day in case of rain. When the painting was exhibited at the Royal Academy in 1852, there were more difficulties. "Hung in a false light, and viewed through the medium of extraneous ideas, the painting was, I think, much misunderstood," the artist wrote in 1865. "I was told that it was impossible to make out what meaning I had in the picture. At the present moment, few people I trust will seek for any meaning beyond the obvious one, that is – a lady, a baby, two lambs, a servant maid, and some grass [...]. This picture was painted out in the sunlight; the only intention being to render that effect as well as my powers in a first attempt of this kind would allow."[1]

Brown's "first attempt" seems to be the earliest nineteenth-century exhibition picture (as opposed to a preliminary sketch or casual study) painted almost entirely in the outdoors. It is also unusually early for a "subjectless" picture – one with the purpose of representing a visual effect rather than telling a story. With this work, Brown was deliberately breaking with established British art, characterized by narrative subject matter, painterly brushwork, and highly artificial studio lighting and coloring. In order to achieve the sense of sunlight and heat (his alternative title for this work was "Summer Heat"), the artist adopted the new painting methods of the Pre-Raphaelite Brotherhood. Avoiding shadows and shading, he painted in brilliant, thin colors directly onto an extremely smooth canvas primed with white. Light falling on the surface of the painting penetrates the thin layers of pigment and reflects from the polished white ground back to the viewer. In this way, the viewer gets a

1 Kenneth Bendiner, *The Art of Ford Madox Brown*, University Park, Pennsylvania 1998, p. 135.
2 Ralph E. Shikes and Paula Harper, *Pissarro: His Life and Work*, New York 1980, p. 130.

more intense experience of light and color – the sunlight effect that the artist wished to suggest.

When the young, radical French artists known today as the impressionists broke with French aesthetic traditions in the 1860s, they too sought the light of the outdoors. Looking for new subjects, the landscape painters concentrated increasingly on light effects, including the challenging problem of bright sunlight. Camille Pissarro's *The Crossroads, Pontoise*, painted in 1872, tackles the problem head on. He depicts a grassy square on a bright, shadowless day – at which point similarities with his Pre-Raphaelite precursor end. Pissarro's canvas is unified and tempered by an even, greyish tonality that is the opposite of Brown's glaring hues. Even more distinctive is the French painting's lack of detail. Pissarro's plot of grass in the foreground is roughly but

convincingly described with broad strokes of green paint; not for him the meticulous drawing of the lawn blade by blade. Like his impressionist colleagues, he believed that bright sunlight flattened detail and diminished color. "There is nothing more cold than the sun at its height in the summer, contrary to what the colorists believe," he wrote to Theodore Duret.[2]

Why did these radical young artists, working with similar goals in similar lighting conditions, paint similar subjects so differently? Why did Brown see more, and more intensely, while Pissarro saw less? Did light behave differently in Britain's notoriously humid atmosphere, as compared to France's drier one? Or did each artist go out into the sunshine expecting to see things differently from certain artists of the past – and consequently each found a different version of the truth?

Camille Pissarro, *The Crossroads, Pontoise*, 1872, Carnegie Museum of Art, Pittsburgh, Acquired through the generosity of the Sarah Mellon Scaife family

Sentimental light

Bierstadt based *Sunlight and Shadow* on an oil study made in Kassel, Germany, in 1855. The study is a dramatic and lively rendition of the play of light and shade on the stone façade of the Gothic Revival Löwenburg chapel, constructed about fifty years earlier. Bierstadt follows Valenciennes in his use of light and shade to model architectural form, but his enjoyment in the irregular tree shadows betrays a romantic love of the ephemeral and unpredictable. The final composition replicates the study's vibrant lighting with great fidelity.

Sunlight and Shadow was the hit of the 1862 National Academy exhibition in New York. As Charles Lanman wrote to the artist soon after seeing it, "The effect of sunlight is truly wonderful, and the pretty girl at the exhibition's door told me this picture attracted more attention and comment than any other on the walls. In my opinion, old fellow, you are bound to lead the brotherhood of American Landscape." The critics praised Bierstadt's lighting effects unanimously: "[...] an effect of sunshine upon the stone wall and balustrade of an old church, and is more perfectly painted than any sunshine we ever saw. [...] the management of the lights and shades in this picture is remarkable."[1]

Yet, however naturalistic the light effects might appear, the critics interpreted them morally and symbolically. One identified the woman seated in the shade as an ill and poverty-stricken embodiment of "shadow;" another envisioned the light as a "benediction." Such sentimental readings were extremely popular in mid-nineteenth-century America in all the art forms. American sentimental novels, for example, frequently bore titles that featured moralistic contrasts similar to Bierstadt's *Sunlight and Shadow*: e.g., *The Lofty and Lowly, Here and Hereafter, Spending or Saving, Blond or Brunette*, and *Tempest and Sunshine*.[2] Read in this context, Bierstadt's title invites us to think morally, sentimentally, and symbolically about light, time, transience, God, and nature.

1 Quoted after Nancy K. Anderson and Linda S. Ferber, *Albert Bierstadt: Art & Enterprise*, exh. cat. New York (The Brooklyn Museum) 1990, p. 166; Katharina and Gerhard Bott, *Vice Versa: Deutsche Maler in Amerika, Amerikanische Maler in Deutschland 1813-1913*, exh. cat. Berlin (Deutsches Historisches Museum) 1996, p. 286.

2 Mary Jane Holmes, *Tempest and Sunshine*, and Maria Susanna Cummins, *The Lamplighter*, ed. Donald A. Koch, New York 1968, p. IX.

Albert Bierstadt, *Sunlight and Shadow*, 1862, Fine Arts Museums of San Francisco, Gift of Mr. and Mrs. John D. Rockefeller 3rd

145 **Sentimental light**

Cosmological controversies

By the mid-nineteenth century, scientists had constructed an account of the origins of the universe completely different from the first days of the Creation described in the Book of Genesis. Light played a fundamental role in each account.

The scientific account, based on observations by telescope and other instruments, described a universe whose dimensions could be measured in light years, containing many millions of stars, and of which the earth was an insignificant and probably not unique particle. The universe was formed over many hundreds of thousands of years from clouds of nebulous, luminous gasses that gradually coalesced into stars and planets in conformity with the laws of gravity and thermodynamics. God was not necessary to the process.

The credibility of this system depended upon the accuracy of the measuring instruments and the sophistication of the mathematics used to interpret and relate the measurements. The great obstacle to public acceptance of these ideas consisted in the abstractness of the mathematics, the incomprehensible scale of the times and distances involved, and the incredibly trivial status of humanity in the new scheme of things. Few non-specialists saw or understood the instruments and experiments that underpinned the concept despite the lectures and publications of science popularizers.

The biblical version of the creation describes a universe composed of the earth and a surrounding watery heaven studded with sun, moon, and stars. All were created by God over a span of six days about 4,000 years before the birth of Christ. The continued acceptance of this view well into the era of modern astronomy has depended upon the emotional power of the biblical text, the dogmatic teachings of the church, and the human centeredness and human scale of the story. It

seems to explain the behavior of sun, moon, and stars as seen by an earthbound observer's unaided eye.

The problems with the biblical version become apparent in Gustave Doré's attempt to depict The Creation of Light for a superbly illustrated edition of the Bible, published in 1865-66. Doré's challenge was to provide convincing, realistic images for a text whose scientific and historical accuracy was in question. The splendid burst of light in his print cap-

tures the grandeur of the text, "And God said, 'Let there be light,' and there was light." (Genesis 1:3) Doré represents the watery heavens cleverly with a magnificent cloudscape, such as one would expect to see in nature at dawn, or at the end of a storm. However, the clouds float above – and dwarf – the darkened globe or void representing the earth, a bewildering mismatch in scale. But the biggest difficulty occurred over God's role in the process. The first French editions of 1866

include God the Father raising his arm in the midst of the flash of light, a straightforward rendition of the text. Yet, in the first English edition, with illustrations modified by the publisher for his Protestant, scientifically advanced readers, God vanishes. He also disappears – camouflaged as a cloud – from the 1874 German/Hebrew edition. In the latter case, the publisher was most likely responding to Jewish law, prohibiting the portrayal of God.

Héliodore-Joseph Pisan after Gustave Doré, *The Creation of Light*, ca. 1865, wood engraving, plate 1 from *La Sainte Bible*, Tours 1866, from the first English edition of 1867, and from the 1874 German edition, Dan Malan, Saint Louis

"Flash, Ye Cities, in Rivers of Fire!"

London did "flash" in celebration of the arrival in England of Princess Alexandra of Denmark on the night of March 7, 1863, and again, three days later, on her marriage to Albert Edward, Prince of Wales. Commentators remarked on the splendid illuminations and immense crowds packed in every square foot of open space along the procession routes on both days. England's poet laureate, Alfred, Lord Tennyson, described the festivities of the night of March 7 in his welcoming tribute addressed to the "sea-king's daughter." The poem evokes the glowing, teeming streets of London with the dramatic phrase, "Flash, ye cities, in rivers of fire!"[1] Its imagery suggests not only the fireworks displays of the Baroque era, but also the volcanic energy of the gas-lit Victorian city and its perilous similarity to the flaming streets of Satan's Pandemonium. The Pre-Raphaelite painter William Holman Hunt witnessed the glory and chaos three days later. "On the night of the marriage of the prince and princess of Wales, I went to the City to see the decorations of the streets through which the royal party had passed. The display made many edifices, by daylight dingy with city smoke, fairylike and gorgeous. Temple Bar was enlivened by hangings of gold and silver tissue [...] and the whole was illuminated by an effulgence of light."[2] Always interested in unusual light effects, Hunt drew some pencil sketches that night and returned a few days later to make color studies. He also read Tennyson's poem, for he refers to it in an early title for this painting – *The Sea-King's Peaceful Triumph on London Bridge, 10th of March 1863*. His painting is lit entirely by the "effulgence of light" generated by the bridge's impressive gas lamps and the incense braziers erected for the occasion. London's thick, smoky atmosphere diffuses the reddish glow, which overwhelms the pale moonlight at upper left. *London Bridge* can appropriately be considered a visual rendition of Tennyson's "river of fire." In London at least, gaslighting was transforming the traditional, torch-lit royal procession and courtly firework display into a modern democratic brawl.

1 Alfred, Lord Tennyson, *The Poems*, ed. Christopher Ricks, 2nd ed. London 1987, vol. 2, no. 331, pp. 649-50.
2 Hunt 1905, vol. 2, p. 24.

William Holman Hunt, *London Bridge on the Night of the Marriage of the Prince and Princess of Wales*, 1863–66, Visitors of the Ashmolean Museum, Oxford

Light in the museum

The illumination of museums' holdings was not only a technical challenge but arose out of the spirit of the Enlightenment. More light was to shine *on* the paintings so that, metaphorically speaking, more light could shine *out* of them. Yet museum visitors have always complained about the quality of the lighting. Even the move from installing galleries in places where they were not originally intended, to creating special buildings to house the collections – beginning in the second half of the eighteenth century – did nothing to solve the lighting problem. It appeared that no matter how carefully you planned the architecture, the glazing, and the artificial lights, in reality, the behavior of the light led to disappointment. One can only speculate about the reasons: perhaps the progress in architecture could not keep pace with the progress in artificial lighting, and thus with the expectations of the public.

Taking the ideal illumination of the studio as their starting point, early museum founders recommended an even, northerly daylight. In the course of the nineteenth century, the debate began to focus on the advantages and disadvantages of lighting works of art from above or from the side. New technology found its way quickly, although sporadically, into the museum. In 1817, the Great Room at the Royal Academy in Somerset House was equipped with gaslight. However, it was evident to con-

temporaries that gas was in no way a cure-all. Apart from the difficulty of installing it, there were also obvious drawbacks, such as the smell and the danger of fire. Still more important in this context was that many viewers found the color of the flame itself to have a negative impact on the works, one that appeared to contradict the painters' intentions. None other than the important English physicist Michael Faraday dealt the deathblow to gaslight in museums when he concluded that it was damaging the pictures in London's National Gallery. The Royal Academy, too, ended its trials with evening openings by gaslight when it became apparent that the paintings were becoming blackened by soot. Consequently, museums made use of artificial light only occasionally until late in the nineteenth century. Picture galleries remained almost entirely dependent on daylight.

Only the introduction of electricity brought about a radical change. This time it was the South Kensington Museum in London – today the Victoria and Albert Museum – that played the leading role. In 1881 arc lamps were installed in the gallery designed to house Raphael's cartoons. (At that time no one was aware that it is not only the type of light but also the amount that damages works of art.) Although one may be tempted to mock the experiments of the nineteenth century, this would be more than a little unfair: even today, complaints about the poor lighting in museums can be heard all over the world.

Roger Fenton, *At the British Museum*, 1860s, albumen print, The Royal Photographic Society, Bath

1 Jeroen Boomgaard, "'Hangt mij op een sterk licht'. Rembrandts licht en de plaatsing van de Nachtwacht in het Rijksmuseum," *Nederlands Kunsthistorisch Jaarboek* 35 (1984), pp. 327-49; compare Compton 1992, pp. 41-43; Perkowitz 1996, p. 98; H. Lank 1992.

Diagrams of daylit galleries, engravings from Eduard Magnus, Über Einrichtung und Beleuchtung von Räumen zur Aufstellung von Gemälden und Sculpturen (On the Installation and Illumination of Rooms for Paintings and Sculptures), Berlin 1864, Rijksmuseum, Amsterdam

In 1864, the German painter Eduard Magnus pointed out that museum architecture was still in its infancy. Much experience had been gained in the previous decades, he claimed, but the problem of illuminating the galleries was still being approached at random. The time had come "for ignorance and volition to be replaced by real knowledge." In what follows, Magnus discusses the placement and size of windows – in fact, daylight is the only kind of lighting he mentions. He felt that illumination from the side was better than from above. Being a curator himself, he then suggested that one-to-one models be built of all the galleries to be installed – a method still recommended today. Another of Magnus's dictums has also withstood the test of time: "You can see that we are forced to maneuver between a variety of evils, whereby aesthetic considerations and good taste should always be given priority."

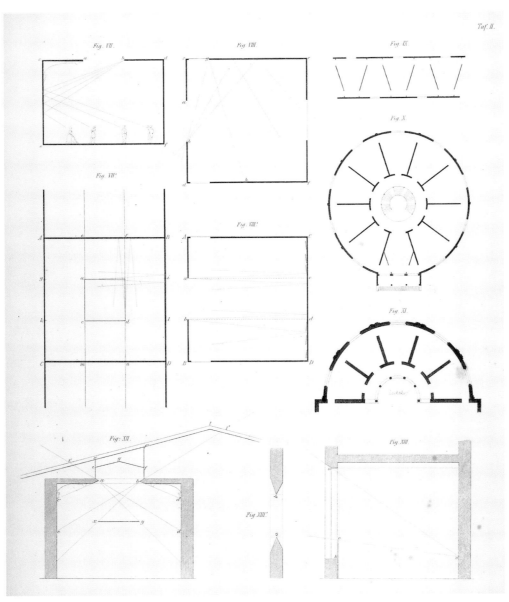

J. Bouman, *The New Extension of the Rijksmuseum, built to accommodate Rembrandt's "Night Watch"*, after 1902, glass slide, Private collection

Occasionally, the proper lighting of a work of art could become a matter of national interest. General dissatisfaction with the presentation of Rembrandt's *Night Watch* in Amsterdam's Rijksmuseum led to the constitution of an official committee. It concluded its report: "On the basis of our extensive research and discussions, the committee has come to the conclusion – one shared by the overwhelming majority of its members – that the best illumination for Rembrandt's *Night Watch* would be a southwesterly lighting from the side [...]."[1]

A closer look at the moon

With the introduction of improved lenses and mirrors, the telescope had been continuously refined since the time of Galileo. Until far into the nineteenth century, however, new discoveries continued to be recorded and disseminated through the traditional means of drawing and engraving. With the invention of photography, scientists hoped they now had a more reliable, and thus more useful, reproductive technique at their disposal. The origins of photography were, in fact, directly linked to astronomy. John Herschel, an astronomer like his famous father, worked closely with William Henry Fox Talbot, and Talbot's first glass-plate photograph, dated 1839, depicts Herschel's renowned forty-foot telescope.

The early days of astronomic photography were, however, characterized by difficulties and disappointment. Being non-reproducible and only visible under certain lighting conditions, daguerreotypes were completely inadequate. The long exposure times still necessary in these decades were even more frustrating, and initially prevented photography from serving a useful purpose in the exploration of the sky. After all, stars and planets could not be made to stand still for the time it took to fix their image on the sensitized plate. Stars were recorded as lines, and the moon transformed into an unfocused oval disk. As in the eighteenth century, scientists sought to resolve

these problems, caused by the motions of the celestial bodies, with the help of clockwork. At that time, heliostats had been used to guarantee that the light reflecting off the microscope mirror was constant. Now, clockworks were to help steer the telescope along the path of the star to be photographed. These were not, however, precise enough to achieve a truly sharp image, and so, even twenty years after its invention, photography remained peripheral to this important branch of science.[1] It was Lewis Morris Rutherfurd (he built an observatory in Manhattan with his own money in 1856), who, after years of struggle, finally managed to capture the heavens in detail and in focus in 1865.

Despite improvements in technology, observers in the nineteenth century were confronted with a problem their eighteenth century predecessors had not known. Air pollution forced the photographer Warren de la Rue to leave London in 1856 and set up his studio in the countryside.[2] The increase in street lighting, too, began to interfere with a clear view of the night sky. To this day, astronomers continue to conduct campaigns to make the night truly dark once again, but with little success. It is, therefore, no accident that both astronomers and artists left the cities at the same time in order to escape air and light pollution, and recapture the natural light of both the day and the night.

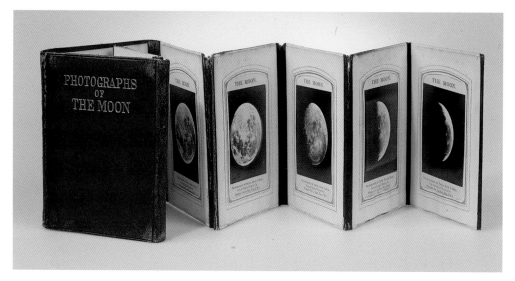

Warren de la Rue, *The Moon*, ca. 1860, album with 12 albumen prints, Rijksmuseum, Rijksprentenkabinet, Amsterdam

1 Rooseboom 1994, pp. 264-66.
2 Ibid., p. 271.

153 **A closer look at the moon**

In the harsh light of naturalism

Degas's famous, deeply troubling masterpiece is built around the light and symbolic values of the lamp and the hearth. Degas called it "my genre painting," thus connecting it to the intimate family interiors of Menzel, Whistler, Bonvin, and other realist and naturalist artists of the mid-nineteenth century. Like Menzel's *Living Room with the Sister of the Artist* (p. 133), it contains the work table, firelight, oil lamp, sewing materials, and warm shadowed spaces that nineteenth-century viewers associated with domestic comfort, virtue, and intimacy. The warmth and light of the hearth was and still is a symbol of home; the carefully tended lamp has represented female virtue ever since the biblical parable of the Wise and Foolish Virgins. As new lamps and fuels improved the brightness and quality of available light, they were becoming increasingly important as centers of the family circle. Indeed, in the nineteenth century, the image of the family group clustered around the glowing lamp had come to represent domestic happiness in general, as exemplified in the frontispiece to Catharine Beecher and Harriet Beecher Stowe's uplifting manual, *The American Woman's Home*. In *Interior*, Degas defied the sentimental domestic themes associated with such conventional light symbolism. His protagonists, a despairing woman and an angrily withdrawn man, may be two of the unhappiest people ever depicted in art. To the nineteenth-century viewer, they appeared at odds with each other and with their environment.

Degas's interest in light effects and light's meanings is also characteristic of the work of the novelist Emile Zola, the painter's contemporary and a champion of impressionist art. Both Degas and Zola considered themselves to be "naturalists," observers and recorders of contemporary urban life in all its gritty reality. For them and their audiences, the new and different forms of artificial light coming in to use provided startling visual effects with unmistakable moral connotations. Today, we can still appreciate the splendor and naturalism of the effects, but we have lost the knowledge that provides the moral insights they took for granted. The connotations were connected to the lights' settings and functions. The oil lamp was a precious domestic possession and symbolized family intimacy, as in this painting and the Zola novel *Therese Raquin* (which may have inspired Degas). Elsewhere, the naturalists contrasted lamplight with the gas and electric lighting used in public spaces, theatres, and street lamps – in both Zola's and Degas's work these are linked with commerce, prostitution and vice.

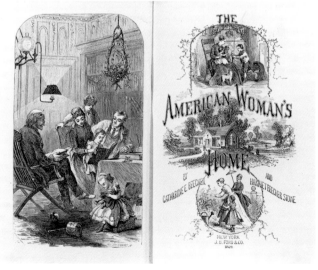

Title page of Catharine E. Beecher and Harriet Beecher Stowe, *The American Woman's Home: or, Principles of Domestic Science; Being a Guide to the Formation and Maintenance of Economical, Healthful, Beautiful, and Christian Homes*, New York 1869, Carnegie Museum of Art, Pittsburgh, Curatorial Library

Sisters and social reformers, the Beechers sought to elevate housekeeping to the status of a learned profession. The frontispiece illustrates the manner in which a gas wall fixture could be modified to serve in lieu of the traditional table lamp.

Edgar Degas, *Interior*, 1868–69,
Philadelphia Museum of Art, The
Henry P. McIlhenny Collection in
memory of Frances P. McIlhenny

Light and public order

During the French Revolution of 1789, mobs destroyed the lanterns installed under the *ancien régime*. In the nineteenth century, the city streets became the most important stage for political protest whenever courts and parliaments were unable to find a solution to the problems arising from the extraordinary pace of economic and social change. Demonstrations, riots and barricades were characteristic of the European revolutions of 1830 and 1848. In Paris, the government sought to prevent such activities by constructing wide boulevards, making it difficult for the rebelling populace to block them off. The changes wrought on the Parisian cityscape by Baron Haussmann, however, also had other purposes. The broad avenues brought light and air into the city, more room was created for traffic, and the expanding population was provided with new and cleaner housing. The boulevards also made it easier for gas lamps to be more efficiently linked to a network. These lanterns transformed the streets into promenades, which in turn led to a whole new culture of night life.

Edouard Manet is generally considered the chronicler of Haussmann's Paris. Like his impressionist colleagues, he made the street his major subject. In 1871, as the German army was approaching the French capital, Manet, like many others, came to witness the end of progress in an era of peace. He captured the days of the Commune, and particularly its defeat, in a series of lithographs that were published only after his death. Here, in *The Barricade*, we see the rebels shot by a firing squad. The street lamp plays the role of mute spectator to these events. Not coincidentally, it is placed exactly at the vanishing point. It is a symbol of modernity and enlightenment, of the rule of law and humanity – principles which here fell victim to willful despotism.

Auguste Gérardin after Manuel Orazi, *Riots in Rome – Pillaging of Shops by the Unemployed*, wood engraving from *Le Monde Illustré* (23 February 1889), Van Gogh Museum, Amsterdam

Precisely one hundred years after street lanterns had become a target for the French revolutionaries, they again fell victim to the destructive energy of an angry mob. The burst glass casing allows a rare glimpse of the fuel supply opening.

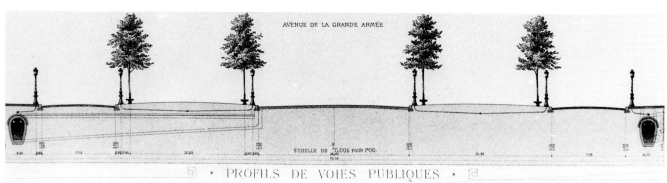

Cross-section of a boulevard, wood engraving from Adolphe Alphand, *Les Promenades de Paris*, Paris 1867–73, vol. 2, Universiteitsbibliotheek Amsterdam

The director of Public Works in Paris presents the city's new streets and roads in loving technical detail in this large and elaborately illustrated two-volume work. This cross-section illustrates all the various facilities found beneath the pavement.

Edouard Manet, *The Barricade*,
1871, lithograph, Van Gogh
Museum, Amsterdam (Vincent
van Gogh Foundation)

Electric light

Despite the introduction of gaslight, there were a number of visionaries who predicted the advent of a still-newer technology in the near future: electric lighting. Even in the eighteenth century, it had been possible to produce short-lived flashes of light using live carbon electrodes. In the first instance, these were (and were to remain for some time to come) "philosophical fireworks" – scientific experiments of the most entertaining sort.[1] Once again, it was the light-thirsty entertainment industry that was responsible for putting the new light source to practical use: the arc lamp was used to increase the intensity of the magic lantern, formerly powered by the much weaker Argand lamp.

One of the first to employ electric light for projection was the ingenious and multi-talented instrument maker Jules Duboscq in 1839.[2] The theater, too, soon exploited the almost immeasurable luminosity of the arc lamp. Initially, it was employed only to produce special effects, since the technology was not yet advanced enough to be used for permanent illumination.[3] The light itself was perceived as volatile, and it had an unpleasant bluish-white color. In the appendix to his 1849 treatise *Gas-lighting: Its Progress and its Prospects*, John Rutter wrote: "As

a philosophical experiment, and especially when seen for the first time, the electric-light is as startling as it is beautiful. Those who have never witnessed its effects are unable to form any correct opinion on the subject. Its intense brilliancy, and the consequent depth, or rather darkness of the shadows, surpasses all the ordinary phenomena of artificial illumination. For a moment, the observer seems to be deprived of the power of vision. To look *at* the light, excepting from a distance, is extremely painful, and to be *in* it, produces sensations which, at first, are anything but agreeable."[4]

Thirty years later a real breakthrough still seemed a long way off. In 1878, the mayor of a small town asked Werner von Siemens if he should build a new gasworks or install electricity. The engineer replied that he should simply go ahead with his plans and not be disconcerted by the inventor's recently developed electric dynamo, which was still too big and heavy to be easily moved around.[5] This, however, changed rapidly, and soon better generators helped solve the problem of local energy supply. Arc lamps could then be used on board ships, in factories, for work in agriculture, and in circus tents. Still, a network like that already used by the gas industry was a long way off.

L. Sautter, Lemonnier & Cie., *Arc lamp*, ca. 1882, EnergeticA, Museum voor Energietechniek, Amsterdam

As contemporaries noted, the light from an arc lamp is so brilliant that it can only be regarded for long periods of time from a certain distance. There was no question of it being used in domestic settings.

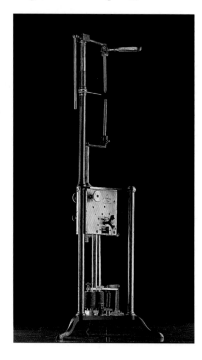

Jules Duboscq, *Arc lamp*, 1852, Teylers Museum, Haarlem

L. Sautter, Lemonnier & Cie., *Gramme generator*, ca. 1882, EnergeticA, Museum voor Energietechniek, Amsterdam

The Belgian engineer Zénobe-Théophile Gramme developed the first commercially viable electrical supplier.

1 Altick 1978, p. 363.
2 Hankins and Silverman 1995, p. 65.
3 Bergman 1977, pp. 277-78.
4 Rutter 1849, pp. 61-62, 277-78.
5 Rebske 1962, p. 183.

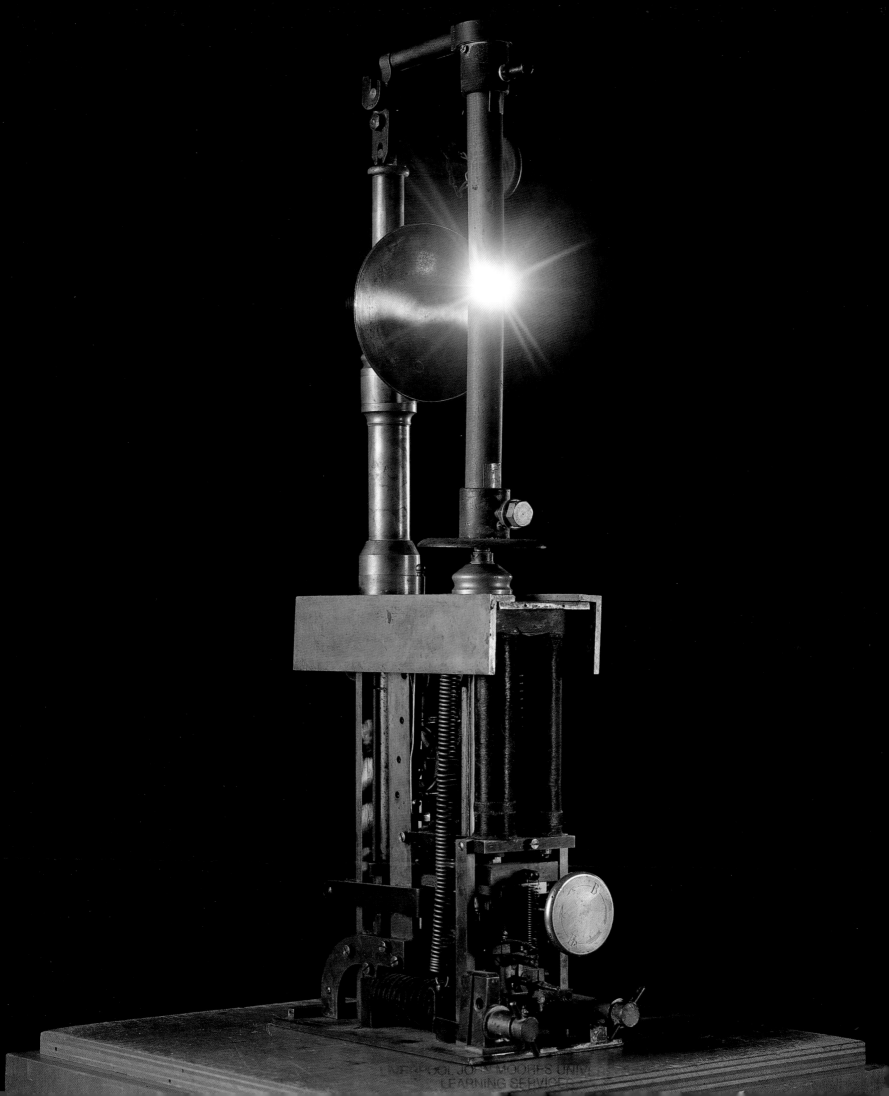

Right shadows, wrong light

Coming upon this painting unprepared, the viewer probably needs some time before he or she deciphers the scene in all its detail. The title indicates that it depicts the view from Golgotha, and in the background we can indeed make out the famous silhouette of Jerusalem. A group of Roman soldiers is shown moving towards the city; several appear to be looking back at something, or someone, located just beyond the picture frame. The three shadows on the sandy hill tell us exactly what they see: Christ on his cross, flanked by the two thieves. Gérôme thus succeeds in recounting one of the best-known stories in the world in a completely new and subtle way. He treats the death of the Saviour as a historical episode like any other, no different from the events of the present. Contemporaries were shocked by the seeming banality of the scene in which the heroism and suffering of Jesus are invisible.

Recent art-historical analyses have focused on the contradiction between the painting's almost photographic realism and its extraordinary dramaturgy.[1] The complicated lighting in the work, however, deserves closer attention.

The Bible describes the atmospheric conditions at the time of Christ's death as follows: "And it was about the sixth hour, and there was a darkness over all the earth until the ninth hour. And the sun was darkened and the veil of the temple was rent in the midst" (Luke 23:44-45). In the painting, the landscape is cast into shadow by a large black cloud approaching from the right. The effect is similar to that of a total eclipse – the experience of which may even explain the biblical description itself. But then the question arises: what is giving off the light that is coming from behind the crucified figures and casting the shadows? Something is definitely amiss here, from both a scientific and a biblical point of view. However, one should not adopt this suspicious point of view, even if Gérôme's fine technique, richness of detail and (presumed) topographical accuracy, invite us to do so. The lighting does nothing more than *suggest* a realistic depiction of an extraordinary event. Since the artist's literary source, the Gospels, leaves much to speculation concerning the cause of the miraculous darkness, Gérôme's artistic license is certainly justified.

John Martin, *The Creation of Light*, 1825/1831, etching, aquatint, mezzotint, Hamburger Kunsthalle, Kupferstichkabinett

1 Fred Leeman, "Shadows over Jean-Léon Gérôme's career," *Van Gogh Museum Journal* (1997-98), pp. 88-99.

Jean-Léon Gérôme, *Golgotha*,
ca. 1868, Van Gogh Museum,
Amsterdam

The bull's eye

The first and greatest tour of hell was described by the Renaissance poet Dante in his imaginative masterpiece, *The Inferno*. Dante's nineteenth-century imitators, artists and writers alike, had only to go across town to find modern nightmares that frequently surpassed what they imagined to be hell's most impressive horrors. Dickens wrote of his wanderings around London's gas-lit streets in *Sketches by Boz* (1839) and started the grotesque fashion of urban underworld tourism. He found a certain glamour and beauty in the night: "But the streets of London, to be beheld in the very height of their glory, should be seen on a dark, dull, murky winter's night, when there is just enough damp gently stealing down to make the pavement greasy, without cleansing it of any of its impurities; and when the heavy lazy mist, which hangs over every object, makes the gas-lamps look brighter, and the brilliantly-lighted shops more splendid, from the contrast they present to the darkness all around."[1]

Dickens went into that darkness, to be followed by social reformers, artists, writers, and gawkers, accompanied by policemen who served as guides and protectors. The practice inspired publication of some sensational pocket guides, beginning with George Foster's *New York by Gas-Light* (1850): "What a task we have undertaken! To penetrate beneath the thick veil of night and lay bare the fearful mysteries of darkness in the metropolis – the festivities of prostitution, the orgies of pauperism, the haunts of theft and murder, the scenes of drunkenness and beastly debauch, and all the sad realities that go to make up the lower stratum – the under-ground story – of life in New York!"[2] Similar guides to London, Paris, and Berlin appeared soon thereafter.

The Bull's Eye represents a grim moment on one such tour of London's Whitechapel district, undertaken by the English writer Blanchard Jerrold and the French artist Gustave Doré in 1869: "From low house to low house we go, picking up some fresh scrap of the history of Poverty and Crime – they must go hand in hand hereabouts – at every turn. At dark corners, lurking men keep close to the wall; and the police smile when we wonder what would become of a lonely wanderer who should find himself in these regions unprotected."[3] The bull's eye of the print's title is actually the name of the oil lamp carried by the policeman. The name derives from the thick, rounded glass lens that magnifies the light and resembles a single, cyclopean eye. In the hands of the police, it was a symbol of power and surveillance.

Héliodore-Joseph Pisan after Gustave Doré, *The Bull's Eye*, from Blanchard Jerrold and Gustave Doré, *London, a Pilgrimage*, London 1872, Van Gogh Museum, Amsterdam

1 Charles Dickens, *Sketches by Boz Illustrative of Every-Day Life and Every-Day People* (1839), London 1991, p. 66.
2 Foster 1850, p. 69.
3 Blanchard Jerrold and Gustave Doré, *London, a Pilgrimage*, London 1872, p. 146.

Bull's eye lantern, American, ca. 1850–75, Carnegie Museum of Natural History, Pittsburgh, George and Lilian Ball Memorial Fund

This lantern was also known as a dark lantern. A sliding metal shutter allowed the user to cut off the light without extinguishing the lamp inside.

Traditional perspective, avant-garde style

In 1882, Vincent van Gogh set out to teach himself to paint. As his vision expanded beyond figure studies to the landscape as a whole, he designed and had made the perspective screen illustrated in this drawing. It consists of an adjustable wooden framework strung with wires to form a grid or, as in Van Gogh's drawing, a one-point perspective scheme. Van Gogh described setting the frame up in his bedroom window in order to make a watercolor of the landscape beyond. "The peculiar effects of perspective intrigue me more than human intrigues," he concluded.[1]

It would seem that four years later, as he was learning new methods of impressionist and pointillist painting in Paris, he made use of the perspective screen again. Perhaps he wished to concentrate on the technical difficulties of new color systems and brushstrokes, instead of on making compositions. He may also have found that the constructed environment of the big city posed more difficult spatial problems than the flat and sparsely occupied Dutch landscape to which he was accustomed. *Vegetable Gardens and the Moulin de Blute-Fin on Montmartre* still shows the faint pencil lines of the perspective grid he laid down on the canvas for a guide. Its horizontal format corresponds to the proportions of the frame, while its neat vertical division (by the fence line, running up the center foreground) and horizontal counterpart (by the horizon line) match the disposition of the wire guidelines. The diagonals, marked on the left by

Van Gogh's signature and a division between two vegetable patches, and on the right by a line of wooden stakes, converge neatly on the small tree in the exact center of the canvas.

Artists had been using perspective frames since the sixteenth century, usually for subjects far more challenging than a windmill on a hill. It was especially helpful for dramatic foreshortenings of the human figure, for example. By the 1870s, however, the perspective frame, and the geometric perspective systems it supported, had been abandoned by most avant-garde painters from Whistler, to Monet, to Gauguin. New theories of light, color, and human perception had outmoded the linear systems of Newtonian physics and classical perspective. Van Gogh's continued reliance upon it betrays a certain provincial naiveté as well as a novice painter's lack of confidence. However, once he had discovered how to create sensations of light and space through color and brushwork, he too left academic perspective behind.

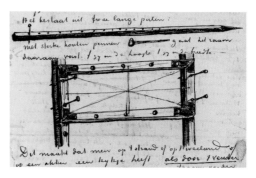

Vincent van Gogh, *Sketch of a perspective frame*, ink, from a letter to his brother Theo, 5 or 6 August 1882 (255/223), Van Gogh Museum, Amsterdam (Vincent van Gogh Foundation)

1 Letter to his brother Theo, 23 July 1882 (251/219).

Vincent van Gogh, *Vegetable Gardens and the Moulin de Blute-Fin on Montmartre*, 1886, Van Gogh Museum, Amsterdam (Vincent van Gogh Foundation)

LIVERPOOL JOHN MOORES UNIVERSITY
LEARNING SERVICES

Lighting the stage II

If discomfort is the mother of invention, then the theater was probably the most important catalyst for the development of new lighting technologies. In the eighteenth century, progressive theater designers looked to painting for inspiration. Francesco Algarotti, whom we have already encountered in connection with the dissemination of Newton's theories, asked if it might not be possible to create lighting effects on stage like those found in the paintings of Rembrandt, Giorgione or Titian.[1] It was still some time before lighting became an integral part of the staging, and even in the Romantic period, stage directions still contained no explicit references to the lighting.[2] In general, the tendency was towards a greater separation between the stage and auditorium; that is, more light on the actors, less on the audience. At Bayreuth in 1876, Richard Wagner decided on total darkness except on stage, much to the initial surprise of the spectators. However, a notice had warned them that it would not be possible to read the libretto during the performance.[3]

Gaslight proved more flexible than the usual oil lamps. Limelight, a type of gaslight, was invented in 1826, and was produced by heating lime to white heat with the help of a compressor. This light was strong enough to be directed. Actors could move freely about the stage, followed by a beam of light. The disadvantages of gas were not only the danger of fire – this was equally the case with oil lamps – but also the smell and heat, which were particularly troubling to spectators in the upper tiers. Electric light offered the solution.

The first theater to convert entirely to electricity seems to have been the California in San Francisco in 1879; two years later, the Savoy in London became the first in Europe.[4] Security and relatively maintenance-free light sources, and – in contrast to flickering gaslight – stability: these were the advantages of the new technology according to the experts.[5] What they forgot to mention, however, was that electricity has a different color spectrum than gas. At the Hoftheater in Vienna in 1883, for example, trials with the lighting revealed that the flats had to be repainted, as they looked entirely different under electric light. Set painters thus came to experience the same problems fine artists had been struggling with for some time.[6] The brilliancy, flexibility and stability of electricity finally allowed directors not only to realize numerous and various effects, but also to use the light itself to convey mood. In 1900, in his *Madame Butterfly*, David Belasco allowed his audience to experience the transition from night to day over a period of fourteen minutes.[7] After the turn of the century, pioneers, such as Adolphe Appia and Edward Gordon Craig, gave the profession of light designer artistic credentials and independence. In their productions light became the most important medium of expression.

The Sun, stage light effect with electric arc light, wood engraving from Georges Moynet, *L'Envers du théâtre*, Paris 1875, Theater Instituut Nederland, Amsterdam

Phantasmagory: arrangement of the plate-glass and position of the ghost, wood engraving from Amedée Guillemin, *La Lumière*, Paris 1882, Private collection

Making phantoms appear on stage was one of the most popular theatrical tricks since the early nineteenth century. The most famous of these illusions were conjured up by Etienne-Gaspard Robertson, whose "phantasmagories," created using mirrors, steam and projections, gave his audience a chilling thrill.

1 Francesco Algarotti, *Saggio sopra l'opera in musica*, ed. Annalisa Bini, Lucca 1989, p. 68.
2 Bergman 1977, pp. 234-35.
3 Ibid., p. 300; Rebske 1962, p. 82.
4 Bergman 1977, pp. 287-88.
5 Deutsche Edison Gesellschaft (ed.), *Elektrische Beleuchtung von Theatern mit Edison-Glühlicht*, Berlin 1884.
6 Rebske 1962, p. 141.
7 Bergman 1977, p. 306.
8 Jean Renoir, *Renoir, My Father*, trans. Randolph and Dorothy Weaver, London 1964, p. 170. Thanks to Fred Leeman.

Edgar Degas, *The Ballet of Robert le Diable*, 1871, The Metropolitan Museum of Art, New York, H. O. Havemeyer Collection, Bequest of Mrs. H. O. Havemeyer

Here Degas depicts the ballet of the ghosts of dead nuns from Meyerbeer's opera, which premiered in 1831. The nuns are lit only by footlights which contribute to the spooky atmosphere. The foreground is so shadowy that it is difficult to distinguish between the people in the front row and the members of the orchestra. And, due to the dim light, the man on the left would have had some difficulty picking out a person in the audience, even with the help of his binoculars. In reference to Richard Wagner's completely dark theater, Degas's colleague Renoir later complained that one no longer had the opportunity to admire a pretty woman among the spectators.[8]

Shadow plays

In every culture, shadows – humankind's dark, mysterious and eternal companion – provoke fear. Shadow plays, on the other hand, are a much-loved form of entertainment throughout the world. This is only apparently a contradiction: when controlled, shadows lose their frightening aspect.

A strong light source is necessary for the puppeteer to be able to tell his stories. In the pre-Industrial Age, a large candle was supposedly enough to illuminate the screen – at least according to the seventeenth-century Dutch painter and theoretician Samuel van Hoogstraten, who described a shadow play in 1678. In the wake of the improvements in lighting technology made at the end of the eighteenth century, the screen could be enlarged. François Dominique Séraphin created automated figures, giving his shadow theater a new dimension and casting his audience into a state of awe and fright. In London, the painter Philippe Jacques de Loutherbourg developed the so-called "Eidophusikon," an enormously popular theater designed for the sole purpose of light projections. Loutherbourg succeeded in "[synthesizing] the clockwork picture, the transparency, and one of the principles of the magic lantern and the Chinese shadows – the concentration of lighting in a confined space – into a new and memorable kind of show."[1]

One hundred years later, shadow plays had lost nothing of their attraction. Technically improved sources of light enabled the creation of all kinds of new effects, and the projections became more stable. So-called ombres chinoises were highly fashionable at the end of the nineteenth century and could be experienced at their best in the lively theater district on Montmartre. Here, the avant-garde enter-tained itself by pushing the genre to its limits, experimenting with increasingly novel projection methods that would soon lead to the invention of cinema. In 1890, Henri Rivière raised the shadow play to an art form in its own right. Dennis Cate has described his performance technique: "Essentially, Rivière created a system in which he placed silhouettes of figures, animals, elements of landscapes, and so forth, within a wooden framework at three distances from the screen: the closest created an absolutely black silhouette, and the next two created gradations of black to gray, thus suggesting recession into space. Silhouettes could be moved across the screens on runners within the frame. [...] Behind the three tiers of silhouettes were sliding structures supporting glass panels, which could be painted in a variety of transparent colors; and finally, at the rear of the work area was the oxyhydrogen flame, which served as the light source."[2] Only film was able to replace this ancient form of entertainment. In many ways, however, the essence of the medium lived on: from Murnau's *Nosferatu* (1921) to Carol Reed's *Third Man* (1949), it is the use of shadow that makes the viewer shiver.

Paul Eudel, *Les Ombres chinoises de mon père*, Paris 1885, Jane Voorhees Zimmerli Art Museum, Rutgers, The State University of New Jersey, Schimmel Fund

Samuel van Hoogstraten, *Shadow Theater*, engraving from *Inleyding tot de hooghe schoole der schilderkonst*, Rotterdam 1678, Rijksmuseum, Amsterdam

1 Altick 1978, p. 120.
2 Cate and Shaw 1996, pp. 58-59; cf. Forgione 1999, p. 508.

Henri Rivière, *The Devil and St. Anthony*, 1887–90, zinc cutout for the shadow-theater play *La Tentation de Saint Antoine*, Jane Voorhees Zimmerli Art Museum, Rutgers, The State University of New Jersey, Gift of the University College New Brunswick Alumni Association

Light and impressionism

Of all the impressionists, Alfred Sisley remained truest to impressionist painting techniques and landscape subjects throughout his career. This luminous view of the village of Saint-Mammès exemplifies the impressionist handling of daylight.

Sisley has placed his easel on the northern shore of the river looking south and east. Working out of doors enabled him to study particular effects and achieve the impressionist goal of bathing the subject in a coherent, unifying light. The early morning sun causes the pale glow along the horizon and the shadowy reflections of houses on the left. To the right, the water in full sunshine reflects the bright blue sky, while in the foreground, dancing gold and orange reflections suggest ripples among reeds bent by a westerly breeze. All of these light effects are true to nature and human perception, in keeping with the impressionist project of observing and recording the landscape as directly as possible.

Unlike preceding generations of painters, the impressionists – Sisley among them – relied on color rather than gradations of shading to suggest both form and light. In this view of Saint-Mammès, for example, the east-facing walls of village houses are painted in warm cream and pale orange, while the north walls are lavender. From these complementary colors, we deduce not only the shapes of the houses, but also the action of the light that falls upon them. The orange strokes of paint on the water in the foreground do the same dual job – defining the ripples and their sparkling reflections.

The broad, thick brushstrokes of the impressionist style also contribute to the overall sense of light and brightness in these landscapes. Each ridge and blob of paint, especially in the lighter areas, reflects light back toward the viewer. The impressionists' preference for white or light colored ground layers also enhances the reflectivity of their canvases.

Light's behavior and representation are consistently important themes in impressionist painting, both landscape and genre. The impressionists' interest in light surely developed from the movement toward plein-air painting that originated with Pierre-Henri de Valenciennes at the beginning of the nineteenth century, and must have received impetus from the explosion of popular interest in the sciences of light, climate, atmosphere, and color perception around mid-century. However, as careful analyses of the impressionist painters' methods and materials have shown, the artists themselves relied most of all on their own observations and their empirical knowledge of the painter's craft.

Alfred Sisley, *Saint-Mammès on the Banks of the Loing*, ca. 1881, Carnegie Museum of Art, Pittsburgh, Purchase

Light in black and white

Imitating light and shade with only two colors is one of the artist's greatest challenges. Only the most practiced dared attempt to depict a sunlit landscape using nothing but black lines and the white of the paper. It is even more difficult – as in the graphic arts – when the colored areas have to be worked up in the negative, that is: when what is meant to be light is actually dark during the entire creative process. In the case of copper engraving, the dark plate itself is a problem, which must be solved using a fine network of thin lines and delicate hatching. Printmakers, however, were rarely discouraged. They even took on fireworks – i.e., light in motion – as a subject. The mezzotint, a widespread technique in the eighteenth century and particularly popular in England, proved to be well adapted to the imitation of tone and mood. It was the best way to replicate the shadows in paintings, and thus became the most common method for engraved reproductions. It was even used for making prints after the complexly lit pictures of Wright of Derby and Constable.

The graphic arts were probably the least affected by developments in lighting technology. Are there more perfect etchings than Rembrandt's, executed long before Argand's oil lamp, gas and electricity? Like painters, however, printmakers were dependent on good lighting. Their workshops closely resembled those of watchmakers. Depictions of engravers' studios almost always show a transparent screen placed in front of the window, installed to diffuse and even out the daylight.

Astonishingly, little research has been done on the influence of photography on the graphic arts. Even long after the invention of the photograph in the 1830s, wood engraving still remained the most important technique for illustrations in the press. Magazines employed whole armies of draftsmen and engravers, who increasingly worked from photographic originals. Only during the course of the 1880s did photomechanical procedures gain the upper hand. The relationship between artists and photographers was a tense one. Painters tended to deny any form of influence, and they refused to recognize photography as an art form. The photographers, in turn, often sought to imitate painting in order to gain recognition for the new medium, rather than concentrating on its unique qualities.

A highly original photographic technique is the "cliché-verre," a favorite of the Barbizon painters in particular. It is a photographic etching process. First, a specially coated glass plate is incised with the drawing, much as one would do for an engraving. The glass plate is then photographically reproduced, like a negative, by laying it on light-sensitive paper. Thus, the creation of the work of art is not mechanical, only the method of reproducing it. When one views the glass plate and the print side by side, the positive-negative effect is more obvious than in all the other techniques – what was white has become black, and vice versa. In contrast to the traditional copper plate, the glass plate could be turned around, so that the image was not reversed. However, when the incised side of the plate faced up away from the paper, the resulting print was slightly fuzzy. Corot created more than sixty cliché-verres, beginning in 1853. Using a free and vibrant line, he created atmospheric landscapes like the one seen here.

Nocturnes, harmonies and waves

The most sophisticated observers and interpreters of light effects in the 1860s to 1880s were John Atkinson Grimshaw and James McNeill Whistler. Together, they invented and perfected the nocturne – the atmospheric, moody, and subdued vision of the modern city at night. The inspiration for their innovative compositions came from two sources: new light technologies that transformed the appearance of the urban landscape, and new scientific theories of light that justified the expressive use of color and apparent lack of narrative subject.

The critical light technology was gaslight. Both Grimshaw and Whistler enjoyed depicting the starry points of light from street lamps contrasted with the gentle glow from illuminated windows. Grimshaw especially studied the complexity of city lighting; his view of the Liverpool docks includes the greenish gleam of a carriage lamp, and the silvery light of the moon overhead, as well as the red-orange glow of gas. The nocturne also benefited from one of gaslighting's unintended consequences – the thickening of the urban atmosphere from burning coal in gas plants and heating fires. The magical luminosity of the urban sky was caused by the refraction and diffusion of gaslight and moonlight in the particle-laden atmosphere. Water, almost always on the ground or in the air in rainy England, acted as another light reflector and eliminated the dark shadows one would otherwise expect in a night scene. The new overall brightness of city streets allowed Grimshaw and Whistler to portray them as unified cityscapes.

The wave theory of light must also have influenced the two artists, especially Whistler. Accepted generally by about 1830 and aggressively popularized in all aspects of culture and education thereafter, the new theory described light as a wave-like motion in the ether, an invisible impalpable substance that acted as a medium – like air does for sound waves; or

James McNeill Whistler, *Nocturne, the River at Battersea*, 1878, lithotint, Carnegie Museum of Art, Pittsburgh, Bequest of Charles J. Rosenbloom

water, for ripples. This theory superceded Newton's concept of light as a stream or ray of particles moving in accordance with the laws of geometry. The wave theory dealt the death blow to classical perspective systems based on ideas of light's geometrical behavior. It also changed the general understanding of how the human eye perceived and responded to light. Both advanced scientists, such as the great physicist Hermann von Helmholtz, and science popularizers emphasized the analogies between the light waves that produced sensations of color and the sound waves that produced sensations of musical tone. It is a very short mental jump to the notion that just as musical harmonies result from complimentary patterns of sound waves, so visual harmonies would result from complimentary patterns of light waves, that is color. Whistler's disciplined and self-conscious search for wave harmonies expressed as color was his greatest and most original contribution to art. The wave theory also justified eliminating narrative or symbolic subjects from visual art. If light waves acted directly on the senses, and therefore on the emotions (as did sound waves), narrative content simply interfered with the direct communication of feeling from work of art to viewer.

Atkinson Grimshaw, *Liverpool
Quay by Moonlight*, 1887, Tate
Gallery, London

The origin of light

In the modern definition, the sun is "a giant, natural thermonuclear reactor that converts hydrogen to helium in its core to produce the heat we sense on our faces as sunshine"[1] – a fairly prosaic description of the origins of light and thus life on earth. The sun has been the subject of scientific investigation since the seventeenth century. One of the most important dates in this chronicle of discovery is 1817, when Joseph von Fraunhofer began his research into the spectra of the sun and planets other than Earth. His so-called dark lines later enabled scientists to determine the sun's elemental composition. Spectroscopy is still the most widely used method for gathering information on the chemistry of the universe.

As was the case with the moon, photography could initially contribute little to the spread of knowledge about the sun, being hampered by the earth's motions. This changed toward the middle of the nineteenth century, when astronomers and photographers began working together to find a solution. One such duo was Secchi and Rutherfurd. Angelo Secchi, a Jesuit priest from Reggio Emilia, had united the study of physics and theology, and even taken a photograph of a solar eclipse in 1860. He was the first to claim that the sun was made up of gases, whose heat became weaker as they progressed outward from the core. His book about the sun, published in French in 1870, was quickly translated into a number of languages, and was probably the most significant work on the subject of the entire century. While Secchi was an astronomer with an interest in photography, Rutherfurd was just the opposite. He took the art of photographing the heavenly bodies to new heights, and it was a great stroke of luck that these two influential representatives of their disciplines found one another. Rutherfurd's photographs were the first to give the layman a vision of the surface of the only star in our solar system. It now appeared not as an illuminated disk, but as a living and breathing organism.

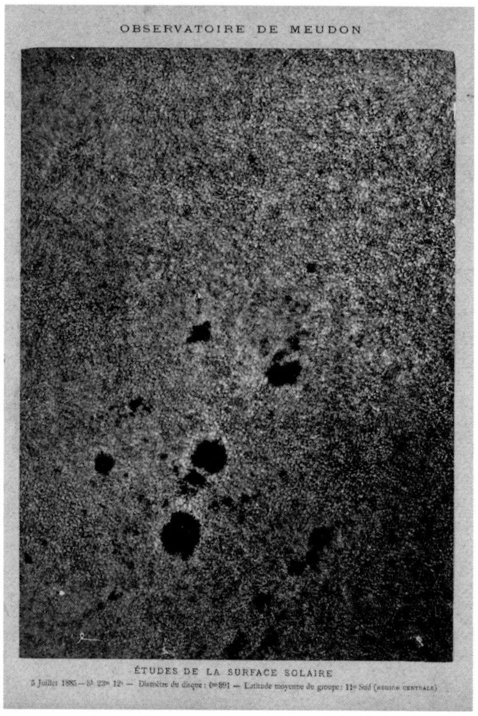

Anonymous, *Study of the Solar Surface*, 1885, albumen print, Rijksmuseum, Rijksprenten-kabinet, Amsterdam

OBSERVATOIRE DE MEUDON

ÉTUDES DE LA SURFACE SOLAIRE

1 An excellent historical overview of the research into the sun (with extensive bibliography) can be found at www.hao.ucar.edu/public/education/sp.sp.html.

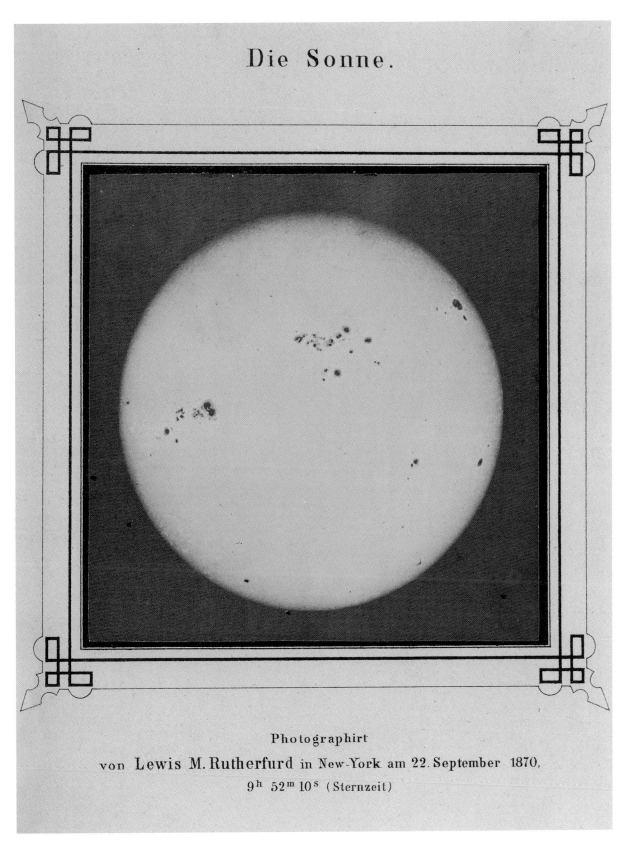

Die Sonne.

Photographirt

von Lewis M. Rutherfurd in New-York am 22. September 1870,

9^h 52^m 10^s (Sternzeit)

Lewis Morris Rutherfurd, *The Sun*,
1870, albumen print, frontispiece
to Pietro Angelo Secchi, *Die
Sonne*, Braunschweig 1872,
Rijksmuseum, Amsterdam

At the eye doctor

Transparencies were not fashionable simply in art, entertainment and popular education, they also had a practical use: translucent and colored glasses were used for all kinds of scientific experiments. In fact, any pair of sunglasses can be considered a transparency, filtering out some of the information provided by light.

Eye doctors and opticians measure patients' eyesight using a series of letters of decreasing size. These "optotypes" were introduced in 1862 by the Utrecht doctor Herman Snellen, and are widely known as "Snellen charts." The example shown here is a variation on the standard chart which, together with a pair of red and green glasses, was designed to test the sight of either the left or right eye. Through the glasses, one eye perceives only green, the other only red letters. The fact that the eye functions much like a camera obscura was already well known. A great leap forward was made in the analysis of the receptors behind the lens when, in 1850, a mirror became available that allowed doctors and scientists to explore the interior of the eye.

Science's new discoveries had value as entertainment as well, particularly the realization that perception is, in fact, rather slow. In the anonymous *Spectropia* of 1864, we find red and green forms which, when stared at long enough, produce an afterimage on the retina in the complementary color. As in the eighteenth century, it was ghosts that played a major role in optical diversions. Perhaps, however, it was this toying with perception that gave science a helping hand. Red and green were also the two colors used for the first gaslit traffic lights, installed in 1868 in front of the Houses of Parliament in London.

Benjamin Martin, *Model of the eye*, ca. 1765, Harvard University Collection of Historical Scientific Instruments, Cambridge, Massachusetts

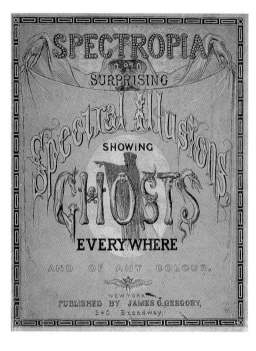

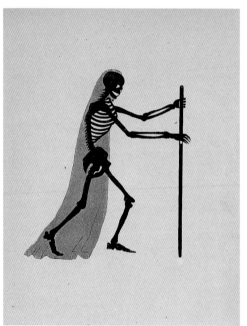

Spectropia or Surprising Spectral Illusions Showing Ghosts Everywhere and of Any Colour, New York 1864, Graphic Arts Technical Foundation, Sewickley, Pennsylvania

Letter display and red-green spectacles, Dutch, 1878,
Universiteitsmuseum Utrecht

Introducing the light bulb

Although the invention of the light bulb is usually dated 1879, it was not possible to install one at home until the the mid 1880s. Not only did techniques for mass production have to be developed, but also power stations and supply networks had to be constructed. By then, Thomas Edison and his competitors in the United States and Europe had also begun to produce the newspaper and magazine stories and popular manuals that promoted the new lights.

The ABC of Electricity, endorsed by Thomas Edison, explained, "You must all have seen electric lights, either in the streets or in some large buildings, for so many electric lights are used now, that there are very few people who have not seen them. But perhaps some of you have only seen the large dazzling lights that are used in the streets, and do not know that there is another kind of electric light which is in a globe about the size of a large pear, and gives about the same light as a good gas jet. [...] The large, dazzling lights which you see in the streets are called 'arc lights', and the small pear-shaped lamps, which give a soft, steady light, are called 'incandescent lights'."[1]

The user's manuals provided basic details: "We have made mention several times of turning on or off one or more lights, and now, perhaps, you would like to know how this is done."[2] And: "Some day, however, from a great variety of obscure causes, the carbon [filament] becomes weak in some particular spot and breaks, and the light ceases. When this happens, we unscrew the lamp and put another one in, and the light goes on as usual."[3] It is hard to imagine how exciting it must have been, in 1885, to replace a light bulb.

Power companies and popular writers stressed the light bulb's advantages over gas: electric light bulbs did not explode, did not throw off heat, smoke and poisonous fumes, and could be turned on quickly from a single point when burglars broke in. They also stressed its soft, even glow, although users accustomed to the warmth and coziness of flickering gas burners did not always admire it. However, one of its strongest selling points was the popular conception, fostered by early science fiction, that electricity was the key to the future.

Park Benjamin, *The Age of Electricity from Amber-Soul to Telephone*, New York 1889, Private collection; Captain E. Ironside Bax, *Popular Electric Lighting: Being Practical Hints to Present and Intending Users of Electric Energy for Illuminating Purposes*, [...], 2nd ed., London 1882, Private collection; Robert Hammond, *The Electric Light in our Homes, Popularly Explained and Illustrated*, London 1884, Carnegie Museum of Art, Pittsburgh, Curatorial Library

Bax's cover design features a light bulb as the head of a comet, drawing energy from the sun, eclipsing the moon and leaving the smoking candle in its dust. An extraterrestrial being – subject of serious debate among astronomers in the 1890s – rides the tail.

The gold tooling on Hammond's cover glitters like a light bulb should. The designer has included four types of bulb, including the most popular, Edison's and Swan's.

Westinghouse Company, *Electric light bulbs*, 1890s, Carnegie Museum of Natural History, Pittsburgh, Gift of Paul Caldwell

1 Quoted after Meadowcroft 1888, p. 49.
2 Ibid., p. 79.
3 Ibid., p. 73.

Gaslight versus arc light

Of all the major cities in Europe and the United States, Paris was one of the slowest to adopt gas street lighting, and one of the first to experiment with electric arc lighting. Gas street lights were not introduced in Paris on a major scale until 1829, and did not become generally available until the 1840s. Parisian street lighting improved markedly with the magnificent gas lamps that illuminated Haussmann's boulevards, constructed in the 1850s and 1860s, and visitors to the Paris Universal Expositions of 1867 and 1878 were overwhelmed by the beauty of the city at night.

In 1867, Julius Rodenberg described the view of Paris from Montmartre in a guidebook for German visitors to the fair: "Right in the middle of the heart of the city there appears a golden dot, another one here, a third there, a fourth – one cannot say how quickly they follow one another, they can no longer be counted. The whole of Paris is studded with golden dots, as closely as a velvet gown with gold glitter. Soon they wink and twinkle everywhere, and you cannot imagine anything more beautiful, and yet the most beautiful is still to come. Out of the dots emerge lines, and from the lines figures, spark lining up with spark, and as far as the eye can see are endless avenues of light."[1] Hippolyte Delpy captured the elegance, mystery, and glamour of these gas-lit Parisian streets in his view of a boulevard in his Montmartre neighborhood. A colleague of the impressionists, he focused on the particular effects created by star-like gas lamps and glowing shop windows as their light was reflected and refracted by falling snow. Patches of brightness animate the snowy street like sunlight falling on a forest floor. Paris's reputation as a city of light began in this era, with scenes such as Delpy's and descriptions such as Rodenberg's.

In 1878, it was still too difficult and expensive to illuminate the grounds of the Exposition Universelle at night. It was the last of the great world's fairs to close its doors at sundown. Visitors to Paris that year spent their evenings viewing another lighting phenomenon: the electric arc lights replacing gaslights in stores and city streets. A visitor from Pittsburgh, Mary Roswell Scaife, reported to her relatives on the latest Paris scenes, including electrically lit stores open until midnight, and a demonstration of the telephone at the Conservatoire des arts et métiers, where "a great many of the rooms were lighted by the electric light, which I think just like moonlight only stronger. Our eyes ached when we would come into the yellow gaslight, the other being so much softer."[2] The Place de la Concorde was even more spectacular. "We went to the Place de la Concorde, and while standing there admiring the stars [...] found a man with a telescope. This was too much for Mother, so we had a look at Saturn and his rings, then went on to the Gardens in the Champs Elysées which are lighted by electricity and are almost bright as day. You would think all creation has gathered here, for every nation and every tongue is represented."[3]

The writer Robert Louis Stevenson hated arc lights when he saw them in Paris and London in 1878. His impassioned "A Plea for Gas Lamps" utterly condemns electricity: "[...] a new sort of urban star now shines out nightly, horribly, unearthly, obnoxious to the human eye; a lamp for a nightmare! Such a light as this should shine only on murders and public crime, or along the corridors of lunatic asylums, a horror to heighten horror. To look at it only once is to fall in love with gas [...]."[4] Nevertheless, Paris staged a third fair in 1881, this time devoted entirely to electricity. There, the electric light bulb would make its triumphant European debut.

Street lamp designs, from Adolphe Alphand, *Les Promenades de Paris*, Paris 1867–73, vol. 2, Universiteits-bibliotheek Amsterdam

1 Julius Rodenberg, *Paris bei Sonnenschein und Lampenlicht: Skizzenbuch zur Weltausstellung*, quoted in Schlör 1998, p. 60.
2 Mary Roswell Scaife, "A Pittsburgh Lady on the Grand Tour (1878)," *Carnegie Magazine* 28 (October 1954), pp. 265-72, 275, here p. 265.
3 Ibid., p. 266.
4 Stevenson 1878, p. 147.

Hippolyte Camille Delpy, *The Boulevard Barbès-Rochechouart in Winter*, 1879, Elisabeth Cumbler

Art under the arc lamp

At home in Denmark, Peder Severin Krøyer, who had studied in France, was a fashionable society painter. Here, he depicts a relaxed gathering at the beer brewer and collector Carl Jacobson's first "Glyptotek." The scene is illuminated by a hard, even, brilliant light emanating from a source at the top of the picture. The sculptures in the background – more or less ignored by the guests – are reproduced in a gleaming white, and throw well-defined shadows on the wall behind them. This indicates that the light source is an arc lamp, a known technology, only recently introduced into the interior. Arc lamps generated a glaring white light from two electrified carbon electrodes heated to incandescence. As the electrodes were consumed, a clockwork mechanism kept them at an even distance, thus maintaining the current and the light. The light burned out when the electrodes were consumed, usually in about eight hours.

Arc lamps had been successfully employed since the 1860s on city streets, in lighthouses, factories, circus tents and anywhere else a strong light was required. Before the introduction of electrical networks, isolated generators served as the source of energy. Beginning in 1877, these lamps were also used to illuminate works of art, namely at the Paris Salon, the great annual art exhibition. Reactions were mixed. Many critics felt the experiment was a failure on the, not insignificant, grounds that the paintings' colors were no longer correct: "[The arc lamp] overemphasizes the violent movements of the brush, while at the same time eliminating every delicacy."[1] While artists and critics viewed this new development with skepticism, technology enthusiasts were pleased. On 15 June 1879, Frank Géraldy reported in detail on the lighting of the Salon in the magazine *La Lumière Électrique*: "The overall sensation is one of subdued, gentle daylight. The effect in the galleries of painting is entirely satisfactory; the globes are placed quite high, and their light concentrated by reflectors on the walls; one easily forgets the time, giving oneself over to examining the paintings with the same tranquility one would by daylight."[2]

It was at just this time that the new republican government in France decided to permanently adopt artificial lighting for the Paris Salon, not out of enthusiasm for either technology or art, but for social reasons. Thanks to the new system, the exhibition was able to stay open longer, giving the working classes a chance to view the paintings and sculptures on display. A large-scale advertising campaign helped make the venture an enormous success. "An announcement has just been made – in large red letters on the official poster – that the Salon will be open every evening, lit by electric light. This is the first step in an inevitable, and regrettable, transformation," the critic Jules Claretie complained.[3] The number of visitors, however, proved the organizers had made the right decision: in comparison to the year before, the figure more than quadrupled, reaching nearly 700,000.[4] That the Salon was now officially a form of mass entertainment, however, was less than pleasing to the critics, and even disturbed most of the participants. The jury itself protested against the new course, but to no avail: the state had already closed a five-year contract with the manufacturer of so-called "Jablochkoff candles," 356 of which illuminated the exhibition at the Palais de l'Industrie.[5]

Daniel Urrabieta y Vierge, *The Salon by Electric Light*, wood engraving from *Le Monde Illustré* (5 July 1879), Van Gogh Museum, Amsterdam

This engraving illustrates the various uses of arc lights at the Salon: those uninterested in the works could at least spend their time reading the newspaper. The gesture of the man at the left shows that the lights were so bright that they were actually blinding.

1 *La Chronique des Arts et de la Curiosité* (9 June 1877), p. 211.
2 pp. 58-59.
3 Jules Claretie, *La Vie à Paris 1880*, Paris 1881, pp. 96-97.
4 Mainardi 1993, pp. 72-74.
5 See the letter from Paul Baudry, President of the Jury of Paintings, to Edmond Turquet, Undersecretary of State for Fine Arts, published in Victor Champier, *L'Année artistique* 3 (1880-1881), pp. 68-69.

Peder Severin Krøyer, *Social
Evening in the Banqueting Hall of
the Carlsberg Glyptotek*, 1888,
Carlsberg Museum, Copenhagen

Electric enlightenment

The metamorphoses of the Statue of Liberty's torch sum up the story of symbolic light in the Industrial Age. The statue was first conceived in the 1860s as an emblem of the historical connection between the eighteenth-century French Enlightenment and American democratic ideals expressed in the Declaration of Independence. The sculptor's original title for the piece was *Liberty Enlightening the World*, a not so subtle assertion of French and American leadership in international and cultural affairs. By the time *Liberty* had been designed, constructed, exported to the United States and dedicated in 1886, it also represented the political affinities between the republican governments of France and the United States. Many other interpretations have been attached to *Liberty* since then; she is one of the most famous icons in the world.

Every element of the imposing figure carries a symbolic message, including her golden torch, symbol of enlightenment. Bartholdi's original plan called for the torch to be gilded. Its precious surface would gleam above New York harbor like a yellow flame embodying the high historical value of liberty and enlightenment. With her golden flame, *Liberty* would function as a traditional sculptural memorial and landmark, but not as a beacon.

Almost immediately, *Liberty*'s golden torch was electrified. This had happened by 1883, when poet Emma Lazarus alluded to it in "The New Colossus:" "Here at our sea-washed, sunset gates shall stand / A mighty woman with a torch, whose flame / Is the imprisoned lightning, and her name / Mother of Exiles. From her beacon-hand / Glows world-wide welcome; [...]."[1] One can well understand why Americans would prefer the Statue of Liberty electrified. Thomas Edison had invented the incandescent light bulb in 1879, and New York City was the first in the world to install a central electric power generating plant for municipal lighting. Mastery of electricity was correctly interpreted at the time as a sign of American dominance in engineering, economics, and ingenuity – it manifested power in a multitude of ways. Shining out from the torch, electric light symbolized a very modern, American form of enlightenment as well – not an eighteenth-century philosophy at all, but a belief in industrialization, political and economic opportunity, and the innovative, questing spirit of the New World. Gold plate could hardly compete.

With her electric torch, the Statue of Liberty took on her now familiar role as lighthouse and beacon, guardian and welcomer: "Send these, the homeless, tempest-tossed to me, / I lift my lamp beside the golden door!"[2]

The end of the story comes with the most recent restoration of the statue in 1984–86. The electric torch was replaced with a new, gilded flame more representative of the sculptor's original intention, but completely missing the point of the early substitution. The decision demonstrates that electric light no longer jolts us with a thrilling sense of modernity, power, and pride. In fact, set against the brilliant backdrop of the modern cityscape, the old electric torch probably seemed anticlimactic and banal. However, if the restorers had respected the technological spirit and nationalistic agenda of the original change to electricity, perhaps they would have considered today's equivalent – lasers – instead.

Frédéric-Auguste Bartholdi, *Liberty Enlightening the World*, 1873, cast 1900, bronze, Sénat de la République Française, Paris (Jardin du Luxembourg)

Mrs. Cornelius Vanderbilt as "The Electric Light," 1883, New York Historical Society, Museum of the City of New York

1 Emma Lazarus, "The New Colossus," (1883).
2 Ibid.

Lights of desire

Theatres, opera houses, and public arenas were among the first structures to adopt electric lighting in their interiors. Edison and other early "electricians" installed the new lighting free of charge in several buildings, whose cavernous spaces absorbed the brightness of arc lighting and also showcased the decorative qualities of light bulbs. The large audiences that packed the halls every night were among the first to see and covet the new technologies.

The Paris Hippodrome, with a glass roof for light by day, was equipped for night by 1883 with Jablochkoff candles (a form of arc light) and Edison bulbs, as well as spotlights. As its name implies, the Hippodrome featured equestrian entertainments that combined elements of the modern circus and antique charioteering. The chariots were driven by young women, theatrically garbed in revealing, vaguely allegorical dresses, equipped with whips, and effortlessly in control of their high-spirited horses. They were among the most visible members of the French demi-monde – perfect subjects for Tissot's series of paintings characterizing "The Parisian Woman." *The Ladies of the Chariots* reveals the strengths and weaknesses of the new lighting. The Hippodrome is as bright as day (a strength), but the audience is also brightly lit (a weakness). To late twentieth-century viewers accustomed to darkened halls and moving spotlights, the effect seems dull. However, nineteenth-century observers admired the lights even more than the ladies, who "if they are not beautiful, at all events under the glamour of electric light and amid the applause of the amphitheatre they seem so. [...] Glamour is everything: the multitude applauds not what it sees but what it thinks it sees."[1]

As electric lighting and power proliferated, it came to serve as a metaphor for life force and sexual desire. Electricity strikes, like a bolt of lightning, in a scene from Alphonse Daudet's racy novel *Sapho* (1884), which may have inspired Tissot to paint *The Ladies of the Chariots*. At a licentious costume ball in a lantern-lit studio, "[...] flashes of electricity, of a bluish tinge, would suddenly pale all those thousands of lights, and cast a frosty gleam, like a ray of moonlight, on the faces and bare shoulders, on all the phantasmagoria of dresses, feathers, spangles, and ribbons, jostling one another in the ball-room [...]."[2]

Electric lighting glamorized not only courtesans, but also mundane items like bath towels. In Emile Zola's novel *Ladies' Delight* set in a Paris department store, new electric lights turned the showroom into consumer heaven: "Six o'clock would soon be striking, the light which was waning outside was retreating from the covered galleries which were dark already, and was fading in the depths of the halls flooded with lingering shadows. In this still not properly extinguished daylight, electric lamps were lighting up one by one, and their translucent white globes were spangling the distant depths of the departments with bright moons. They shed a white brightness of blinding fixity, like a reflection from some colourless star, which was killing the dusk. Then, when all the lamps were alight, the crowd gave a murmur of rapture; beneath this new lighting the great display of white took on the fairy-like splendor of a transformation scene [...]. A white gleam was sparkling from the linens and calicoes [...]."[3] In 1880s Paris, it would seem that almost anything viewed under electric light became a desirable commodity.

James Tissot, *The Ladies of the Chariots*, 1883-85, Museum of Art, Rhode Island School of Design, Providence, Rhode Island, Gift of Walter Lowry

1 Quoted in Nancy Rose Marshall and Malcolm Warner, *James Tissot: Victorian Life/ Modern Love*, exh. cat. New Haven (Yale Center for British Art) & Buffalo (Albright Knox Art Gallery) 1999-2000, p. 159.

2 Michael J. Wentworth, *James Tissot: Catalogue Raisonné of His Prints*, exh. cat. Minneapolis (Minneapolis Institute of Arts) and Williamstown, Massachusetts (Sterling & Francine Clark Art Institute) 1978; Alphonse Daudet, *Sapho* (1884), introduction by Carl van Doren, New York n.d. (1930s), p. 3.

3 Emile Zola, *Ladies' Delight (Au Bonheur des dames)*, trans. April Fitzlyon, London & New York 1958, p. 401.

The Paris Hippodrome, wood engraving from Em. Alglave and J. Boulard, *La Lumière électrique*, Paris 1882, Universiteits-bibliotheek Amsterdam

189 **Lights of desire**

Under the gaslight

Throughout the nineteenth century, gaslighting was the hallmark of working class leisure, culture, and vice. In London, blazing street lamps identified the gin palaces, the only bright, warm, and inviting environments to be found in the city's grimmest slums and neighborhoods. The poor entered them seeking comfort, companionship, and forgetfulness; the affluent came for the thrill and the novelty. In Paris, the same role was filled by the café, which supported the leisure activities of numerous social classes, as well as the professional careers of cardsharps, entertainers, and prostitutes. This was the world recorded in the prints and paintings of one of its most distinguished habitués, the artist Henri de Toulouse-Lautrec.

The Moulin Rouge was the most famous café in 1890s Paris, favored by Toulouse-Lautrec as well as dancers and singers, such as La Gouloue, Jane Avril, Yvette Guilbert, and May Milton, whose disturbing face appears at the far right of Lautrec's painting. The room is lit by gas lamps, their light reflected and amplified by the huge mirrors panelling the café walls. The green tones of the glass alter the color of reflected light, perhaps accounting for the bluish-green shadows found throughout the composition. The yellow light warms the brown wood railing, the red hair of Jane Avril, the yellow hair of May Milton, and the polished marble table top. The women's exaggerated make-up – whitened skin, carmine lips, vivid hair – more than compensates for gaslight's notorious color-dampening effects. In fact, their faces seem to capture and reflect light even more effectively than the surrounding mirrors.

Georges Seurat's many paintings and drawings of cafés and gas-lit cabarets emphasize the ways in which gaslighting diminished or modified color. In this subtle drawing, the colors of the singer's costume have been reduced to tones of grey, cream, and white; the singer herself is outshone by the chandeliers and footlights surrounding the stage. For both artists, capturing the peculiar color effects of gaslight was critical to their larger goal of evoking the nocturnal world of the Paris café. In their paintings, they seem to agree that within an overall greenish, murky atmosphere, gaslight browned out the dark shades and heightened the light ones. Toulouse-Lautrec uses this discovery in *At the Moulin Rouge* to create a dramatic, indeed lurid, image of café denizens. Seurat adapts the same idea in his drawing and suggests with it the unbreachable distance between performer and audience.

Georges Seurat, *Eden-Concert*, 1887, black chalk, Van Gogh Museum, Amsterdam (Vincent van Gogh Foundation)

Henri de Toulouse-Lautrec, *At the Moulin Rouge*, 1894–95, Art Institute of Chicago, Helen Birch Bartlett Memorial Collection

The truth about lightning

An amateur photographer is credited with taking the first known photographs of lightning, dated ca. 1880–85. He proudly (and perhaps a bit misleadingly) recorded his achievement in a small notebook. "In 1880, W. N. Jennings, of Philadelphia, noticed that Artists only depicted one form of lightning – an awkward zig-zag, and he decided to see what the camera would show. For over fifteen years he made lightning photographs in various parts of the world; no two of which were alike, and none 'zig-zag.' For this pioneer work he was awarded the John Price Wetherill Medal by the Franklin Institute."[1] Jennings illustrated his notebook with the drawing of lightning, and a series of photographs of lightning bolts.

Artists had been depicting lightning as zigzags ever since antiquity, and the convention is still recognized and used today. It has endured despite the fact that the identity of lightning and electricity had been proved by Benjamin Franklin in 1752, and published in 1767. The true form of electrical discharges had been diagrammed and published by the end of the eighteenth century. The information necessary to draw lightning correctly had been available for many years when Benjamin West, celebrating Franklin's brilliant experiment, drew it wrong in 1816–17, to be followed by many others, including John Martin. Even realist painters of the latter half of the nineteenth century inserted conventional artist's lightning into otherwise close descriptions of nature and atmosphere.

Throughout the nineteenth century, scientific research disproved artists' claims to be nature's most faithful students and portraitists. The new optical instruments, such as photometers, cameras and ophthalmoscopes, were revealing the limits and fallibility of the human eye and brain. They were beginning to portray a world that humans could not see for themselves.

Benjamin West, *Portrait of Benjamin Franklin*, ca. 1816–17, Philadelphia Museum of Art, Gift of Mr. and Mrs. Warton Sinkler

1 William N. Jennings, "Jove's Thunderbolt," manuscript notebook with photographs, ca. 1885, p. 1, George Eastman House, Rochester, New York, Gift of 3M Company, inv. 83:679:1.

Artists lightning

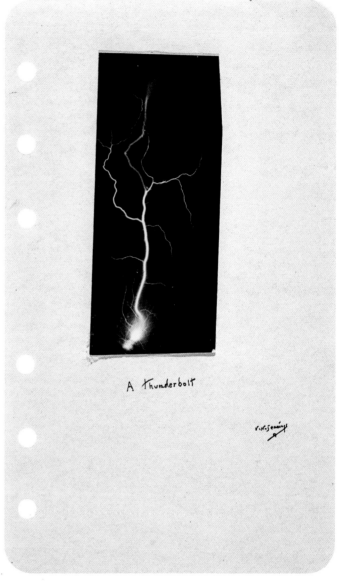

A Thunderbolt

William N. Jennings, *Artist's Lightning*, ca. 1885, pen and ink, George Eastman House, Rochester, New York, Gift of 3M Company

William N. Jennings, *A Thunderbolt*, ca. 1885, gelatin silver print, George Eastman House, Rochester, New York, Gift of 3M Company

By the light of the lamp

Van Gogh hoped to establish himself as an artist with this painting, and to achieve recognition.[1] It is an ambitious work, not only in format and composition, but also in terms of the lighting. Van Gogh took as his subject a family of Brabant peasants, eating the potatoes they had dug from the earth after a hard day's work: "I wanted to convey the idea that these people eating their potatoes by the light of a lamp had used the same hands with which they now take food from the plate to work the land [...]," Vincent wrote to his brother Theo at the end of April 1885.[2]

The kerosene lamp is the only source of light in the interior. It is a kind of simple ceiling lamp found almost everywhere at the time. The flame was painted using strong brushstrokes and a bright orange color, giving it a real physical presence. Emanating from the base, rays of light appear to spread in all directions. Reproducing these always remained a difficult task for Van Gogh, although he devoted himself to it as no other artist had before him. The light produced by the flame bounces off the lamp's reflector, illuminating the figures and objects in the room. Everything is defined by this rather weak reflected light. Van Gogh's early, if somewhat awkward, genius reveals itself precisely here, however, in the way he modeled the beams, jugs, headdresses and, finally, the potatoes themselves using only a few, strategically placed highlights. In the background, the light can be perceived only as a faint gleam on the walls. It is this half-darkness that makes the peasants' plight, their utter destitution, obvious to the viewer. The brightest and darkest portions of the canvas – the lamp and the head of the girl with her back to us – are placed close together at the center of the composition. This is a highly refined detail, and one that makes it clear that Van Gogh's reading of academic art treatises paid off. Unfortunately, he did not yet have the manual skill to convince even his most well-meaning critics of his talent.

Vincent van Gogh, *The Potato Eaters*, 1885, lithograph, Van Gogh Museum, Amsterdam (Vincent van Gogh Foundation)

Vincent van Gogh, *The Potato Eaters*, sketch in a letter to his brother Theo, 11 April 1885 (495/399), Van Gogh Museum, Amsterdam (Vincent van Gogh Foundation)

Van Gogh executed this lithograph after completing the painting. The colorless print gives an excellent impression of the distribution of light and shade in the original canvas. The figure seen from the back is set quite dramatically in shadow. The lamplight falls on the table, reflecting back onto the figures gathered around it, creating an effect reminiscent of old masters such as Caravaggio or his Dutch followers of the Utrecht School.

1 Louis van Tilborgh, *The Potato Eaters by Vincent van Gogh*, exh. cat. Amsterdam (Van Gogh Museum) 1993; Louis van Tilborgh and Marije Vellekoop, *Vincent van Gogh: Paintings, Dutch Period, 1881-1885*, Blaricum 1999, pp. 136-45, no. 26.
2 Letter to his brother Theo, ca. 30 April 1885 (501/404).

Vincent van Gogh, *The Potato Eaters*, 1885, Van Gogh Museum, Amsterdam (Vincent van Gogh Foundation)

Zones of light

Charles Angrand belonged to a group of artists known as divisionists or neo-impressionists that also included Georges Seurat, Paul Signac, and Camille Pissarro. Their method of painting, divisionism consisted of flat dots or strokes of pure color juxtaposed with complementary and contrasting hues to create form and the sensation of light. Their ideas were based on nineteenth-century optical and color theories synthesized in manuals such as Michel Eugène Chevreul, *Des Couleurs et leurs applications dans les arts industrielles* (1864), Charles Blanc, *Grammaire des arts du dessin* (1867), and Ogden Rood, *Modern Chromatics* (1879). The neo-impressionists, working during the brief moment in the 1880s when scientific authorities believed that light had been fully understood, sought to formulate their own laws of color, light, and form for art. The history of their movement might be defined as a struggle to reconcile the abstract laws of optics with the conflicting and complex realities of human visual experience.

The visual experience that is the subject of *The Accident* is the way zones of light organize city spaces and social encounters. Urban engineers, working with the different capacities of gas and electric street lighting, were beginning to understand how they influenced street life and architecture, something realist and naturalist writers and painters had noticed already. Angrand's painting shows a crowd gathered in front of an apothecary shop with its traditional globes filled with colored water in the window. The writer Elizabeth Gaskell had first pointed out how beautiful these globes looked in illuminated windows at night forty years before: "It is a pretty sight to walk through a street with lighted shops; the gas is so brilliant, the display of goods so much more vividly shown than by day, and of all shops a druggist's looks the most like the tales of our childhood, from Aladdin's garden of enchanted fruits to the charming Rosamund with her purple jar."[1] In the middle distance, a white cab horse is profiled against the dark coats and umbrellas of the onlookers, and in the foreground a woman in red glances curiously in their direction as she crosses the street.

This enigmatic painting – the nature of the accident cannot be determined – captures the randomness of urban night life played out under the gaslights. Angrand's combination of light sources – gas street light, glowing shop windows, and cab lights – had been typical of the urban nocturne since the work of Atkinson Grimshaw and James McNeill Whistler in the 1860s and 1870s. However, rather than present a unified, atmospheric cityscape, Angrand divides his street into lighted zones. The most distant zone, the space behind the shop window, presents a remarkably ambitious study of luminous effects. The red, yellow and bluish-green apothecary globes reflect the streetlight outside the shop, as well as the lamps within. At the same time, the shop's large plate glass window shines with reflections and the space within the store is defined by spreading, overlapping, differently colored pools and spheres of light. Angrand's treatment of light in the background of this painting seems a perfect illustration of the aesthetic implications of the wave theory of light, which compared the motion of light waves to ripples spreading through water.

In contrast to the magical illuminations behind the plate glass window, street-side lighting in *The Accident* defines the pedestrians' world. The street lamp is a conventional point source of light, like the candles, lamps, and suns in the perspective treatises. Light falls on black-garbed pedestrians and the white horse in carefully measured angles; its warm color brightens up the dark coats and creates contrasting greyish blue shadows on the animal. The street itself is in shadow. An unseen light source illuminates the face and red dress of the woman in the foreground; most probably it is cast by a street lamp near the viewer. We know that she is about to enter another light zone.

Street illumination diagram from Heinrich Lux, *Die öffentliche Beleuchtung von Berlin*, Berlin 1896, Carnegie Library, Pittsburgh

1 Elizabeth Gaskell, *Mary Barton: A Tale of Manchester Life* (1848), London 1970, p. 101.

Charles Angrand, *The Accident*,
1887, Private collection

From light to color

Between June and November 1888, Van Gogh painted three versions of *The Sower*. This may be the second of the series, a careful study for the large composition now in the Bührle Collection, Zurich. Despite its small size, *The Sower* exerts an enormous visual and spiritual impact on most viewers. Its powerful diagonals and contrasting purples and yellows, greens and pinks catch the eye. The juxtaposition of setting sun and sowing peasant evokes the recurring birth and death cycles of nature, a constant theme in Van Gogh's personal brand of Christian pantheism.

Van Gogh drew on several artistic prototypes for this composition. Most obvious are the repeated images of the sower by his hero Millet. Van Gogh often praised the religious intensity of Millet's nearly monochromatic peasant scenes, with their subtle and powerful light effects. Translating Millet into color had been one of the goals of his move to Arles, where the pure air and brilliant sunlight would reveal color in all its variety and intensity. As he wrote to his brother Theo in May 1888, "[...] the painter of the future will be a colorist the like of which has never yet been seen."[1] In addition, he was looking closely at Japanese prints and at the symbolist paintings of his friend Gauguin, who joined him in Arles that October.

Whatever its symbolic and emotional content, *The Sower* also represents real twilight effects that can be linked with light phenomena specific to the early evening and the atmosphere in the south of France. The most prominent is the green sky. In May and June 1888, as he was working on his first version of *The Sower* (Kröller-Müller Museum, Otterlo), Van Gogh remarked on it twice. In a letter to Theo, he wrote, "When good old Corot said a few days before his death, 'Last night in a dream, I saw landscapes with skies all pink,' well, they've arrived, haven't they, those pink skies, and yellow and green ones into the bargain, in the impressionist landscape? Which means that some things one can foresee in the future do indeed come about."[2] And a few weeks later, he mentioned seeing again "the green azure of the white-hot sky" in Provence.[3]

Similarly, the oversized yellow sun on the horizon corresponds to a twilight phenomenon known as the "moon illusion." In this dramatic optical illusion, the setting sun or rising moon appears to be approximately three times its normal size while it is close to the horizon.[4] Finally, the unusual blueness of the landscape, evident in the lavender and indigo tones of the fields, tree, and peasant's jacket, may result from the so-called Purkinje shift, which occurs in the human eye as the environment gradually brightens or darkens. During the half-hour period while the retina adjusts between reliance on its cones (for daylight vision) to its rods (for night vision), its ability to perceive tones in the blue range increases significantly.

Therefore, it seems plausible that Van Gogh's *Sower* combines natural light phenomena that the artist observed at different times during his sojourn in Arles. All the same, his goals had moved far from the naturalistic representation of light typical of impressionism. As he wrote about *The Sower* in June 1888, "[...] I couldn't care less what the colors are in reality. I'd sooner do those naïve pictures out of old almanacs, old farmers' almanacs where hail, snow, rain, and fine weather are depicted in a wholly primitive manner [...]."[5] The final irony being that the almanacs, however naïve, were also accurate.

1 Letter to his brother Theo, ca. 4 May 1888 (606/482).
2 Letter to his brother Theo, ca. 20 May 1888 (613/489).
3 Letter to his brother Theo, 12-13 June 1888 (627/497).
4 Lynch and Livingston 1995, p. 226. Current theory explains the phenomenon as an illusion caused by the brain's tendency to interpret an object on the horizon as farther away than a similar sized object high in the sky. Thus, although the size of the solar disk does not change as it rises or sets, the brain registers the disk on the horizon as farther away – and therefore larger – than the same disk at midday.
5 Letter to Emile Bernard, ca. 18 June 1888 (630/B7).

Vincent van Gogh, *The Sower*,
1888, Van Gogh Museum,
Amsterdam (Vincent van Gogh
Foundation)

Reviewing the day's work

Anna and Michael Ancher,
Reviewing the Day's Work, 1883,
Statens Museum for Kunst,
Copenhagen

The ideal light for painting, as any artist will confirm, is daylight, which has a constant color spectrum that includes all the shades of the rainbow in a gentle curve. Depending on its type, artificial light, on the other hand, has a variety of spectrums, leaving painters with the dilemma that oil, gas and arc light either suppress or overemphasize certain colors. In this double portrait, the Danish artists Anna and Michael Ancher depict themselves studying an unfinished canvas. As the title states, they are reviewing the day's work. The only source of light is an oil lamp, its flame shaded by a matte-glass globe. Such globes, which not only shielded the light but also were highly decorative, had come into fashion in the 1850s. Here, the lamp occupies the center of the composition, standing between the easel and the artist-couple. Lost in silence and thought, they take a moment to inspect their achievements. As painters working for the free market rather than a patron, it was only possible for them to judge the composition with any certainty: the appearance of the colors depended entirely on where the picture was eventually hung. It is also possible, that the couple is checking to see if the work looks as good in the evening, by the light of a lamp, as it did during the day. The size of the work in progress seems to indicate that it was indeed intended for a domestic setting.

In the Segantini, it is not the painter, but rather his models, who are shown studying a recently completed canvas. By the light of a lantern, the boy and girl peer intently at the picture on the easel. Their relative poverty (they were employed in the artist's household) stands in sharp contrast to the wealthy society for which the painting was finally intended. Segantini, who also referred to this work as a "lantern effect," was particularly interested in what he called "the mysterious division of color," which, in his opinion, was nothing less than the "pure study of light."[1] His method of painting appears to have been almost scientific, and he was distressed by what he perceived to be the progressive alienation of art and science: "You, men of science and philosophers, do not flee from us but instead approach; only together can we create a new culture, one we may call 'the culture of the sun.'"[2] Like many of his contemporaries, Segantini was searching for the meaning of art, much as his models seek out their likenesses in the picture within the picture.

1. Giovanni Segantini, *Schriften und Briefe*, Zurich 1935, p. 91.
2. Ibid., p. 59.

Giovanni Segantini, *My Models*,
1888, Kunsthaus Zurich

Gaslight effect

In the nineteenth century, artists suddenly found themselves confronted with a new dilemma: the lighting conditions in which their works would be seen could no longer be predicted. The American painter Thomas Eakins remarked in 1874: "One ought to know where the work is going to be exhibited before one even begins to paint it."[1] In a moving passage in *L'Oeuvre*, Emile Zola describes how the painter Claude Lantier, the novel's hero, discovers his painting hung at the Paris Salon: "As if drawn and held by some invisible force, he stood glaring in astonishment at his picture. He hardly recognized it hanging there in that room. It was certainly not the work he had seen in his studio. It looked yellower in the light that filtered through the white cotton screen; it looked somehow smaller, too, and cruder, and yet at the same time more laboured."[2]

Gas bracket, French, ca. 1880–1900, Lumière de l'oeil, Paris

Vincent van Gogh, *The Yellow House*, 1888, Van Gogh Museum, Amsterdam (Vincent van Gogh Foundation)

Vincent van Gogh's brief artistic career coincided with one of the most important decades in the history of lighting, when gas, kerosene and electricity were fighting for market dominance. He painted *Gauguin's Chair*, a still life of a chair and candle, in Arles in 1888, one of the key works in his *oeuvre*.

While the candle on Gauguin's chair has led to all kinds of speculation regarding the symbolic nature of Van Gogh's art, the second light source in the picture – the open gas flame in the background – has been treated only cursorily. The gaslight has robbed the candle of its practical function, thus reinforcing the notion that the latter has a more abstract and symbolic character. In fact, however, the case is somewhat more complicated. Van Gogh mentioned gaslight so often in his letters that it seems safe to say it had a particular meaning for him. At the beginning of one of his letters to Theo, from the second half of October 1888, he wrote that he had just had gas pipes laid in his studio and in the kitchen of the Yellow House. He justifies the outlay spent with the claim that he and Gauguin would now be able to paint in the evenings as well as during the day, stating that within a fortnight they would have recouped the twen-

ty-five francs invested.[3] Not only did nothing of the sort come to pass, the following January he was forced to inform Theo that the gas company had begun charging for its product.[4]

It seems probable that sometime during September or early October, the private households on Van Gogh's street were connected to the gas network. The view of the Yellow House, dating from September 1888, shows some kind of digging work in the foreground – perhaps the laying of a pipeline. We can thus assume that the painter, hoping to profit from the situation, had his own residence linked up as well. The house itself is placed at the center of the composition; to the left, we see the street lights on the Place Lamartine, while to the right, a train crosses a bridge. It is certainly no accident that these two icons of modernity – street lamps and the railroad – frame the picture. Van Gogh often integrated them into his paintings and drawings; he clearly saw his house as an integral part of the urban system.

Nighttime street scenes and interiors clearly fascinated Van Gogh during September 1888: such well-known works as *The Night Café* and the *Café Terrace at Night* date to just this period. Several times Van Gogh mentioned in his letters that the *Starry Night on the Rhône* was painted by gaslight, and in October he appears to have become completely obsessed with its effects. He fantasized about painting the gas-lit boulevards of Paris and a short time later he told Theo how nice his studio looked in this light, by which he hoped to paint portraits – "that seems to me something that still needs to be done."[5] *Gauguin's Chair* is the first evidence of the modernization of Van Gogh's studio. The gas flame has a kind of aura that clearly differentiates it from the candle – a flame that does not radiate, reduced to a symbol with no luminosity of its own. Only modern gaslight was capable of illuminating the surroundings. Perhaps the artist believed that in depicting gaslight in this way he was creating something entirely original, something never seen before that could even become the trademark of his art, helping to open new markets for his pictures.

1 Kathleen A. Foster, *Thomas Eakins Rediscovered: Charles Bregler's Thomas Eakins Collection at the Pennsylvania Academy of the Fine Arts*, New Haven & London 1997, pp. 76-77.
2 Emile Zola, *The Masterpiece*, translated by Thomas Walton, London 1950, p. 127.
3 Letter to his brother Theo, ca. 21 October 1888 (714/556).
4 Letter to his brother Theo, 19 January 1889 (742/572).
5 Letters to his brother Theo, 10 October 1888 (707/550); 10 October 1888 (706/549); 28 October 1888 (719/558b).

Van Gogh's painting *Gauguin's Chair* seen by gaslight, reproduced by Kevin McGuire, Tailored Lighting, Inc., Rochester, New York

Vincent van Gogh, *Gauguin's Chair*, 1888, Van Gogh Museum, Amsterdam (Vincent van Gogh Foundation

American lights

Even as Americans were flocking to Europe to acquire culture, sophistication, and taste, European connoisseurs were viewing American industrial design with admiration and envy. In the field of lamps and lighting, Americans were considered the world's leading innovators. German scholar, critic, and museum director Wilhelm Bode was deeply impressed by American exhibits at the Chicago World's Columbian Exposition of 1893: "In America, the character of incandescent light was correctly grasped right from the beginning, and as a result the lamps were constructed and shaped in the most varied and imaginative – often even fantastic – ways. The American has accomplished the task of supplying full-strength, gentle, and uniform light to all parts of the room, while at the same time protecting the eye against glare, in the most productive and versatile ways."[1]

Samuel Bing, another European reporting on American manufacturers, loved the work of Tiffany in particular: "[Electric] light, so intense in its naked state, was sometimes shaded into an opalescent glow, at other times diffused into brilliant beams refracted by the hundred prisms of multicolored glass. In this kind of fixture, glass, revealing its most magical effects, takes on the role of marvelous collaborator [...] and always so designed so as to disperse a soft, even light, while unlit in daytime, they still constitute ornaments in perfect harmony with their surroundings. Sometimes, in a particularly lavish interior, the mysterious gleam of a luminous wall emerges from the shadows, magical in its harmonies, and whose appearance, stimulating the imagination, transports it to enchanted dreams."[2]

In an effort to revitalize tradition-bound French manufacturing, Bing commissioned avant-garde painters to design stained glass walls for exhibition and sale in his Salon de l'Art Nouveau in Paris. The brilliantly colored, decorative styles of French artists adapted well to decorative lighting designs. When com-

Tiffany & Co., *Table lamp*, ca. 1899–1902, Carnegie Museum of Art, Pittsburgh, Gift of Mr. Arthur E. Braun

Tiffany's richly colored glass imitated the saturated colors of Byzantine mosaics and gothic stained glass windows. However, his natural motifs, such as the dragonflies in this example, are typical of late nineteenth-century art nouveau.

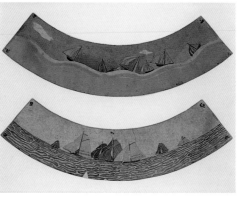

Félix Vallotton, *Lamp shades*, ca. 1898, tempera on parchment, Private collection, Paris

bined with the new electric lights, they represented a cutting-edge union of art and technology. Toulouse-Lautrec's *Papa Chrysanthème* was manufactured for Bing in Tiffany's New York studios. It makes luxurious use of Tiffany's variegated glass to imitate Lautrec's swirling, multi-colored brushstrokes.

The new fashions even inspired artists to furnish their old-fashioned kerosene and oil lamps with new shades. Félix Vallotton, one of the group of Nabi painters patronized by Bing, made his own lampshades with paint on parchment that compensate for their humble materials with whimsy and charm.

1 Wilhelm Bode, "Modern Art in the United States of America: Impressions Following a Visit to the Universal Exposition in Chicago," quoted in Holt 1988, vol. 1, p. 100.
2 Samuel Bing, *Artistic America, Tiffany Glass, and Art Nouveau* (1895), Cambridge, Massachusetts, & London 1970, pp. 178-83.

Henri de Toulouse-Lautrec and
Louis Comfort Tiffany, *Au
Nouveau Cirque, Papa Chrysanthème*, 1894–95, stained glass,
cabochons, Musée d'Orsay, Paris

Lautrec's design represents a
scene from a Japanese-
themed ballet performed at
the Nouveau Cirque.

Starry nights

The Night Sky over Paris, lithograph from Amédée Guillemin, *The Heavens*, Paris 1866, Carnegie Museum of Art, Pittsburgh, Curatorial Library

In September 1888, Vincent van Gogh became fixated with the idea of painting the night sky. In a letter to his sister, Willemien, he claimed that he often found the night – with its violet, blue and intense green tones – more colorful than the day. The stars, too, seemed to shine in different colors, alternating between lemon yellow, pink, green and forget-me-not blue. Merely painting white dots against a blue-black background could not do justice to reality.[1] By the end of the month he was ready to begin: "finally, the starry night," he wrote to Theo. He later described the work as a view of Arles seen from the banks of the Rhône and showing the town lit by gaslight; the city itself had been done in blue and violet, the gaslight in yellow, and its reflection in tones ranging from red-gold to a bronze green. He painted the Great Bear in green and red against a green-blue sky, pale in comparison to the blazing gold of the gaslight.[2]

It is difficult to imagine a more complicated lighting situation. Nonetheless, Van Gogh had no qualms about setting himself the task of painting a scene that had no precedent even in the long tradition of the nocturne: a view of an artificially lit town under a starry sky and its mirror image in water. The work can only be compared to the bravura landscapes of the eighteenth century, with their variety of light sources and complex reflections. The artist clearly aimed to reproduce the scene accurately, capturing both the colors of the gaslight and the stars themselves. In reference to the latter, art historian Albert Boime has suggested the artist may have been inspired by popular science. Although unable to prove this thesis, Boime did set the painter's interest within the context of the late nineteenth-century fascination with the then recent progress in astronomy.[3]

More interesting than the similarities, however, are the differences between the scientific and artistic interpretations of the night sky. One is amazed by the exactitude of the illustrations and prints made in the decades preceding Van Gogh's picture. Two celebrated French books of the period offer some excellent examples. Amédée Guillemin pictured the night sky above Paris, a motif similar to Van Gogh's view of Arles; the Dutchman's painting, however, has nowhere near the amount of detail found in the illustration. In comparison with this one and other illustrations, Van Gogh's reproduction of the star-filled sky seems rather awkward. Naturally, this is not an accusation; the painter was, in fact, pursuing entirely different goals. He was primarily interested in the variety of colors a sensitive person could perceive if he or she looked closely enough at nature. His painting is an *effet de nuit*, a painterly exercise not intended to generate scientific knowledge. Perhaps it is true that Van Gogh's interest in, and enthusiasm for, the night sky was born of the same spirit that made Guillemin and Flammarion into best-selling authors. Their visual interpretation of starlight could not, however, be more different. Here, art and science went their separate ways.

1 Letter to his sister Willemien, 9 and 16 September 1888 (681/W7).
2 Letter to his brother Theo, ca. 29 September 1888 (695/543).
3 Boime 1984.

Vincent van Gogh, *Starry Night on
the Rhône River*, 1888, Musée
d'Orsay, Paris

Under the street lantern

The history of street lamp design has yet to be written. One only occasionally finds references in local historical publications to the designers of the lamps used in a particular area. Nonetheless, important artists have put their hand to the task, beginning in the seventeenth century with Jan van der Heyden, whose oil lamps first illuminated the city of Amsterdam. Certain streetlights in Berlin have been ascribed to the architect Karl Friedrich Schinkel, although there is no proof of his authorship. Most famous perhaps are the Art Nouveau lights decorating the entrances of many a metro station in Paris, the work of Hector Guimard. Despite their relatively short history, all these lamps have undergone a number of important transformations – with more or less successful results. Often, these changes were merely technical in nature, such as replacing the gas flame with an electric light bulb. The arc light, however, required a completely different casing: due to the glare of the light, it had to be placed at a higher level, and had to be able to house all kinds of spools, springs and wires for keeping the carbon electrodes apart. In the twentieth century, many a street lamp has been consigned to the scrap heap. Until recently, there was little interest in the preservation of historic public spaces. Old lamps are occasionally cast anew, but only rarely are they used for their original type of lighting.

Contemporaries were well aware of innovations and their impact on the urban scenery. Even the paintings of the impressionists and post-impressionists occasionally have a street light as the central focus – as the works of Gustave Caillebotte, Claude Monet, and Paul Signac demonstrate. Van Gogh, too, painted an entire row of street lamps on Montmartre, which take up half the canvas. These pictures generally show the lamps by daylight, and are, unfortunately, no help in determining how effective they actually were in the dark of the night.

Vincent van Gogh, *Belvedère Overlooking Montmartre*, 1886–87, Art Institute of Chicago, Helen Birch Bartlett Memorial Collection

Etienne Moreau-Nélaton, *Bec Auer*, 1895, color lithograph, Kunsthalle Bremen

Moreau-Nélaton is better known as a collector of the impressionists than as painter and graphic artist. Here, he has created an advertisement for the Bec Auer Company, whose gas mantles helped delay the final triumph of electricity.

The marketplace of light

At the end of the nineteenth century, international fairs had become international competitions, in which the host countries invited all nations to put their arts, industries, and cultures on display and on the line. Each fair outdid its predecessor in size and splendor, thanks in large part to increasingly sophisticated and imaginative uses of the new electric lighting technologies. Thomas Edison, innovative promoter of the electric light bulb, was instrumental in the production of these elaborate spectacles that would convince consumers of their need for electric lighting at home.

These great displays stunned audiences with their brilliance, color, and scale. Fireworks, searchlights, illuminated fountains, and magical vistas composed of twinkling lights reduced visitors to speechless awe. Reproducing these spectacles proved to be beyond the scope of the stationary black and white image in the popular press. At the 1889 Paris exposition, with its controversial Eiffel

Tower, the boldly colored light effects could not be conveyed by conventional wood engravings, although colored prints came closer. Even so, Georges Garen tried his best to capture the motion, sparkle, and transformations created by light.

A view of the electrical spectaculars at the 1900 Paris exposition succeeds better with glittery materials (fashionable in the eighteenth century) added to colored lithographic prints. Ground up mica, a highly reflective, glass-like rock, was adhered to the lighted areas to suggest the dazzling glare of arc and incandescent lighting. Large colored lamps are represented by stamped tinfoil stars in red and blue, and small beads of colored, translucent paste glued onto the paper. Displayed in strong light, this print shines and glitters in an amusing and suggestive fashion. It could not be reproduced for mass consumption however, as some background coloring and glitter materials had to be added individually by hand.

Georges Garen, *Illumination of the Eiffel Tower during the Universal Exposition, Paris 1889*, 1889, colored wood engraving, Musée d'Orsay, Paris, fonds Eiffel

The Universal Exposition, Paris 1900: The Palais de l'Electricité Illuminated at Night, photograph, Roger-Viollet

Theodor-Josef Hoffbauer, *The
Universal Exposition, Paris 1900:
The Palais de l'Electricité and the
Château d'Eau*, 1900, handcolored
lithograph, with mica chips and
stamped tinfoil, Private collection

The dark side of street light

Since its introduction by Lieutenant De la Reynie on 2 September 1667, Paris's public lighting system had been the concern of the police.[1] It was not only designed to improve the navigability of the city's streets, but also to insure that they were safe. This naturally had drawbacks as well. Many innocent citizens, for whom the light was supposed to be an improvement, came to believe that illuminating the night would only make the work of burglars that much easier.[2] In 1819, the *Kölnische Zeitung* reported anxiously on the establishment of a gasworks in Paris, believing it would lead to a deterioration of morals: "Artificial light dispels the fear of darkness that prevents many a weakling from committing sins. The light assures the drinker that he can stay in the bar until nightfall, and it debilitates couples in love [...]."[3]

One profession the police certainly had no interest in promoting profited like no other from the introduction of the street lamp: prostitution. The illuminated boulevard became the whore's favored territory. Under the light of the gas flame, and in imitation of the *flaneur*, she ruled the streets or so it was

believed. City guides warned of the dangers lurking around every corner, thus stimulating the tourist's curiosity: "No where are the Nymphs of the *pavé* to be seen in greater force than on the Boulevards. As soon as the lamps are lit, they come pouring through the passages and the adjacent *rues*, an uninterrupted stream, until past midnight."[4]

By the 1860s, the underworld was so indelibly associated with gaslight that it gave rise to a whole new literary genre – referred to as "Under the Gaslight" novels. Soon artists, too, discovered the connection between street lights and streetwalkers, transforming it into a subject for painting. The enormous number of representations, only a tiny selection of which we show here, allows only one conclusion: the new lanterns and the prostitution they "brought to light" were quintessential symbols of urban night life. Sin and morality, once depicted in allegories of a classicizing bent, were now "translated" into the present. Such themes also allowed the artist to express his anti-bourgeois stance, to show himself a true bohemian to whom nothing human was foreign and who was not afraid to socialize with (other) outsiders.

Medardo Rosso, *Kiss under the Lamppost*, 1882–83, bronze, Museo Medardo Rosso, Barzio (Como)

Théophile-Alexandre Steinlen, *A Prostitute's Prayer*, 1894, lithograph, Rijksmuseum, Rijksprentenkabinet, Amsterdam

"Marmite" (literally "cooking pot") from the original French title is slang for the mistress of a pimp. In her "church," altar candles have been replaced by street lights.

Emile Bernard, *Girl in a Paris Street*, 1888, watercolor, Van Gogh Museum, Amsterdam (Vincent van Gogh Foundation)

This is probably the most artistically radical equation of streetwalker and street lamp: in this drawing they have become one.

1 Knapp 1879, p. 7.
2 Griffiths 1992, p. 278.
3 Quoted after Rebske 1962, p. 37.
4 *Paris after Dark: Night Guide for Gentlemen*, ca. 1870, quoted after Clayson 1991, p. 93.

Jacobus van Looy, *Paris by Night*,
ca. 1886–87, pastel, Instituut
Collectie Nederland, on loan to
the Van Gogh Museum,
Amsterdam

Modern science, modern art

Vincent van Gogh, *Trunks of Trees with Ivy*, 1889, Van Gogh Museum, Amsterdam (Vincent van Gogh Foundation)

In 1889, Vincent van Gogh left Paris for Arles in the south of France; his friend and colleague Signac moved to nearby St. Tropez in 1892. Both artists wished to work in the brilliant Mediterranean sunlight that illuminated the Algerian landscapes painted thirty years earlier by their hero Eugène Delacroix.

These two landscapes were painted in the south of France. Their subject is the play of light through foliage on a hot summer day, and the contrast of cool foreground shadows with the baking yellow heat of a distant landscape. Each artist noted, in his own way, the intensification of color in shaded spaces, the blueness of shadows, and the bleaching of tone in intense light. Both artists applied color with isolated, discreet brushstrokes to simulate the dazzling effects of sunshine.

Like many impressionist paintings, Van Gogh's *Trunks of Trees with Ivy* is a wonderfully

direct observation of nature, and its goal is the naturalistic representation of light and atmosphere. However, much of its impact depends on strong brushwork. The prominent diagonal strokes in the foreground suggest not only individual leaves, but also the movement of sunshine falling from the upper left. Thick blobs and ridges of paint scatter light to create a scintillating effect in the eye of the viewer. Thus, Van Gogh created glowing patches of dancing sunshine despite the limited light/dark contrasts achievable through oil pigments.

Signac took almost the opposite approach. *Places des Lices* is painted with uniform, flat dots of pure hue. Each tiny dot mixes with nearby dots of complimentary and contrasting hues to create the colors perceived by the viewer. The resulting impressions of intense sunlight and cool shadows overwhelm the ostensible subject of a city square. Signac's tech-

1 Paul Signac, "From Eugène Delacroix to Neo-impressionism," trans. Willa Silverman, in Floyd Ratliff, *Paul Signac and Color in Neo-impressionism*, New York 1992, pp. 206, 208.

2 Minnaert 1993, pp. 1-4.

Paul Signac, *Place des Lices, St. Tropez*, 1893, Carnegie Museum of Art, Pittsburgh, Acquired through the generosity of the Sarah Mellon Scaife family

nique, divisionism, had been invented by Georges Seurat in the mid 1880s and developed further by Signac after Seurat's death in 1892. As Signac explained in his influential treatise *D'Eugène Delacroix au Néo-Impressionisme*, "[...] these painters came to their technique because of their desire to achieve a maximum of brightness, color, and harmony which seemed to them unobtainable by any other mode of expression [...].To obtain this luminous, colored brilliance, the Neo-Impressionists use only pure colors, which, insofar as matter can come close to light, approximate all the colors of the prism."[1]

Signac believed that the neo-impressionists' rigorous, disciplined application of the rules of divisionism merited comparison with contemporary scientific methods. He was proud of the artists' adaptations of theories of Newton, Young, and Helmholtz on spectral color and optical mixing. In *Place des Lices*, Signac also made use of scientists' observations of how sunlight falling through narrow openings (such as those between the individual leaves of trees), projects elliptical images of the sun itself on flat surfaces (such as a dusty city square).[2] Like many of his generation, Signac seems to have believed that scientific discoveries and methods were the key to the future, offering new solutions to problems as old as the proper depiction of color, light, and shade.

Round and elliptical images of the sun seen through foliage, wood engraving from Amedée Guillemin, *La Lumière*, Paris 1882, Private collection

The economy of light

Ever since mankind first tamed fire, light has been a commercial product. What is produced, however, is not the light itself, but rather the means for making it: oil, wax, gas, kerosene, and electric energy. Like most other goods until the end of the Baroque period, light was available in cheap and expensive forms in anything from primitive tallow to luxurious wax candles. A large amount of light was naturally a status symbol, and it was only at court that one could afford to be lavish with it. This changed with the advent of the Industrial Age. Substantial quantities of light were necessary for traffic and factory work. The real revolution in light production, however, came with the separation of the light source from the location where the supply (gas or electricity) was produced.

Gasworks, and later electrical plants, were located far away from the consumer; a single unit could serve thousands of customers. An abstract relationship between producer and consumer – codified by law, and controlled by contracts and the monopolies of third parties – characterizes the beginning of the networked era in which we still live today. The gas turned on at home was delivered by a closely interconnected system of pipes; these had their origin in gigantic tanks situated at the edges of the city, which, in turn, were connected by railroad tracks to the mines in other parts of the country. Here, the raw material of light (coal) was extracted, a process that could only take place efficiently under the proper lighting conditions. This circuit and the mutual dependencies thus created, gave rise to a new class of entrepreneurs. The feudal powers were left with no choice but to either take part in the process and adapt to bourgeois values, or to remain as they were, dreaming of the old days in the candlelight glow of their chandeliers.

Examined more closely, the overall picture is undoubtedly more complicated; yet, the history of light production can certainly be considered a case study in nineteenth-century capitalism. In almost no other area was the pace of change so fast. One technological improvement followed upon the heels of another, all needing to be digested by an amazed public that barely had time to get used to one new light source before being confronted with the next. Gas managed to hold on to its monopoly on remote-supplied light, although this did not mean it held the monopoly on lighting in general. Most private homes continued to be lit by oil. Since the 1850s, the production of kerosene had offered a cheaper alternative. It was only with the advent of electric lighting that the gas era finally came to an end. Following the publication of several early experiments around 1873, the announcement of the invention of the light bulb on 11 October 1878 caused gas prices to plummet, creating panic among shareholders.[1] In an effort to keep their product viable, gas producers responded with much-needed technical improvements. Finally, the inventors and exploiters of gas, kerosene and electricity entered into fierce competition. Innovation by one led the others to try and catch up or even surpass them through imitation. The pace of development increased steadily at the end of the nineteenth century, with light becoming ever faster and brighter. Truly, light had become the bearer and symbol of progress.

Auguste Tilly, *The Nightmare of a Gas-Factory Director*, 1882, wood engraving

This wood engraving was so popular that it was reproduced in numerous magazines all over the world between 1882 and 1884. It shows the inventors of electricity haunting gas manufacturer's dreams. Edison can be seen in the upper middle, while Swan is shown riding his namesake below. The large number of now-forgotten figures demonstrates how much competition gaslighting was facing at just this time.

Stock certificates, American, between 1858 and 1890, Private collection

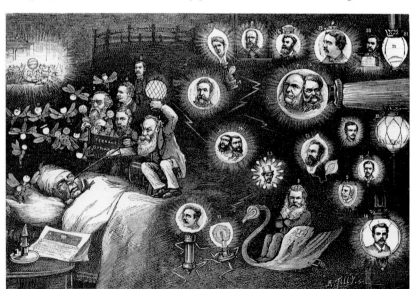

1 Rebske 1962, p. 88; Urbanitzky 1883, p. 6.

The orange glow of decadence

Vincent van Gogh, *Stuffed Kalong Bat (Flying Dog)*, 1886, Van Gogh Museum, Amsterdam (Vincent van Gogh Foundation)

The translucent wings function like a parchment lamp shade, dimming, coloring, and diffusing the light.

Emile Gallé, *Bat lamp*, ca. 1900, glass and bronze, Collection Neumann, Gingins (Switzerland)

Multiple layers and colors of glass create the effect of bats silhouetted against an orange evening sky.

In 1884, Joris-Karl Huysmans published *Against Nature*, the story of the aesthete des Esseintes and his attempt to live a life of total decadence. While furnishing his house in his new style, the hero gave highest priority to his selection of lighting and color: "What he wanted was colours which would appear stronger and clearer in artificial light. He did not particularly care if they looked crude or insipid in daylight, for he lived most of his life at night, holding that night afforded greater intimacy and isolation and that the mind was truly roused and stimulated only by awareness of the dark [...]".[1] Des Esseintes dismissed the cool tones – blues, purples, grays – and pale warm tones such as pinks, which fared poorly in artificial light. He then correlated each color with the artistic temperament most responsive to it. Eliminating tasteful conventionality (blues and greys), and robust energy (reds and yellows), des Esseintes was left with one temperament, the decadent. "As for those gaunt, febrile creatures of feeble constitution and nervous disposition whose sensual appetite craves dishes that are smoked and seasoned, their eyes almost always prefer that most morbid and irritating of colors, with its acid glow and unnatural splendor – orange. There could be no doubt whatsoever about des Esseintes's final choice [...]".[2]

Throughout the nineteenth century, but gaining impetus after 1850, scientists conducted serious research into the physiology and psychology of the senses, including color perception. As it became possible to measure light and sensory responses more accurately, there were numerous efforts to gauge the effects of colored light on everything from human health to plant growth. In both science and art theory, reds, oranges and yellows were believed to have an exciting effect on the nerves and psyche which could be injurious if overdone. As early as 1857, housekeeping manuals recommended avoiding orange wall hangings, especially because the color "is too fatiguing for the eye."[3] The red and orange flames of oil and gas lamps damaged eyes and nerves, causing inflammation or palsy of the retina, and subsequent blindness.[4]

The orange light transmitted through Van Gogh's bat wings and Gallé's glass lampshade decorated with fluttering bats would have fit right into des Esseintes's décor. Van Gogh was reading the novels and essays of Huysmans, de Maupassant and other naturalist writers at the time he executed his *Stuffed Kalong Bat*, and his admiration for them is recorded in his letters and still life paintings of the period. Bats were also symbols of decadence – strange, delicate creatures that flew by night, like des Esseintes himself and the fin de siècle flaneurs strolling the streets of Paris. Emile Gallé's *Bat lamp* also pays homage to the decadents while addressing new aesthetic problems created by the incandescent electric light bulb. Its cool, bright light was completely out of harmony with the desired orange glow of decadence.

1 Joris-Karl Huysmans, *Against Nature (A Rebours)* (1884), trans. Robert Baldick, New York 1959, p. 28.
2 Ibid., p. 30.
3 Youmans 1857, pp. 103-04.
4 Ibid., pp. 146-47.

Projections II

The Ionic Order, educational art history slide, French, ca. 1900–1910, Private collection

It would seem that the last professionals to use slides for study and teaching purposes were precisely those most dependent on visual material, namely art historians. Although photographic glass slides had been available since 1849, they were only introduced into art history lectures in the United States in 1882; Europe followed suit a year later. Initially, however, there was little enthusiasm for the invention. And yet slides had one enormous advantage: one could use them to compare works of art that were normally never seen together.[1]

In the nineteenth century, the popularity of magic lanterns continued and even increased. Improvements in lighting allowed for larger projections at greater distances, and thus for bigger audiences. They were still mainly used for entertainment and popular education, the two often going hand in hand. According to Hankins and Silverman, projections began to be used to educate the lower ranks of society in France as early as 1839.[2] One of the most important pioneers in this field was the Abbé Moigno. His memoirs describe the administrative difficulties he encountered trying to set up a night school. He believed that only knowledge presented through experiment or images would really take root. The program offered at his Salle de Progrès was enormously varied: in any given week one could enjoy lectures on music, science, geography, developments in optics, the miracle of creation and, at the end, a concert of religious music.[3] Various kinds of projections, using limelight, magnesium or electricity, helped Moigno achieve his ambitious goals. Such "theaters of science" were known throughout Europe and America, and probably even beyond – British explorer David Livingstone, for example, fascinated audiences in Africa with his projections, writing: "It was the only mode of instruction I was ever asked to repeat."[4]

The magic lantern soon found its way into private households. Looking back in 1895, one author described the impression such projection made on him in his youth: "How thrilled we were as children when our father or 'big

Painting a panorama from a projected image, wood engraving from *L'Exposition de Paris* (*Encyclopédie du Siècle*), 3 vols., Paris 1900, Private collection

brother' promised to take out the magic lantern after supper. We sat together in the oh-so mysterious darkness, giggling in anticipation. A sheet or large napkin – perfectly clean, of course, large and stiff and folded in four – was pinned to the wall, while our father or brother set about moving the furniture in order to create a stand. A few suppressed groans from the operator, caused by burned fingertips, and the performance could begin. Boos and hisses if the pictures were upside down, countered by the most solemn assurances that the slide had indeed been put in the right way."[5] Magic lantern clubs sprang up everywhere, and by the end of the century, the first historians of the medium had also appeared on the scene – a sure sign that the era was coming to an end. Moving pictures had taken the place of the static lantern slides.

Lapierre, *Magic Lantern*, ca. 1880, Haags Documentatie Centrum Nieuwe Media, The Hague

1 Grimm 1892; Dilly 1975; Leighton 1984.
2 Hankins and Silverman 1995, p. 65.
3 Moigno 1872, pp. I-X.
4 Quoted in David Robinson's foreword to Hecht 1993, p. VII.
5 Ign. Bispinck, "Iets over projecteren," *Fotografisch Jaarboek* 4 (1895), pp. 59-68, here p. 59. Thanks to Ingeborg Leijerzapf.

Invisible light

As more and more information became available on the actual physics of light, the phenomenon itself became more and more puzzling. It was increasingly apparent that what the human eye perceives is not always what is really there. Particularly in the last decade of the nineteenth century, artists sought to give visual expression to the invisible. The painters, sculptors and graphic artists usually grouped together under the generic name "symbolists" were, in fact, extraordinarily diverse, not only in the techniques they employed, but also in their choice of subject matter. The only thing they truly had in common was a supposed rejection of the real, objective world.

However, the symbolists were unable to free themselves entirely from the sensual reality that surrounded them. Odilon Redon, for example, combined his love of the occult with a fascination for contemporary scientific research and its discoveries. Although removed from their everyday context and integrated into the artist's own fantasy world, many of his compositions deal with themes discussed in scientific magazines, or have their origins in natural history. Light and light rays are continually reoccurring subjects. His figures are often surrounded by a kind of aura or nimbus, a motif he derived from both traditional Christian iconography and the then current fashion for "spirit photography." In this lithograph, Redon alludes to a projection on canvas. Here, light itself, which is in fact ungraspable, takes the form of a giant head. This transformation into something palpable, however, only serves to make the phenomenon appear more mysterious.

In contrast to Redon, Eugène Carrière was no dreamer, but rather a man with deep-seated social convictions. He made a name for himself with highly individual, misty, brownish portraits. His lithographs take this reduction of color one step further. In this piece, entitled *Sleep*, one can barely disentangle the head of the sleeping girl from the curving lines. Here, too, "occult photography" may have played a role, although there is no evidence that Carrière was interested in it. Another source for his fascination with diffuse light effects may have been the work of the Würzburg doctor Wilhelm Röntgen, who accidentally discovered the principle of the x-ray in 1895. This breakthrough, as scientifically important as it was, had a profoundly disturbing effect on the prevailing positivist worldview. The idea of examining the inside of the human body was simply beyond the contemporary imagination. It is therefore not surprising that the invisible and the unconscious, sleep and dreams, became increasingly interesting to both scientists and artists.

Eugène Carrière, *Sleep*, 1897, lithograph, Rijksmuseum, Rijksprentenkabinet, Amsterdam

Odilon Redon, *Light*, 1893, lithograph, Van Gogh Museum, Amsterdam

223 **Invisible light**

Time and light

Before clocks and watches became commonplace, people used light to measure time. The light of the sun changed in height, direction, and color over the course of the day; sunrise, noon, and sunset signified day's beginning, middle, and end. At night, the motions of the moon, planets, and stars allowed observers to track the hours, months, and years. Sundials and sextants permitted more sophisticated and arbitrary temporal distinctions, but they still measured out light. Some of the great cathedrals of Europe served as light-based timekeepers as well.

Claude Monet's famous series of views of Rouen Cathedral is loaded with paradoxes related to time and light. The most famous, of course, is Monet's representation of this enduring stone monument as an immaterial screen of evanescent, diaphanous light effects. A second paradox concerns its aesthetic goal and Monet's working methods. Intended to record the artist's observations of light on the Cathedral façade from moment to moment, the series was in fact completed in Paris with the aid of a photograph and the artist's memory and imagination. A third paradox is that Monet should have selected this subject – the relationship between daylight and time – just as rising standards of living and industrial working hours were finishing it off in urban society. In 1890s Paris, day was separated from night by the illumination or extinction of street lights, and the hours were told by bells

Claude Monet, *Rouen Cathedral: Façade and the Tour d'Albane (Morning Effect)*, 1893, Museum of Fine Arts, Boston, Tompkins Collection

1 Charles Stuckey, *Claude Monet 1840-1926*, exh. cat. Chicago (Art Institute of Chicago) 1995, p. 228.

Claude Monet, *Rouen Cathedral:*
Façade and the Tour d'Albane
(Morning Effect), 1894, Fondation
Beyeler, Riehen/Basel

and clocks. One final paradox: In 1895, twenty of these great studies of natural light effects were exhibited at the Durand-Ruel Gallery, to be viewed at least some of the time by gas or electric light.

The critic Georges Clemenceau complained that at the Durand-Ruel exhibition, the *Cathedrals* did not appear in chronological order. Viewers could not reconstruct the sweep of light across and around the Cathedral over the course of a day by looking at the paintings one after the other.[1] From this, we may conclude that Monet was not attempting to analyze time and the motion of the sun in any scientific sense that would be comparable to another great nineteenth-century series on time and motion, namely the human and animal studies by the photographer Eadweard Muybridge. Yet, when we place two morning views of the Cathedral side by side, as Clemenceau would have wished, we do perceive the shadows lightening, deep blues fading into warmer aquas tinged with yellow and orange, and the stone surfaces beginning to sparkle as they emerge into the light. Monet's expressive use of color and prominent brushstrokes convey the onset of morning with a directness that affects not just the eyes, but also the emotions. Less objective, less detached, more personal and more decorative than Monet's landscapes of the 1870s, the *Cathedrals* explore the workings of light on the human senses and psyche.

Aurora

For centuries, light had been a symbol of truth and progress. The conquest of darkness was an important motif in the rich light symbolism of the Christian church. The Enlightenment in particular proclaimed the triumph of light over the evils of superstition. In the nineteenth century, many, sometimes incompatible, ideologies made use of similar symbols. The international workers' movements, for example, adopted the pictorial language of the French Revolution. In a flood of treatises and songs, they made use of light as a symbol of a glorious future when the chains of slavery would be broken and the working classes would take destiny into their own hands.

The thirst for light, however, was not merely abstract. The conditions in most factories and lodgings deprived the worker of natural light. Already in 1867, health problems among the members of certain professions appeared that could be traced back to a lack of light: "It may be enunciated as an indisputable fact, that all who live and pursue their calling in situations where the minimum degree of light is permitted to penetrate, suffer seriously in bodily and mental health." Forbes Winslow, author of *Light: Its Influence on Life and Health*, published in London, used his experiments with animals as proof.[1] Ironically, it was artificial light that had made the long working hours in windowless factories possible in the first place.

The majority of illustrations in socialist magazines and pamphlets had little or no artistic pretensions. Some representatives of the avant-garde, however – painters and graphic artists like Camille Pissarro or Théophile Steinlen – aligned themselves with the political Left, putting their art more or less regularly at the disposal of its causes and organizations. Henri de Toulouse-Lautrec and Eugène Carrière made posters for the radical magazines *L'Aube* and *L'Aurore*. The titles both refer to the dawn. In his poster for *L'Aube*, Toulouse-Lautrec depicts an exhausted family arriving in the city, all their possessions in a cart; a street lamp casts a ray of hope on the otherwise depressing scene. Carrière was best known for his murky, almost monochrome portraits. Politically, he counted himself a leftist. His lithograph announces the first edition of Georges Clemenceau's *Aurore*. The magazine was founded on 19 October 1897, and became famous a year later with the publication of Emile Zola's commentary on the Dreyfus Affair, "J'accuse."

One clever manufacturer knew how to turn the yearning for the sun to his own and others' advantage: William Lever introduced a soap he named "Sunlight" in the 1880s. He used some of the profits from its sales to improve the housing of his workers. His model workers' town, Port Sunlight on the Mersey River near Liverpool, even includes a museum, the Lady Lever Art Gallery, in its center. Natural light and enlightenment through education are here united.

Henri de Toulouse-Lautrec, *L'Aube*, 1896, lithograph, Kunsthalle Bremen

1 Winslow 1867, p. 6.

Form versus function

Concours de Lampes électriques

Lamp design published by the French Magazine *Art et Décoration* (April 1898), Rijksmuseum, Amsterdam

No one has yet written a stylistic history of the lamp. This is certainly not because lamps are there only to shed light on more beautiful things while not drawing attention to themselves. As an integral part of the domestic interior, designers create them to fit with the style of their surroundings, like chairs or cabinets. Chandeliers, candlesticks, and lamps are thus subject to the same laws of style and taste as all other crafted objects in the home. It appears, however, that the aesthetics of the lamp is limited to the packaging. The form of the candle and the shape of the light bulb are determined by their function, and little attention has been paid to their design. Since the Enlightenment, the development of lighting technology has been the province of technicians, engineers, and chemists, rather than artists. In contrast to all other furnishings, whose forms are determined by designers, the lamp is the only object in the living room whose appearance depends primarily on its technology. Its "aesthetic" is something additional, based on technical givens. Leaving aside the locomotive, there is no other instance where form and function are so difficult to combine as in the lamp – but, unlike the lamp, one is not forced to look at a locomotive day and night. From Argand to Tiffany, the reconciliation of form and function was one of the greatest challenges to lamp designers – and one that they could not always meet.

In the case of the Argand lamp, the oil container and the shade were the biggest aesthetic problems. Classical decorative elements helped conceal the fact that the overall form originated in the chemist's laboratory. In the early days of gaslight new technology was forced into an old mold before developing a formal vocabulary of its own. The main problem here was the unsightly duct that stuck out of the wall. In 1851, the German architect Gottfried Semper complained about the tendency to disguise it by making the gas lamp look like a candle or oil lamp.[1] Many contemporaries found the open flame too bright, and those who could afford to, surrounded it with elaborately decorated glass globes. Only a short time later, the arc lamp appeared on the scene, the "aesthetic horror of electrical technology." All efforts to give it an appealing form failed, due, Wilke wrote, to its "[...] obstinacy. 'Dress me up too much and I won't shine!'"[2]

The light bulb inaugurated the era of flameless illumination. Engineers and inventors could finally leave the field to designers. With the instruments of the eighteenth century in mind, this separation of technology and form represented a remarkable development. The designers now had more freedom than ever. They could turn the light source in every conceivable direction, with no concern for pipes or flames. Nonetheless, the results of the early efforts in uniting taste and electricity were less than satisfactory, not only from our point of view, but in the eyes of contemporaries as well. When the magazine *Art et Décoration* announced the results of a lamp design competition in 1898, not only did the editors refuse to award the first prize, they were also forced to admit that the submissions were "ugly and not in harmony with their use."

Change came with the lamps of art nouveau. The masters of the Nancy School – Majorelle, Gallé and Daum – turned to organic forms and used the arbitrary placement of the light bulb to great advantage. They were the first to give electric light its own aesthetic. What they produced, however, were in fact illuminated objets d'art rather than masterly light sources. Translucent shades made the light so low that the gloom was barely relieved.[3] This was actually intentional: those who were shocked by the presence of arc lights, reflectors and other horrors on the street and at the Salon wanted both comfortable and atmospheric lighting at home.

Willem Kromhout, *Swan lamp*, 1899–1902, bronze, Kunsthandel Frans Leidelmeijer, Amsterdam

Only about twenty years after its invention, it became fashionable in lamp design to reveal the naked light bulb.

1 Semper 1851, pp. 12-13.
2 Wilke 1893, pp. 610-11.
3 Alastair Duncan, *Louis Majorelle: Master of Art Nouveau Design*, London 1991, p. 146.

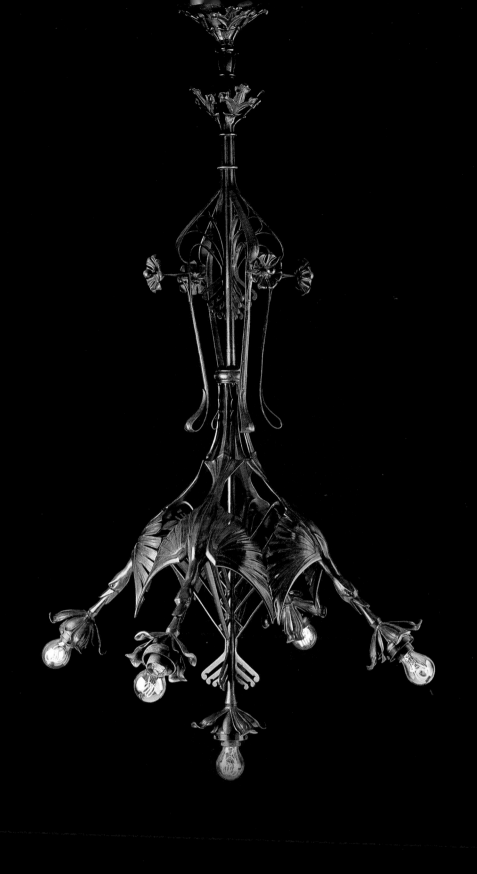

War

Stronger light sources and better reflectors and lenses, which helped concentrate light rays, were a catalyst to the development of projection technology. Its applications appeared endless: from the magic lantern to the cinema, from the theater stage to the floodlights used to light the World's Fairs. It was most useful, however, at sea – not only in the form of lighthouses, but on board the ships themselves. In 1867, Prince Napoleon's yacht, the *Reine-Hortense*, could sail into a harbor at night unaided. Thanks to its own searchlights, the ship no longer had to lie offshore awaiting the break of day. This had been made possible by the new technologies of local energy supply; generators were now small and light enough to be taken on board.[1]

The military, too, put these new technologies to use. During the Franco-Prussian War of 1870–71, for example, electric arc lamps were used to illuminate the battlefield, and were employed by both sides not only for lighting but also for signaling as well.[2] The warring factions also considered trying to blind each other's soldiers, who were accustomed to the total darkness of night, a tactic known from antiquity, when advancing armies (so we are told) were dazzled by reflected sunlight.

One of the extremely rare artistic depictions of such military light projection is Winslow Homer's *Searchlight on Harbor*

Projecting microscopic messages during the Siege of Paris 1871, wood engraving from Amédée Guillemin, *La Lumière*, Paris 1882, Private collection

One military use for projection technology is shown here: the enlargement of a microfilm, which could be sent by carrier pigeon.

War material – telegraph and light projections, wood engraving from *Le Monde Illustré, Supplément au no. 1282*, 1881, Van Gogh Museum, Amsterdam

Entrance. Painted in 1901, it depicts an event of 1898, when the Americans prevented the Spanish fleet at Santiago de Cuba from fleeing. Four ships took turns illuminating the coastline with searchlights: "This shift was necessary because of the rapid heating up of the light, and because it was very exacting and fatiguing to the men in charge, so that a light could not long be maintained by a single man, though only the most expert men were employed," reported Read Admiral William T. Sampson in *Century* magazine.[3] Homer painted the scene from the shore, thus setting the viewer in the position of the Spanish. Their old-fashioned cannon appears powerless against the immaterial weapon of light. The episode became topical once again when Admiral Sampson and his comrade-in-arms Schley fought a court battle against each other in 1901 to determine who deserved the credit for defeating the Spanish. Homer knew the details of the action only from reports in the press, not from his own experience. The blinding light illuminates the coastline, bathing the palm trees in an almost surrealistic silvery glow. The artist's fascination with technology is also demonstrated by his depiction of the moon, which seems weak and pale in comparison to the artificial light. The triumph over nature appears to be complete; in the new century, mankind would know no bounds.

1 Alglave and Boulard 1882, pp. 390-91.
2 Ibid., p. 395.
3 "The Atlantic Fleet in the Spanish War," *The Century* 57 (November 1898-April 1899), pp. 886-913, here p. 901. See also Nicolai Cikovsky, Jr., and Franklin Kelly, *Winslow Homer*, exh. cat. Washington, D.C. (National Gallery of Art), Boston (Museum of Fine Arts) & New York (The Metropolitan Museum of Art) 1995-96.

Winslow Homer, *Searchlight on
Harbor Entrance, Santiago de
Cuba*, 1901, The Metropolitan
Museum of Art, New York, Gift of
George A. Hearn

Ethereal photography

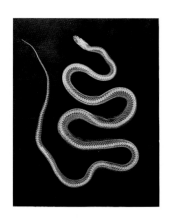

Josef Maria Eder, *Aesculapius Snake*, 1896, photogravure print, George Eastman House, Rochester, New York, Gift of Eastman Kodak Company, plate 15 from Josef Maria Eder and Eduard Valenta, *Versuche über Photographie [...]*, Vienna 1896

This photographic print was made from stereoscopic negatives taken by x-rays.

Not long after the invention of photography, camera users discovered ways to make pictures of things invisible to the naked eye. The mysteries, curiosity, excitement, discoveries, and fakery generated by such photographs were often tied to controversies about the strange, light-bearing substance called ether, or to the rapidly evolving chemistry and optics of photographic processes.

The concept of the ether appears in the writings of the Greek philosopher Aristotle, was endorsed by Newton, and was aggressively researched throughout the nineteenth century. Ether was thought to be an invisible, impalpable substance pervading the universe and serving as the medium transmitting light waves through space. Its existence could not be proven or disproven, and the famous effort to detect it experimentally by the American physicists Michelson and Morley was at first considered a failure when their instruments measured nothing in 1887. Albert Einstein was among the first to conclude that the experiment worked, and proved that ether did not exist after all.

Throughout the nineteenth century, enigmatic and unsuspected effects occasionally turned up on photographic negatives. As glass plate negatives replaced daguerreotype plates, the phenomenon known today as the double exposure appeared, and was soon exploited by unscrupulous photographers claiming to capture ghostly images of the dear departed. The "scientific" explanation for these spirit manifestations was the ether: Presumably, just as it could transmit light vibrations from the subject to the photographic plate, so it could also transmit spiritual vibrations from heaven. At this point in time, cosmological theory had not ruled out the possibility that heaven and hell might be located on distant planets or stars,

clearly within communication range via the ether. Serious physicists, notably Sir Oliver Lodge in the 1890s, spent years trying to prove the scientific validity of ethereal communication, lending support to popular spiritualist movements of the late nineteenth and early twentieth centuries.

Ether also became an issue for chemists using photographic plates in their laboratories. Some found that plates became exposed despite being protected from ordinary light. Their conclusion – that invisible, ether-borne rays were penetrating the plates' protective wrappings – led to the identification of x-rays in 1895 and gamma rays in 1896. The identification of these rays was of immense importance to many kinds of scientific research in the twentieth century, but also encouraged the spiritualists' belief, for a time, that similar, but still undetected, rays carried ghostly human communications.

Adolphe Neyt, *Photomicrograph of a Flea* (?), ca. 1865, albumen print, George Eastman House, Rochester, New York, Gift of 3M Company

Photomicrographs vastly improved the detail and accuracy of knowledge of the microscopic world. They contributed to popular perceptions of the camera's magical abilities to see more, differently.

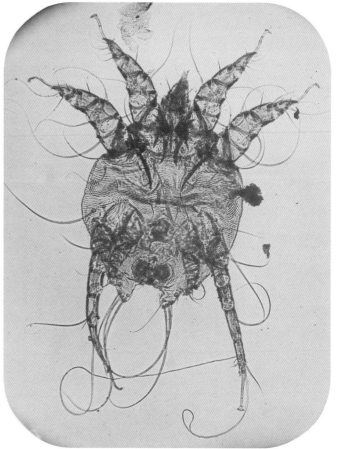

Woman's Spirit behind Table with Photograph, ca. 1865, albumen print, George Eastman House, Rochester, New York, Museum Purchase

In this image made by exposing the negative at two different times, a ghostly woman appears to hover beside a table.

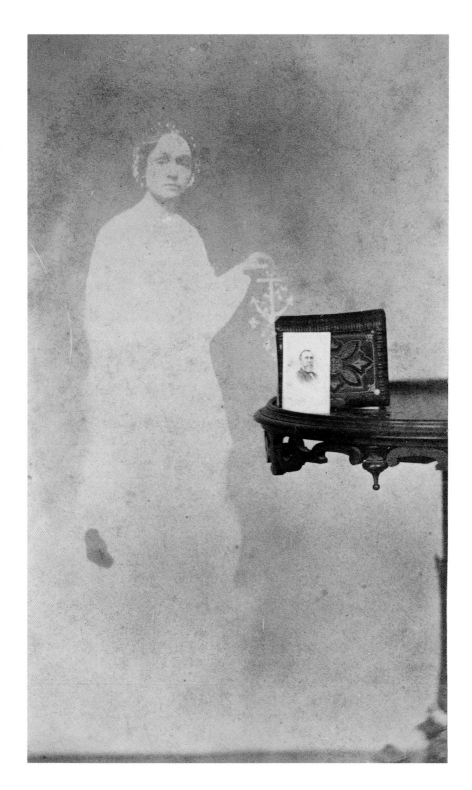

Nostalgia

Contemporaries experienced the technological developments of the nineteenth century as if in a kind of frenzy. A person seventy years of age in 1900 had lived through the euphoric beginnings of gaslight as a child and, as an adult, the widespread use of the kerosene lamp, the arc light and finally the invention of the light bulb. With the arrival of this inexpensive, clean, bright, safe and constant light, the dreams of the pioneers from Ami Argand onward seemed to have been fulfilled. The problem of artificial light had been solved; the time had come to take an historical view. The 1900 World's Fair in Paris celebrated one hundred years of progress with the appropriate pomp and ceremony.

The turn of the century was a time of reflection and nostalgia. The scientists and engineers of the eighteenth and nineteenth centuries already possessed an awareness of the importance of their own contributions, and often saw their innovations in historical context. One need simply remember Newton's famous saying that he had only been able to see further because he had stood on the shoulders of giants. Already in 1767, Joseph Priestley had published an historical overview of the research on light, introducing it with a graphic chart of all the great figures who had aided in its understanding. The technical treatises of the nineteenth century also began with historical reviews, for example, Eugène Peclet's *Traité de l'éclairage* of 1827 or the important *La Lumière électrique* by Alglave and Boulard of 1882. From France, too, came the first great history of lighting fixtures, Henry-René d'Allemagne's *Histoire du luminaire depuis l'époque Romaine jusqu'au XIX siècle*, published in 1891. The lamp had finally become a serious subject for historians.

John Frederick Peto's painting *Lights of Other Days* captures the nostalgia many of his contemporaries felt in the face of a rapidly changing modern world. Peto's work is not only a beautiful still life in the American tradition and a painted encyclopedia of outmoded light sources, it is also an allegory of the past.

Peto's picture evokes memories of the (supposedly) good old days, when life was leisurely and cozy. But not only the light sources looked different in 1906, the year Peto executed his painting: art, too, had changed. Only a short time later, Pablo Picasso would develop Cubism.

Hand in hand with these historical reflections came an interest in the preservation of light's more old-fashioned manifestations, albeit hesitatingly and intermittently. As early as 1928, Guillaume Apollinaire demanded the establishment of a street lamp museum, where at least one example of every type would be kept.[1] Some cities still preserve old fixtures in their historical districts, seeking to attract tourists with the romantic half-light of the gas lamp. All too often, however, we find instead antique gas replica lampposts with the light supplied by electricity, which makes about as much sense as fitting a horse-drawn carriage with a BMW motor.

The lighting of historical buildings also remains in its infancy. As early as 1902, Louis Bell, in his *Art of Illumination*, warned against overuse of the bright, new lights in existing buildings. He was concerned that inappropriate applications of the latest lighting fashions damaged the harmony of interiors.[2] Today, the recently restored Saltram House in Devon has come to be regarded as one of the rare successful examples of the use of historical lighting, and in the United States much attention has been paid to the lighting of locations where the country's past can be experienced, complete with actors in historical costume (for example, Colonial Williamsburg or Plymouth Plantation).[3] In the wake of Stanley Kubrick's revolutionary *Barry Lyndon* (1975), the film industry, too, has made an occasional effort to evoke historical lighting situations. It remains a question, however, if something as contingent and fleeting as styles of illumination can be reconstructed at all. Much is already gained, though, when preservationists, museologists, architects, city planners and filmmakers at least take the issue into consideration.

Ch. Baude and Edmond Morin, *The Great Stages of Electricity*, wood engraving from *Le Monde Illustré, Supplément au no. 1282*, 1881, Van Gogh Museum, Amsterdam

1 Guillaume Apollinaire, *Le Flâneur des deux rives* (1928), Paris 1975, pp. 15-16; cf. Thézy 1993, p. 19.
2 Bell 1902, pp. 301, 312.
3 Phillips 1997, p. 45; cf. Myers 1978.

John Frederick Peto, *Lights of
Other Days*, 1906, Art Institute of
Chicago, Goodman Fund

Chronology

1675 British scientist Isaac Newton's letter to the Royal Society, London, announces his discovery that sunlight, when refracted through a prism, is composed of different colored lights: red, golden, yellow, green, blue, indigo, violet.

1690 In his *Traité de la lumière*, Dutch scientist Christiaan Huygens proposes that light travels in the form of rays, contradicting Newton's particle theory of light.

1704 Newton publishes the results of his investigation of light in *Opticks*. His theories of light will dominate scientific research and theory until ca. 1830.

1708 The *Traité de la Peinture en Miniature*, attributed to French artist Claude Boutet is one of the earliest known art treatises to be based on Newton's *Opticks*.

1720 Dutch scientist Willem Jacob 's Gravesande publishes a textbook of Newtonian science that includes instructions for demonstrations and experiments. It disseminates Newton's experimental method throughout Europe.

1729 French physicist Pierre Bouguer publishes the results of his study of photometry (light measurement); his methods of determining relative brightness will be used by physicists, astronomers, engineers, chemists, and artists for more than a century.

1733 In *Lettres philosophiques*, French philosopher Voltaire argues that Newtonian science is fundamental to intellectual enlightenment.

1750 Benjamin Franklin's kite experiment proves that lightning and electricity are the same.

1751 Beginning of publication of the great French *Encyclopédie*. Its entry on light adopts Newton's theories in full; its definition is repeated in dictionaries and encyclopedias for the next fifty years.

1758 London optician John Dollond creates achromatic lenses for telescopes by combining different kinds and colors of glass with different indices of refraction; improved clarity of the image leads to advances in astronomy and navigation.

1763 The French Académie des Sciences organizes a competition for improved streetlights; the winning design, the reverbère generates extra brightness from multiple wicks and a hemispherical reflector.

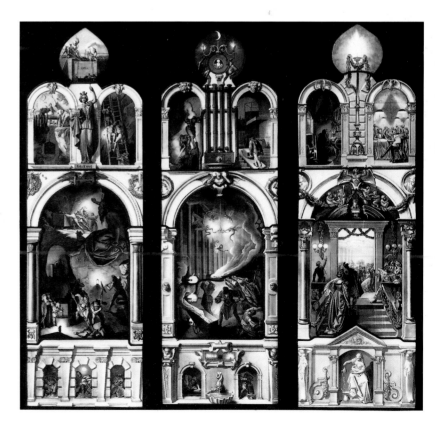

August von Kreling and Hermann Kellner, *The Extraction and the Blessings of Gaslight*, 1863, stained glass window, Germanisches Nationalmuseum, Nuremberg

Monuments for inventors of gaslight: *Frederick Albert Winsor*, 1830, Père-Lachaise cimetery, Paris, photograph Harlingue-Viollet; *Philippe Lebon*, ca. 1904, Chaumont (lost), photograph Boyer-Viollet; *Johann Peter Minckelers*, ca. 1902, Maastricht

1770s French chemist Antoine Louis Lavoisier's theory of combustion triggers major improvements in artificial lighting, e.g. the Argand lamp. The new lamp employs Lavoisier's discovery with its innovative hollow wick that doubles the air supply to the flame, thus creating brighter, less sooty light.

1780 In art academies, museums and collections, it becomes fashionable to study sculpture under artificial light.

1781 Using telescopes of his own design powerful enough to discern starlight, British astronomer William Herschel discovers the planet Uranus.

1789 In Paris, French revolutionaries hang aristocrats from street lamps. The destruction of street lighting in cities is subsequently seen as symbolic of popular revolt against surveillance.

1791 First performance of Mozart's *Magic Flute*, employing Masonic light symbolism.

1792 British engineer William Murdoch lights his office and house in Redruth, Cornwall, with gas. His methods of distilling, distributing, and burning coal gas for light become the basis for the nineteenth-century gaslighting industry.

1794 At the Royal Society, London, the scientist Sir Benjamin Thompson, Count Rumford, delivers a paper about a new design of the photometer.

1799 William Herschel discovers infra-red radiation, showing that light exists beyond the visible spectrum.

1800 French artist Pierre-Henri de Valenciennes publishes a treatise on perspective for landscape painters, advocating careful study of Newton's *Opticks*. His system of geometrical and atmospheric perspective encourage artists to observe and paint light effects out of doors.

1800 British chemist Humphry Davy is first to observe the light produced by a discharge of electric current between two carbon electrodes: arc light.

1800 Count Rumford invents the lampshade to moderate the brightness of improved lamps, such as the Argand.

1800 British artist and poet William Blake denounces Newton in his writings. His renunciation of scientific theories of light characterizes the attitude of many Romantic artists.

1801 British scientist Thomas Young lectures "On the Theory of Light and Colors" to the Royal Society, London. His ideas on interference, the wave-like behavior of light, and red, blue, and yellow as the primary colors of light contradict the basic principles of Newton's *Opticks*.

1802 Influential public exhibitions of gaslighting in London and Paris.

1805 William Murdoch lights a British cotton mill with gas, one of the earliest known permanent gaslighting installations.

1806 English physicist William Hyde Wollaston patents the camera lucida, a device that uses a prism to reflect an object or scene onto a piece of drawing paper. Small and portable, it could be used for drawing out of doors in daylight.

1809 Pall Mall, Westminster, is the first street to be permanently illuminated with gas. Its lights attract tourists, satirists, artists, and poets.

1814 German scientist Joseph von Fraunhofer plots dark lines, i.e. gaps in the solar spectrum, which would be used to analyze the chemical composition of sunlight.

1816 American artist-entrepreneur Rubens Peale creates a gaslit display at Peale's Philadelphia Museum and sculptor William Rush promotes the introduction of gaslighting in the same city's Chestnut Street Theater.

1816 British engineer Thomas Drummond invents limelight, an incandescent light emitted by burning lime, widely used in theaters for spotlights and special effects.

1817 British scientist David Brewster patents the kaleidoscope. Thousands of the optical toys will be sold in less than three years.

1819 French scientist Augustin-Jean Fresnel's work on diffraction and interference supports Thomas Young's view of light as a wave.

1820 Painting by artificial light at night becomes common studio practice.

1821 Fresnel invents a lens that will be used to project light from lighthouses across the horizon.

1825 Bohemian physiologist Jan Evangelista Purkinje notes shift in the perceived intensity of colors at twilight as the retina of the eye shifts from rod to cone vision.

1827 British astronomer John Herschel's treatise on "Light" in the *Encyclopaedia Metropolitana* is the first full-scale scientific textbook article on post-Newtonian theories of light. Herschel accepts the wave theory.

1830s French landscape painters work in the forest near Fontainebleau, forming the School of Barbizon. Their works depict atmospheric natural light effects, although they are mainly painted indoors.

1835 German chemist Justus von Liebig discovers a process to deposit silver on glass to produce mirrors of superior brilliance. His discovery improves mirrors in use in everday life and in telescopes.

1839 French artist and inventor Louis-Jacques-Mandé Daguerre publishes his photographic process, ensuring the new medium's immediate popularity.

1841 In Paris, police prohibit prostitutes on public streets until half an hour after the time set for the lighting of the lamps.

1844 The Place de la Concorde, Paris, is illuminated by electric arc light.

Joseph Nicéphore Niépce, *Cardinal d'Amboise*, 1826, heliograph on pewter, The Royal Photographic Society, Bath

One of the earliest known photographic images.

Illumination of the Place de la Concorde in Paris with electric arc light in 1844, wood engraving from *L'Exposition de Paris*, Paris 1900, Private collection

Candle makers tool, Dutch, ca. 1850–1875, Nederlands Openluchtmuseum, Arnhem

Paul Morane Aîné, *Candle molding machine "Parisienne,"* 1880, Musée national des arts et métiers du CNAM, Paris

Despite the new lighting technologies, candles remained popular in the domestic interior throughout the nineteenth century.

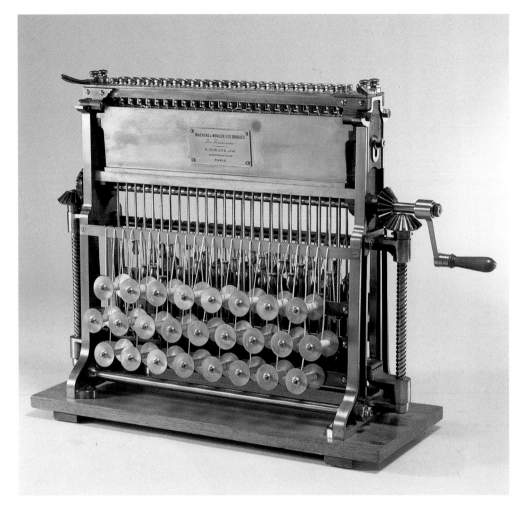

Lace maker's globe, French, ca. 1800–50, Carnegie Museum of Natural History, Pittsburgh, George and Lilian Ball Memorial Fund

The globe, filled with water, magnifies the light of a candle or lamp.

1846 In an address to the Royal Society, British scientist Michael Faraday suggests that the vibrations called "light" are not vibrations of the ether, but rather the vibrations of physical lines of force in an electromagnetic field.

1849 French physicist Armand-Hippolyte-Louis Fizeau makes first land-based estimate of the speed of light.

1849 Performance of Italian composer Giacomo Meyerbeer's opera *Le Prophète* in Paris uses electric arc light to simulate sunrise; the sensational effect astounds the critics.

1850 Pope Pius IX forbids gaslight in the Vatican because it would outshine votive candles.

1850 In England, Burghley House is among the earliest private homes to light paintings with gas picture lights.

1850 American journalist George Foster writes a guidebook to New York by gaslight, encouraging the fashion for urban tourism after dark.

1851 Pre-Raphaelite artist Ford Madox Brown begins work on the first exhibition painting to be painted entirely in daylight.

1851 The Crystal Palace, main building of the Great Exhibition, London, is constructed entirely of glass, so that the exhibits inside can be seen in shadowless light.

1851 Introduction in the United States of paraffin and kerosene, the first petroleum-based lamp fuels.

1853 British photographer Warren de la Rue photographs the moon and produces the first astronomical photographs of scientific value.

Camille Pissarro, *Crystal Palace,* 1871, Art Institute of Chicago, Gift of Mr. and Mrs. B. E. Bensinger

Gas discharge tubes, ca. 1860–90, Universiteitsmuseum Utrecht

1855 German glassmaker Johann Heinrich Wilhelm Geissler makes gas-filled tubes that glow colorfully when electric current is applied. His bulbs demonstrate the basic principles of neon lighting and the cathode ray tube, the essential component of the television set.

1856 German physiologist and physicist Hermann von Helmholtz publishes his *Handbook of Physiological Optics* on the sensory problems of human vision, including the retina's limited perception of light.

1857 French physics teacher Jules Jamin publishes an article on his use of photometry to measure light in paintings, demonstrating that artists cannot replicate the brightness of sunlight. For the rest of the century, artists and critics would debate the usefulness, to art, of scientific discoveries about light.

1859 American artist Frederic Edwin Church exhibits his painting, *Heart of the Andes*, in New York City with provisions for gaslight illumination.

1859 British scientist Michael Faraday reports to the Lords of the Privy Council on Education on "Lighting Picture Galleries by Gas;" however, difficulties with sulfuric acid produced by burning coal gas prevents substantial use in art galleries.

1860 German philosopher and physicist Gustav Theodor Fechner publishes *Elements of Psychophysics* with results of attempts to measure human perceptions and sensations, including the perception of light.

1865 British physicist James Clerk Maxwell defines light as "an electromagnetic disturbance propagating through the field according to electromagnetic laws."

1870 Invention of the Gramme dynamo gives a practicable source of electric current for lighting.

1874 The Impressionist group show in Paris is open in the evenings so that gallery visitors may view paintings under gaslight.

A gallery in New York, illuminated by Edison light bulbs, wood engraving from Em. Alglave and J. Boulard, *La Lumière électrique,* Paris 1882, Universiteitsbibliotheek Amsterdam.

1876 German composer Richard Wagner eliminates house lighting during performances of his operas at his theater in Bayreuth; the new fashion will transform the staging and the reception of musical and theatrical drama.

1878 Joseph Wilson Swan in England and Thomas Edison in the United States develop incandescent electric light bulbs suitable for use in the home. The price of gas shares in London collapses following announcements of their advances in electric lighting.

1879 The Paris Salon exhibition is lit with Jablochkoff candles (electric arc lights) to the dismay of many participating artists.

1880 Novelist and critic Emile Zola's review of "Naturalism at the Salon" in Paris defines impressionist painting as the study of light.

1881 The International Electrical Exhibition at the Palais de l'Industrie, Paris, establishes the commercial dominance of Edison's incandescent electric light.

1883 French critic Jules Laforgue, writing about impressionist art, uses the term "plein-air" to designate any light (such as sun, gaslight, electric light) different from traditional studio light.

1885 Austrian chemist and engineer Carl Auer, Freiherr von Welsbach puts the gas mantle into commercial use to compete with electric light.

1885 Engineers working for American industrialist George Westinghouse develop the modern transformer for alternating electric current (AC), improving the transmission of electric current over long distances and launching a bitter commercial rivalry with Thomas Edison.

1886 The Statue of Liberty, torch-bearing symbol of enlightenment and republican values, is dedicated in New York harbor.

1887 Two Americans, the physicist Albert Michelson and the chemist Edward Morley together perform an experiment designed to detect the existence of the ether. They find nothing.

1889 A proposal for a light tower for the 1889 Paris Universal Exposition leads to construction of the Eiffel Tower equipped with spotlights and thousands of gas jets for evening illuminations.

1893 Edison's kinetoscope gives first public demonstration of a motion picture at the Brooklyn Institute of Arts and Sciences.

1893 American dancer Loïe Fuller uses diaphanous draperies and electric light effects in her performances.

1895 German physicist Wilhelm Conrad Röntgen discovers x-rays; their use in medicine follows immediately.

1899 British scientist Lord Rayleigh publishes the definitive paper on the transmission of light through the atmosphere, recognizing importance of molecular light scattering and explaining why the sky is blue and sunsets are red.

1900 German physicist Max Planck develops quantum theory, allowing light to act like either a wave or a particle.

1905 Albert Einstein publishes his work on the principle of relativity.

Electric lighting by the Swan system at Sir William Armstrong's residence, Cragside, wood engraving from *The Graphic*, 2 April 1881, Van Gogh Museum, Amsterdam

Electric filament lamps on rack, 1881–82, Teylers Museum, Haarlem

Jehan Rictus, *Paul Verlaine!*, ca. 1895, pen and ink, Jane Voorhees Zimmerli Art Museum, Rutgers, The State University of New Jersey, New Brunswick, Acquired with The Herbert D. and Ruth Schimmel Museum Library Fund

Vignette from Edward Orme, *Essay on Transparent Prints [...]*, London 1807, Rijksmuseum, Amsterdam

Catalogue

Objects are divided into the following categories:

Painting, sculpture and decorative arts

Prints and drawings

Photographs

Instruments and optical toys

Light sources

Books and periodicals

Objects are organized chronologically within each category. All dimensions are given height before width before depth.

(Amsterdam) or (Pittsburgh) at the end of an entry indicates a loan to that venue only.

Paintings, sculpture and decorative arts

Giovanni Battista Pittoni, Italian, 1687-1767, *An Allegorical Monument to Sir Isaac Newton*, 1727-30, oil on canvas, 231.6 x 138.4 cm; 91 1/4 x 54 1/2 in., Fitzwilliam Museum, Cambridge, inv. PD.52-1973

Franz Anton Maulbertsch, German, 1724-1796, *Allegory of Light and Truth*, ca. 1750, oil on canvas, 67 x 53 cm; 26 3/4 x 21 in., Wallraf-Richartz-Museum, Cologne, inv. 2521 (Amsterdam)

Simon-Mathurin Lantara, French, 1729-1778, *The Spirit of the Lord Moved Upon the Waters*, 1752, oil on canvas, 52 x 64 cm; 20 1/2 x 25 1/4 in., Musée de Grenoble, inv. MG 2.404

Jean Siméon Chardin, French, 1699-1779, *Glass of Water and Coffee Pot*, ca. 1761, oil on canvas, 32.4 x 41.3 cm; 12 3/4 x 16 1/4 in., Carnegie Museum of Art, Pittsburgh, Howard A. Noble Collection, inv. 66.12

Anna Dorothea Therbusch, German, 1721-1782, *A Drinker - Light Effect*, 1767, oil on canvas, 108 x 91 cm; 42 1/2 x 35 3/4 in., Ecole nationale supérieure des beaux-arts, Paris, inv. MRA 124

Joseph Wright of Derby, British, 1734-1797, *An Academy by Lamplight*, ca. 1769, oil on canvas, 127 x 101 cm; 50 x 39 3/4 in., Lord Somerleyton, Somerleyton Hall, Lowestoft, Suffolk (Amsterdam)

Pierre-Jacques Volaire, French, 1728-1809, *Eruption of Vesuvius*, 1771, oil on canvas, 77.5 x 115.7 cm; 30 1/2 x 45 1/2 in., Private collection, courtesy Rafael Valls Limited, London (Amsterdam)

Joseph Wright of Derby, British, 1734-1797, *The Blacksmith's Shop*, 1771, oil on canvas, 125.7 x 99 cm; 49 1/2 x 39 in., Derby Museum and Art Gallery, inv. DBYMU 1979-598

Joseph Wright of Derby, British, 1734-1797, *The Annual Girandola at the Castel Sant'Angelo, Rome*, 1775-76, oil on canvas, 138 x 173 cm; 54 1/4 x 68 in., Walker Art Gallery, Liverpool, inv. 1428

Pierre-Henri de Valenciennes, French, 1750-1819, *View of Ara Coeli*, ca. 1785, oil on paper on cardboard, 17.2 x 26 cm; 6 3/4 x 10 1/4 in., Musée du Louvre, Département des Peintures, Paris, inv. RF 3027

Pierre-Henri de Valenciennes, French, 1750-1819, *View of Ara Coeli*, ca. 1785, oil on paper on cardboard, 19.5 x 25.5 cm; 7 3/4 x 10 in., Musée du Louvre, Département des Peintures, Paris, inv. RF 3013

Januarius Zick, German, 1730-1797, *Newton's Contribution to Optics*, ca. 1790, oil on canvas, 62.5 x 72.5 cm; 24 1/2 x 28 1/2 in., Niedersächsisches Landesmuseum, Hanover, inv. PAM 897 (Amsterdam)

Philippe Jacques de Loutherbourg, British, 1740-1812, *Coalbrookdale by Night*, 1801, oil on canvas, 68 x 107 cm; 26 3/4 x 42 in., Science Museum, London, inv. 1952-452

Samuel Mohn, German, 1761-1815, *Covered cup with silhouettes*, 1807, enamel painting on crystal, 21.5 cm; 8 1/2 in., Museum für Angewandte Kunst, Frankfurt am Main, inv. 5646

Georg Friedrich Kersting, German, 1785-1847, *The Painter Friedrich Matthäi in his Studio*, 1812, oil on canvas, 52 x 40.7 cm; 20 1/2 x 16 in., Kunstsammlungen Chemnitz, inv. 505

Caspar David Friedrich, German, 1774-1840, *The Cross on the Baltic Sea*, 1815, oil on canvas, 44.7 x 32 cm; 17 1/2 x 12 1/2 in., Stiftung Preussische Schlösser und Gärten Berlin-Brandenburg, Potsdam (Schloss Charlottenburg, Berlin), inv. GK I 30203 (Amsterdam)

Decoration for a Master of the Masonic Lodge "L'Union Frédéric" in The Hague, Dutch, ca. 1816, silver, diameter 9.4 cm; 3 3/4 in., Verzamelingen van de Orde van Vrijmetselaren (CMC), The Hague, inv. 3331

Anton Kothgasser, Austrian, 1769-1851, *Night cup*, ca. 1820, enamel painting on glass, 12 cm; 4 3/4 in., Staatliche Museen zu Berlin, Preussischer Kulturbesitz, Kunstgewerbemuseum, inv. W-1971,67

John Constable, British, 1776-1837, *Cloud Study with Horizon of Trees*, 1821, oil on paper on board, 24.8 x 29.2 cm; 9 3/4 x 11 1/2 in., Royal Academy of Arts, London

Adèle Chavassieu d'Audebert, French, 1788-after 1831, after **François-Louis Dejuinne**, French, 1786-1844, *Girodet Painting "Pygmalion and his Statue,"* 1822, oil on enamel, 16 x 13.2 cm; 6 1/4 x 5 1/4 in., Pinacoteca di Brera, on loan to the Galleria d'Arte Moderna, Milan, inv. 1080/13

Franz Anton Siebel, German, 1777-1842, *David and Samson*, 1825, enamel painting on glass, wood, 38.5 x 22 cm; 15 1/4 x 8 3/4 in., Rijksmuseum, Amsterdam, inv. BK NM-709

Wilhelm Bendz, Danish, 1804-1832, *The Life Class in the Academy of Fine Arts*, 1826, oil on canvas, 57.5 x 82.5 cm; 22 1/2 x 32 1/2 in., Statens Museum for Kunst, Copenhagen, inv. KMS 54

Wilhelm Bendz, Danish, 1804-1832, *A Tobacco Party: Justitsråd Jürgensen's Sunday Gathering*, 1828, oil on canvas, 98.5 x 85 cm; 38 3/4 x 33 1/2 in., Ny Carlsberg Glyptotek, Copenhagen, inv. 1881

Eduard Daege, German, 1805-1883, *The Invention of Painting*, 1832, oil on canvas, 176.5 x 135.5 cm; 69 x 53 1/4 in., Staatliche Museen zu Berlin, Preussischer Kulturbesitz, Nationalgalerie, inv. A I 216

Joseph Mallord William Turner, British, 1775-1851, *Sun Setting over a Lake*, ca. 1840, oil on canvas, 91 x 122.5 cm; 35 7/8 x 48 1/4 in., Tate Gallery, London, inv. N 04665

Hippolyte Michaud, French, 1813-1886, *Spectators at the Theater*, ca. 1840-60, oil on canvas, 22 x 27 cm; 8 3/4 x 10 1/2 in., Rijksmuseum, Amsterdam, inv. SK-A-1745

John Martin, British, 1789-1854, *Pandemonium*, 1841, oil on canvas, 123.2 x 184.2 cm; 48 1/2 x 72 1/2 in., The FORBES Magazine Collection, New York (Pittsburgh)

Alexandre-Gabriel Decamps, French, 1803-1860, *A Turkish School*, 1846, oil on canvas, 117 x 94 cm; 46 x 37 in., Amsterdams Historisch Museum (Fodor Collection), on loan to the Van Gogh Museum, Amsterdam, inv. S 156 B/1996 (SA 2940)

Adolph Menzel, German, 1815-1905, *The Living Room with the Sister of the Artist*, 1847, oil on paper on cardboard, 46.1 x 31.7 cm; 18 1/4 x 12 1/2 in., Bayerische Staatsgemäldesammlungen, Neue Pinakothek, Munich, inv. 8499 (Amsterdam)

Auguste Vinchon, French, 1789-1855, *Louis-Philippe and the Royal Family Visit the Statue of Joan of Arc by Marie d'Orléans in the Galerie de Pierre (1839)*, 1848, oil on canvas, 190 x 150 cm; 75 3/4 x 59 in., Musée National des Châteaux de Versailles et de Trianon, inv. MV 5695

Frederic Edwin Church, American, 1826-1900, *Twilight, "Short arbiter 'twixt day and night,"* 1850, oil on canvas, 81.9 x 121.9 cm; 32 1/4 x 48 in., The Newark Museum, Wallace M. Scudder Bequest Fund, inv. 56.43 (Amsterdam)

Cast of the *Venus de Milo*, ca. 1850-1900, plaster, 204 cm; 80 1/4 in., Collectie Rijksakademie, on loan to the Allard Pierson Museum, Amsterdam (Amsterdam); Carnegie Museum of Art, Pittsburgh (Pittsburgh)

Ford Madox Brown, British, 1821-1893, *The Pretty Baa Lambs*, 1854, oil on canvas, 61 x 76.2 cm; 24 x 30 in., Birmingham City Museums and Art Gallery, inv. 1956P9

Petrus van Schendel, Dutch, 1806-1870, *Night Market in Antwerp*, 1861, oil on canvas, 124 x 102 cm; 48 3/4 x 40 1/4 in., The Richard Green Gallery, London, inv. AS 102 VE (Amsterdam)

Albert Bierstadt, American, 1830-1902, *Sunlight and Shadow*, 1862, oil on canvas, 99.1 x 85 cm; 41 1/2 x 35 1/2 in., Fine Arts Museums of San Francisco, Gift of Mr. and Mrs. John D. Rockefeller 3rd, inv. 1979.7.10

William Holman Hunt, British, 1827-1910, *London Bridge on the Night of the Wedding of the Prince and Princess of Wales*, 1863-66, oil on canvas, 65.4 x 98.1 cm; 25 3/4 x 38 1/2 in., The Visitors of the Ashmolean Museum, Oxford, inv. A 268

Jean-Léon Gérôme, French, 1824-1904, *Golgotha*, ca. 1868, oil on canvas, 63.5 x 98 cm; 25 x 38 1/2 in., Van Gogh Museum, Amsterdam, inv. S 453 S/1995

Edgar Degas, French, 1834-1917, *Interior*, 1868-69, oil on canvas, 81 x 116 cm; 32 x 45 3/4 in., Philadelphia Museum of Art, The Henry P. McIlhenny Collection in memory of Frances P. McIlhenny, inv. 1986-026-010

Claude Monet, French, 1840-1926, *An Interior after Dinner*, 1868-69, oil on canvas, 50 x 65 cm; 19 3/4 x 25 1/2 in., National Gallery of Art, Washington, D.C., Mr. and Mrs. P. Mellon 1983, inv. 1983-1-25

Edgar Degas, French, 1834-1917, *The Ballet from "Robert le Diable,"* 1871-72, oil on canvas, 66 x 54.3 cm; 26 x 21 1/4 in., The Metropolitan Museum of Art, New York, H.O. Havemeyer Collection, Bequest of Mrs. H.O. Havemeyer, 1929, inv. 29.100.552

Camille Pissarro, French, 1830-1903, *The Crossroads, Pontoise*, 1872, oil on canvas, 54.9 x 94 cm; 21 1/4 x 37 in., Carnegie Museum of Art, Pittsburgh, Acquired through the generosity of the Sarah Mellon Scaife family, inv. 71.7

Frédéric-Auguste Bartholdi, French, 1834-1904, *Liberty Enlightening the World*, 1873, cast 1900, bronze, 274.3 cm; 108 in., Sénat de la République Française, Paris, inv. 91-01412/RF 3878 (Amsterdam)

Hippolyte Camille Delpy, French, 1841-1910, *The Boulevard Barbès Rochechouart in Winter*, 1879, oil on canvas, 109 x 154.9 cm; 43 x 61 in., Elisabeth Cumbler

Jean-Georges Vibert, French, 1840-1902, *The Sketching Class*, 1881, oil on panel, 61.5 x 45.2 cm; 24 1/8 x 17 7/8 in., Cleveland Museum of Art, inv. 1980.202 (Pittsburgh)

Alfred Sisley, French, 1839-1899, *Saint-Mammès on the Banks of the Loing*, ca. 1881, oil on canvas, 54 x 73.7 cm; 21 1/4 x 29 in., Carnegie Museum of Art, Pittsburgh, Purchase, inv. 99.7

Heinrich Geuer, German, 1841-1904, workshop, *Apelles*, 1882, stained glass, 265 x 105 cm; 104 1/4 x 41 1/4 in., Rijksmuseum, Amsterdam, inv. BK-1999-87-B (Amsterdam)

Medardo Rosso, Italian, 1858-1928, *Kiss under the Lamppost*, 1882-83, bronze, 28.5 cm; 11 1/4 in., Museo Medardo Rosso, Barzio (Como)

Anna Ancher, Danish, 1859-1935, and Michael Ancher, Danish, 1849-1927, *Reviewing the Day's Work*, 1883, oil on canvas, 83.5 x 103 cm; 32 3/4 x 40 1/2 in., Statens Museum for Kunst, Copenhagen, inv. KMS 1806

James Tissot, French, 1836-1903, *The Ladies of the Chariots*, 1883-85, oil on canvas, 146 x 101 cm; 57 1/2 x 39 5/8 in., Museum of Art, Rhode Island School of Design, Providence, Rhode Island, Gift of Walter Lowry, inv. 58.186 (Pittsburgh)

Felician Freiherr von Myrbach, Austrian, 1853-1940, *The Print Shop*, 1884, oil on canvas, 64.3 x 80.5 cm; 25 1/4 x 31 3/4 in., Van Gogh Museum, Amsterdam, inv. S 432 M/1992 (Amsterdam)

Vincent van Gogh, Dutch, 1853-1890, *The Potato Eaters*, 1885, oil on canvas, 82 x 114 cm; 32 1/4 x 44 3/4 in., Van Gogh Museum, Amsterdam (Vincent van Gogh Foundation), inv. S 05 V/1962 (Amsterdam)

John Atkinson Grimshaw, British, 1836-1893, *Liverpool Quay by Moonlight*, 1886, oil on canvas, 61 x 91.4 cm; 24 x 36 in., Tate Gallery, London

Vincent van Gogh, Dutch, 1853-1890, *Stuffed Kalong Bat (Flying Dog)*, 1886, oil on canvas, 41 x 79 cm; 16 1/4 x 31 in., Van Gogh Museum, Amsterdam (Vincent van Gogh Foundation), inv. S 136 V/1973

Vincent van Gogh, Dutch, 1853-1890, *Vegetable Gardens and the Moulin de Blute-Fin on Montmartre*, 1886, oil on canvas, 44.8 x 81 cm; 17 3/4 x 32 in., Van Gogh Museum, Amsterdam (Vincent van Gogh Foundation), inv. S 15 V/1962 (Amsterdam)

Charles Angrand, French, 1854-1926, *The Accident*, 1887, oil on canvas, 50 x 64 cm; 19 3/4 x 25 1/4 in., Private collection

Peder Severin Krøyer, Danish, 1851-1909, *Social Evening in the Banqueting Hall of the Carlsberg Glyptotek*, 1888, oil on canvas, 144 x 172 cm; 56 3/4 x 67 3/4 in., Carlsberg Museum, Copenhagen (Amsterdam)

Vincent van Gogh, Dutch, 1853-1890, *Gauguin's Chair*, 1888, oil on canvas, 90.5 x 72 cm; 35 1/2 x 28 1/4 in., Van Gogh Museum, Amsterdam (Vincent van Gogh Foundation), inv. S 48 V/1962

Vincent van Gogh, Dutch, 1853-1890, *The Sower*, 1888, oil on canvas, 32 x 40 cm; 12 1/2 x 15 3/4 in., Van Gogh Museum, Amsterdam (Vincent van Gogh Foundation), inv. S 29 V/1961

Vincent van Gogh, Dutch, 1853-1890, *Starry Night on the Rhône River*, 1888, oil on canvas, 72.5 x 92 cm; 28 1/2 x 36 1/4 in., Musée d'Orsay, Paris, donation sous réserve d'usufruit de M. et Mme. Robert Kahn-Scriber, en souvenir de M. et Mme. Fernand Moch, inv. 1975.19 (Amsterdam)

Giovanni Segantini, Italian, 1858-1899, *My Models*, 1888, oil on canvas, 65.5 x 92.5 cm; 25 3/4 x 36 1/2 in., Kunsthaus Zurich, on permanent loan from the Vereinigung Zürcher Kunstfreunde

Vincent van Gogh, Dutch, 1853-1890, *Trunks of Trees with Ivy*, 1889, oil on canvas, 74 x 92 cm; 29 1/4 x 36 1/4 in., Van Gogh Museum, Amsterdam (Vincent van Gogh Foundation), inv. S 51 V/1962

Paul Signac, French, 1863-1935, *Place des Lices, St. Tropez*, 1893, oil on canvas, 65.4 x 81.8 cm; 25 3/4 x 32 1/4 in., Carnegie Museum of Art, Pittsburgh, Acquired through the generosity of the Sarah Mellon Scaife family, inv. 66.24.2

Claude Monet, French, 1840-1926, *Rouen Cathedral: Façade and the Tour d'Albane (Morning Effect)*, 1893, oil on canvas, 106 x 74 cm; 41 3/4 x 29 1/4 in., Museum of Fine Arts, Boston, Tompkins Collection, inv. 24.6

Claude Monet, French, 1840-1926, *Rouen Cathedral: Façade and the Tour d'Albane (Morning Effect)*, 1894, oil on canvas, 107 x 74 cm; 42 x 29 1/4 in., Fondation Beyeler, Riehen/Basel, inv. 82.2

Henri de Toulouse-Lautrec, French, 1864-1901, *At the Moulin Rouge*, 1894-95, oil on canvas, 123 x 141 cm; 48 1/2 x 55 1/2 in., Art Institute of Chicago, Helen Birch Bartlett Memorial Collection, inv. 1928.610 (Pittsburgh)

Henri de Toulouse-Lautrec, French, 1864-1901, and **Louis Comfort Tiffany**, American, 1848-1933, *Au Nouveau Cirque, Papa Chrysanthème*, 1894-95, stained glass, cabochons, 120 x 85 cm; 47 1/4 x 33 1/2 in., Musée d'Orsay, Paris, don Henry Dauberville au nom de ses enfants, Béatrice et Guy-Patrice, 1979, inv. OAO 338

Winslow Homer, American, 1838-1910, *Searchlight on Harbor Entrance, Santiago de Cuba*, 1901, oil on canvas, 77.5 x 128.3 cm; 30 1/2 x 50 1/2 in., The Metropolitan Museum of Art, New York, Gift of George A. Hearn, 1906, inv. 06.1282

John Frederick Peto, American, 1854-1907, *Lights of Other Days*, 1906, oil on canvas, 77.5 x 114.9 cm; 30 1/2 x 45 1/4 in., Art Institute of Chicago, Goodman Fund, inv. 56.125

Prints and drawings

Jan Caspar Philips, Dutch, 1700-1773, *Fireworks on the Vijver, The Hague, 13 June 1749, in Celebration of the Peace of Aix-la-Chapelle*, 1749, engraving, 41.5 x 49.5 cm; 16 1/4 x 19 1/2 in., Rijksmuseum,

Rijksprentenkabinet, Amsterdam, inv. RP-P-OB-60.037 (Amsterdam)

William Hogarth, British, 1697-1764, *Cruelty in Perfection*, 1751, etching and engraving, 38.8 x 31.8 cm; 15 1/4 x 12 1/4 in., Rijksmuseum, Rijksprentenkabinet, Amsterdam, inv. RP-P-OB 18.775

William Pether, British, 1738-1821, after **Joseph Wright of Derby**, British, 1734-1797, *The Orrery*, 1768, mezzotint, 48.4 x 58 cm; 19 x 22 3/4 in., Rijksmuseum, Rijksprentenkabinet, Amsterdam, inv. RP-P-OB 33.704 (Amsterdam); Carnegie Museum of Art, Pittsburgh, Leisser Art Fund, inv. 1996.16 (Pittsburgh)

James Watson, British, 1740-1790, after **Henry Robert Morland**, British, ca. 1730-1797, *The Ballad Singer*, ca. 1770-90, mezzotint, 33 x 22.6 cm; 13 x 9 in., Rijksmuseum, Rijksprentenkabinet, Amsterdam, inv. RP-P-OB 33.507 (Amsterdam)

Richard Earlom, British, 1743-1822, after **Joseph Wright of Derby**, British, 1734-1797, *An Iron Forge*, 1771, mezzotint, 60.8 x 43.3 cm; 24 x 17 in., Rijksmuseum, Rijksprentenkabinet, Amsterdam, inv. RP-P-OB 33.678 (Amsterdam)

Cornelis Buijs, Dutch, 1745-1826, *Study of a Male Nude*, 1771, red chalk, 55.2 x 31.9 cm; 21 3/4 x 12 1/2 in., Rijksmuseum, Rijksprentenkabinet, Amsterdam, inv. RP-T-00-2760 (Amsterdam)

Pieter Wagenaar, Dutch, active ca. 1770-1780, *Study of a Male Nude*, 1771, black chalk, 55.3 x 31.3 cm; 21 3/4 x 12 1/4 in., Rijksmuseum, Rijksprentenkabinet, Amsterdam, inv. RP-T-00-2761 (Amsterdam)

Daniel du Pré, Dutch, 1752-1817, *Study of a Male Nude*, 1771, black chalk, heightened with white, 52 x 39.1 cm; 20 1/2 x 12 1/2 in., Rijksmuseum, Rijksprentenkabinet, Amsterdam, inv. RP-T-00-2762 (Amsterdam)

C. Bogerts, Dutch, active 1772-1815, after **Pieter Barbiers**, Dutch, 1717-1780, *The Fire of the Amsterdam Theater on 11 May 1772, seen from Keizersgracht*, after 1772; *The Fire on the Stage of the Amsterdam Theater, 11 May 1772*, after 1772; *The Amsterdam Theater Burning, 11 May 1772*, after 1772, three colored engravings, each 21 x 33.5 cm; 8 1/4 x 13 1/4 in., Collectie Theater Instituut Nederland, Amsterdam, inv. A 1976-189 (14), (12), (13) (Amsterdam)

William Pether, British, 1738-1821, after **Joseph Wright of Derby**, British, 1734-1797, *Study of the Antique by Artificial Light*, 1778, mezzotint, 48.2 x 55.6 cm; 19 x 22 in., Rijksmuseum, Rijksprenten-kabinet, Amsterdam, inv. RP-P-OB 33.704 (Amsterdam)

Fireworks, Austrian, ca. 1780-90, colored engraving, 27.6 x 41 cm; 10 3/4 x 6 1/4 in., Collectie Theater Instituut Nederland, Amsterdam, inv. A 1976-189 (26)

Three masonic emblems, French, ca. 1785: *The Degree of the Royal Arches*, pen and ink, watercolor, 21.2 x 31.5 cm; 8 1/4 x 12 1/2 in., *The Initiated*, pen and ink, watercolor, 20.5 x 15.3 cm; 8 x 6 in., *Chamber of Preparation for the Knight of Phoenix*, watercolor, 26.3 x 35 cm; 10 1/4 x 13 3/4 in., Verzamelingen van de Orde van Vrijmetselaren (CMC), The Hague, inv. MDH 40, 41, 43

C. H. Koning, Dutch, active ca. 1780-1790, *Electrical Discharge*, 1785, engraving with copper plate, each 50 x 41 cm; 19 3/4 x 16 1/4 in., Martinus van Marum, *Description d'une très grande machine électrique, placée dans le muséum de Teyler à Haarlem, et des expériments faits par le moyen de cette machine*, Haarlem: Joh. Enschedé en Zoonen, en Jan van Walré 1785, pl. IV, Teylers Museum, Haarlem, inv. 22A and 1990.06 (plate) (Amsterdam)

Joseph Adolf Schmetterling, Austrian, 1751-1828, *Couple Sitting at the Tea Table*, ca. 1790, pen and ink, 19.2 x 24.3 cm; 7 1/2 x 9 1/2 in., Rijksmuseum, Rijksprentenkabinet, Amsterdam, inv. RP-T-1904-16 (Amsterdam)

The Return of the Aristocrats from the London Racetrack, French, ca. 1790, etching, 21.5 x 24 cm; 8 1/2 x 9 1/2 in., Bibliothèque Nationale de France, Cabinet des Estampes, Paris, inv. Qb1 1790 (07 juillet) (Amsterdam)

Pierre Gabriel Berthault, French, 1748-1819, after **Jean Louis Prieur**, French, 1759-1795, *Celebrations and Illuminations on the Champs-Elysées on 18 July 1790*, 1790-91, etching, 24 x 29 cm; 9 1/2 x 11 1/2 in., Bibliothèque Nationale de France, Cabinet des Estampes, Paris, inv. Qb1 1790 (18 juillet) (Amsterdam)

Michel Honoré Bounieu, French, 1740-1814, *France Sacrificing to Reason*, 1791-92, mezzotint, 56 x 40 cm; 22 x 15 3/4 in., Bibliothèque Nationale de France, Cabinet des Estampes, Paris, inv. Qb1 1791 (14 juillet) (Amsterdam)

Noach van der Meer the Younger, Dutch, ca. 1740-after 1814, and **Reinier Vinkeles**, Dutch, 1741-1816 after **Jacques Kuijper**, Dutch, 1761-1808, and **Pieter Barbiers**, Dutch, 1717-1780, *Felix Meritis*, 1791/1801, four etchings and engravings, each ca. 45 x 54 cm; 17 3/4 x 21 1/4 in., Rijksmuseum, Rijksprentenkabinet, Amsterdam, inv. RP-P-FM 5124

Declaration of the Rights of Man (French edition), French, 1793, engraving, 43 x 29 cm; 17 x 11 1/2 in., Bibliothèque Nationale de France, Cabinet des Estampes, Paris, inv. Qb1 1793 (10 août) (Amsterdam)

Lambert Antoine Claessens, Belgian, 1763-1834, *Declaration of the Rights of Man (Dutch edition)*, 1795, etching, 46 x 26 cm; 18 x 10 1/4 in., Rijksmuseum, Rijksprentenkabinet, Amsterdam, inv. RP-P-FM 5342A (Amsterdam)

Jean-Baptiste Chapuy, French, ca. 1760-1802, after **Louis Simon Boizot**, French, 1743-1809, *Liberty Armed with the Scepter of Reason Suppresses Ignorance and Fanaticism*, 1793-95, etching, 44.5 x 58.5 cm; 17 1/2 x 23 in., Bibliothèque Nationale de France, Cabinet des Estampes, Paris, inv. Hennin 12178 ft 4 (Amsterdam)

Francisco Goya, Spanish, 1746-1828, *Sleep Delivers Them*, 1797-98, etching and aquatint, 21.8 x 15.3 cm; 8 1/2 x 6 in., plate 34 of the *Caprichos*, Carnegie Museum of Art, Pittsburgh, Gift of Mr. and Mrs. Charles J. Rosenbloom, inv. 57.23 (Pittsburgh)

Franz Niklaus König, Swiss, 1765-1832, *The St. James Fires at Lake Brienz, The City of Berne by Moonlight, The Area around Interlaken by Moonlight*, ca. 1810, three watercolors, each 84.5 x 119 cm; 33 1/4 x 46 3/4 in., Kunstmuseum Bern, inv. A 9494, A 9501, A 9504

Johann Friedrich Jügel, German, d. 1833, after **Karl Friedrich Schinkel**, German, 1781-1841, *Stage designs for Friedrich Schiller's "Don Carlos" and "Die Braut von Messina,"* 1822, two aquatints, each 22.5 x 35 cm; 8 3/4 x 13 3/4 in., Collectie Theater Instituut Nederland, Amsterdam, inv. TL 43-29, TL 43-31

William Blake, British, 1757-1827, *When the Morning Stars Sang Together, & All the Sons of God Shouted for Joy*, 1825, engraving, 19.2 x 15.1 cm; 7 1/2 x 6 in., plate 14 of *Illustrations for the Book of Job*, Carnegie Museum of Art, Pittsburgh, Purchase, inv. 34.4.15 (Pittsburgh)

John Martin, British, 1789-1854, *The Creation of Light*, 1825/1831, etching, aquatint, mezzotint, 19.1 x 21.9 cm; 7 1/2 x 8 1/2 in., Hamburger Kunsthalle, Kupferstichkabinett, inv. 1976/32

David Lucas, British, 1802-1881, after **John Constable**, British, 1776-1837, *Summer, Afternoon - After a Shower*, ca. 1830, mez-

zotint, 14.3 x 18.9 cm; 5 1/2 x 7 1/2 in., Rijksmuseum, Rijksprentenkabinet, Amsterdam, inv. RP-P-1954-434 (Amsterdam)

William Henry Fox Talbot, British, 1800-1877, *View towards Lecco*, ca. 1833, camera lucida drawing, The Royal Photographic Society, Bath, inv. 025140 (Amsterdam)

Nine designs for the competition for the lantern posts on Dam Square in Amsterdam, ca. 1844, pencil, 38 x 29.7 cm; 15 x 11 3/4 in. (inv. M 105-28); pencil, 49 x 29 cm; 19 1/4 x 11 1/2 in. (inv. M 109-2); watercolor, pencil, 71 x 49.5 cm; 28 x 19 1/2 in.(inv. G 129-2); watercolor, pencil, 66.5 x 49.5 cm; 26 1/4 x 19 1/2 in. (inv. G 129-3); watercolor, pencil, 33 x 21 cm; 13 x 8 1/4 in. (inv. K 147-14); pencil, 52.3 x 38.5 cm; 20 1/2 x 15 1/4 in. (inv. M 109-8); pencil, 48.5 x 29 cm; 19 x 11 1/2 in. (inv. M 105-29); pencil, 48.7 x 29 cm; 19 x 11 1/2 in. (inv. M 105-24); watercolor, 36 x 21 cm; 14 1/4 x 8 1/4 in. (inv. K 147-15); winning design attributed to **Martin Gerard Tetar van Elven**, Dutch, b. 1803, Gemeentearchief Amsterdam (Amsterdam)

Silhouette Portrait of drs. Vincent van Gogh (1789-1874), Dutch, ca. 1850, pen and ink, 15.5 x 10.9 cm; 6 x 4 1/4 in., Van Gogh Museum, Amsterdam (Vincent van Gogh Foundation), inv. P 764 V/1992 (Amsterdam)

Jean-Baptiste Camille Corot, French, 1796-1875, *The Young Girl and Death*, 1854, cliché verre, 18.3 x 14 cm; 7 3/16 x 5 1/2 in., Carnegie Museum of Art, Pittsburgh, inv. 22.11.4 (Pittsburgh)

James McNeill Whistler, American, 1834-1903, *Reading by Lamplight*, 1858, etching and drypoint, 15.8 x 11.8 cm; 6 1/4 x 4 3/4 in., Rijksmuseum, Rijksprentenkabinet, Amsterdam, inv. RP-P-1962-287 (Amsterdam)

Ten stock certificates, American, between 1858 and 1900, engravings, various sizes, *Birmingham,*

East Birmingham & South Pittsburgh Gas Company, ca. 1858, *The South Pacific Mining Company*, ca. 1880, *Chicago Gas Company*, 1890, *Ohio and Indiana Consolidated Natural and Illuminating Gas Company*, ca. 1890, *Consolidated Gas Company of the City of Pittsburgh*, ca. 1890, *The North New York Lighting Co.*, 1890, *East End Electric Light Company*, ca. 1890, *Durham Coal & Iron Co.*, ca. 1895, *The United States Light & Heating Company*, ca. 1900, *Mount Carmel Gas Light Company of Mount Carmel, Pennsylvania*, ca. 1900, Private collection

Adolph Menzel, German, 1815-1905, *Departure after the Party*, 1860, gouache, 26.7 x 33.5 cm; 10 1/2 x 13 1/4 in., Carnegie Museum of Art, Pittsburgh, Heinz Family Acquisition Fund, inv. 92.8

François Bonvin, French, 1817-1887, *The Engraver*, 1861, drypoint, 21.4 x 16.2 cm; 8 1/2 x 6 1/4 in., Rijksmuseum, Rijksprentenkabinet, Amsterdam, inv. RP-P-1971-214 (Amsterdam)

Héliodore-Joseph Pisan, French, 1822-1890, after **Gustave Doré**, French, 1832-1883, *The Creation of Light*, 1866, wood engraving, 24.8 x 20 cm; 9 3/4 x 7 7/8 in., *La Sainte Bible: traduction nouvelle selon la Vulgate par MM. J.-J. Bourassé et P. Janvier [...]*, 2 vols., Tours: Alfred Mame et fils 1866, vol. 1, Universiteitsbibliotheek Amsterdam, inv. 203 A 13 (Amsterdam); *La Sainte Bible: traduction nouvelle selon la Vulgate par MM. J.-J. Bourassé et P. Janvier [...]*, 2 vols., Tours: Alfred Mame et fils 1866, vol. 1; *The Holy Bible Containing the Old and New Testaments, According to the Authorized Version, with Illustrations by Gustave Doré*, 2 vols., London & New York: Cassel Petter and Galpin, n.d. (1867); *Die Heilige Schrift der Israeliten, [...]*, n.p.: Hallberger 1874, Dan Malan, Saint Louis (Pittsburgh)

Edouard Manet, French, 1832-1883, *The Barricade*, 1871, lithograph, 46.5 x 33.4 cm; 18 1/4 x 13

1/4 in., Van Gogh Museum, Amsterdam, inv. P 57 V/1962

Héliodore-Joseph Pisan, French, 1822-1890, after **Gustave Doré**, French, 1832-1883, *The Bull's Eye*, 1872, wood engraving, 23.5 x 18.5 cm; 9 1/4 x 7 1/4 in., Blanchard Jerrold and Gustave Doré, *London, a Pilgrimage*, London: Grant and Co. 1872, Van Gogh Museum, Amsterdam, inv. BVG 134 (Amsterdam); Carnegie Museum of Art, Pittsburgh, Gift of Graham Shearing, inv. 1998.40 (Pittsburgh)

Louis-Joseph-Amédée Daudenarde, French, active 1869-1882, after **Frédéric-Théodore Lix**, French, 1830-1897, *Visit of H. M. Naser od-Din Shah to the Louvre*, 1873, wood engraving, 31.2 x 21.8 cm; 12 1/4 x 8 1/2 in., *Le Monde Illustré*, 26 July 1873, Foundation Artificial Light in Art, Eindhoven

Jean-Baptiste Camille Corot, French, 1796-1875, *The Dreamer under the Large Trees*, 1874, cliché-verre with its glass plate, 17.6 x 13.1 cm; 7 x 5 1/4 in., Bibliothèque Nationale de France, Cabinet des Estampes, Paris, Legs E. Moreau-Nélaton, 1927, inv. Dc 282 i rés. boîte 14; inv. Rés., musée, Corot, plaque de verre no. 133 (Amsterdam)

Daniel Urrabieta y Vierge, Spanish, 1851-1904, *The Salon by Electric Light*, 1879, wood engraving, 32 x 14 cm; 12 1/2 x 5 1/2 in., *Le Monde Illustré* 23, no. 1162, 5 July 1879, Van Gogh Museum, Amsterdam, inv. BVG 6282

Félix Bracquemond, French, 1833-1914, *The Storm Cloud*, 1879-87, etching (sixth state), 24 x 33.7 cm; 9 1/2 x 13 1/4 in., Rijksmuseum, Rijksprentenkabinet, Amsterdam, inv. RP-P-1953-414 (Amsterdam)

HWB, *Electric Lighting in the City*, 1881, wood engraving, 30 x 22.6 cm; 11 3/4 x 9 in., *The Graphic* 23, 9 April 1881, Van Gogh Museum, Amsterdam, inv. BVG 5214/23

Edmond Morin, French, 1824-1882, *The Queen of Today*, 1881, wood engraving, 27 x 22 cm; 10 1/2 x 8 1/2 in., *Le Monde Illustré*, no. 1273, 20 August 1881, Van Gogh Museum, Amsterdam, inv. BVG 6285

Auguste Lepère, French, 1849-1918, after **Edmond Morin**, French, 1824-1882, *Electricity*, 1881, wood engraving, 27.5 x 22.5 cm; 10 3/4 x 8 3/4 in., title page of *Le Monde Illustré, Numéro spécial exclusivement consacré à l'Exposition de l'Electricité*, 1881, Van Gogh Museum, Amsterdam, inv. BVG 6286

Vincent van Gogh, Dutch, 1853-1890, *The Potato Eaters*, 1885, lithograph, 26.9 x 31.8 cm; 10 1/2 x 12 1/2 in., Van Gogh Museum, Amsterdam (Vincent van Gogh Foundation), inv. P 477 V/1992 (Amsterdam); inv. P 16 V/1962 (Pittsburgh)

Auguste Lepère, French, 1849-1918, *The Rue de la Montagne Sainte-Geneviève*, 1886, wood engraving, 40.5 x 23 cm; 16 x 9 in., Jane Voorhees Zimmerli Art Museum, Rutgers, The State University of New Jersey, New Brunswick, New Jersey, David A. and Mildred H. Morse Art Acquisition Fund, inv. 85.075.016.011

Jacobus van Looy, Dutch, 1855-1930, *Paris by Night*, ca. 1886-87, pastel, 51 x 56 cm; 20 x 22 in., Instituut Collectie Nederland, on loan to the Van Gogh Museum, Amsterdam, inv. D 05 B/1986 (AB 3338)

Emile Bernard, French, 1868-1941, *Girl in a Paris Street*, 1888, pen and ink, watercolor, 31 x 19.9 cm; 12 1/4 x 7 3/4 in., Van Gogh Museum, Amsterdam (Vincent van Gogh Foundation), inv. D 638 V/1962

Henri Boutet, French, b. 1851, *A Corner of Paris at Night*, 1888, etching, 37.5 x 20.4 cm; 14 3/4 x 8 in., Jane Voorhees Zimmerli Art Museum, Rutgers, The State

University of New Jersey, New Brunswick, New Jersey, David A. and Mildred H. Morse Art Acquisition Fund, inv. 85.075.016.008

Georges Garen, French, b. 1854, *Illumination of the Eiffel Tower during the Universal Exposition, Paris 1889*, 1889, colored wood engraving, 65 x 45.3 cm; 25 1/2 x 17 3/4 in., Musée d'Orsay, Paris, fonds Eiffel, don de Mlle. Solange Granet, de Mme. Bernard Granet et ses enfants, inv. ARO 1981-144

Auguste Gérardin, French, b. 1849, *The Opening of the Universal Exposition, Paris 1889*, 1889, wood engraving, 30 x 45.5 cm; 11 3/4 x 18 in., *Le Monde Illustré*, no. 1676, 11 May 1889, Van Gogh Museum, Amsterdam, inv. BVG 6299

Charles Clément, French, active ca. 1880-1900, after **Daniel Urrabieta y Vierge**, Spanish, 1851-1904, *The Universal Exposition, Paris 1889: The Last Beam of the Luminous Fountains*, 1889, wood engraving, 20.3 x 28.2 cm; 8 x 11 in., *Le Monde Illustré*, no. 1702, 9 November 1889, Van Gogh Museum, Amsterdam, inv. BVG 6300

Auguste Gérardin, French, b. 1849, after **Manuel Orazi**, Italian, 1860-1934, *Riots in Rome - Pillaging of Shops by the Unemployed*, 1889, wood engraving, 28 x 20 cm; 11 x 7 3/4 in., *Le Monde Illustré*, no. 1665, 23 February 1889, Van Gogh Museum, Amsterdam, inv. BVG 6299

Henri-Gabriel Ibels, French, 1867-1936, *Sketch of a Street Scene (verso of "Le Devoir")*, 1892, gouache on card, 28 x 34 cm; 11 x 13 1/4 in., Van Gogh Museum, Amsterdam, inv. D 1077 S/1997 (Amsterdam)

Käthe Kollwitz, German, 1867-1945, *Self-portrait at the Table*, ca. 1893, etching and aquatint, 17.8 x 12.8 cm; 7 x 5 in., Rijksmuseum, Rijksprentenkabinet, Amsterdam, inv. RP-P-1953-417 (Amsterdam)

Odilon Redon, French, 1840-1916, *Light*, 1893, lithograph, 39.2 x 27.2 cm; 15 1/2 x 10 3/4 in., Van Gogh Museum, Amsterdam, inv. P 879 N/1996 (Amsterdam)

Théophile-Alexandre Steinlen, Swiss, 1859-1923, *Mothu and Doria*, 1893, lithograph, 120 x 91 cm; 47 1/4 x 35 3/4 in., Kunsthalle Bremen (Amsterdam)

Théophile-Alexandre Steinlen, Swiss, 1859-1923, *A Prostitute's Prayer*, 1894, lithograph, 25.5 x 18.3 cm; 10 x 7 1/4 in., Rijksmuseum, Rijksprentenkabinet, Amsterdam, inv. RP-P-1950-431

Etienne Moreau-Nélaton, French, 1859-1927, *Bec Auer*, 1895, color lithograph, 172.5 x 91.5 cm; 68 x 36 in., Kunsthalle Bremen (Amsterdam)

Edvard Munch, Norwegian, 1863-1949, *Moonlight*, 1895, drypoint and aquatint, 31 x 25.3 cm; 12 1/4 x 10 in., Rijksmuseum, Rijksprentenkabinet, Amsterdam, inv. RP-P-1949-49 (Amsterdam)

Jehan Rictus, French, 1867-1933, *Paul Verlaine!*, ca. 1895, pen and ink, 21.5 x 14.4 cm; 8 1/2 x 5 3/4 in., Jane Voorhees Zimmerli Art Museum, Rutgers, The State University of New Jersey, New Brunswick, New Jersey, Acquired with The Herbert D. and Ruth Schimmel Museum Library Fund, inv. 1994.0086

Henri de Toulouse-Lautrec, French, 1864-1901, *"L'Aube,"* 1896, lithograph, 60 x 79.5 cm; 23 3/4 x 31 1/4 in., Kunsthalle Bremen (Amsterdam)

Eugène Carrière, French, 1849-1906, *"L'Aurore,"* 1897, lithograph, 203 x 136.5 cm; 80 x 53 3/4 in., Kunsthalle Bremen (Amsterdam)

Emile Berchmans, Belgian, 1867-1947, *"La Lampe belge,"* before 1897, colored lithograph, 70 x 100.5 cm; 27 1/2 x 39 1/2 in., Kunsthalle Bremen (Amsterdam)

Eugène Carrière, French, 1849-1906, *Sleep*, 1897, lithograph, 33.8 x 43 cm; 13 1/4 x 17 in., Rijksmuseum, Rijksprentenkabinet, Amsterdam, inv. RP-P-1949-274 (Amsterdam)

Félix Vallotton, Swiss, 1865-1925, *The Exit*, ca. 1897, woodcut, 16.1 x 20 cm; 6 1/4 x 7 3/4 in., Rijksmuseum, Rijksprentenkabinet, Amsterdam, inv. RP-P-1947-66 (Amsterdam)

Félix Vallotton, Swiss, 1865-1925, *Lamp shade*, ca. 1898, tempera on parchment, 13 x 60 cm; 5 x 23 1/2 in., Private collection, Paris

George Randolph Barse, American, b. 1861, *Moths*, ca. 1900, pencil, 115.6 x 95.3 cm; 45 1/2 x 37 1/2 in., Carnegie Museum of Art, Pittsburgh, Andrew Carnegie Fund, inv. 06.24

Theodor Josef Hubert Hoffbauer, German, b. 1839, *The Universal Exposition, Paris 1900: The Palais de l'Electricité and the Château d'Eau*, 1900, handcolored lithograph, with mica chips and stamped tinfoil, 29.5 x 46.2 cm; 11 5/8 x 18 1/6 in., Private collection

Charles-Henri Toussaint, French, 1849-1911, *The Universal Exposition, Paris 1900: The Palais des Illusions*, 1900, handcolored lithograph, with mica chips and stamped tinfoil, 31.5 x 47 cm; 12 3/8 x 18 1/2 in., Private collection

Photographs

Joseph Nicéphore Niépce, French, 1765-1833, *Cardinal d'Amboise*, 1826, heliograph on pewter, 16.5 x 13.1 cm; 6 1/2 x 5 1/4 in., The Royal Photographic Society, Bath (Amsterdam)

Soleil Opticien, Paris, *Daguerreotype camera with accessories*, 1840, Universiteitsmuseum Utrecht, inv. LI 148 (Amsterdam)

Set of four daguerreotypes, nationality unknown, ca. 1840-50, Rijksmuseum, Rijksprenten-

kabinet, Amsterdam, inv. RP-F-14404 A-D (Amsterdam)

Eduard Isaac Asser, Dutch, 1909-1894, *Daguerreotype*, ca. 1840-50, 9 x 7.2 cm; 3 1/2 x 2 3/4 in. (quarter plate), Rijksmuseum, Rijksprentenkabinet, Amsterdam, inv. RP-F-AB 12294 (Amsterdam)

Louis-Auguste Bisson, French, 1814-1876, *Portrait of a Man*, ca. 1843, daguerreotype, 8.1 x 6.1 cm; 3 1/4 x 2 1/2 in. (sixth plate), Rijksmuseum, Rijksprentenkabinet, Amsterdam, inv. RP-F-14596 (Amsterdam)

Louis-Jacques-Mandé Daguerre, French, 1787-1851, *Portrait of an Artist (Hippolyte Sebron?)*, ca. 1843, daguerreotype, 15.6 x 13 cm; 6 1/4 x 5 1/4 in. (quarter plate), George Eastman House, Rochester, New York, Gift of Eastman Kodak Company, inv. 76:0168:0151 (Pittsburgh)

William Henry Fox Talbot, British, 1800-1877, *Lace*, ca. 1845, salted paper print, 23 x 18.8 cm; 9 x 7 1/2 in., irregular, George Eastman House, Rochester, New York, Gift of Dr. Walter Clark, inv. 81:2836:0001 (Pittsburgh)

Lewis-style daguerreotype camera with Harrison lens, American, ca. 1848, wood, brass, leather, 18 x 16 x 49 cm; 7 x 6 1/4 x 19 1/4 in., George Eastman House, Rochester, New York, Museum Collection, inv. 77:0850:08 (Pittsburgh)

C. Humbert, French, *Camera*, ca. 1850-75, wood, brass, canvas, 55 x 53 x 106 cm; 21 3/4 x 20 3/4 x 41 3/4 in., height of stand 80 cm; 31 1/2 in., Musée Nicéphore Niépce, Ville de Chalons-sur-Saône, France, inv. MNN 75.45.1

Warren de la Rue, British, 1815-1889, *The Moon*, ca. 1860, album with 12 albumen prints, each 6.4 x 5.3 cm; 2 1/2 x 2 in., Rijksmuseum, Rijksprentenkabinet, Amsterdam, inv. RP-F-F-25451 A-L

Woman's Spirit behind Table with Photograph, American, ca. 1865, albumen print carte-de-visite, 9.8 x 5.6 cm; 3 3/4 x 2 1/4 in., George Eastman House, Rochester, New York, Museum Purchase, inv. 68:0325.0004 (Pittsburgh)

Adolphe Neyt, Belgian, 1830-1893, *Photomicrograph of a Flea*, ca. 1865, albumen print, 19.8 x 15.1 cm; 7 3/4 x 6 in., George Eastman House, Rochester, New York, Gift of 3M Company, inv. 77:0638:0009 (Pittsburgh)

Lewis Morris Rutherfurd, American, 1816-1892, *The Moon*, 1865, albumen print, 57.2 x 43.2 cm; 22 1/2 x 17 in., Stephen White Collection II, Los Angeles

Timothy H. O'Sullivan, American, 1840-1882, *Gould Curry Mine, Comstock Lode, Virginia City, Nevada*, 1868, albumen print, 17.7 x 21.9 cm; 7 x 8 1/2 in., George Eastman House, Rochester, New York, Gift of Harvard University, inv. 81:1887:0017 (Pittsburgh)

Lewis Morris Rutherfurd, American, 1816-1892, *The Sun*, 1870, albumen print, 9.2 x 9.2 cm; 3 1/2 x 3 1/2 in., Pietro Angelo Secchi, *Die Sonne*, ed. H. Schellen, Braunschweig: George Westermann 1872, Rijksmuseum, Amsterdam, inv. BI-350-D-1

William N. Jennings, American, 1860-1946, *Artist's Lightning*, 1885, pen and ink, 4.5 x 2.5 cm; 1 3/4 x 1 in., George Eastman House, Rochester, New York, Gift of 3M Company, inv. 83:0679:0003 (Pittsburgh)

William N. Jennings, American, 1860-1946, *A Thunderbolt*, ca. 1885, gelatin silver print, 7.9 x 3.4 cm; 3 x 1 1/4 in., George Eastman House, Rochester, New York, Gift of 3M Company, inv. 83:0679:0006 (Pittsburgh)

Study of the Solar Surface, French, 1885, carbon print, 23 x 16.9 cm; 9 x 6 3/4 in., Rijksmuseum, Rijksprentenkabinet, Amsterdam, inv. RP-F-1997-50

Peter Henry Emerson, British, 1856-1936, *Gathering Water-lilies*, ca. 1885, platinum print, 19.6 x 28.6 cm; 7 3/4 x 11 1/4 in., P. H. Emerson and T. F. Goodall, *Life and Landscape on the Norfolk Broads*, London: Sampson Low, Marston, Searle and Rivington, 1886, plate IX, George Eastman House, Rochester, New York, Gift of William C. Emerson, inv. 79:4338:0019 (Pittsburgh)

Paul Pierre Henry, French, 1848-1905, and **Prosper Mathieu Henry**, French, 1849-1903, *A Lunar Region*, 1887, albumen print, 11 x 8.4 cm; 4 1/4 x 3 1/4 in., E. Mouchez, *La Photographie astronomique à l'Observatoire de Paris et la carte du ciel*, Paris: Gauthier-Villars 1887, Rijksmuseum, Amsterdam, inv. BI-350-D-12

Josef Maria Eder, Austrian, 1855-1944, and **Eduard Valenta**, Austrian, 1857-1937, *Aesculapius Snake*, 1896, photogravure print, 27.0 x 21.7 cm; 10 1/2 x 8 1/2 in., Josef Maria Eder and Eduard Valenta, *Versuche über Photographie mittelst der Röntgen'schen Strahlen*, Vienna: R. Lechner 1896, plate 15, George Eastman House, Rochester, New York, Gift of Eastman Kodak Company, inv. 79:3352:0002 (Pittsburgh)

Three prints from x-rays, German, 1896: *Left Hand of a Man with a Bullet in his Wrist*, *An Egyptian Cat Mummy*, *Hand of a Lady with a Bunch of Flowers*, photogravure prints, each ca. 60 x 35.5 cm; 23 1/2 x 14 in., Walter König, *14 Photographien mit Röntgen-Strahlen aufgenommen im Physikalischen Verein zu Frankfurt a. M.*, Leipzig: Johann Ambrosius Barth 1896, Deutsches Röntgen-Museum, Remscheid (Amsterdam)

Prestwich Manufacturing Company, British, *Prestwich cinematograph*, 1898, various metals, wood, glass, 40.5 x 22 x 45 cm; 16 x 8 5/8 x 17 3/4 in., George Eastman House, Rochester, New York, Museum Collection, inv. 78:1651:0011 (Pittsburgh)

Siegmund Lubin, American, 1851-1923, *Lubin projector*, ca. 1900, metal, wood, glass, 90 x 45 x 102 cm; 35 3/8 x 17 3/4 x 40 1/8 in., George Eastman House, Rochester, New York, Museum Collection, inv. 78:1674:0084 (Pittsburgh)

Instruments and optical toys

Large prismatic cell, Dutch, ca. 1720, wood, glass, 35 x 26 x 21 cm; 13 3/4 x 10 1/4 x 8 1/4 in., Museum Boerhaave, Leiden, inv. 9222

Jan van Musschenbroek, Dutch, 1687-1748, attributed, *Projection lantern*, ca. 1720, wood, glass, metal, 180 x 80 cm; 70 3/4 x 31 1/2 in., Museum Boerhaave, Leiden, inv. 10916 (Amsterdam)

Jan van Musschenbroek, Dutch, 1687-1748, attributed, *Optical trough*, ca. 1720-40, wood, glass, 9 x 22 x 15 cm; 3 1/2 x 8 1/2 x 6 in., Museum Boerhaave, Leiden, inv. 7924

Jacob van der Cloesen, Dutch, ca. 1690-1766, *Heliostat*, ca. 1720-40, brass, wood, 40 x 50 x 24 cm; 15 3/4 x 19 3/4 x 9 1/2 in., Museum Boerhaave, Leiden, inv. 9233 (Amsterdam)

Viewer of optical prints, Dutch, ca. 1725-75, wood, glass, 53.5 cm; 21 in., Rijksmuseum, Rijksprentenkabinet, Amsterdam, inv. RP-OUD BEZIT

Viewer of optical prints, Dutch, ca. 1725-75, wood, glass, 70 cm; 27 1/2 in., Rijksmuseum, Rijksprentenkabinet, Amsterdam, inv. RP-DO-1980-61

Microscope, possibly Swedish, before 1730, wood, ivory, brass, glass, paper, 35.6 cm; 14 in.; diameter 20.3 cm; 8 in., Carnegie Museum of Natural History, Pittsburgh, Henrici Bequest, inv. 8923-1a-h (Pittsburgh)

James Short, British, 1710-1768, *Pepperell telescope, with heliometer*, ca. 1750, brass, glass, silver, 50.8 cm, 20 in., Harvard University Collection of Historical Scientific Instruments, Cambridge, Massachussetts, inv. 0002 (Pittsburgh)

Lens, Dutch, ca. 1750-75, wood, brass, glass, 32.5 cm; 12 3/4, diameter 14 cm; 5 1/2 in., Teylers Museum, Haarlem, inv. 345 (Amsterdam)

Portable theater, Dutch, ca. 1750-75, oil on glass, 32.5 x 40 x 10.6 cm; 12 3/4 x 15 3/4 x 4 1/4 in., Collectie Theater Instituut Nederland, Amsterdam

Nathaniel Hill, British, active 1746-1764, and **George Adams, Sr.**, British, 1704-1772, *Orrery (Tellurium)*, ca. 1754, brass, 43 x 44 x 29 cm; 17 x 17 1/4 x 11 1/2 in., Nederlands Scheepvaartsmuseum, Amsterdam, inv. B.0028 (01) 03 (Amsterdam)

Prism in holder, Dutch, ca. 1750-75, glass, wood, brass, 22 cm; 8 3/4 in., Universiteitsmuseum Utrecht, inv. LI 85 (Amsterdam)

Microscope, Dutch, ca. 1750-75, wood, glass, leather, 40 cm; 17 3/4 in., Museum Boerhaave, Leiden, inv. 4424

Viewer of optical prints, Dutch, ca. 1750-75, oak, 34 x 45.2 x 54 cm; 13 1/4 x 17 3/4 x 21 1/4 in., Collectie Theater Instituut Nederland, Amsterdam

Camera obscura, French, ca. 1750-1800, wood, 29 x 15 x 19 cm; 11 1/2 x 6 x 7 1/2 in. (closed), Musée Nicéphore Niépce, Ville de Chalons-sur-Saône, France, Don de Bernard Lefebvre, inv. MNN 30.11.77 no. 23

Solar microscope, Dutch, ca. 1750-1800, brass, glass, length of tube 20.5 cm; 8 in., Museum Boerhaave, Leiden, inv. 7352

Mirror, French, ca. 1750-1800, wood, brass, glass, 166 x 50 x 80.5

cm; 65 1/4 x 19 1/2 x 31 3/4 in., Musée des arts et métiers du CNAM, Paris, inv. 1734

Projection lantern, British, ca. 1760, wood, brass, iron, 112 x 75.6 x 28.8 cm; 44 x 29 3/4 x 11 1/4 in., Harvard University Collection of Historical Scientific Instruments, Cambridge, Massachusetts, inv. 00089 (Pittsburgh)

Camera obscura, British, ca. 1760-80, wood, leather, iron, brass, glass, paper, ca. 83 x 64 x 55 cm; 32 3/4 x 25 1/4 x 21 3/4 in. (open), Science Museum, London, inv. 1875-28

Benjamin Martin, British, 1704-1784, *Orrery (Tellurium and Lunarium)*, ca. 1765, brass, height to cylinder surface 31.7 cm; 12 1/2 in., diameter of cylinder 23.5 cm; 9 1/4 in., Harvard University Collection of Historical Scientific Instruments, Cambridge, Massachusetts, inv. 00052 (Pittsburgh)

Benjamin Martin, British, 1704-1784, *Two glass prisms*, ca. 1765, glass, brass, length 19.7 cm; 7 3/4 in (A), 14.6 cm; 5 3/4 in. (B), Harvard University Collection of Historical Scientific Instruments, Cambridge, Massachusetts, inv. 00085, A, B (Pittsburgh)

Benjamin Martin, British, 1704-1784, *Model of the eye*, ca. 1765, brass, glass; 22.9 cm; 9 in., diameter, 7.6 cm; 3 in., Harvard University Collection of Historical Scientific Instruments, Cambridge, Massachusetts, inv. 00011 (Pittsburgh)

Benjamin Martin, British, 1704-1784, attributed, *Apparatus for the angle of incidence*, ca. 1765, brass, 52.1 cm; 20 1/2 in., Harvard University Collection of Historical Scientific Instruments, Cambridge, Massachusetts, inv. 00087 (Pittsburgh)

Prism with decorative shape, Dutch, ca. 1775-1800, glass, wood, brass, 16 cm; 6 1/4 in., Universiteitsmuseum Utrecht, inv. LI 6 (Amsterdam)

Jan van Deijl, Dutch, ca. 1715-1801, and **Harmanus van Deijl**, Dutch, 1738-1809, *Achromatic telescope*, 1781, mahogany, brass, glass, 140 cm; 55 in., Teylers Museum, Haarlem, inv. 352 (Amsterdam)

Gerard Hulst van Keulen, Dutch, active before 1801, *Sextant*, between 1792-1801, brass, glass, 13 x 40 x 55 cm; 5 x 15 3/4 x 21 3/4 in., Nederlands Scheepvaartsmuseum, Amsterdam, inv. 1996.0005 (Amsterdam)

Lay figure, Dutch, ca. 1775-1800, wood, 85 x 24 x 13 cm; 33 1/2 x 9 1/2 x 5 1/4 in., Rijksuniversiteit Utrecht, Kunsthistorisch Instituut, inv. KHI.SW.194/95

Concave mirror, French, 1800, glass, wooden frame, 71 x 34 cm; 28 x 13 1/4 in., diameter 46 cm; 18 in., Musée des arts et métiers du CNAM, Paris, inv. 1738

Robert Bate, British, 1782-1847, *Polyangular kaleidoscope with stand*, ca. 1820, brass, glass, ca. 30 cm; 11 3/4 in., Science Museum, London, inv. 1928-881

West London camera lucida, British, ca. 1830-40, brass, glass, 26 cm; 10 1/4 in., George Eastman House, Rochester, New York, Museum Collection, inv. 88:0988:2 (Pittsburgh)

François jeune, French, *Fresnel lens*, 1835, glass, wood, brass, 160 x 110 cm; 63 x 43 1/4, diameter 82 cm; 32 1/4 in., Musée des arts et métiers du CNAM, Paris, inv. 2820

Camera lucida, Dutch, ca. 1850-75, brass, glass, 25.5 x 54 x 38 cm; 10 x 21 1/4 x 15 in. (box), Teylers Museum, Haarlem, inv. 378 (Amsterdam)

Soleil Opticien, Paris, *Camera lucida*, ca. 1825-75, brass, 35 cm; 13 3/4 in., Musée Nicéphore Niépce, Ville de Chalons-sur-Saône, France, inv. Prov. 22.01.76, no. 6

Egg on a stand, Dutch, ca. 1850-1900, wood, metal, 36 cm; 14 1/4 in., Rijksuniversiteit Utrecht, Kunsthistorisch Instituut, inv. KHI.SW.66/95

Cast of a foot, Dutch, ca. 1850-1900, biscuit porcelain, 13.5 x 10 x 24.5; 5 1/4 x 4 x 9 1/2 in., Rijks-universiteit Utrecht, Kunsthistorisch Instituut, inv. KHI.SW.31b/95

Ecorché with measuring device, Dutch, ca. 1850-1900, plaster, wood, 46 x 24 x 8.5 cm; 85 1/4 x 9 1/2 x 3 1/4 in., Rijksuniversiteit Utrecht, Kunsthistorisch Instituut, inv. KHI.SW.163/95

Black mirror, Dutch, ca. 1850-1900, wooden box, leather, black glass, 12.5 x 9.7 cm; 5 x 3 3/4 in., Rijksuniversiteit Utrecht, Kunsthistorisch Instituut, inv. KHI.SW.61/95

Perspective model, French, ca. 1860, plaster, wood, 35.4 x 27.5 x 7 cm; 14 x 10 3/4 x 2 3/4 in., Musée des arts et métiers du CNAM, Paris, inv. 7087

Jules Duboscq, French, 1817-1886, *Grease spot photometer*, ca. 1860, wood, paper, 27.9 x 30.5 cm; 11 x 12 in., National Museum of American History, Smithsonian Institution, Washington, D.C., Transferred from the Smithsonian Astrophysical Laboratory, 1956, inv. 314,956 (Pittsburgh)

E. Zimmermann, German, active ca. 1875-1900, *Rotating mirror apparatus*, ca. 1875-1900, iron, mirrors, 47 x 29.8 x 18 cm; 18 1/2 x 11 3/4 x 7 1/8 in., National Museum of American History, Smithsonian Institution, Washington, D.C., Gift of the Physics Department of Fordham University, 1964, inv. 325,687 (Pittsburgh)

Red-green letter display, Dutch, 1878, wood, glass, 12 x 59 cm; 4 3/4 x 23 1/4 in., Universiteits-museum Utrecht, inv. 19.04.110 (Amsterdam)

Red-green spectacles, Dutch, 1878, copper, glass, width 11.3 cm; 4 1/4 in., Universiteitsmuseum Utrecht, inv. 19.08.020 (Amsterdam)

Lapierre, French, *Magic lantern*, ca. 1880, tin, glass, 63 x 16 x 27 cm; 24 3/4 x 6 1/4 x 10 1/2 in., Haags Documentatie Centrum Nieuwe Media, The Hague

Henri Rivière, French, 1864-1951, *The Devil and St. Anthony*, 1887-90, zinc cutout, 75 x 42 cm; 29 1/2 x 16 1/2 in., Jane Voorhees Zimmerli Art Museum, Rutgers, The State University of New Jersey, New Brunswick, New Jersey, Gift of University College Rutgers New Brunswick Alumni Association, inv. 1986.0081

Light sources

Candelabrum, British, ca. 1725, cut glass and metal, 64.8 cm; 25 1/2 in., Carnegie Museum of Art, Pittsburgh, Gift of Ailsa Mellon Bruce, inv. 70.32.2250

Double crusie grease lamp, American, ca. 1750, iron, 38.1 x 19.5 x 10.2 cm; 15 x 7 1/2 x 4 in., Carnegie Museum of Natural History, Pittsburgh, Gift of Arthur B. Van Buskirk, inv. 19458-112

Argand lamp, British, 1784-89, brass, paper, zinc, 38.5 cm; 15 1/4 in., Teylers Museum, Haarlem, inv. 213 (Amsterdam)

Matthew Boulton, British, 1728-1809, *Argand lamp*, ca. 1790-1805, silver plate, glass, 55.2 x 41.3 cm; 21 1/4 x 16 1/4 in., Winterthur Museum, Garden and Library, Winterthur, Delaware, inv. 59.671.1 (Pittsburgh)

Thomas Hope, British, 1769-1831 (designer) and **Alexis Decaix**, French, d. 1811 (maker), attributed, *Pair of candlesticks*, ca. 1807, gilt bronze, 31.8 cm; 12 1/2 in., Carnegie Museum of Art, Pittsburgh, Museum Purchase, Gift of Ailsa Mellon Bruce, by exchange, and Ailsa Mellon Bruce Fund, inv. 95.111.1-2

Lace maker's globe, Dutch, ca. 1800-50, glass, ca. 40 cm; 15 1/2 in., Nederlands Openlucht-museum, Arnhem, inv. 7344-48 (Amsterdam)

Lace maker's globe, French, ca. 1800-50, glass, 39.4 cm; 15 1/2 in., Carnegie Museum of Natural History, Pittsburgh, George and Lilian Ball Memorial Fund, 1969, inv. 23781-20 a (Pittsburgh)

Candleholder, American, ca. 1800-50, iron, 26.7 cm; 10 1/2 in., Carnegie Museum of Natural History, Pittsburgh, Gift of George and Lilian Ball, inv. 13997/14 (Pittsburgh)

Splintholder, American, ca. 1800-50, iron, 15.9 x 19 x 7 cm; 6 1/4 x 7 1/2 x 2 3/4 in., Carnegie Museum of Natural History, Pittsburgh, George and Lilian Ball Memorial Fund, inv. 13997/78 (Pittsburgh)

Oil lamp, Dutch, ca. 1800-50, copper, 61.5 cm; 24 1/4 in., Nederlands Openluchtmuseum, Arnhem, inv. 21330-54 AB (Amsterdam)

Miner's lamp, British, ca. 1825-50, brass, 6.8 x 3.8 x 6 cm; 2 2/3 x 1 1/2 x 2 1/3 in., Carnegie Museum of Natural History, Pittsburgh, Gift of Arthur B. Van Buskirk, inv. 19458/122 (Pittsburgh)

Whale oil lamp, American, ca. 1830-40, metal, glass, 26.7 cm; 10 1/2 in., Carnegie Museum of Art, Pittsburgh, Gift of Edward Duff Balken, inv. 50.1.4

Königliche Porzellanmanufaktur Berlin, German, *Candleholder with lithophane shade*, ca. 1835-44, iron and biscuit porcelain, 44.5 x 22.2 x 12.7 cm; 17 1/2 x 8 3/4 x 5 in., Carnegie Museum of Natural History, Pittsburgh, George and Lilian Ball Memorial Fund, inv. 18810-20a-d

Solar lamp, German?, 1842, bronze, crystal, 65 cm; 25 1/2 in., Lumière de l'oeil, Paris

Trainman's lantern, American, ca. 1845, tin, glass, steel, 26 x 12.4 x 12.4 cm; 10 1/4 x 4 7/8 x 4 7/8 in., Carnegie Museum of Natural History, Pittsburgh, Gift of John L. Herring, inv. 1381 (Pittsburgh)

Presentation railroad lantern, American, ca. 1850, brass, glass, 40.2 cm; 15 7/8 in., diameter 16 cm; 6 1/4 in., Mrs. Hattie Ward Frew, courtesy of the Carnegie Museum of Natural History, Pittsburgh, inv. L-208 (Pittsburgh)

Gas table lamp, French, ca. 1850, cast iron, brass, clear and opalized crystal, ceramic, 56 cm; 22 in., Lumière de l'oeil, Paris

Jules Duboscq, French, 1817-1886, *Arc lamp*, 1852, brass, 83 cm; 32 3/4 in., Teylers Museum, Haarlem, inv. 620 (Amsterdam)

Dietz & Company, American, *Kerosene lamp*, ca. 1855, gilded metal, marble, 16 cm; 6 1/4 in.; diameter 11.5 cm; 4 1/2 in., Carnegie Museum of Natural History, Pittsburgh, George and Lilian Ball Memorial Fund, inv. 23781-6 (Pittsburgh)

Bull's eye lantern, American, ca. 1850-75, japanned tin, glass, steel, brass, wood, 22.9 x 20.3 x 10.2 cm; 9 x 8 x 4 in., Carnegie Museum of Natural History, Pittsburgh, George and Lilian Ball Memorial Fund, 1969, inv. 23781-13

Gas facade lantern, French, ca. 1850-1900, copper, glass, ceramic, 65 x 38 x 50 cm; 25 1/2 x 15 x 19 3/4 in., Lumière de l'oeil, Paris

Q. Harder, Dutch, *Model for a lighthouse on the island of Texel, Netherlands*, 1863, wood, brass, 138.5 cm; 54 1/2 in., Rijksmuseum, Amsterdam, inv. NG-MC-1149

Gieterij Prins van Oranje, Dutch, *Model for a lighthouse on the island of Java, Indonesia*, ca. 1870, brass, wood, glass, 81 cm; 31 3/4 in., Rijksmuseum, Amsterdam, inv. NG-MC-1280

Street lantern, Dutch, ca. 1870-80, cast iron, glass, 95 cm; 37 1/2 in., EnergeticA, Museum voor Energietechniek, Amsterdam (Amsterdam)

Dietz & Company, American, *Pocket lantern*, ca. 1875, tin, glass, steel, 21.5 x 7.5 x 4.5 cm; 8 3/8 x 3 x 1 3/4 in., Carnegie Museum of Natural History, Pittsburgh, George and Lilian Ball Memorial Fund, inv. 23781-2 (Pittsburgh)

Kerosene hanging lamp, German, ca. 1875-1900, metal, ceramic, glass, 60 cm; 23 1/2 in., Van Gogh Museum, Amsterdam, inv. V 077 M/1992 (Amsterdam)

Kerosene table lamp, Austrian, ca. 1875-1900, spelter, brass, crystal, 64 cm; 25 1/4 in., Lumière de l'oeil, Paris

Vesta lamp, German, 1878, brass, glass, 65 cm; 25 1/2 in., Lumière de l'oeil, Paris

Nederlandsche Stoomboot Maatschappij Feijenoord, Dutch, *Model for a lighthouse on the island of Sumatra, Indonesia*, 1879, brass, wood, 155 cm; 61 in., Rijksmuseum, Amsterdam, inv. NG-MC-1413

Paul Morane Aîné, French, *Candle molding machine "Parisienne,"* 1880, steel, wood, bronze, wax, iron, textile, 67 x 29.5 x 75.5 cm; 26 1/2 x 11 1/2 x 29 3/4 in., Musée des arts et métiers du CNAM, Paris, inv. 9796

Kerosene lamp, European, ca. 1880, brass, glass, tin, 38.1 x 15.2 x 14 cm; 15 x 6 x 5 1/2 in., Carnegie Museum of Natural History, Pittsburgh, George and Lilian Ball Memorial Fund, 1966, inv. 21832-5a&b (Pittsburgh)

Grand-Val, American, *Time-indicating lamp*, ca. 1880-90, glass, brass, 22.9 cm; 9 in., diameter 6.7 cm; 2 2/3 in., Carnegie Museum of Natural History, Pittsburgh, George and Lilian Ball Memorial Fund, inv. 13997-57

Allegorical gas bracket, British, ca. 1880-1900, brass, crystal, 42 cm; 16 1/2 in., Lumière de l'oeil, Paris

Gas bracket, French, ca. 1880-1900, brass, length 17 cm; 6 3/4 in., Lumière de l'oeil, Paris

Electric filament lamps on rack, various nationalities, ca. 1881-82, mahogany, glass, 26.5 x 44.5 cm; 10 1/2 x 17 1/2 in. (rack), Teylers Museum, Haarlem, inv. 624/1 (Amsterdam)

L. Sautter, Lemonnier & Cie., French, *Gramme generator*, ca. 1882, iron, copper, 60 x 88 x 40 cm; 23 1/2 x 34 1/2 x 15 3/4 in., EnergeticA, Museum voor Energietechniek, Amsterdam (Amsterdam)

L. Sautter, Lemonnier & Cie., French, *Arc lamp*, ca. 1882, brass, 81 cm; 32 in., EnergeticA, Museum voor Energietechniek, Amsterdam

Gas table lamp, Dutch, ca. 1890-1900, brass, iron, glass, 55 cm; 21 3/4 in., EnergeticA, Museum voor Energietechniek, Amsterdam (Amsterdam)

Arc lamp, Dutch, ca. 1890-1900, iron, glass, ca. 70 cm; 27 1/2 in., EnergeticA, Museum voor Energietechniek, Amsterdam (Amsterdam)

Westinghouse Company, American, *Electric light bulbs*, ca. 1890-1900, glass, brass-plated copper, porcelain, each 13.3 cm; 5 1/4 in., diameter 6 cm; 2 3/8 in., Carnegie Museum of Natural History, Pittsburgh, Gift of Paul Caldwell, inv. 20090/2 and 20090/3 (Pittsburgh)

Gas discharge tube, British, ca. 1891, glass, wood, 28 cm; 11 in., Universiteitsmuseum Utrecht, inv. LI 159 (Amsterdam)

Willem Kromhout, Dutch, 1864-1940, *Swan lamp*, 1899-1902, bronze, 153 cm; 60 1/4 in., diameter 82 cm; 32 1/4 in., Kunsthandel Frans Leidelmeijer, Amsterdam (Amsterdam)

Tiffany & Co., American, *Table lamp*, ca. 1899-1902, bronze, glass, 66 cm; 26 in., diameter 53.3 cm; 21 in., Carnegie Museum of Art, Pittsburgh, Gift of Mr. Arthur E. Braun, inv. 76.46a-c

William Arthur Smith Benson, British, 1854-1924, *Gas pendant*, before 1900, brass, copper, glass, 128 cm; 50 1/2 in., Lumière de l'oeil, Paris

Gas and electric incandescent lamp, French, ca. 1900, brass, crystal, glass, 55 cm; 21 3/4 in., Lumière de l'oeil, Paris

Emile Gallé, French, 1846-1904, *Bat lamp*, ca. 1900, glass, bronze, 33.7 cm; 13 1/4 in., Collection Neumann, Gingins (Switzerland), inv. J-409 (Amsterdam)

Books and periodicals

Christiaan Huygens, *Traité de la lumière: ou sont expliquées les causes de ce qui luy arrive dans la reflexion, & dans la refraction [...]*, Leiden: Pierre van der Aa 1690, Universiteitsbibliotheek Amsterdam, inv. 720 C 10 (Amsterdam); Harvard University, Houghton Library, Cambridge, Massachusetts, inv. Hollis# ALQ1811/bks (Pittsburgh)

Isaac Newton, *Opticks, or, a Treatise of the Reflexions, Refractions, Inflexions and Colours of Light [...]*, London: Sam. Smith and Benj. Walford 1704, Universiteitsbibliotheek Amsterdam, inv. OG 80-21 (Amsterdam); American Philosophical Society, Philadelphia, inv. 535N48 (Pittsburgh)

Willem Jacob 's Gravesande, *Physices elementa mathematica, experimentis confirmata: sive introductio ad philosophiam Newtonianam*, 2 vols. in 1, Leiden: Peter van der Aa, 1721, Universiteitsbibliotheek Amsterdam, inv. OG 80-43 (Amsterdam); *Mathematical Elements of Natural Philosophy Confirm'd by*

Experiments, 6th ed., 2 vols., London: W. Innys, T. Longman, T. Shewell, and M. Senex 1747, American Philosophical Society, Philadelphia, inv. 530SG6 (Pittsburgh)

Voltaire, *Elémens de la philosophie de Neuton, mis à la portée de tout le monde*, Amsterdam: Etienne Ledet & Compagnie 1738, Universiteitsbibliotheek Amsterdam, inv. 2486 D 19 (Amsterdam); *Elements of Newton's Philosophy*, London: Stephen Austin 1738, American Philosophical Society, Philadelphia, inv. 508Z88E.R. (Pittsburgh)

Francesco Algarotti, *Sir Isaac Newton's Theory of Light and Colours and his Principle of Attraction: Made Familiar to the Ladies in Several Entertainments [...]*, London: G. Hawkins 1742, American Philosophical Society, Philadelphia, inv. 535AL3S.C (Pittsburgh); *De Newtoniaansche wysbegeerte voor de vrouwen, of samenspraaken over het licht, de kleuren en de aantrekkingskracht. In het Italiaansch beschreven door den heer Algarotti. Vermeerderd met een Voorreden van een voornaam Natuur-kenner*, 2nd ed., Utrecht: A. Stubbe 1775, Universiteitsbibliotheek Amsterdam, inv. 2397 H 27 (Amsterdam)

Pierre Bouguer, *Traité d'optique sur la gradation de la lumière*, Paris: H. L. Guerin and L. F. Delatour 1760, Carnegie Library, Pittsburgh, inv. qr 535 B65

Benjamin Martin, *The Young Gentleman and Lady's Natural Philosophy*, 2nd ed., vol. 2, London: W. Owen and Benjamin Martin 1772, University of Pittsburgh, Darlington Memorial Library, inv. Q157.M379 (Pittsburgh)

Denis Diderot and **Jean d'Alembert** (eds.), *Encyclopédie ou Dictionnaire raisonné des sciences, des arts et des métiers [...]*, vol. 1, Paris 1772, Universiteitsbibliotheek Amsterdam, inv. 1290 A 1 (Amsterdam)

Joseph Priestley, *The History and Present State of Discoveries Relating to Vision, Light, and Colours*, London: J. Johnson 1772, Carnegie Library, Pittsburgh, inv. qr535 P94

Edmé Guyot, *Nouvelles récréations physiques et mathematiques, contenant toutes celles qui ont été découvertes & imaginées dans ces derniers temps, sur l'aiman, les nombres, l'optique, la chymie, &c, nouvelle édition*, 4 vols., Paris: Gueffier, vol. 3: 1774, University Library, Nijmegen (Netherlands)

Martin Frobenius Ledermüller and Adam Wolfang Winterschmidt, *Mikroskoopische vermaaklykheden [...]*, 4 vols. in 2, Amsterdam: Erven van F. Houttuyn 1776, Universiteitsbibliotheek Amsterdam, inv. 1734 C 5-6 (Amsterdam)

Johann Caspar Lavater, *Over de physiognomie*, 4 vols., Amsterdam: Johannes Allart, 2nd ed. 1784, Rijksmuseum, Amsterdam, inv. BI-21-G-10-13 (Amsterdam)

Edward Orme, *Essay on Transparent Prints and on Transparencies in General*, London: Printed for and sold by the author 1807, Rijksmuseum, Amsterdam, inv. BI-89-A-57

Rudolph Ackermann, *Microcosm of London*, 3 vols., London: R. Ackermann 1808-11, University of Pittsburgh, Darlington Memorial Library, inv. FDA683.M62 (Pittsburgh)

Frederick Accum, *A Practical Treatise on Gas-light: exhibiting a summary description of the apparatus and machinery best calculated for illuminating streets, houses and manufactures with carburetted hydrogen, or coal-gas [...]*, London: R. Ackermann 1815, Carnegie Museum of Art, Pittsburgh, Heinz Architectural Center

Pierre-Henri de Valenciennes, *Elémens de perspective pratique, à l'usage des artistes [...]*, Paris: A. Payen 1820, University of Pittsburgh, Frick Fine Arts Library, inv. N7430.V15

Eugène Peclet, *Traité de l'éclairage*, Paris: Malher 1827, Museum Boerhaave, Leiden, inv. 8679

Alfred-Henri Darjou, *Silhouettes faciles, ombres amusantes produites par l'arrangement des mains et les doigts placés entre une lumière et la muraille dessinés par Darjou*, Paris: Au Bureau du Journal Amusant, ca. 1840, Cooper-Hewitt, National Design Museum Branch, Smithsonian Institution Libraries, New York, inv. f 6V 1218 55 D37 CHM

William Henry Fox Talbot, *The Pencil of Nature*, London: Longman, Brown, Green and Longmans 1844, The Royal Photographic Society, Bath (Amsterdam)

Thomas Webster and Mrs. Parkes, *An Encyclopedia of Domestic Economy [...]*, New York: Harper & Brothers 1845, Carnegie Museum of Art, Pittsburgh, Curatorial Library (Pittsburgh)

Pieter Jan Kaiser, *De toepassing der photographie op de sterrekunde: academisch proefschrift [...]*, Leiden: Academische Boekhandel van P. Engels 1862, Rijksmuseum, Amsterdam, inv. BI-350-D-2

Eduard Magnus, *Über Einrichtung und Beleuchtung von Räumen zur Aufstellung von Gemälden und Sculpturen: Ein Vortrag, gehalten in der Königlichen Akademie der Künste am 27. November 1863*, Berlin: Ernst & Korn 1864, Rijksmuseum, Amsterdam, inv. BI-48-B-25

Spectropia or Surprising Spectral Illusions Showing Ghosts Everywhere and of Any Color, New York: James G. Gregory 1864, Graphic Arts Technical Foundation, Sewickley, Pennsylvania

Amédée Guillemin, *The Heavens: An Illustrated Handbook of Popular Astronomy*, ed. J. Norman Lockyer, London: Richard Bentley 1866,

Carnegie Museum of Art, Pittsburgh, Curatorial Library

Charles Blanc, *Grammaire des arts du dessin: architecture, sculpture, peinture [...]*, Paris: Jules Renouard 1867, Van Gogh Museum, Amsterdam, inv. BVG 4872 (Amsterdam); Carnegie Library, Pittsburgh, inv. qr 701 B53 (Pittsburgh)

Adolphe Alphand, *Les Promenades de Paris: histoire, description des embellissements, dépenses de création et d'entretien des Bois de Boulogne et de Vincennes, Champs-Elysées, parcs, squares, boulevards, places plantées [...]*, 2 vols., Paris 1867-73, vol. 2, Universiteitsbibliotheek Amsterdam, inv. 2757 A 8,9 (Amsterdam)

Catherine E. Beecher and Harriet Beecher Stowe, *The American Woman's Home: or, Principles of Domestic Science; Being a Guide to the Formation and Maintenance of Economical, Healthful, Beautiful, and Christian Homes*, New York: J. B. Ford and Co. 1869, Carnegie Museum of Art, Pittsburgh, Curatorial Library

Ernest Hareux, *L'Outillage et le matériel nécessaire à l'atelier ou en plein air: cours complet de peinture à l'huile*, Paris: Librairie Renouard n.d., ca. 1870-90, Van Gogh Museum, Amsterdam, inv. BVG 13936

François-Napoléon-Marie Moigno, *L'Art des projections*, Paris: Au Bureau du Journal Les Mondes et Chez M. Gauthier-Villars, 1872, University Library, Nijmegen (Netherlands), inv. Tz c 14427

Amédée Guillemin, *The Forces of Nature*, trans. Mrs Norman Lockyer, 2nd ed., New York: Scribner's 1873, Carnegie Library, Pittsburgh, inv. r 530 G96f (Pittsburgh)

Camille Flammarion, *The Atmosphere*, trans. James Glaisher, New York: Harper's 1874, Carnegie Library, Pittsburgh, inv. qr 551.5 F61

Georges Moynet, *L'Envers du théâtre: machines et décorations*, Paris: Hachette et Cie. 1875, Collectie Theater Instituut Nederland, Amsterdam, inv. Spec H 28

La Lumière Electrique, vol. 1, 1879, Carnegie Library, Pittsburgh, inv. qr 621.305 L97

Camille Flammarion, *Astronomie populaire*, Paris: C. Marpon et E. Flammarion 1881, University of Pittsburgh, Hillman Library, inv. q QB44.F59

A. Müller, *Die Gasbeleuchtung im Haus*, Vienna, Pest & Leipzig: A. Hartleben 1881, Carnegie Library, Pittsburgh, inv. r665.7 M95

Em. Alglave and J. Boulard, *La Lumière électrique: son histoire, sa production, son emploi dans l'éclairage public ou privé, les phares, les théâtres, l'industrie, les travaux publics, les opérations militaires et maritimes*, Paris: Librairie de Firmin-Didot et Cie 1882, Universiteitsbibliotheek Amsterdam, inv. 2348 F 20 (Amsterdam)

Captain E. Ironside Bax, *Popular Electric Lighting: Being Practical Hints to Present and Intending Users of Electric Energy for Illuminating Purposes [...]*, 2nd ed., London: Biggs & Co. 1882, Private collection

Camille Flammarion, *Les Etoiles et les curiosités du ciel: description complète du ciel visible à l'oeil nu et de tous les objets célestes faciles à observer*, Paris: C. Marpon et E. Flammarion 1882, Van Gogh Museum, Amsterdam, inv. BVG 12239

Amédée Guillemin, *La Lumière*, Paris: Hachette 1882, Private collection

Amédée Guillemin, *El mundo físico*, transl. by D. Manuel Aranda y Sanjuan, vol. 2, Barcelona: Montaner y Simon 1883, Carnegie Library, Pittsburgh, inv. qr 530 696 (Pittsburgh)

Robert Hammond, *The Electric Light in our Homes, Popularly Explained and Illustrated*, London: Frederick Warne and Co. 1884, Carnegie Museum of Art, Pittsburgh, Curatorial Library

Paul Eudel, *Les Ombres chinoises de mon père*, Paris: Editions Rouveyre, 1885, Jane Voorhees Zimmerli Art Museum, Rutgers, The State University of New Jersey, New Brunswick, New Jersey, Gift of Herbert D. and Ruth Schimmel, inv. 1990.0251

Philibert Delahaye, *L'Industrie moderne: L'Eclairage dans la ville et dans la maison*, Paris: G. Masson 1886, Carnegie Library, Pittsburgh, inv. qr 628.9 D38

Alexis Lemaistre, *L'Ecole des beaux-arts dessinée et racontée par un élève*, Paris: Firmin-Didot 1889, Van Gogh Museum, Amsterdam, inv. 3 C 1

G. Berger, *Das Licht in seinen verschiedenen Erscheinungen und Wirkungen aus den natürlichen Ursachen derselben wissenschaftlich erklärt. Zur praktischen Anwendung auf das Studium der Malerei: Ein Leitfaden für angehende Künstler und Dilettanten*, 2nd ed., Leipzig: Karl Scholtze, n.d. ca. 1890, Van Gogh Museum, Amsterdam, inv. 25 B 30

Henry-René d'Allemagne, *Histoire du luminaire depuis l'époque Romaine jusqu'au XIXe siècle*, Paris: Alphonse Picard 1891, Rijksmuseum, Amsterdam, inv. BI-40-C-16

Arthur Wilke, *Die Elektrizität, ihre Erzeugung und ihre Anwendung in Industrie und Gewerbe*, Leipzig & Berlin: Otto Spamer 1893, Universiteitsbibliotheek Amsterdam, inv. 350 A 9 (Amsterdam)

Heinrich Lux, *Die öffentliche Beleuchtung von Berlin*, Berlin: S. Fischer 1896, Carnegie Library, Pittsburgh, inv. qr 628.9 L98

Art et Décoration, 3, April 1898, Rijksmuseum, Amsterdam, inv. BI-TS-0442

Rapport aan Hare Majesteit de Koningin: uitgebracht door de Rijks Commissie tot het nemen van proeven betreffende de verlichting van Rembrandt's 'Nachtwacht' (Corporaalschap van Banning Cocq), Amsterdam 1902, Van Gogh Museum, Amsterdam, inv. 25 A 33 (Amsterdam)

Select bibliography

The bibliography is divided into the following categories:

Sources before 1900

General and interdisciplinary studies

Science and history of science

History, social history and history of technology

History of lighting

Philosophy and light symbolism

Art

Spectacles and entertainment

Sources before 1900

A. M., *Light without a Wick: A Century of Gas-Lighting, 1792-1892. A Sketch of William Murdoch, the Inventor*, Glasgow 1892.

Accum, Frederick, *A Practical Treatise on Gas-light: Exhibiting a Summary Description of the Apparatus and Machinery Best Calculated for Illuminating Streets, Houses and Manufactures with Carburetted Hydrogen, or Coal-gas: with Remarks on the Utility, Safety, and General Nature of this New Branch of Civil Economy*, London 1815.

Ackermann, Rudolph, *Microcosm of London*, 3 vols., London 1808-11.

Ackermann, Rudolph, *Instructions for Painting Transparencies*, London 1799.

Algarotti, Francesco, *Il Newtonianismo per le dame, ovvero dialoghi sopra la luce e i colori*, Venice 1737.

Alglave, Em., and J. Boulard, *La Lumière électrique: son histoire, sa production, son emploi dans l'éclairage public ou privé, les phares, les théâtres, l'industrie, les travaux publics, les opérations militaires et maritimes*, Paris 1882.

Allemagne, Henry-René d', *Histoire du luminaire depuis l'époque Romaine jusqu'au XIXe siècle*, Paris 1891.

Alphand, A., *Les Promenades de Paris: histoire, description des embellissements, dépenses de création et d'entretien des Bois de Boulogne et de Vincennes, Champs-Elysées, parcs, squares, boulevards, places plantées. Etude sur l'art des jardins et arboretum*, 2 vols., Paris 1867-73.

Anonymous, *Observations sur l'illumination de Paris*, Paris 1789.

Anonymous, *An Heroic Epistle to Mr. Winsor, the Patentee of the Hydro-carbonic Gas Lights, and Founder of the National Light and Heat Company*, London 1808.

Anonymous, "La Recherche de la lumière dans la peinture," *L'Art Moderne* 7 (26 June 1887), pp. 201-02.

Arago, Dominique François, "Report of the Commission of the Chamber of Deputies [...]" (1839), in Alan Trachtenberg (ed.), *Classic Essays on Photography*, New Haven 1980, pp. 15-25.

Arnold, Matthew, *Culture and Anarchy* (1869), reprint Cambridge 1969.

Baader, Franz von, "Über den Blitz als Vater des Lichts (1815)," *Sämtliche Werke*, ed. Franz Hoffmann, vol. 2, Leipzig 1851, pp. 27-46.

Baraduc, Hippolyte-Ferdinand, *L'Ame humaine, ses mouvements, ses lumières et l'iconographie de l'invisible fluidique*, Paris 1896.

Baudelaire, Charles, *The Painter of Modern Life and Other Essays*, trans. Jonathan Mayne, New York 1964.

Becquerel, Edmond, *La Lumière: ses causes et ses effets*, 2 vols., Paris 1867-68.

Benjamin, Park, *The Age of Electricity from Amber-Soul to Telephone*, New York 1889.

Berger, G., *Das Licht in seinen verschiedenen Erscheinungen und Wirkungen aus den natürlichen Ursachen derselben wissenschaftlich erklärt. Zur praktischen Anwendung auf das Studium der Malerei: Ein Leitfaden für angehende Künstler und Dilettanten*, 2nd ed., Leipzig n.d.

Bernstein, Alex, *Die electrische Beleuchtung*, Berlin 1880.

Bischoff, Wilhelm Ferdinand, *Die Steinkohlen-Gasbeleuchtung: Populäre Belehrung über Einrichtung und Betrieb von Gaswerken nebst kurzer Anweisung für Gas-Consumenten, möglichst viel Gas zu sparen*, Berlin 1864.

Blanc, Charles, *Grammaire des arts du dessin: architecture, sculpture, peinture [...]*, Paris 1867.

Blochmann, Georg Moritz Sigismund, *Beiträge zur Geschichte der Gasbeleuchtung*, Dresden (1871).

Bonnefont, Gaston, *La Règne de l'électricité*, Tours 1895.

Bouguer, Pierre, *Traite d'Optique sur la gradation de la lumiere: ouvrage posthume de M. Bouguer [...]*, Paris 1760.

Bracquemond, Félix, *Du Dessin et de la couleur*, Paris 1885.

Brewster, David, *A Treatise on the Kaleidoscope*, Edinburgh & London 1819.

Brown, Ford Madox, *The Diary of Ford Madox Brown*, ed. Virginia Surtees, New Haven & London 1981.

Chadwick, William Isaac, *The Magic Lantern Manual*, London 1878.

Chatel jeune, A., *Notice sur les différentes systèmes d'éclairage depuis les temps anciens jusqu'à nos jours*, Paris 1859.

Couture, Thomas, *Méthode et entretiens d'atelier*, Paris 1867.

Delahaye, Ph., *L'Eclairage dans la ville et dans la maison*, Paris 1885-90.

Delboeuf, J., "Etude psycho-physique: recherches théoriques et experimentales sur la mesure des sensations et spécialement des sensations de lumière et de fatigue," *Mémoires couronnés et autres mémoires publiées par l'Académie Royale des Sciences, des Lettres et des Beaux-Arts de Belgique*, vol. 23, Brussels 1873.

Descartes, René, *Le Monde, ou Traité de la lumière* (1664), ed. Micheal Sean Mahoney (bilingual edition), New York 1979.

Diderot, Denis, and Jean d'Alembert (eds.), *Encyclopédie, ou dictionnaire raisonné des sciences, des arts et des métiers*, 35 vols., Paris 1751-80.

Dolbear, Amos Emerson, *The Art of Projecting: A Manual of Experimentation in Physics, Chemistry, and Natural History with the Porte Lumière and Magic Lantern*, Boston 1892.

Elektrische Beleuchtung von Theatern mit Edison-Glühlicht, Berlin 1884.

Encyclopedia Britannica or A Dictionary of Arts and Sciences, 3 vols., Edinburgh 1771.

Ernouf, Baron, *Les Inventeurs du gaz et de la photographie: Lebon d'Humbersin, Nicéphore Niépce, Daguerre*, Paris 1877.

Euler, Leonhard, *Lettres à une princesse d'Allemagne* (1768), ed. Andreas Speiser, 2 vols., Thur 1960.

Exposition internationale d'électricité: administration, jury, rapport, Paris 1881, 2 vols., Paris 1883.

Faraday, Michael, *A Course of Six Lectures on the Chemical History of a Candle to which is Added a Lecture on Platinum*, London 1861.

Fechner, Gustav, *Elements of Psychophysics*, vol. 1, trans. Helmut E. Adler, ed. Davis H. Bowles and Edwin G. Boring, New York 1966.

Flammarion, Camille, *Lumen*, Paris 1867.

Flammarion, Camille, *Astronomie populaire*, Paris 1879.

Flammarion, Camille, *Les Etoiles et les curiosités du ciel: description complète du ciel visible à l'oeil nu et de tous les objets célestes faciles à observer*, Paris 1882.

Flammarion, Camille, *Dans le ciel et sur la terre: tableaux et harmonies*, Paris 1886.

Flammarion, Camille, *Omega: The Last Days of the World* (1894), reprint Lincoln, Nebraska, & London 1999.

Fontaine, Hippolyte, *Eclairage à l'électricité*, Paris 1877.

Foster, George G., *New York by Gas-light and other Urban Sketches* (1850), ed. Stuart M. Blumin, Berkeley, Los Angeles & Oxford 1990.

Fournier, Edouard, *Les Lanternes de Paris: histoire de l'ancien éclairage, suivi de la réimpression de quelques poèmes rares*, Paris 1854.

Fourtier, Henri, *La Pratique des projections: étude méthodique des appareils. Les accessoires, usages et applications diverses des projections*, 2 vols., Paris 1892-93.

Fourtier, Henri, *Les Lumières artificielles en photographie: étude méthodique et pratique des différentes sources artificielles de lumière, suivie de recherches inédites sur la puissance des photopoudres et des lampes au magnésium*, Paris 1895.

Fresnel, Augustin-Jean, *Mémoire sur un nouveau système d'éclairage des phares*, Paris 1822.

Galine, Louis, *Traité général d'éclairage: huile, pétrole, gaz, électricité*, Paris 1894.

Grasset, E., "Concours des lampes électriques," *Art et Décoration* 3 (April 1898) pp. 163-67.

's Gravesande, Willem Jacob, *Physices elementa mathematica, experimentis confirmata: sive introductio ad philosophiam Newtonianam*, 2 vols., Leiden 1725 (English edition: *Mathematical Elements of Natural Philosophy, Confirm'd by Experiments: Or, an Introduction to Sir Isaac Newton's Philosophy*, trans. J. T. Desaguliers, 6th ed., London 1747.

Grimm, Herman, "Die Umgestaltung der Universitätsvorlesungen für neuere Kunstgeschichte durch die Anwendung des Skioptikons (1892)," *Beiträge zur deutschen Culturgeschichte*, Berlin 1897, pp. 276-395.

Guillemin, Amédée, *The Heavens: An Illustrated Handbook of Popular Astronomy*, ed. J. Norman Lockyer, 2nd ed., London 1866.

Guillemin, Amédée, *Le Ciel: notions d'astronomie, à l'usage des gens du monde et de la jeunesse*, Paris 1877.

Guillemin, Amédée, *La Lumière et les couleurs*, 3rd ed., Paris 1879.

Guillemin, Amédée, *Le Monde physique*, 5 vols., Paris 1881-85.

Guyot, Edmé, *Nouvelles récréations physiques et mathématiques, contenant toutes celles qui ont été découvertes & imaginées dans ces derniers temps, sur l'aiman, les nombres, l'optique, la chymie, &c. & quantité d'autres qui n'ont jamais été rendues publiques. Ou l'on a joint leurs causes, & l'amusement qu'on peut en tirer pour étonner agréablement*, 4 vols., Paris 1769-70.

Hammond, Robert, *The Electric Light in our Homes*, London 1884.

Hareux, Ernest, *L'Outillage et le matériel nécessaires à l'atelier ou en plein air: cours complet de peinture à l'huile*, Paris n.d. (1870-90)

Harris, John, *Lexicon Technicum: Or, An Universal English Dictionary of Arts and Sciences; Explaining Not Only the Terms of Art, but the Arts Themselves*, 5th ed., London 1736.

Helmholtz, Hermann von, "Optisches über Malerei," *Populäre wissenschaftliche Vorträge*, Braunschweig 1876, pp. 55-97.

Helmholtz, Hermann von, *Science and Culture: Popular and Philosophical Essays*, ed. David Cahan, Chicago & London 1995.

Herschel, John F. W., *A Preliminary Discourse on the Study of Natural Philosophy* (1830), London 1996.

Hoogstraten, Samuel van, *Inleyding tot de hooge schoole der schilderkonst; anders de zichtbare werelt*, Rotterdam 1678.

Hopkins, Albert Allis, *Magic Stage Illusions and Scientific Diversions Including Trick Photography* (1898), reprint New York 1967.

Humboldt, Alexander von, *Cosmos: A Sketch of the Physical Description of the Universe*, 2 vols., trans. E. C. Otte (1858), Baltimore & London 1997.

Hunter, Henry, *The Origin, Nature, and Properties of Light: A Sermon Preached before the Society for Promoting Religious Knowledge*, London 1793.

Hunter, James, *On the Influence of Artificial Light in Causing Impaired Vision, and on some Methods of Preventing, or Lessening, its Injurious Action on the Eye*, Edinburgh, London & Glasgow 1840.

Huygens, Christiaan, *Traité de la lumière. Ou sont expliquées les causes de ce qui luy arrive dans la reflexion, & dans la refraction. Et particulierement dans l'etrange refraction du cristal d'Islande, par C.H.D.Z. Avec un discours de la cause de la pesanteur*, Leiden 1690 (English edition: *Treatise on Light*, trans. Silvanus P. Thompson [1912], New York 1962).

Jamin, Jules, "L'Optique et la peinture," *La Revue des Deux Mondes* (February 1855), pp. 624-42.

Jamin, Jules, *Cours de physique de l'Ecole polytechnique*, 2nd ed., vol. 3, Paris 1869.

Kaiser, Pieter Jan, *De toepassing der photographie op de sterrekunde*, Leiden 1862.

Kircher, Athanasius, *Ars magna lucis et umbrae in X libros digesta. Quibus admirandae lucis & umbrae in mundo, atque adeò universa natura, vires effectusque uit nova, ita varia novorum reconditiorumque speciminum exhibitione, ad varios mortalium usus, panduntur*, Amsterdam 1671.

Knapp, Friedrich Ludwig, "Geschichte der Gasbeleuchtung," in Nikolaus Heinrich Schilling, *Handbuch für Steinkohlen-Gasbeleuchtung* (1860), 3rd ed., vol. 1, Munich 1879, pp. 1-29.

Lacassagne, J., and Rodolphe Thiers, *Nouveau système d'éclairage électrique, ses avantages, ses instruments, ses principes scientifiques et ses applications industrielles*, Paris & Lyons 1857.

Lambert, Johann Heinrich, *Photometria, sive de mesura et gradibus luminis colorum et umbrae* (1760), ed. E. Anding, 3 vols., Leipzig 1892.

Lambert, Johann Heinrich, *Merkwürdigste Eigenschaften der Bahn des Lichts durch die Luft und überhaupt durch verschiedene sphärische und concentrische Mittel, nebst der Auflösung verschiedener Aufgaben, welche sich darauf beziehen, als die astronomische und Erdstrahlenbrechung und was davon abhängt*, Berlin 1773.

Le Breton, Joséphine, *Histoire et applications de l'électricité*, Paris 1884.

Lebon, Philippe, *Thermolampes, ou poêles qui chauffent, éclairent avec economie, inventés par Philippe Lebon*, Paris 1801.

Ledermüller, Martin Frobenius, and Adam Wolfang Winterschmidt, *Mikroskoopische vermaak-* *lykheden, zo voor de ogen als voor den geest, behelzende de afbeeldingen van veelerley voorwerpen, zo van dierlyke lichaamen, als van planten en delfstoffen, die of geheel of gedeeltelyk ten naauwkeurigste onderzogt, en in sterke vergroting met hunne natuurlyke kleuren afgebeeld, als ook omstandig beschreeven zyn*, 4 vols., Amsterdam 1776.

Lemaistre, Alexis, *L'Ecole des beaux-arts dessinée et racontée par un élève*, Paris 1889.

Lemer, Julien, *Paris au gaz*, Paris 1861.

La Lumière Edison: système d'éclairage électrique, transmission de la force motrice a domicile, 3rd ed., Paris 1882.

Lux, Heinrich, *Die öffentliche Beleuchtung von Berlin: Eine geschichtliche, technische und wirthschaftliche Darstellung des öffentlichen Beleuchtungswesens in Berlin, sowie des Beleuchtungseffectes auf den Berliner Strassen*, Berlin 1896.

Magnus, Eduard, *Über Einrichtung und Beleuchtung von Räumen zur Aufstellung von Gemälden und Sculpturen*, Berlin 1864.

Mallarmé, Stephane, "The Impressionists and Edouard Manet," (1876) reprinted in *The New Painting: Impressionism 1874-1886*, exh. cat. San Francisco (The Fine Arts Museums of San Francisco) & Washington, D.C. (National Gallery of Art) 1983, pp. 27-35.

Marat, Jean-Paul, *Découvertes de M. Marat, (Docteur en Médecine & Médecin des Gardes-du-Corps de Monseigneur le Comte d'Artois) sur la Lumière [...]*, 2nd ed., London 1780.

Maréchal, Henri, *L'Eclairage à Paris: Étude technique des divers modes d'éclairage employés à Paris sur la voie publique, dans les promenades et jardins, dans les monuments, les gares, les théâtres, les grands magasins, etc. et dans les maisons particulières. Gaz, électric-* *ité, pétrole, huile, etc. [...]*, Paris 1894.

Martin, Benjamin, *The Young Gentleman and Lady's Philosophy, in a Continued Survey of the Works of Nature and Art; By Way of a Dialogue*, 2nd ed., London 1772.

McCabe, James D., Jr., *Paris by Sunlight and Gaslight: A Work Descriptive of the Mysteries and Miseries, the Virtues, the Vices, the Splendors, and the Crimes of the City of Paris, Illustrated with over 150 Fine Engravings by Gustave Doré and other Celebrated Artists of France*, Philadelphia 1869.

McCabe, James, *Light and Shadows of New York, or, The Sights and Sensations of the Great City*, n.p. 1872.

Meadowcroft, William, *The ABC of Electricity*, New York 1888.

Minckelers, Johann Peter, *Mémoire sur l'air inflammable tiré des différentes substances* (1784), reprint 's Hertogenbosch 1905.

Mitchell, Vance & Co., *Picture Book of Authentic Mid-Victorian Gas Lighting Fixtures: A Reprint of the Historic Mitchell, Vance & Co. Catalog, ca. 1876, with over 1000 Illustrations*, Introduction by Denys Peter Myers, New York 1984.

Moigno, François-Napoléon-Marie, *L'Art des projections*, Paris 1872.

Morse, Samuel F. B., *Lectures on the Affinity of Painting with the other Fine Arts*, ed. Nicolai Cikovsky, Jr., Columbia, Missouri & London 1983.

Mouchez, E., *La Photographie astronomique à l'Observatoire de Paris et la carte du ciel*, Paris 1887.

Moxon, Joseph, *Practical Perspective; or Perspective Made Easie [...]*, London 1670.

Moynet, Georges, *L'Envers du théâtre*, Paris 1875.

Moynet, Georges, *Trucs et décors: explication raisonnée de tous les moyens employés pour produire les illusions théâtrales*, Paris ca. 1890.

Murphy, Shirley Foster (ed.), *Our Homes, and How to Make them Healthy*, London, Paris & New York 1883.

Newton, Isaac, *Opticks, or, A Treatise of the Reflexions, Refractions, Inflexions and Colours of Light. Also Two Treatises of the Species and Magnitude of Curvilinear Figures*, London 1704.

Nollet, Jean-Antoine, *Leçons de physique experimentale*, 6 vols., Amsterdam 1754-56.

Orme, Edward, *Essay on Transparent Prints and on Transparencies in General*, London 1807.

Paillot de Montabert, Jacques Nicolas, *Traité complet de peinture*, 10 vols., Paris 1829-51.

Paiva, Adriano de, *La Télescopie électrique basée sur l'emploi du sélénium*, Porto 1880.

Parville, Henri de, *L'Electricité et ses applications: exposition de Paris*, Paris 1882.

Peclet, Eugène, *Traité de l'éclairage*, Paris 1827.

Peclet, Eugène, *Die Kunst der Gebäude-, Zimmer- und Straßenerleuchtung durch Oel, Talg, Wachs und Gas* (1829), 3rd ed., Weimar 1853.

Pepper, John Henry, *The Boy's Playbook of Science*, London ca. 1860.

Pepper, John Henry, *Scientific Amusements for Young People*, London 1864.

Pisko, Franz Joseph, *Licht und Farbe: Eine gemeinfaßliche Darstellung der Optik*, Munich 1869.

Pleasanton, Augustus J., *The Influence of the Blue Ray of the*

Sunlight and of the Blue Colour of the Sky in Developing Animal and Vegetable Life, in Arresting Disease, and in Restoring Health in Acute and Chronic Disorders to Human and Domestic Animals, as Illustrated by the Experiments of Gen. A. J. Pleasanton, and Others, between the Years 1861 and 1876, Philadelphia 1877.

Poe, Edgar Allan, "Philosophy of Furniture," (1840), Collected Works of Edgar Allan Poe: Tales and Sketches, 1831-1842, ed. T. O. Mabbott, vol. 2, Cambridge, Massachusetts 1978, pp. 495-99.

Priestley, Joseph, The History and Present State of Discoveries Relating to Vision, Light, and Colours, London 1772.

Proctor, Richard A., Other Worlds than Ours: The Plurality of Worlds Studied under the Light of Recent Scientific Researches, New York 1896.

Richter, Henry, Day-Light: A Recent Discovery in the Art of Painting. With Hints on the Philosophy of the Fine Arts, and on That of the Human Mind, as First Dissected by Emanuel Kant, London 1817.

Robertson, Etienne-Gaspard, Mémoires récréatifs scientifiques et anecdotiques du physicien-aéronaute E. G. Robertson, connu par ses expériences de fantasmagorie et par ses ascensions aérostatiques dans les principales villes de l'Europe; ex-professeur de physique, 2 vols., Paris 1840.

Robida, Albert, Le vingtième siècle: la vie électrique, Paris 1892.

Rodenberg, Julius, et al., Paris bei Sonnenschein und Lampenlicht: Ein Skizzenbuch zur Weltausstellung, Leipzig 1867.

Rumford, Benjamin Thomson, Collected Works of Count Rumford, vol. IV: Light and Armament, ed. Sanborn C. Brown, Cambridge, Massachusetts 1970.

Rutter, John Obadiah Newell, Gas-Lighting: Its Progress and its Prospects; With Remarks on the Rating of Gas-Mains, and a Note on the Electric-Light, London 1849.

Sala, George Augustus, Gaslight and Daylight, With some London Scenes They Shine Upon, London 1872.

Secchi, P. A., Die Sonne: Die wichtigen neuen Entdeckungen über ihren Bau, ihre Strahlungen, ihre Stellung im Weltall, und ihr Verhältnis zu den übrigen Himmelskörpern [...], ed. H. Schellen, Braunschweig 1872.

Semper, Gottfried, Wissenschaft, Industrie und Kunst: Vorschläge zur Anregung nationalen Kunstgefühls bei dem Schlusse der Londoner Industrie-Ausstellung, Braunschweig 1852.

Smith, Robert, A Compleat System of Opticks In Four Books, viz. A Popular, a Mathematical, a Mechanical, and a Philosphical Treatise [...], Cambridge 1738.

Stevenson, Robert Louis, "A Plea for Gas Lamps" (1878), Virginibus Puerisque & Other Papers, Harmondsworth 1946, pp. 153-57.

Stewart, James Haldane, Thoughts upon the Attractive Light of the Wise Virgins, London 1847.

Stowe, Catherine E. Beecher, and Harriet Beecher Stowe, The American Woman's Home: Or, Principles of Domestic Science; Being a Guide to the Formation and Maintenance of Economical, Healthful, Beautiful, and Christian Homes, New York 1869.

Talbot, William Henry Fox, The Pencil of Nature, London 1844-46.

Thomas, Ernest, Histoire de l'éclairage depuis des temps les plus reculés jusqu'à nos jours: monographie complète de tous les genres d'éclairages à Paris, Paris 1890.

Tyndall, John, Six Lectures on Light Delivered in the United States in 1872-1873, 4th ed., London 1885.

Urbanitzky, Alfred von, Die elektrischen Beleuchtungsanlagen, Vienna, Pest & Leipzig 1883.

Valenciennes, Pierre-Henri de, Elémens de perspective pratique, à l'usage des artistes, suivi de réflexions et conseils à un élève sur la peinture, et particulièrement sur le genre de paysage, Paris An VIII (1800), 2nd ed. Paris 1820.

Varley, Cornelius, A Treatise on Optical Drawing Instruments, by Cornelius Varley, Artist, Member of The Society of Arts, The Microscopical Society, etc., also, A Method of Preserving Pictures in Oil and in Water Colours, London 1845.

Vivarez, Henry, "La lumière électrique et l'art," La Vie Moderne (26 December 1879), pp. 605-06.

Voltaire, Elémens de la philosophie de Neuton, mis à la portée de tout le monde, Amsterdam 1738.

W. T. C. (ed.), Five Black Arts: A Popular Account of the History, Processes of Manufacture, And Uses of Printing, Gas-Light, Pottery, Glass, Iron, Condensed from the Encyclopaedia Britannica, Columbus, Ohio 1861.

Walker, Adam, An Account of the Eiduranion, or Transparent Orrery, 4th ed., London 1784.

Walker, Adam, A System of Familiar Philosophy: In Twelve Lectures; Being the Courses Usually Read by Mr. A. Walker. Containing the Elements and Practical Uses to Be Drawn from the Chemical Properties of Matter [...], London 1799.

Walsh, J. H., A Manual of Domestic Economy Suited to Families Spending from £ 100 to £ 1000 a Year, 2nd ed., London 1857.

Webster, Thomas, and Mrs. Parks, An Encyclopaedia of Domestic Economy: Comprising such Subjects as are most Immediately Connected with Housekeeping [...], New York 1845.

The Welsbach Light or the Evening Beautiful, Philadelphia (1896), reprint The Rushlight Club 1984.

Whewell, William, Astronomy and General Physics Considered with Reference to Natural Theology, London 1839.

Wilke, Arthur, Die Elektrizität, ihre Erzeugung und ihre Anwendung in Industrie und Gewerbe, Leipzig & Berlin 1893.

Winslow, Forbes, Light: Its Influence on Life and Health, London 1867.

Wood, John, Elements of Perspective: Containing the Nature of Light and Colours, and the Theory and Practice of Perspective [...], London 1799.

Youmans, Edward L., The Hand-Book of Household Science: A Popular Account of Heat, Light, Air, Aliment, and Cleansing, in their Scientific Principles and Domestic Applications, with Numerous Illustrative Diagrams, New York 1857.

Zacharias, Johannes, Die Glühlampe, ihre Herstellung und Anwendung in der Praxis, Vienna, Pest & Leipzig 1890.

General and interdisciplinary studies

Baltrusaitis, Jurgis, Le Miroir: révélations, science-fiction et fallacies, Paris 1978.

Béguet, Bruno, et al., La Science pour tous, exh. cat. Paris (Musée d'Orsay) 1994.

Burnie, David, Light, London 1992.

Clair, Jean (ed.), Cosmos: From Romanticism to the Avant-garde, exh. cat. Montreal (The Montreal Museum of Fine Arts) & Barcelona (Centre de Cultura Contemporània) 1999-2000.

Goldberg, Benjamin, *The Mirror and Man*, Charlottesville 1985.

Hankins, Thomas L., and Robert J. Silverman, *Instruments and the Imagination*, Princeton 1995.

Kranzberg, Melvin, and Carroll W. Pursell, Jr. (eds.), *Technology in Western Civilization: The Emergence of Modern Industrial Society. Earliest Times to 1900*, New York, London & Toronto 1967.

Lepenies, Wolf, *Das Ende der Naturgeschichte: Wandel kultureller Selbstverständlichkeiten in den Wissenschaften des 18. und 19. Jahrhunderts*, Frankfurt am Main 1978.

Lumières, je pense à vous, exh. cat. Paris (Centre Georges Pompidou) 1985.

Maag, Georg, *Kunst und Industrie im Zeitalter der ersten Weltausstellungen: Synchronistische Analyse einer Epochenschwelle*, Munich 1986.

Mathieu, Caroline, *1889: La Tour Eiffel et l'Exposition Universelle*, exh. cat. Paris (Musée d'Orsay) 1889.

Miller, Jonathan, *On Reflection*, exh. cat. London (National Gallery) 1998.

Richardson, John Adkins, *Modern Art and Scientific Thought*, Urbana 1971.

Robin, Harry, *The Scientific Image: From Cave to Computer*, New York 1992.

Schivelbusch, Wolfgang, *Lichtblicke: Zur Geschichte der künstlichen Helligkeit im 19. Jahrhundert*, Frankfurt am Main 1986 (English edition: *Disenchanted Night*, Oxford, New York & Hamburg 1988).

Schivelbusch, Wolfgang, *Licht, Schein und Wahn: Auftritte der elektrischen Beleuchtung im 20. Jahrhundert*, Berlin 1992.

Smith, Merritt Roe, and Leo Marx, *Does Technology Drive History? The Dilemma of Technological Determinism*, Cambridge, Massachusetts & London 1994.

Stafford, Barbara M., "'Fantastic' Images: From Unenlightening to Enlightening 'Appearances' Meant to Be Seen in the Dark," Frederick Burwick and Walter Pape (eds.), *Aesthetic Illusion: Theoretical and Historical Approaches*, Berlin & New York 1990, pp. 158-79.

Stafford, Barbara M., *Artful Science: Enlightenment, Entertainment and the Eclipse of Visual Education*, Cambridge, Massachusetts & London 1994.

Stanjek, Klaus (ed.), *Zwielicht: Die Ökologie der künstlichen Helligkeit*, Munich 1989.

Sterk, Harald, *Stadtlichter: Die Erhellung von Alltag und Kunst durch Elektritizität mit 235 Abbildungen aus Wissenschaft, Technik, Wirtschaft und Kunst*, Vienna 1991.

Sternberger, Dolf, *Panorama oder Ansichten vom 19. Jahrhundert* (1938), Frankfurt am Main 1974.

Stoichita, Victor I., *A Short History of the Shadow*, London 1997.

Sypher, Wylie, *Literature and Technology: The Alien Vision*, New York 1968.

Turner, Frank Miller, *Between Science and Religion: The Reaction to Scientific Naturalism in Late Victorian England*, New Haven & London 1974.

Wagner, Fritz, "Zur Apotheose Newtons: Künstlerische Utopie und naturwissenschaftliches Weltbild im 18. Jahrhundert," *Bayerische Akademie der Wissenschaften, Philosophisch-Historische Klasse, Sitzungsberichte 10*, Munich 1974.

Wosk, Julie, *Breaking Frames: Technology and the Visual Arts in the Nineteenth Century*, New Brunswick, New Jersey 1992.

Science and history of science

Baas, Michael (ed.), *Handbook of Optics*, 2 vols., 2nd. ed., New York 1995.

Baierlein, Ralph, *Newton To Einstein: The Trail of Light. An Excursion to the Wave-Particle Duality and the Special Theory of Relativity*, Cambridge 1992.

Boyer, Carl B., *The Rainbow: From Myth to Mathematics*, Houndmills & London 1987.

Bradbury, S., *The Microscope Past and Present*, Oxford & London 1968.

Brennan, Pip, *The Camera Obscura and Greenwich*, n.p., n.d.

Buchwald, Jed Z., *The Rise of the Wave Theory of Light: Optical Theory and Experiment in the Early Nineteenth Century*, Chicago 1989.

Bud, Robert, and Deborah Jean Warner (eds.), *Instruments of Science: An Historical Encyclopedia*, New York & London 1998.

Burke, James, *Connections*, Boston, New York & London 1995.

Buttman, Guenther, *The Shadow of the Telescope: A Biography of John Herschel*, New York 1970.

Cantor, Geoffrey N., *Optics after Newton: Theories of Light in Britain and Ireland 1704-1840*, Manchester 1983.

Cantor, Geoffrey N., "Light and Enlightenment: An Exploration of Mid-Eighteenth-Century Modes of Discourse," David Lindberg and Geoffrey Cantor, *The Discourse of Light from the Middle Ages to the Enlightenment*, Los Angeles 1985, pp. 69-104.

Clercq, Peter de, *The Leiden Cabinet of Physics: A Descriptive Catalogue*, Leiden 1997.

Cohen, I. Bernard, *Benjamin Franklin's Science*, Cambridge, Massachusetts & London 1990.

Cohen, I. Bernard, *Science and the Founding Fathers: Science in the Political Thought of Jefferson, Franklin, Adams, and Madison*, New York & London 1995.

Coley, Noel G., and Vance M. D. Hall (eds.), *Darwin To Einstein: Primary Sources on Science and Belief*, New York 1980.

Crowe, Michael J., *The Extraterrestrial Life Debate, 1750-1900: The Idea of a Plurality of Worlds from Kant to Lowell*, Cambridge 1986.

Dale, Peter Allan, *In Pursuit of a Scientific Culture: Science, Art, and Society in the Victorian Age*, Madison 1989.

Daum, Andreas, *Wissenschaftspopularisierung im 19. Jahrhundert: Bürgerliche Kultur, naturwissenschaftliche Bildung und die deutsche Öffentlichkeit, 1818-1914*, Munich 1998.

Daumas, Mauris, *Scientific Instruments of the Seventeenth and Eighteenth Centuries*, trans. and ed. Mary Holbrook, New York & Washington, D.C. 1972.

Dawkins, Richard, *Unweaving the Rainbow: Science, Delusion, and the Appetite for Wonder*, Boston & New York 1998.

Eather, Robert H., *Majestic Lights: The Aurora in Science, History and the Arts*, Washington, D.C. 1980.

Elenbaas, W., *Light Sources*, London 1972.

Emsley, John, *The Shocking History of Phosphorus: A Biography of the Devil's Element*, London 2000.

Feynman, Richard P., *QED: The Strange Theory of Light and Matter*, Princeton 1985.

Forbes, R. J., et al. (eds.), *Martinus van Marum: Life and Work*, 6 vols., Haarlem 1969-76.

Greenler, Robert, *Rainbows, Halos, and Glories*, Cambridge 1980.

Gregory, Richard, *Mirrors in Mind*, New York 1997.

Gribbin, John, *Schrödinger's Kittens and the Search for Reality*, London 1999.

Gross, Paul R., Norman Levitt and Martin W. Lewis (eds.), *The Flight from Science and Reason*, New York 1996.

Hall, Alfred Rupert, *All was Light: An Introduction to Newton's Opticks*, Oxford 1993.

Hammond, John H., *The Camera Obscura: A Chronicle*, Bristol 1981.

Hammond, John H., and Jill Austin, *The Camera Lucida in Art & Science*, Bristol 1987.

Heering, Peter, et al., *Welt erforschen Welten konstruieren: Physikalische Experimentierkultur vom 16. Bis zum 19. Jahrhundert*, exh. cat. Oldenburg (Staatliches Museum für Naturkunde und Vorgeschichte und Carl von Ossietzky-Universität) 1998.

Helden, Anne C. van, and Rob H. van Gent, *The Huygens Collection*, Leiden 1995.

Inkster, Ian, *Science and Technology in History: An Approach to Industrial Development*, New Brunswick, New Jersey 1991.

Jacob, Margaret C., *Scientific Culture and the Making of the Industrial West*, New York & Oxford 1997.

Jaspers, P. A. Th. M., *J. P. Minckelers, 1748-1824*, Maastricht 1983.

Jolly, W. P., *Sir Oliver Lodge: Psychical Researcher and Scientist*, Rutherford, Madison & Teaneck, New Jersey 1975.

King, H. C., *Exploration of the Universe: The Story of Astronomy*, London 1964.

Klamt, Johann-Christian, "'Hier ist ein Tubus oder großes Perspektiv': Zur Symbolik des Fernrohrs," *Münchner Jahrbuch der bildenden Kunst* 30 (1979), pp. 187-97.

Klamt, Johann-Christian, *Sternwarte und Museum im Zeitalter der Aufklärung: Der Mathematische Turm zu Kremsmünster (1749-1758)*, Mainz 1998.

Kuhn, Thomas S., *The Structure of Scientific Revolutions* (1962), Chicago 1996.

Lightman, Bernard (ed.), *Victorian Science in Context*, Chicago 1997.

Lummer, Otto, *Grundlagen, Ziele und Grenzen der Leuchttechnik: Auge und Lichterzeugung* (1903), Munich 1918.

Lynch, David K., and William Livingston, *Color and Light in Nature*, Cambridge, Massachusetts 1995.

Mauray, Jean-Pierre, *Newton: Understanding the Cosmos*, London 1992.

Meinel, Aden, and Marjorie Meinel, *Sunsets, Twilights and Evening Skies*, Cambridge, Massachusetts 1993.

Minnaert, Marcel, *The Nature of Light and Color in the Open Air*, New York 1954 (*Light and Color in the Outdoors*, trans. Len Seymour, Berlin 1993).

Mitchell, William J., *The Reconfigured Eye: Visual Truth in the Post-Photographic Era*, Cambridge, Massachusetts & London 1992.

Morton, Alan Q., *Science in the 18th Century: The King George III Collection*, London 1993.

Newtons erfenis: Nederland, de natuurwetenschappen en de Verlichting, Leiden 1989.

North, John, *The Norton History of Astronomy und Cosmology*, New York & London 1995.

Park, David, *The Fire within the Eye: A Historical Essay on the Nature and Meaning of Light*, Princeton 1997.

Perkowitz, Sidney, *Empire of Light: A History of Discovery in Science and Art*, New York 1996.

Planck, Max, *Das Wesen des Lichts*, 2nd ed. Berlin 1920.

Rohr, René R. J., *Die Sonnenuhr: Geschichte, Theorie, Funktion*, Munich 1982.

Rooseboom, Hans, "P. J. Kaiser, of: het gebruik van de fotografie in de sterrenkunde, 1839-1880," *Bulletin van het Rijksmuseum* 42 (1994), no. 3, pp. 263-86.

Sabra, A. I., *Theories of Light: From Descartes to Newton*, London 1967.

Schaaf, Larry J., *Tracings of Light: Sir John Herschel & the Camera Lucida, Drawings from the Graham Nash Collection*, San Francisco 1989.

Schaaf, Larry J., *Out of the Shadows: Herschel, Talbot & The Invention of Photography*, New Haven & London 1992.

Sepper, Dennis L., *Newton's Optical Writings: A Guided Study*, New Brunswick, New Jersey 1994.

Shapin, Steven, *The Scientific Revolution*, Chicago & London 1996.

Shlain, Leonard, *Art and Physics: Parallel Visions in Space, Time and Light*, New York 1991.

Silverman, Mark P., *Waves and Grains: Reflections on Light and Learning*, Princeton 1998.

Sobel, Michael I., *Light*, Chicago 1987.

Stafford, Barbara M., "Images of Ambiguity: Eighteenth-Century Microscopy and the Neither/Nor," David Philip Miller and Peter Hanns Reill (eds.), *Visions of Empire: Voyages, Botany, and Representations of Nature*, Cambridge 1994, pp. 230-57.

Thomson, Ann et al., *Beauty of Another Order: Photography in Science*, exh. cat. Ottawa (National Gallery of Canada) 1997-98.

Tonkelaar, Isolde den, et al., *Eye and Instruments: Nineteenth-Century Ophthalmologic Instruments in the Netherlands*, Amsterdam 1996.

Turner, Gerard L'E., and T. H. Levere, Van Marum's Scientific Instruments in Teyler's Museum, Leiden 1973 (E. Lefebvre and J. G. De Bruijn [eds.], *Martinus van Marum: Life and Work*, 6 vols., Leiden 1973, vol. 4).

Turner, Gerard L'E., *Nineteenth-Century Scientific Instruments*, London 1983.

Turner, Gerard L'E., *The Practice of Science in the Nineteenth Century: Teaching and Research Apparatus in the Teyler Museum*, Haarlem 1996.

Warner, Deborah Jean, *Alvan Clark and Sons: Artists in Optics*, Washington, D.C. 1968.

Weiss, Richard J., *A Brief History of Light and Those That Lit the Way*, Singapore, New Jersey 1996.

Wheatland, David P., *The Apparatus of Science at Harvard 1765-1800: Collection of Historical Scientific Instruments, Harvard University*, Cambridge, Massachusetts 1968.

White, Michael, *Isaac Newton: The Last Sorcerer*, Reading, Massachusetts 1997.

Wilson, Robert, *Astronomy through the Ages: The Story of the Human Attempt to Understand the Universe*, London 1997.

Zajonc, Arthur, *Catching the Light: The Entwined History of Light and Mind*, New York & Oxford 1993.

History, social history and history of technology

Alvarez, A., *Night: An Exploration of Night Life, Night Language, Sleep & Dreams*, London 1995.

Asendorf, Christoph, *Batterien der Lebenskraft: Zur Geschichte der Dinge und ihrer Wahrnehmung im 19. Jahrhundert*, Gießen 1984 (English edition: *Batteries of Life*, Berkeley, Los Angeles & London 1993).

Asendorf, Christoph, *Ströme und Strahlen: Das langsame Verschwinden der Materie um 1900*, Gießen 1989.

Asman, Carrie, "Georg Simmels Psychologie des Schmucks: Vom Diamanten zur Glübirne," *Frauen Kunst Wissenschaft* 17 (May 1994), pp. 14-22.

Baldwin, Neil, *Edison: Inventing the Century*, New York 1995.

Beltran, Alain, *La Fée Electricité*, Paris 1991.

Bernheimer, Charles, *Figures of Ill-repute: Representing Prostitution in Nineteenth-Century Paris*, Cambridge, Massachusetts, & London 1989.

Birkefeld, Richard, and Martina Jung, *Die Stadt, der Lärm und das Licht*, Seelze 1994.

Bouman, Mark J., "Luxury and Control: The Urbanity of Street

Lighting in Nineteenth-Century Cities," *Journal of Urban History* 14, no. 1 (November 1987), pp. 7-37.

Bremen wird hell: 100 Jahre Leben und Arbeiten mit Elektrizität, exh. cat. Bremen (Bremer Landesmuseum für Kunst und Kulturgeschichte, Focke Museum) 1993-94.

Briggs, Asa, *Victorian Cities*, London 1963.

Brimblecombe, Peter, *The Big Smoke: A History of Air Pollution in London since Medieval Times*, London & New York 1987.

Buddensieg, Tilman, and Henning Rogge (eds.), *Die nützlichen Künste: Gestaltende Technik und Bildende Kunst seit der Industriellen Revolution*, exh. cat. Berlin (Messegelände am Funkturm) 1981.

Corbin, Alain, *Les Filles des noces: misère sexuelle et prostitution (19e et 20e siècles)*, Paris 1978.

Falkus, M. E., "The British Gas Industry before 1850," *Economic History Review* 20, no. 3 (1967), pp. 494-508.

Falkus, M. E., "Lighting in the Dark Ages of English Economic History: Town Streets before the Industrial Revolution," in D. C. Coleman and A. H. John (eds.), *Trade, Government and Economy in Pre-Industrial England: Essays Presented to F. J. Fisher*, London 1976, pp. 248-73.

Falkus, M. E., "The Early Development of the British Gas Industry 1790-1815," *Economic History Review* 35 (1982), pp. 217-34.

Garrett, Elizabeth Donaghy, *At Home: The American Family 1750-1850*, New York 1989.

Giles, Colum, and Ian H. Goodall, *Yorkshire Textile Mills: The Building of the Yorkshire Textile Mills 1770-1930*, London 1992.

Götz, Matthias, and Bruno Haldner (eds.), *Licht*, exh. cat. Basel (Museum für Gestaltung) 1990-91.

Gordon, Colin, *By Gaslight in Winter: A Victorian Family History through the Magic Lantern*, London 1980.

Haine, W. Scott, *The World of the Paris Café: Sociability among the French Working Class 1789-1914*, Baltimore & London 1996.

Harrison, Michael, *London by Gaslight, 1861-1911*, London 1963.

Hazen, Margaret Hindle, and Robert M. Hazen, *Keepers of the Flame: The Role of Fire in American Culture 1775-1925*, Princeton 1992.

Inwood, Stephen, *A History of London*, New York 1998.

Johnson, Paul, *The Birth of the Modern: World Society 1815-1830*, New York 1991.

Jordan, David P., *Transforming Paris: The Life and Labors of Baron Haussmann*, Chicago 1995.

Laing, Alastair, *Lighting: The Arts and Living*, London 1982.

Leach, William, "Strategists of Display and the Production of Desire," in Simon J. Bronner (ed.), *Consuming Visions: Accumulation and Display of Goods in America 1880-1920*, Winterthur, Delaware, New York & London 1989, pp. 99-132.

Leach, William, *Land of Desire: Merchants, Power, and the Rise of a New American Culture*, New York 1993.

Let There Be Light, introduction William O'Dea, exh. cat. Hartford (Wadsworth Atheneum) 1964.

Lindberg, Richard, *Chicago by Gaslight: A History of Chicago's Netherworld, 1880-1920*, Chicago 1996.

Marcus, Leonard S., *The American Store Window*, London 1978.

Marvin, Carolyn, *When Old Technologies Were New: Thinking about Electric Communication in Late Nineteenth Century*, New York & Oxford 1988.

Moskowitz, Sam, *Science Fiction by Gaslight: A History and Anthology of Science Fiction in the Popular Magazines 1891-1911*, Westport, Connecticut 1968.

Nye, David E., *Electrifying America: Social Meanings of a New Technology, 1880-1940*, Cambridge, Massachusetts & London 1990.

Nye, David E., *American Technological Sublime*, Cambridge, Massachusetts & London 1994.

Pacey, Arnold, *The Maze of Ingenuity: Ideas and Idealism in the Development of Technology*, New York 1975.

Pacey, Arnold, *Technology in World Civilization: A Thousand-Year History*, Cambridge, Massachusetts 1990.

Perrot, Michelle (ed.), *A History of Private Life IV: From the Fires of Revolution to the Great War*, Cambridge, Massachusetts & London 1990.

Praz, Mario, *An Illustrated History of Interior Decoration from Pompeii to Art Nouveau* (1964), New York 1994.

Rolt, L. T. C., *Victorian Engineering*, London 1970.

Rose, Mark H., *Cities of Light and Heat: Domesticating Gas and Electricity in Urban America*, University Park, Pennsylvania 1995.

Schlör, Joachim, *Nachts in der großen Stadt*, Munich 1991 (English edition: *Nights in the Big City: Paris, Berlin, London 1840-1930*, London 1998).

Sindal, Rob, *Street Violence in the Nineteenth Century: Media Panic or Real Danger?*, Leicester, London & New York 1990.

Tann, Jennifer, *The Development of the Factory*, London 1970.

Tarr, Joel A., and Josef W. Konvitz, "Patterns in the Development of the Urban Infrastructure," Howard Gillette, Jr., and Zane L. Miller, *American Urbanism: An Historiographical Review*, New York, Westport, Connecticut & London 1987, pp. 195-226.

Warner, Marina, *Monuments and Maidens: The Allegory of the Female Form*, London 1985.

Williams, Raymond, *The Country and the City*, New York 1973.

Williams, Rosalind H., *Dream World: Mass Consumption in Late 19th-Century France*, Berkeley, Los Angeles & London 1982.

Wilson, A. N., *God's Funeral*, New York & London 1999.

Wolff, Janet, "The Invisible Flâneuse: Women and the Literature of Modernity," *Canadian Journal of Political and Social Theory* 2 (1985), no. 3, pp. 37-46.

Woolf, Vivienne, "Morality of Flowers," *Country Life* (19 April 1990), pp. 150-51.

History of lighting

Bacot, H. Parrott, *Nineteenth-Century Lighting: Candle-Powered Devices, 1783-1883*, West Chester, Pennsylvania 1987.

Bazerman, Charles, *The Languages of Edison's Light*, Cambridge, Massachusetts 1999.

Beck, Wilhelm August, *Die Elektrizität und ihre Technik: Eine gemeinverständliche Darstellung der physikalischen Grundbegriffe und der praktischen Anwendung der Elektrizität*, 3 vols., 7th ed., Leipzig 1906.

Bell, Louis, *The Art of Illumination*, New York 1902.

Böhm, Richard, *Das Gasglühlicht: Seine Geschichte, Herstellung und Anwendung, Ein Handbuch für die Beleuchtungsindustrie*, Leipzig 1905.

Bourne, Jonathan, and Vanessa Brett, *Lighting in the Domestic Interior: Renaissance to Art Nouveau*, London 1991.

Bowers, Brian, *A History of Electric Light and Power*, Stevenage & New York 1982.

Bowers, Brian, *Lengthening the Day: A History of Lighting Technology*, Oxford, New York & Tokyo 1998.

Caspall, John, *Fire and Light in the Home, pre-1820*, Woodbridge, Suffolk 1995.

Chandler, Dean, *Outline of History of Lighting by Gas*, London 1936.

Country House Lighting 1660-1890, exh. cat. Leeds (Leeds City Art Gallery) 1992.

Devogelaere, Antoon, *Van gaslamp tot gloeilicht*, Kapellen 1987.

Duncan, Alastair, *Art Nouveau and Art Deco Lighting*, London 1978.

Duncan, Alastair, *Light Opera: Virtuosity in Lighting Design*, exh. cat. Miami (The Mitchell Wolfson Jr. Collection of Decorative and Propaganda Art, Miami-Dade Community College) 1987.

L'Electricité dans l'histoire: problèmes et méthodes, Actes du colloque Paris 11-13 October 1983, organisé par L'Association pour l'histoire de l'électricité en France, Paris 1985.

Elton Bt., Sir Arthur, "Gas for Light and Heat," in Charles Singer et al. (eds.), *A History of Technology*, vol. IV: *The Industrial Revolution c1750-c1850*, Oxford 1958, pp. 258-76.

Feldstein, William, Jr., and Alastair Duncan, *The Lamps of Tiffany Studios*, New York 1983.

Feuer und Flamme für Berlin: 170 Jahre Gas in Berlin, 150 Jahre Städtische Gaswerke, exh. cat. Berlin (Deutsches Technikmuseum) 1997.

Finn, Bernard, "The Incandescent Electric Light," in Margaret Latimer, Brooke Hindle, Melvin Kranzberg (eds.), *Bridge to the Future: Annals of the New York Academy of Sciences*, vol. 424 (1984), pp. 247-63.

Friedel, Robert D., and Paul Israel, *Edison's Electric Light: Biography of an Invention*, New Brunswick, New Jersey 1986.

Fürst, Artur, *Das elektrische Licht: Von den Anfängen bis zur Gegenwart, nebst einer Geschichte der Beleuchtung*, Munich 1926.

Gas Journal Centenary Volume 1849-1949, London 1949.

Gilbert, Christopher, and Anthony Wells-Cole, *The Fashionable Fire Place 1660-1840*, exh. cat. Leeds (Leeds City Art Galleries) 1985.

Gledhill, David, *Gas Lighting*, Aylesbury 1981.

Griffiths, John, *The Third Man: The Life and Times of William Murdoch, 1754-1839, The Inventor of Gas Lighting*, London 1992.

Hague, Douglas B., and Rosemary Christie, *Lighthouses: Their Architecture, History and Archaeology*, Llandysul 1975.

Hayward, Arthur H., *Colonial and Early American Lighting* (1923), 3rd ed., New York 1962.

Hobson, Anthony, *Lanterns that Lit our World: How to Identify, Date and Restore Old Railroad, Marine, Fire, Carriage, Farm and other Lanterns*, Spencertown, New York 1997.

Horst, Dick van der, "De Amsterdamse stadsverlichting I: de periode tot 1883," *Amsterdamse Monumenten*, no. 1 (May 1985).

Horst, Dick van der, "De Amsterdamse stadsverlichting II: de periode 1883-1930," *Amsterdamse Monumenten*, no. 2 (July 1985).

Hughes, Thomas P., *Networks of Power: Electrification in Western Society, 1880-1930*, Baltimore 1983.

Hunt, Charles B., *A History of the Introduction of Gas-Lighting*, London 1907.

Koch, André, et al., *Struck by Lighting: An Art-Historical Introduction to Electrical Lighting Design for the Domestic Interior*, Rotterdam 1994.

Körting, Johannes, *Geschichte der deutschen Gasindustrie: Mit Vorgeschichte und bestimmenden Einflüssen des Auslandes*, Essen 1963.

Linde, Antoinet van de, *Het oude licht: straatlantaarns en straatverlichting door de eeuwen heen*, Eindhoven 1972.

Luckiesh, Matthew, *The Lighting Art: Its Practice and Possibilities*, New York 1917.

Luckiesh, Matthew, *Artificial Light: Its Influence upon Civilization*, New York 1920.

Lux, Heinrich, *Das moderne Beleuchtungswesen*, Leipzig & Berlin 1914.

Mackenzie, Compton, *The Vital Flame*, London 1947.

McKinstry, E. Richard, *Trade Catalogues at Winterthur: A Guide to the Literature of Merchandising*, New York & London 1984.

Mac Lean, J., *Geschiedenis der gasverlichting in Nederland*, Zutphen 1977.

Maril, Nadja, *American Lighting 1840-1940*, Atglen, Pennsylvania 1995.

Maril, Nadja, *Antique Lamp Buyer's Guide: Identifying Late 19th and 20th Century American Lighting*, Atglen, Pennsylvania 1998.

Mattausch, Daniel W., "David Melville and the First American Gas Light Patents," *The Rushlight*, vol. 64, no. 4 (December 1998), pp. 2-9.

Moss, Roger W., *Lighting for Historic Buildings: A Guide to Selecting Reproductions*, New York 1988.

Myers, Denys Peter, *Gaslighting in America: A Guide for Historic Preservation*, Washington, D.C. 1978.

O'Dea, William T., *Darkness into Daylight: An Account of the Past, Present and Future of a Man-Made Illumination*, exh. cat. London (Science Museum) 1948.

O'Dea, William T., *The Social History of Lighting*, London 1958.

Phillips, Derek, *Lighting Historic Buildings*, Oxford 1997.

Plettenburg, Hermanna W. M., *Licht in huis: kienspaan - kaars - olielamp*, Arnhem 1968.

Rebske, Ernst, *Lampen, Laternen, Leuchten: Eine Historie der Beleuchtung*, Stuttgart 1962.

Reibel, Patricia B., "Lighting through the Ages," *Carnegie Magazine* 50 (September 1979), pp. 38-41.

Romaine, Lawrence B., *A Guide to American Trade Catalogues 1744-1900*, New York 1960.

Schmidt, Fritz, *Die Leuchtgaserzeugung und die moderne Gasbeleuchtung*, Braunschweig 1911.

Schrøder, Michael, *The Argand Burner, Its Origin and Development in France and England 1780-1800: An Epoch in the History of Science, Illustrated by the Life and Work of the Physicist Ami Argand (1750-1803)*, Odense 1969.

Smith, John P., *The Art of Enlightenment: A History of Glass Chandelier Manufacture and Design*, London 1994.

Stoer, G., *History of Light and Lighting*, Eindhoven 1986.

Taylor, Robert S., "Swan's Electric Light at Cragside," *National Trust Studies* (1981), pp. 27-34.

Thézy, Marie de, *Charles Marville réverbères*, Paris 1993.

Thuro, Catherine M. V., *Oil Lamps: The Kerosene Era in North America*, Radnor, Pennsylvania 1992.

Thwing, Leroy, *Flickering Flames: A History of Domestic Lighting Through the Ages*, London 1958.

Webber, William Hopgood Young, *Town Gas and its Uses for the Production of Light Heat and Motive Power*, New York 1907.

Wechssler-Kümmel, Sigrid, *Schöne Lampen, Leuchter und Laternen*, Heidelberg 1962.

Wirtler, Ulrike (ed.), *Lampen, Leuchter & Laternen: Die Bestände des Kölnischen Stadtmuseums*, Cologne 1991.

Wolfe, John J., *Brandy, Balloons, and Lamps: Ami Argand 1750-1803*, Carbondale & Edwardsville 1999.

Worthington, William E., Jr., *Beyond the City Lights: American Domestic Gas Lighting Systems*, exh. cat. Washington, D.C. (Smithsonian Institution) 1985.

Zahn, G. P., *De geschiedenis der verlichting van Amsterdam*, Amsterdam 1911.

Philosophy and light symbolism

Blumenberg, Hans, "Licht als Metapher der Wahrheit: Im Vorfeld der philosophischen Begriffsbildung," *Studium Generale* 10 (1957), pp. 432-47.

Dillon, Wilton S., and Neil G. Kotler (eds.), *The Statue of Liberty Revisited: Making a Universal Symbol*, Washington, D.C. & London 1994.

Düriegl, Günter, and Susanne Winkler (eds.), *Freimaurer: Solange die Welt besteht*, exh. cat. Vienna (Historisches Museum der Stadt Wien) 1992.

Herding, Klaus, *Im Zeichen der Aufklärung: Studien zur Moderne*, Frankfurt am Main 1989.

Hofmann, Werner (ed.), *Europa 1789: Aufklärung, Verklärung, Verfall*, exh. cat. Hamburg (Hamburger Kunsthalle) 1989.

Liberty: The French-American Statue in Art and History, exh. cat. New York (New York Public Library) & Paris (Musée des arts décoratifs) 1986-87.

Neugebauer-Wölk, Monika, "Die utopische Struktur gesellschaftlicher Zielprojektionen im Illuminatenbund," Monika Neugebauer-Wölk and Richard Saage (eds.), *Die Politisierung des Utopischen im 18. Jahrhundert: Vom utopischen Systementwurf zum Zeitalter der Revolution*, Tübingen 1996, pp. 169-97.

Paulson, Ronald, *Representations of Revolution (1789-1820)*, New Haven & London 1983.

Petzina, Dietmar (ed.), *Fahnen, Fäuste, Körper: Symbolik und Kultur der Arbeiterbewegung*, Essen 1986.

La Revolution Française et l'Europe 1789-1799, 3 vols., exh. cat. Paris (Galeries nationales du Grand Palais) 1989.

Starobinski, Jean, *1789: Les Emblèmes de la raison*, Paris 1973.

Trachtenberg, Marvin, *The Statue of Liberty*, New York 1986.

Art

Ackerman, James S., "Alberti's Light," in Irving Lavin and John Plummer (eds.), *Studies in Late Medieval and Renaissance Painting in Honor of Millard Meiss*, New York 1978, pp. 1-28.

Alpers, Svetlana, *The Art of Describing: Dutch Art in the Seventeenth Century*, Chicago 1984.

Antonelli, Giorgio, *Light Signs: A Light Path through Posters and Advertising 1890-1940*, Milan 1995.

Ayres, James, *The Artist's Craft: A History of Tools, Techniques and Materials*, Oxford 1985.

Bajac, Quentin, and Agnès de Gouvion Saint-Cyr, *Dans le champ des étoiles: les photographies du ciel, 1850-2000*, exh. cat. Paris (Musée d'Orsay) 2000

Bailey, Anthony, *Standing in the Sun: A Life of J. M. W. Turner*, New York 1997.

Batchen, Geoffrey, *Burning with Desire: The Conception of Photography*, Cambridge, Massachusetts 1997.

Baticle, Jeannine, and Pierre Georgel (eds.), *Technique de la peinture: l'atelier*, Paris 1976.

Bätschmann, Oskar, "Belebung durch Bewunderung: Pygmalion als Modell der Kunstrezeption," Mathias Mayer and Gerhard Neumann (eds.), *Pygmalion: Die Geschichte des Mythos in der abendländischen Kultur*, Freiburg im Breisgau 1997, pp. 325-70.

Baxandall, Michael, *Shadows and Enlightenment*, New Haven & London 1995.

Bell, Janis Callen, "Light," Jane Shoaf Turner (ed.), *The Dictionary of Art*, 34 vols., London 1996, vol. 19, pp. 351-59.

Bendix, Deanna Marohn, *Diabolical Designs: Paintings, Interiors, and Exhibitions of James McNeill Whistler*, Washington, D.C. & London 1995.

Bignamini, Ilaria, and Martin Postle, *The Artist's Model: Its Role in British Art from Lely to Etty*, exh. cat. Nottingham (University Art Gallery) & Kenwood (The Iveagh Bequest) 1991.

Blaugrund, Annette, *The Tenth Street Studio Building: Artist-Entrepreneurs from the Hudson River School to the American Impressionists*, exh. cat. Southampton, New York (Parrish Art Museum) 1997.

Boime, Albert, "Van Gogh's Starry Night: A History of Matter and a Matter of History," *Arts Magazine* 59 (December 1984), pp. 86-103.

Boime, Albert, *The Academy and French Painting in the Nineteenth Century*, New Haven & London 1986.

Bomford, David, et al., *Art in the Making: Impressionism*, exh. cat. London (National Gallery) 1990-91.

Bouret, Claude (ed.), *Corot: le génie du trait, estampes et dessins*, exh. cat. Paris (Bibliothèque nationale de France) 1996.

Busch, Werner, *Joseph Wright of Derby, Das Experiment mit der Luftpumpe: Eine Heilige Allianz zwischen Wissenschaft und Religion*, Frankfurt am Main 1986.

Callen, Anthea, "Immaterial Views? Science, Intransigence and the Female Spectator of Modern French Art in 1879," in Brian Rigby (ed.), *French Literature, Thought and Culture in the Nineteenth Century: A Material World*, London 1993, pp. 184-97.

Callen, Anthea, "Impressionist Techniques and the Politics of Spontaneity," *Art History* 14 (December 1991), pp. 599-608.

Callen, Anthea, *Techniques of the Impressionists*, Secaucus, New Jersey 1982.

Choné, Paulette, *L'Atelier des nuits: histoire et signification du nocturne dans l'art d'Occident*, Nancy 1992.

Clark, T. J., *The Painting of Modern Life: Paris in the Art of Manet and his Followers*, New York 1985.

Clayson, Hollis, *Painted Love: Prostitution in French Art of the Impressionist Era*, New Haven & London 1991.

Conisbee, Philip, et al., *In the Light of Italy: Corot and Early Open-Air Painting*, exh. cat. Washington, D.C. (National Gallery of Art), Brooklyn (The Brooklyn Museum) & Saint Louis (The Saint Louis Art Museum) 1996-97.

Crary, Jonathan, *Techniques of the Observer: On Vision and Modernity in the Nineteenth Century*, Cambridge, Massachusetts & London 1990.

Daniel, Malcolm, et al., *Edgar Degas, Photographer*, exh. cat. New York (The Metropolitan Museum of Art), Los Angeles (The J. Paul Getty Museum) & Paris (Bibliothèque Nationale de France) 1998-99.

Daniels, Stephen, "Louther-bourg's Chemical Theatre: Coalbrookdale by Night," John Barrell (ed.), *Painting and Politics of Culture: New Essays on British Art 1700-1850*, Oxford & New York 1992, pp. 195-230.

Dilly, Heinrich, "Lichtbildprojek-tion: Prothese der Kunstbetrach-tung," Irene Below (ed.), *Kunst-wissenschaft und Kunstvermittlung*, Gießen 1975, pp. 153-72.

Dulon, Guy, and Christophe Duvivier, *Louis Hayet 1864-1940:*
peintre et théoricien du néo-impres-sionisme, Pontoise 1991.

Eder, Josef Maria (ed.), *Quellen-schriften zu den frühesten Anfängen der Photographie bis zum XVIII. Jahrhundert* (1913), reprint Niederwalluf 1971.

Egerton, Judy, et al., *Wright of Derby*, exh. cat. London (Tate Gallery), Paris (Galeries nationales du Grand Palais) & New York (The Metropolitan Museum of Art) 1990.

Feaver, William, *The Art of John Martin*, Oxford 1975.

Filipzak, Z. Zaremba, "New Light on Mona Lisa: Leonardo's Optical Knowledge and his Choice of Lighting," *Art Bulletin* 59 (1977), pp. 518-23.

Ford, John, *Ackermann 1783-1983: The Business of Art*, London 1983.

Forgione, Nancy, "Shadow and Silhouette in Late Nineteenth-Century Paris," *Art Bulletin* 81 (September 1999), no. 3, pp. 490-512.

Foucart, Bruno, "Histoire de l'art et histoire de l'électricité," *L'Electricité dans l'histoire: prob-lèmes et méthodes, Actes du colloque Paris 11-13 October 1983, organisé par L'Association pour l'histoire de l'électricité en France*, Paris 1985, pp. 147-54.

Frelinghuysen, Alice Cooney, *Louis Comfort Tiffany at the Metropolitan Museum of Art*, exh. cat. New York (The Metropolitan Museum of Art) 1998.

Gage, John, *Color in Turner: Poetry and Truth*, New York 1969.

Gage, John, *Colour and Culture: Practice and Meaning from Antiquity to Abstraction*, London 1993.

Gage, John, *Color and Meaning: Art, Science, and Symbolism*, Berkeley & Los Angeles 1999.

Georgel, Chantal (ed.), *La Jeunesse des musées: les musées de France au XIXe siècle*, exh. cat. Paris (Musée d'Orsay) 1994.

Gernsheim, Helmut, and Alison Gernsheim, *L. J. M. Daguerre: The History of the Diorama and the Daguerreotype*, New York 1968.

Gombrich, Ernst H., *Shadows: The Depiction of Cast Shadows in Western Art*, exh. cat. London (National Gallery) 1995.

Green, Nicholas, *The Spectacle of Nature: Landscape and Bourgeois Culture in Nineteenth-Century France*, Manchester & New York 1990.

Hamilton, James, *Turner and the Scientists*, exh. cat. London (Tate Gallery) 1998.

Haskell, Francis, "The Apotheosis of Newton in Art," in Robert Palter (ed.), *The Annus Mirabilis of Sir Isaac Newton 1666-1966*, Cambridge, Massachusetts & London 1970, pp. 302-21.

Herbert, Robert L., et al., *Georges Seurat 1859-1891*, exh. cat. Paris (Galeries nationales du Grand Palais) & New York (The Metropolitan Museum of Art) 1991-92.

Holt, Elizabeth Gilmore, *The Expanding World of Art 1874-1902*, vol. I: *Universal Expositions and State-Sponsored Fine Arts Exhibitions*, New Haven & London 1988.

Homer, William Innes, *Seurat and the Science of Painting*, New York 1985.

Hopmans, Anita, "Het elektrisch licht als artistieke bron," *Kunst-schrift* 37 (January/February 1993), pp. 26-33.

Hunt, William Holman, *Pre-Raphaelitism and the Pre-Raphaelite Brotherhood*, 2 vols., London 1905.

Hutter, Heribert, *Lichteffekte in der Malerei des XVII. und XVIII. Jahrhunderts*, exh. cat. Vienna (Gemäldegalerie der Akademie der bildenden Künste) 1971.

Im Reich der Phantome: Fotografie des Unsichtbaren, exh. cat. Mönchengladbach (Städtisches Museum Abteiberg), Krems (Kunsthalle Krems) & Winterthur (Fotomuseum) 1998.

Jaffe, Michael, *The European Fame of Isaac Newton*, exh. cat. Cambridge (Fitzwilliam Museum) 1973-74.

Jansen, Johan, *"Het Electrisch": van lamplicht tot lichtsculptuur*, exh. cat. Leeuwarden (Museum het Princessehof) 1991.

Jansen, Johan, and Otto Lührs, *Art in Light*, Deventer 1985.

Joppien, Rüdiger, *Philippe Jacques de Loutherbourg, RA, 1740-1812*, exh. cat. Kenwood (The Iveagh Bequest) 1973.

Kahsnitz, Rainer, "Das Licht aus dem Dunkel und der Glanz der neuen Zeit - Ein Glasfenster aus der Nürnberger Gasanstalt," in Tilman Buddensieg and Henning Rogge (eds.), *Die nützlichen Künste: Gestaltende Technik und Bildende Kunst seit der Industriellen Revolution*, exh. cat. Berlin (Messegelände am Funkturm) 1981, pp. 99-104.

Kaufmann, Thomas DaCosta, "The Perspective of Shadows: The History of the Theory of Shadow Projection," *Journal of the Warburg and Courtauld Institutes* 38 (1975), pp. 258-87.

Keisch, Claude, and Marie Ursula Riemann-Reyher (eds.), *Adolph Menzel 1815-1905: Das Labyrinth der Wirklichkeit*, exh. cat. Paris (Musée d'Orsay), Washington, D.C. (National Gallery of Art) & Berlin (Staatliche Museen zu Berlin, Preussischer Kulturbesitz, Nationalgalerie and Kupferstichkabinett) 1996-97.

Kelly, Francis, *The Studio and the Artist*, Newton Abbot 1974.

Kelly, Franklin, et al., *Frederic Edwin Church*, exh. cat. Washington, D.C. (National Gallery of Art) 1989-90.

Kemp, Martin, *The Science of Art: Optical Themes in Western Art from Brunelleschi to Seurat*, New Haven & London 1990.

Kent, Neil, *Light and Nature in Late 19th-Century Nordic Art and Literature*, Uppsala 1990.

Klingender, Francis D., *Art and the Industrial Revolution*, London 1947.

Klonk, Charlotte, *Science and the Perception of Landscape: British Landscape Art in the Late Eighteenth and Early Nineteenth Centuries*, New Haven & London 1996.

Koschatzky, Walter, *Die Kunst der Photographie: Technik, Geschichte, Meisterwerke*, Munich 1987.

Lank, Herbert, "The Function of Natural Light in Picture Galleries," *Burlington Magazine* 126 (January 1984), pp. 4-6.

Lank, Herbert, "The Display of Paintings in Public Galleries," *Burlington Magazine* 136 (March 1992), pp. 165-71.

Leighton, Howard B., "The Lantern Slide and Art History," *History of Photography* 8 (April-June 1984), pp. 107-18.

Levitine, George, "Addenda to Robert Rosenblum's 'The Origin of Painting: A Problem in The Iconography of Romantic Classicism'," *Art Bulletin* 40 (1958), pp. 329-31.

Lochnan, Katherine A., *The Etchings of James McNeill Whistler*, New Haven & London 1984.

Longmore, James, "Lighting," Jane Shoaf Turner (ed.), *The*

Dictionary of Art, 34 vols., London 1996, vol. 19, pp. 361-68.

Maas, Jeremy, *Holman Hunt and the Light of the World*, Aldershot 1984.

Mainardi, Patricia, *The End of the Salon: Art and the State in the Early Third Republic*, Cambridge 1993.

Malan, Dan, *Gustave Doré Adrift on Dreams of Splendor: A Comprehensive Biography and Bibliography*, Saint Louis 1995.

Malhotra, Ruth, Marjan Rinkleff, and Bernd Schälicke, *Das frühe Plakat in Europa und den USA*, 2 vols., Berlin 1977.

Mantura, Bruno, and Geneviève Lacambre (eds.), *Pierre-Henri de Valenciennes 1750-1819*, exh. cat. Spoleto (Palazzo Racani Arroni) 1996.

Marmor, Michael F., and James G. Ravin (eds.), *The Eye of the Artist*, St. Louis 1997.

Martin-Nagy, Gilberte, *La Découverte de la lumière des primitifs aux impressionistes*, exh. cat. Bordeaux (Musée des Beaux-Arts) 1959.

Mayne, Jonathan, "Thomas Gainsborough's Exhibition Box," *Victoria and Albert Museum Bulletin* 1-2 (July 1965), pp. 16-24.

Milner, John, *The Studios of Paris: The Capital of Art in the Late Nineteenth Century*, New Haven & London 1988.

Moffett, Charles S., et al., *The New Painting: Impressionism 1874-1886*, exh. cat. San Francisco (The Fine Arts Museums of San Francisco) & Washington, D.C. (National Gallery of Art) 1986.

Murphy, Alexandra R., *Visions of Vesuvius*, exh. cat. Boston (Museum of Fine Arts) 1978.

Muther, Richard, "Was ist Freilichtmalerei?", *Studien*, ed.

Hans Rosenhagen, Berlin 1925, pp. 379-88.

Die Nacht, exh. cat. Munich (Haus der Kunst) 1998-99.

Nead, Lynda, "Seduction, Prostitution, Suicide: On the Brink by Alfred Elmore," *Art History* 5 (September 1982), pp. 310-22.

Neve, Christopher, "To Pandemonium by Train, John Martin (1789-1854)," *Country Life* (30 October 1975), pp. 1148-49.

Newall, Christopher, *The Victorian Imagination*, exh. cat. Tokyo (Bunkamura Museum of Art), Shizuoka (Shizuoka Prefectural Museum of Art), Kobe (Daimaru Museum) & Ibaraki (Tsukuba Museum of Art) 1998.

Nicolson, Benedict, *Joseph Wright of Derby: Painter of Light*, 2 vols., London 1986.

Nowald, Karlheinz, *Carl Gustav Carus "Malerstube im Mondschein" (1826)*, Kiel 1973.

Oettermann, Stephan, *The Panorama: History of a Mass Medium*, trans. Deborah Lucas Schneider, New York 1997.

Okkultismus und Avantgarde: Von Munch bis Mondrian 1900-1915, exh. cat. Frankfurt am Main (Schirn Kunsthalle) 1995.

Olson, Donald W., and Russell L. Doescher, "Van Gogh, Two Planets, and the Moon," *Sky and Telescope* (October 1988), pp. 406-08.

Olson, Roberta J. M., *Fire and Ice: A History of Comets in Art*, New York 1985.

Pachter, Irwin J., *Kawase Hasui and his Contemporaries: The Shin Hanga (New Print) Movement in Landscape Art*, exh. cat. Syracuse (Everson Museum of Art) 1986.

Parris, Leslie, and Ian Fleming-Williams, *Constable*, New York, London & Paris 1991.

Parris, Leslie (ed.), *The Pre-Raphaelites*, exh. cat. London (Tate Gallery) 1994.

Paulson, Ronald, *Literary Landscape: Turner and Constable*, New Haven & London 1982.

Paviot, Alain, *Le Cliché-verre: Corot, Delacroix, Millet, Rousseau, Daubigny*, exh. cat. Paris (Musée de la Vie Romantique) 1994-95.

Peppiatt, Michael, and Alice Bellony-Rewald, *Imagination's Chamber: Artists and their Studios*, London 1983.

Photography from 1839 to Today: George Eastman House, Rochester, New York & Cologne 1999

Picone, Maria Causa, "Volaire," *Antologia di Belle Arti* 2 (March 1978), pp. 24-48.

Radisich, Paula Rae, *Eighteenth-Century Landscape Theory and the Work of Pierre-Henri de Valenciennes* (Ph.D. University of California, Los Angeles 1977), Ann Arbor, Michigan 1978.

Rapport aan Hare Majesteit de Koningin: uitgebracht door de Rijks Commissie tot het nemen van proeven betreffende de verlichting van Rembrandt's "Nachtwacht" (Corporaalschap van Banning Cocq), Amsterdam 1902.

Rendezvous for Taste: Peale's Baltimore Museum 1814-1830, exh. cat. Baltimore (Peale Museum) 1956.

Rieth, Adolf, *Der Blitz in der bildenden Kunst*, Munich 1953.

Robertson, Alexander, *Atkinson Grimshaw*, London 1996.

Rosenblum, Robert, "The Origin of Painting: A Problem in the Iconography of Romantic Classicism," *Art Bulletin* 39 (1957), pp. 279-90.

Rowell, Christopher, "Display of Art," Jane Turner (ed.), *The Dictionary of Art*, 34 vols., London 1996, vol. 9, pp. 11-33.

Schmit-Burkhart, Astrit, *Sehende Bilder: Die Geschichte des Augen-motivs seit dem 19. Jahrhundert*, Berlin 1993.

Schöne, Wolfgang, *Über das Licht in der Malerei* (1954), 4th ed., Berlin 1977.

Schulze, Simone, *Pierre-Henri de Valenciennes und seine Schule: "Paysage historique" und der Wandel in der Naturauffassung am Anfang des 19. Jahrhunderts*, Frankfurt am Main 1996.

Schwartz, Heinrich, "The Mirror in Art," *Art Quarterly* 15 (Summer 1952) pp. 97-118.

Schweizer, Paul D., "John Constable's Rainbow Science and English Color Theory," *Art Bulletin* 64 (1982), pp. 424-45.

Seager, S. Hurst, *The Lighting of Picture Galleries and Museums*, London 1923.

Sedlmayr, Hans, "Das Licht in seinen künstlerischen Manife-stationen," *Studium Generale* 13 (1960), H. 6, pp. 313-24.

Sedlmayr, Hans, "Der Tod des Lichts: Eine Bemerkung zu Adalbert Stifters 'Sonnen-finsterniß am 8. July 1842'," *Der Tod des Lichts: Übergangene Perspektiven zur modernen Kunst*, Salzburg 1964, pp. 9-17.

Seidel, Katrin, *Die Kerze: Motivgeschichte und Ikonologie*, Hildesheim, Zurich & New York 1996.

Sellers, Charles Colman, *Mr. Peale's Museum: Charles Willson Peale and the First Popular Museum of Natural Science and Art*, New York 1980.

Sharpe, William, "New York, Night, and Cultural Mythmaking: The Nocturne in Photography, 1900-1925," *Smithsonian Studies in American Art* 2, no. 3 (Fall 1988), pp. 3-22.

Sharpe, William, "The Nocturne in fin-de-siècle Paris," Barbara T. Cooper and Mary Donaldson-Evans (eds.), *Modernity in Late Nineteenth-Century France*, Newark, London & Toronto 1991, pp. 108-28.

Sharpe, William, *Interior or Exterior? The Gaslit Street as Spectacle in Haussmann's Paris*, unpublished ms., October 1991.

Sheon, Aaron, "French Art and Science in the Mid-Nineteenth Century: Some Points of Contact," *Art Quarterly* 34 (Winter 1971), pp. 434-55.

Smith, Paul, *Seurat and the Avant-garde*, New Haven & London 1997.

Stafford, Barbara M., "Endymion's Moonbath: Art and Science in Girodet's Early Masterpiece," *Leonardo* 15 (1982), no. 3, pp. 193-98.

Staiti, Paul J., *Samuel F. B. Morse*, Cambridge & New York 1989.

Staley, Allen, *The Pre-Raphaelite Landscape*, Oxford 1977.

Stengel, Walter, "Eine Freilicht-Prophezeiung," *Kunst und Künstler* 4, 1905/06, pp. 204-10.

Turner 1775-1851, exh. cat. London (Tate Gallery) 1974.

Turner, Janet (ed.), *Light in Museums and Galleries*, London n.d.

Vaassen, Elgin, *Glasgemälde zwischen 1780 und 1870*, Munich 1997.

Varnedoe, Kirk, *Northern Light: Nordic Art at the Turn of the Century*, New Haven & London 1988.

Ward, Martha, "Impressionist Installations and Private Exhibitions," *Art Bulletin* 73 (December 1991), pp. 599-622.

Ward, Martha, *Pissarro, Neo-Impressionism and the Spaces of the Avant-Garde*, Chicago & London 1995.

Waterfield, Giles (ed.), *Palaces of Art: Art Galleries in Britain 1790-1990*, exh. cat. London (Dulwich Picture Gallery) & Edinburgh (The National Gallery of Scotland) 1991-92.

Wees, J. Dustin, "Darkness Visible," *The Prints of John Martin*, exh. cat. Williamstown, Massachusetts (Sterling and Francine Clark Art Institute) 1986.

Whiteley, J. J. L., "Light and Shade in French Neo-Classicism," *Burlington Magazine* 117 (December 1975) 768-73.

Wilhelm Bendz 1804-1832: A Young Painter of the Danish Golden Age, exh. cat. Copenhagen (The Hirschsprung Collection) 1996.

Wille, Hans, "Die Erfindung der Zeichenkunst," *Beiträge zur Kunstgeschichte: Eine Festgabe für Heinz Rudolf Rosemann zum 9. Oktober 1960*, Munich 1960, pp. 279-300.

Wilmerding, John, et al., *American Light: The Luminist Movement, 1850-1875, Paintings, Drawings, Photographs*, exh. cat. Washington, D.C. (National Gallery of Art) 1980.

Wright, Christopher, *The Masters of Candlelight: An Anthology of Great Masters Including Georges de La Tour, Godfried Schalcken, Joseph Wright of Derby*, Landshut 1995.

Spectacles and entertainment

Allen, Ralph G., "The Eidophusikon," *Theatre Design & Technology* 7 (December 1966), pp. 12-16.

Altick, Richard D., *The Shows of London*, Cambridge, Massachusetts & London 1978.

Baumann, Carl Friedrich, *Licht im Theater: Von der Argand-Lampe bis zum Glühlampen-Scheinwerfer*, Stuttgart 1988.

Bergman, Gösta M., *Lighting in the Theatre*, Stockholm 1977.

Buddemeier, Heinz, *Panorama, Diorama, Photographie: Entstehung und Wirkung neuer Medien im 19. Jahrhundert*, Munich 1970.

Cate, Phillip Dennis, and Mary Shaw (eds.), *The Spirit of Montmartre: Cabarets, Humor, and the Avant-Garde, 1875-1905*, exh. cat. New Brunswick, New Jersey (Jane Voorhees Zimmerli Art Museum) 1996.

Cook, Olive, *Movement in Two Dimensions: A Study of the Animated and Projected Pictures which Preceeded the Invention of Cinematography*, London 1963.

Crompton, Dennis, David Henry and Stephen Herbert (eds.), *Magic Images: The Art of Handpainted and Photographic Lantern Slides*, London 1990.

Danzker, Jo-Anne Birnie (ed.), *Loïe Fuller: Getanzter Jugendstil*, exh. cat. Munich (Museum Villa Stuck) 1995-96.

Felderer, Brigitte (ed.), *Wunschmaschine Welterfindung: Eine Geschichte der Technikvisionen seit dem 18. Jahrhundert*, exh. cat. Vienna (Kunsthalle) 1996.

Füsslin, Georg, et al., *Der Guckkasten: Einblick - Durchblick - Ausblick*, Stuttgart 1995.

Ganz, Thomas, *Die Welt im Kasten: Von der Camera obscura zur Audiovision*, Zurich 1994.

Hecht, Hermann, *Pre-Cinema History: An Encyclopedia and Annotated Bibliography of the Moving Image before 1896*, ed. Ann Hecht, London, Melbourne, Munich & New Jersey 1993.

Herzogenrath, Wulf, et al. (eds.), *TV Kultur: Fernsehen in der bildenden Kunst seit 1879*, Dresden 1997.

Hoffmann, Detlef, and Almut Junker, *Laterna Magica: Lichtbilder aus Menschenwelt und Götterwelt*, Berlin 1982.

Hrabalek, Ernst, *Laterna Magica: Zauberwelt und Faszination des optischen Spielzeugs*, Munich 1985.

Hyde, Ralph, *Panoramania! The Art and Entertainment of the "All-Embracing" View*, exh. cat. London (Barbican Art Gallery) 1988.

Inventaire des collections: Lanterne magique et fantasmagorie, Conservatoire National des Arts et Métiers, Musée National des Techniques, Paris 1990.

Kaldenbach, C. J., "De optica, een leerzaam kijkvermaak," *De Boekenwereld* 1 (January 1985), no. 2, pp. 3-12, and 1 (March 1985), no. 3, pp. 4-12.

Kohler, Georg (ed.), *Die schöne Kunst der Verschwendung: Fest und Feuerwerk in der europäischen Geschichte*, Zurich & Munich 1988.

Le Men, Ségolène, et al., *Lanternes magiques, tableaux transparents*, exh. cat. Paris (Musée d'Orsay) 1995-96.

Levie, Françoise, *Étienne-Gaspart Robertson: la vie d'un fantasmagore*, Lougueil, Quebec 1990.

Liesegang, Franz Paul, *Das lebende Lichtbild: Entwicklung, Wesen und Bedeutung des Kinematographen*, Leipzig 1910.

Liesegang, Franz Paul, *Dates and Sources: A Contribution to the History of the Art of Projection and to Cinematography*, trans. and ed. Hermann Hecht, London 1986.

Lotz, Arthur, *Das Feuerwerk: Seine Geschichte und Bibliographie. Beiträge zur Kunst- und Kulturgeschichte der Feste und des Theaterwesens in sieben Jahrhunderten*, Leipzig 1941.

Mannoni, Laurent, *Le grand art de la lumière et de l'ombre: archéologie du cinéma*, Paris 1994.

Mannoni, Laurent, *Trois siècles de cinéma: de la lanterne magique au Cinématographe, Collections de la Cinémathèque française*, exh. cat. Paris (Espace Électra) 1995-96.

Mannoni, Laurent, *Le Mouvement continue: catalogue illustré de la collection des appareils de la Cinémathèque française*, Paris 1996.

Mannoni, Laurent, Donata Pesenti Campagnoni, and David Robinson, *Light and Movement: Incunabula of the Motion Picture 1420-1896*, Pordenone 1995.

Milner, Max, *La Fantasmagorie: essai sur l'optique fantastique*, Paris 1982.

Musser, Charles, *Edison Motion Pictures 1890-1900: An Annotated Filmography*, Washington, D.C. 1997.

Penzel, Frederick, *Theater Lighting before Electricity*, Middletown, Connecticut 1978.

Perriault, Jacques, *Mémoires de l'ombre et du son: une archéologie de l'audio-visuel*, Paris 1981.

Rees, Terence, *Theatre Lighting in the Age of Gas*, London 1978.

Remise, Jac, Pascale Remise and Régis van de Walle, *Magie lumineuse: du théâtre d'ombres à la lanterne magique*, Paris 1979.

Robinson, David, *The Lantern Image: Iconography of the Magic Lantern 1420-1880*, London 1993.

Salatino, Kevin, *Incendiary Art: The Representation of Fireworks in Early Modern Europe*, exh. cat. Los Angeles (The Getty Research Institute for the History of Art and the Humanities) 1997-98.

Schönewolf, Herta, *Play with Light and Shadow: The Art and Techniques of Shadow Theater*, New York 1968.

Sehsucht: Das Panorama als Massenunterhaltung des 19. Jahrhunderts, Bonn (Kunst- und Ausstellungshalle der Bundesrepublik Deutschland) 1993.

Storch, Ursula (ed.), *Illusionen: Das Spiel mit dem Schein*, exh. cat. Vienna (Hermesvilla im Lainzer Tiergarten) 1995-96.

Verwiebe, Birgit, *Lichtspiele: Vom Mondscheintransparent zum Diorama*, Stuttgart 1997.

Weil, Theodor, *Die elektrische Bühnen- und Effektbeleuchtung: ein Überblick über die Methoden und neuesten Apparate der elektrischen Bühnenbeleuchtung*, Vienna & Leipzig 1904.

Zotti Minici, Carlo Alberto (ed.), *Il mondo nuovo: le meraviglie della visione dal 700 alla nascità del cinema*, exh. cat. Città di Bassana del Grappa (Museo Civico) 1988.

Lenders to the exhibition

Denmark
Copenhagen
  Carlsberg Museum
  Ny Carlsberg Glyptotek
  Statens Museum for Kunst

France
Chalons-sur-Saône
  Musée Nicéphore Niépce
Grenoble
  Musée de Grenoble
Paris
  Bibliothèque Nationale de
    France
  Ecole nationale supérieure
    des beaux-arts
  Lumière de l'oeil
  Musée des arts et métiers du
    CNAM
  Musée du Louvre
  Musée d'Orsay
  Sénat de la République
    Française
Versailles
  Musée National des Châteaux
    de Versailles et de Trianon

Germany
Berlin
  Staatliche Museen zu Berlin,
    Preussischer Kulturbesitz,
    Kunstgewerbemuseum
    Nationalgalerie
Bremen
  Kunsthalle Bremen
Chemnitz
  Kunstsammlungen
    Chemnitz
Cologne
  Wallraf-Richartz-Museum
Frankfurt am Main
  Museum für Angewandte
    Kunst
Hamburg
  Hamburger Kunsthalle
Hanover
  Niedersächsisches
    Landesmuseum
Munich
  Bayerische Staatsgemälde-
    sammlungen, Neue
    Pinakothek
Potsdam
  Stiftung Preussische
    Schlösser und Gärten
    Berlin-Brandenburg

Remscheid
  Deutsches Röntgen-Museum

Italy
Barzio (Como)
  Museo Medardo Rosso
Milan
  Pinacoteca di Brera

The Netherlands
Amsterdam
  Amsterdams Historisch
    Museum
  EnergeticA, Museum voor
    Energietechniek
  Gemeentearchief
  Instituut Collectie Nederland
  Kunsthandel Frans
    Leidelmeijer
  Nederlands Scheepvaarts-
    museum
  Rijksakademie
  Rijksmuseum
  Theater Instituut Nederland
  Universiteitsbibliotheek
  Van Gogh Museum
  Vincent van Gogh
    Foundation
Arnhem
  Nederlands
    Openluchtmuseum
Eindhoven
  Foundation Artificial Light
    in Art
Haarlem
  Teylers Museum
The Hague
  Haags Documentatie
    Centrum Nieuwe Media
  Verzamelingen van de Orde
    van Vrijmetselaren (CMC)
Leiden
  Museum Boerhaave
Nijmegen
  University Library
Utrecht
  Rijksuniversiteit Utrecht,
    Kunsthistorisch Instituut
  Universiteitsmuseum

Switzerland
Bern
  Kunstmuseum Bern
Gingins
  Collection Neumann

Riehen/Basel
  Fondation Beyeler
Zurich
  Kunsthaus Zurich

United Kingdom
Bath
  The Royal Photographic
    Society
Birmingham
  Birmingham City Museums
    and Art Gallery
Cambridge
  Fitzwilliam Museum
Derby
  Derby Museum and Art
    Gallery
Liverpool
  Walker Art Gallery
London
  The Richard Green Gallery
  Royal Academy of Arts
  Science Museum
  Tate Gallery
  Private Collection, courtesy
    of Rafael Valls Limited
Lowestoft, Suffolk
  Lord Somerleyton,
    Somerleyton Hall
Oxford
  Ashmolean Museum

United States of America
Boston
  Museum of Fine Arts
Cambridge, Massachusetts
  Harvard University,
    Collection of Historical
    Scientific Instruments
    Houghton Library
Chicago
  Art Institute of Chicago
Cleveland
  Cleveland Museum of Art
Los Angeles
  Stephen White Collection II
Newark
  The Newark Museum
New Brunswick, New Jersey
  Jane Voorhees Zimmerli Art
    Museum, Rutgers,
    The State University of
    New Jersey
New York
  Cooper-Hewitt, National
    Design Museum,

    Smithsonian Institution
  The FORBES Magazine
    Collection
  The Metropolitan Museum
    of Art
Philadelphia
  American Philosophical
    Society
  Philadelphia Museum of Art
Pittsburgh
  Carnegie Library
  Carnegie Museum of Art
  Carnegie Museum of Natural
    History
  Mrs. Hattie Ward Frew,
    courtesy of the Carnegie
    Museum of Natural
    History
  University of Pittsburgh,
    Darlington Memorial
    Library
  Falk Library
  Frick Fine Arts Library
  Hillman Library
  Library
Providence, Rhode Island
  Museum of Art, Rhode
    Island School of Design
Rochester, New York
  George Eastman House
Saint Louis
  Dan Malan
San Francisco
  Fine Arts Museums of San
    Francisco
Sewickley, Pennsylvania
  Graphic Arts Technical
    Foundation
Washington, D.C.
  National Gallery of Art
  National Museum of
    American Art,
    Smithsonian Institution
  National Museum of
    American History,
    Smithsonian Institution
Winterthur, Delaware
  Winterthur Museum, Garden
    and Library

  Elisabeth Cumbler

and private lenders who wish to
remain anonymous.

Index

Photographs